MARGINAL COMMENT

ALSO AVAILABLE FROM BLOOMSBURY

Greek Homosexuality, K. J. Dover
Scholarship and Controversy: Centenary Essays on the Life and Work of Sir Kenneth Dover, edited by Stephen Halliwell and Christopher Stray
What Is a Jewish Classicist?, Simon Goldhill

MARGINAL COMMENT

A Memoir Revisited

Kenneth Dover

reissued with editorial material by
Stephen Halliwell and Christopher Stray

BLOOMSBURY ACADEMIC
LONDON • NEW YORK • OXFORD • NEW DELHI • SYDNEY

BLOOMSBURY ACADEMIC
Bloomsbury Publishing Plc
50 Bedford Square, London, WC1B 3DP, UK
1385 Broadway, New York, NY 10018, USA
29 Earlsfort Terrace, Dublin 2, Ireland

BLOOMSBURY, BLOOMSBURY ACADEMIC and the Diana logo are trademarks of
Bloomsbury Publishing Plc

First published in 1994 by Gerald Duckworth & Co. Ltd.
This edition published by Bloomsbury Academic, 2023

Copyright © Sir Kenneth Dover, Stephen Halliwell and Christopher Stray, 2023

Sir Kenneth Dover, Stephen Halliwell and Christopher Stray have asserted their
right under the Copyright, Designs and Patents Act, 1988, to be identified as
Author of this work.

For legal purposes the Acknowledgements on p. 22 constitute an extension of
this copyright page.

Cover illustration by Margaret-Anne Hutton

All rights reserved. No part of this publication may be reproduced or transmitted
in any form or by any means, electronic or mechanical, including photocopying,
recording, or any information storage or retrieval system, without prior
permission in writing from the publishers.

Bloomsbury Publishing Plc does not have any control over, or responsibility for,
any third-party websites referred to or in this book. All internet addresses given in
this book were correct at the time of going to press. The author and publisher
regret any inconvenience caused if addresses have changed or sites have
ceased to exist, but can accept no responsibility for any such changes.

A catalogue record for this book is available from the British Library.

Library of Congress Control Number: 2022946873

ISBN: HB: 978-1-3502-9583-4
PB: 978-1-3502-9582-7
ePDF: 978-1-3502-9584-1
eBook: 978-1-3502-9585-8

Typeset by RefineCatch Limited, Bungay, Suffolk
Printed and bound in Great Britain

To find out more about our authors and books visit www.bloomsbury.com
and sign up for our newsletters.

CONTENTS

List of Figures   vii
Editorial Foreword   viii

Introduction: The Conception and Reception of *Marginal Comment*
 (Stephen Halliwell)   1
Preface   21
Acknowledgements   22

1 On Autobiography   23

2 Forebears   29

3 Escape Routes 1920–1932   35

4 Body and Soul 1926–1934   43

5 Exotica 1933–   51

6 Reconstitution 1935–1936   57

7 Transition 1936–1940   67

8 Intermission 1940–1945   79

9 Women, Children and Work 1940–1951   93

10 History, Comedy and Other Things 1949–   113

11 Migration 1951–1960   125

12 People and Power 1955–1966   139

13 Mind and Body 1958–   153

14 Plato and After 1962–1989   161

15 Tributaries 1962–   171

16 The Public 1964–1980   179

17 Fruition 1966–1968   189

18 Revolutions (Fringe) 1968–1975   199

19 Right and Wrong 1969–1983   211

20 Elevations 1970–1993   225

21 Dovers 1972–1982   237

22 College and University 1975–1986   245

23 Style 1977–1994   263

24 Excursions 1979–1984   271

25 The Blunt Affair 1979–1981   279

26 The Aston Affair 1980–1985   291

27 Admissions 1982–1984   303

28 Best Before 1983–   311

29 At Large 1984–1992   319

30 The Thatcher Affair 1985   327

31 A History Man   333

32 Epimetron 1994   339

Index   341

FIGURES

New no	Old no	Caption	
1	4	Bessie Millson (great aunt), 1935	33
2	3	Kenneth Healey (uncle), 1935	44
3	5	Near Khasia, Attica, with Alistair Matthews, March 1938. *Photo: George Bean*	71
4	8	Eduard Fraenkel, with young Italian classicists	73
5	1	Percy Dover (father), 1943	100
6	2	Dorothy Dover, née Healey (mother), 1941	101
7	11	Wedding of Hugh Latimer (brother-in-law) and Moira Sketch, 1949. Kenneth and Audrey at far right, Cicely (Audrey's mother) next to them, Helen (Audrey's sister) next to Moira	103
8	13	Entretien on Archilochus, Vandoeuvres, 1963. Denys Page second from left, Bruno Snell centre in bow-tie. *Photo: Mary Rochat*	122
9	17	Vecoli, 1973. Much of *Greek Popular Morality* was typed at the table on the grass	218
10	20	Leverhulme Trustees and Research Awards Advisory Committee, *c.* 1972. In front row, Asa Briggs third from left, Bill Holford far right, Helen Gardner next to him. In back row, Anthony Blunt third from right	226
11	16	At Installation as Chancellor, 1981, with Leland Lyons, Anna Davies, Ken Loach and Steven Watson. *Photo: Peter Adamson*	233
12	19	Percy Dover (father) and Lillian (Dover) Lipscombe (aunt), Glen Clova, 1975	240
13	Previous frontispiece (cropped)	Kenneth and Audrey in their St Andrews garden, May 1990. *Photo: Joy Russell (wife of Donald Russell)*	317

EDITORIAL FOREWORD

Autobiographies, like all forms of writing about the past, quickly acquire the status of historical documents in their own right. Almost thirty years after its original publication, Kenneth Dover's memoir is no exception to this rule. In reviewing *Marginal Comment* in the *London Review of Books* for 9 February 1995, Mary Beard, not the book's greatest admirer, anticipated that it would become 'a major source for the history of Classics, and of university life in general, in the second half of the 20th century' (a dimension of the work, it should be noted, that the author himself thought only 'incidental': see p. 24). This new edition is designed to make it a little easier and more profitable for readers both old and new to appreciate the book in a historical perspective and to reconsider its strengths and weaknesses as the uncompromisingly frank self-portrait of a remarkable scholar in his time and place. The memoir deals, among much else, with a number of controversies in which Dover became involved; it also aroused controversy itself on its first appearance, as the Introduction to this edition sets out in some detail. All this is of interest in multiple respects, but with the passage of time it has become increasingly possible and appropriate to ponder the issues in question without (one might hope, at least) simply taking sides over what was at stake.

Marginal Comment was originally published in early November 1994 by Duckworth, whose owner, Colin Haycraft, had died just a fortnight before its appearance. It was reprinted in 1995 with corrections and expanded addenda ('expanded', because there were already some addenda in the first printing). The text of the present edition is essentially that of the 1995 reprint, but it incorporates a few further corrections of small errors, moves the contents of the most important addenda into the annotations, and improves the book's originally rather deficient index. We have also resolved a few minor inconsistencies of spelling, e.g. between Sub-faculty, sub-faculty and Subfaculty, 'word order' and 'word-order', 'funnel chest' and 'funnel-chest', 'lectureship' and 'lecturership' (the latter actually Dover's preferred form, but we have abandoned it on the grounds that it is now likely to strike most readers as a misprint), though we have not attempted to eliminate anomalies systematically. Where, occasionally, the 1995 text differed from that of 1994 in consequential ways, we have drawn attention to the fact.

The guiding policy behind our editorial footnotes is (i) to provide basic information about some of the things (people, places, institutions, etc.) which Dover takes for granted or explains insufficiently (which is often the case), (ii) to shed further light on the significance of certain details in the text, (iii) to provide some cross-references that may help readers to navigate the book's complex chronological organization (discussed in the Introduction), and (iv) to highlight a selection of other salient elements of the text (including some curious errors and obscurities). We have been conscious of the need to avoid smothering Dover's words with annotation, though some parts of the book call for, or benefit from, elucidation more than others. We naturally cannot satisfy the needs of every category of readers: what puzzles some may be obvious to others. But we hope that in exercising our judgement about what matters most we have struck a reasonable balance. It is now easier than ever, of course, to look up information about (almost) everything online, but there is plenty of misinformation out there as well; we have tried always to draw on reliable sources. Readers with further interest in Dover's life and work will certainly want to explore the volume of essays, *Scholarship and Controversy* (see below), which is being published in conjunction with this reissued memoir.

Three special sources exploited by our annotations need to be mentioned here: first, extracts and details from the supplementary notes to his autobiography, involving both additions and corrections, which Dover left in a typescript deposited at Corpus Christi College, Oxford (see below); second, Dover's letters to his parents between 1938 and 1963 (see p. 25, but specifying a longer period of correspondence); third, a few marginalia in Dover's own copy of *Marginal Comment*, which he inscribed and presented to one of the editors (SH) not long before his death. SH would like to put on record that the present edition has greatly profited from the work undertaken on the first two of those sources by Chris Stray in particular. As regards photographs, we have kept slightly more than half of those contained in the first edition, including the original frontispiece, incorporating them (with expanded captions in some cases) at appropriate points in the text.

We would like to express our thanks to Catherine Brown, Kenneth Dover's daughter, for permission to quote from the letters home mentioned above; to Julian Reid (Archivist) and the President and Fellows of Corpus Christi College, Oxford, for permission to cite from the college's archive of Dover papers, including the supplementary notes to his memoir; to Martin Maw (Archivist) and the Secretary to the Delegates of Oxford University Press for permission to cite the original readers' reports on *Marginal Comment* (editorial file OP2693/19078); to Sir Keith Thomas for lending CS his copy of the typescript of *Marginal Comment* originally submitted to OUP; and, for help with individual points, to Deborah Blake, Paul Cartledge, Elizabeth Craik, Sir Brian Harrison, Sian Lewis, Lily Mac Mahon, Helen Moore, Hilary O'Shea, Christopher Pelling, Tim Rood, Richard Rutherford and Alice Wright.

The following abbreviations are used in the Introduction and editorial footnotes:

BG	H. Lloyd-Jones, *Blood for the Ghosts: Classical Influences in the Nineteenth and Twentieth Centuries* (London, 1982)
BMF	*Biographical Memoirs of Fellows of the British Academy* (available with open access at https://www.thebritishacademy.ac.uk/publishing/memoirs/)
CCH	T. Charles-Edwards and J. Reid, eds, *Corpus Christi College, Oxford: A History* (Oxford, 2017)
CSBE	W.W. Briggs and W.M. Calder III, eds, *Classical Scholarship: A Biographical Encyclopedia* (New York, 1990)
DBC	R.B. Todd, ed., *Dictionary of British Classicists*, 3 vols (Bristol, 2004)
G&G	K.J. Dover, *Greek and the Greeks: Collected Papers Vol. I* (Oxford, 1987)
G&L	K.J. Dover, *The Greeks and their Legacy: Collected Papers Vol. II* (Oxford, 1988)
GH	K.J. Dover, *Greek Homosexuality* (London, 1978; updated and with a new postscript, Cambridge Mass., 1989; reprinted (1989 ed.) with Forewords by S. Halliwell, M. Masterson and J. Robson, London, 2016)
GPM	K.J. Dover, *Greek Popular Morality* (Oxford, 1974)
HUO	*The History of the University of Oxford*, vol. 8, ed. B.H. Harrison (Oxford, 1994)
ICNA	*In Conversation with Naim Attallah* (London, 1998); the interview with Dover appears on pp. 91–111
IPC	A. Clare, *In the Psychiatrist's Chair III* (London, 1998); the interview with Dover appears on pp. 81–115
KJD	D.A. Russell and S. Halliwell, 'Kenneth James Dover 1920–2010', *Biographical Memoirs of Fellows of the British Academy* XI (2012) 153–75, with a contribution by P.W.H. Brown (available online: see under *BMF* above)
MC	*Marginal Comment*; page references, unless otherwise indicated, are to the present edition
MP	E.R. Dodds, *Missing Persons: An Autobiography* (Oxford, 1977)
OA	E.M. Craik, ed., *Owls to Athens: Essays on Classical Subjects for Sir Kenneth Dover* (Oxford, 1990)
OC	C. Stray, ed., *Oxford Classics: Teaching and Learning 1800–2000* (London, 2007)
ODNB	*Oxford Dictionary of National Biography* (https://www.oxforddnb.com/)
PBA	*Proceedings of the British Academy* (vols 51–111 available with open access at http://publications.thebritishacademy.ac.uk/pubs/proc/volumes/index.html)
QR	D. Cannadine, ed., *A Question of Retribution? The British Academy and the Matter of Anthony Blunt* (Oxford, 2020; reprinted 2021 with a change to p. 6 n. 36)

S&C   S. Halliwell and C. Stray, eds, *Scholarship and Controversy: Centenary Essays on the Life and Work of Sir Kenneth Dover* (London, 2023)

SN   Dover's supplementary typescript notes to *Marginal Comment*: these form part of the Dover papers at Corpus Christi College, Oxford, archival reference B/14/13/1

S.H. and C.S.
June 2022

NOTE: Kenneth Dover's own occasional footnotes are identified by symbols; all numbered footnotes are editorial.

INTRODUCTION: THE CONCEPTION AND RECEPTION OF *MARGINAL COMMENT*

Stephen Halliwell

nec ego ipse capio totum quod sum.

AUGUSTINE, Confessions

Voilà ce que j'ai fait, ce que j'ai pensé, ce que je fus.

ROUSSEAU, Confessions[1]

Kenneth Dover was, in certain respects, an unlikely autobiographer. In the course of a career devoted to scholarship, teaching and university administration at the highest levels, his single-minded dedication to academic virtues had shaped a life which few would have expected to lend itself to an extensive memoir for a general readership. In his professional and public conduct Dover had always exhibited a judicious, carefully measured temperament which could hardly have struck most observers as a promising basis for autobiographical self-disclosure, let alone for the glaring light of intimate revelations. The temperament in question was formed at an early age. In a letter written to his parents on 19 January 1939, during his first year as an Oxford undergraduate, he said of himself, 'Yes, I think I'm extraordinarily undemonstrative on personal things, because they interest me less than impersonal ones.'[2] That is a

---

[1] 'I myself cannot understand the whole of what I am', Augustine, *Confessions* 10.8.15; 'Here is what I have done, what I have thought, what I have been', Rousseau, *Confessions*, Book I.
[2] For Dover's letters home, see the Editorial Foreword.

description many of his later colleagues and acquaintances might have recognized as authentic, especially since, on his own admission, he 'always put work first and friends second' (*MC* 59).³ But the leaning of his interests towards impersonal things was not really the root of his 'undemonstrative' manner. For most of his life, Dover's public demeanour, though affable and courteous, was marked by an ingrained emotional guardedness, an ability to conceal 'even the most turbulent and agonising emotion' (32), which he himself explained in terms of a 'stoicism' consciously cultivated from adolescence onwards (58, 80).

Dover's stoic self-fashioning is itself one of *Marginal Comment*'s revelations. He identifies two main causes of it: one, the sense of 'inferiority' and 'deformity' associated with his funnel chest, so privately physical that it is impossible to add to what he says about it himself (25, 48, 58); the other, a deep-seated reaction, even revulsion, against his father, so strong in its psychological ramifications that it might well be thought the key to his character. If he consciously learned to live, as he tells us, 'within a shell impermeable both to my emotions on the way out and to other people's on the way in' (58–9), that was the very opposite of the example set by his incorrigibly irascible father, a figure so foul-tempered and unlovable that his son would have felt nothing other than 'relief if he had died or vanished' (36), and whose wrathful menace he even superimposed onto his early image of the Judeo-Christian God (45). The implications of this unhappy state of affairs for Dover's personality were complex, and in ways that would eventually influence the kind of autobiography he chose to write. If he reacted from an early age to his father's 'unpredictable explosions of rage and hatred' (36) by suppressing signs of his own emotions, he could hardly eliminate the emotions as such. In fact, some aspects of his father's behaviour aroused, he tells us, his *own* (inner) 'rage, hatred and despair' (31), a telling mirror-effect made all the more significant as 'the strongest emotion that I have experienced in my life'. The net result was a partially conflicted disposition where personal self-expression was concerned, a conflict exacerbated by an only partly submerged awareness that there was 'a bit more of my father in me than I could bring myself to acknowledge' (107–8, cf. 60). If the suppression of strong emotion is a psychological burden, it is not unreasonable to infer that Dover's eventual decision to write a highly, even shockingly, candid memoir was, in part, a deliberate compensation for the lifelong tensions of his relationship with his father: liberation from a lifetime's pressure of containment.⁴

---

³The philosopher Colin McGinn, who became a fellow of Corpus Christi College, Oxford, in the penultimate year of Dover's presidency, found him 'simultaneously relaxed and unspontaneous': 'he exuded iron self-control, and the feeling that it was seriously needed' ('A Don's Confession', *Lingua Franca* Jan.-Feb. 1995, 48, introducing extracts from *MC*). Cf. Ewen Bowie's description, in his contribution to *S&C*, of Dover's 'indefinable remoteness'.

⁴For a reading of the results as *over*-compensation for the factors, paternal and others, which had induced lifelong habits of emotional self-control, see Martha Nussbaum, 'A stoic's confessions', *Arion* 4 (1997) 149–60, at 158–9.

It is equally justifiable to see that point as reinforced by Dover's very different relationship with his mother. The memoir consistently presents his parents as polar opposites in character, with his mother oppressed and threatened by the same failings on her husband's part as perpetually distressed her son. Dover wrote elsewhere of his mother, immediately after her death in 1973, as having always shown him how 'the unfailing spontaneity of a warm heart' could be combined with 'a truly fair and open mind'.[5] The most important part of what he felt he owed her was a vital attachment to the value of truthfulness, 'a virtue to which I respond with inordinate warmth' (218): he had spent his life trying, he said, to live up to her habit of telling the truth 'whether it was welcome to her or not' (37). Truthfulness is not, of course, exactly the same thing as choosing to write an autobiography which exposes even the most intimate elements of one's life to unknown readers. But if *Marginal Comment* takes this type of self-exposure to an extreme, that can be interpreted as a sort of intensified homage to the mother, just as it was an emphatic liberation from the father. This makes all the more sense in the light of the paradoxical fact that one side-effect of the strength of Dover's anti-paternal feelings was that he was unable to give fulfillingly explicit form to the affection he felt for his mother, a circumstance which, retrospectively at least, caused him 'anguished' regret (59). The memoir tried to make belated amends for that fact, as well as implicitly emulating his mother's commitment to truthfulness with a wholehearted, not to say wilful, directness, even where the truth might strike some as 'nasty' (26).[6]

There were, then, powerful psychological forces at work in the writing of *Marginal Comment*, and I have started from them because they underlie the way in which Dover approached the venture of a retrospective reckoning with his life. The degree of uncensored expression entailed by this approach is a prime reason why Dover considered his autobiography 'experimental',[7] a description which makes less sense with reference to the putative norms of the genre (after all, 'the whole point of an autobiography is to tell the truth'[8]) than to the special respects in

---

[5] *GPM* xiv; cf. p. 217 below.
[6] Truthfulness and 'nastiness' *qua* unfiltered honesty about one's feelings should not be confused with the specifically linguistic issue of non-euphemistic sexual language (see n. 15 to p. 89), though the two sometimes arise in the same context. Such language partly reflects what Dover called his 'natural streak of coarseness' (89), though he had rarely resorted to it in public except when discussing obscenity in Greek comedy: for a rare exception, at a moment of heightened tension, see p. 289.
[7] He did not use this term in the book itself but in speaking to the journalist John O'Leary, *The Times*, 26 November 1994, p. 3 (cf. n. 40 below). The book was also called 'experimental' in the reviews by Mary Beard in the *LRB* (n. 55 below) and Christopher Stray in *Classical Review* 46 (1996) 195–6.
[8] Dover in telephone conversation with journalist John Darnton, quoted in 'A scholar's memoirs raise some ghosts at Oxford', *The New York Times*, 28 November 1994, pp. 1 and 6. Cf. p. 13 below. *The Times*' leader of 30 November 1994, p. 23, while critical of Dover's handling of the Aston affair (see 12 below), nonetheless acknowledged that the book's 'shocking candour suggests how contrived most autobiographies probably are'.

which he was aware of diverging from his own lifelong habits of public circumspection and self-control. But there was a more general consideration in play here as well. Dover was determined that his memoir would be something other than an 'academic autobiography', a categorization of the book he firmly repudiated, preferring 'an autobiography *simpliciter*', with the characteristically dry comment that 'academics are non-academics for a large part of their waking lives', so that the autobiography of an academic can legitimately encompass a much larger slice of life than the purely professional.[9] It was to be fundamental to *Marginal Comment* that strictly academic activities, while bulking large, would be treated as pieces of a larger, more complex mosaic of the whole of its author's life. In this regard, Dover's memoir was at the opposite end of the spectrum from an intellectual autobiography such as that of the idealist philosopher R.G. Collingwood, a book, certainly known to Dover, which starts its Preface with the declaration, 'The autobiography of a man whose business is thinking should be the story of his thought', and provides so few dates or personal details that it does indeed seem to float in a world of disembodied ideas.[10] Dover, by contrast, as a self-described 'English empiricist to the core' (202, cf. 337), wanted to reconstruct his life in all its particularity of time, place, and circumstance, even where ideas themselves were involved. This concern for particulars ran deep: in some notes which Dover sent to Donald Russell for use in public comment when he was awarded his knighthood in 1977, he wrote that 'I am devoted to *particulars* – a beautiful insect or flower, a brief moment of breeze on a hillside – and repelled by metaphysics.'[11] This made *Marginal Comment* far more abundant in specificities than most memoirs by academics. It is the conjunction of this abundance of detail with the quasi-confessional[12] frankness already highlighted which gives the book much of its distinctive piquancy.

Dover did, however, have at least one partial model to hand for his memoir. He was very familiar with E.R. Dodds' *Missing Persons* (1977), the work of a Hellenist of

---

[9] The quotations are from Dover's response, in a letter of 9 February 1994 to Hilary O'Shea, the Classics Editor of Oxford University Press, to one of the readers' reports commissioned by the Press when the book was originally submitted to them: see further at n. 24 below.

[10] R.G. Collingwood, *An Autobiography* (Oxford, 1939); cf. Roy Pascal, *Design and Truth in Autobiography* (London, 1960) 108–10. Dover's familiarity with Collingwood's autobiography is attested by his reference to it on the first page of his British Academy memoir of W.L. Lorimer, his predecessor in the chair of Greek at St Andrews, *PBA* 53 (1967) 437.

[11] Russell had requested these notes, dated 14 May 1977, to help him plan a speech at a faculty celebration of Dover's knighthood; Russell shared the notes with SH many years later. For the emphasis on particulars, cf. his 1976 Classical Association Presidential Address (*G&L* 311): 'To value linguistic phenomena … for their self-sufficient particularity, as one might value a tropical beetle or the movement of a bear, is one way of loving life.'

[12] Although many have understandably referred to parts of *MC* as 'confessional', Dover himself told the journalist Cassandra Jardine, *à propos* the Trevor Aston affair (pp. 9–15 below), 'I didn't set out to confess for the sake of confessing. It has not preyed on my conscience': *The Daily Telegraph*, 25 November 1994, p. 19.

comparable stature to himself as well as a personal friend, and it is not hard to suppose that it was at least a subliminal influence at various points in his own book.[13] Dodds and Dover admired one another greatly. Dodds was disappointed, and tried hard to persuade Dover to change his mind, when the latter turned down the chance to become Dodds' successor as Regius Professor of Greek at Oxford in 1960 – an ironic juncture of events, given that Dodds had come to regret his own acceptance of the Regius chair in 1936, dwelling on the thought that what preceded it were the twelve 'happiest' years of his life, whereas Dover decided to stay in St Andrews in 1960 precisely, in large part, because he was happy there.[14] Although there are salient contrasts in style and ethos of self-presentation between *Marginal Comment* and *Missing Persons*, as well as undeniably far-reaching differences between the social, political and cultural backgrounds of the two men, the subtle threads of connection between the two works should not be underestimated. Dodds' book was, after all, a precedent, from someone Dover had known well for several decades, for an attempt to trace the interweaving, or at any rate entanglement, of the private and public strands of an outstanding scholar's life, and in the process Dodds had broached a number of personal factors – being an only child with a strong sense of difference from others, having a problematic father, discarding religious belief as a teenager, reading Freud, discerning significance in one's dreams, to mention some token examples – which must have struck a chord with Dover, over and above numerous professional and other points of contact between their lives. Dodds had found a way of opening up vistas of the 'whole' life, not just its academic core, and this offered a basic template for Dover to work with, though he was determined to take its possibilities much further in both scale (*MC* is almost twice the length of *MP*) and candour (not for him, among other things, Dodds' silence about his wife's mental decline).[15] Dodds had, for sure, undertaken his autobiography in a rather diffident, wistful spirit; at the end of it, he was left with a predominant sense of a patchwork of contingency ('I find it as bitty and episodic as a badly constructed novel'), though with a lingering awareness of a mysterious personal agency – his 'daemon', as he called it, with overtones of the Neoplatonic philosophy he had studied so intensively – which seemed to intervene at crucial moments.[16] Dover, by

---

[13] Dodds' name was somehow omitted from the original index of *MC*; it was added in the second impression of 1995.

[14] For Dover's refusal of the chair in 1960, see *MC* 137–8; for Dodds' feelings about his move from Birmingham to Oxford, see *MP* 124–6 (with 86 for his twelve 'happiest' years).

[15] See *MP* 194 for Dodds' refusal to describe his wife's last illness; contrast Dover's discussion of his wife's depression in *MC* ch. 13.

[16] The 'episodic' verdict is at *MP* 192, the 'daemon' at 194–5 (cf. 62, 71, for other uses). There are brief but apt remarks on *MP* in C. Pelling and C. Stray, 'Introduction: A Missing Person?', in C. Stray, C. Pelling, S. Harrison, eds, *Rediscovering E. R. Dodds* (Oxford, 2019) 1–9, though, *pace* 7, Dodds' daemon is less Socratic than Neoplatonic. An informative view of the book is provided by R.B. Todd, *Quaderni di storia* 53 (2001) 233–45. Dover's reference to *MP* at *MC* 39, notes Dodds' 'characteristic charity and reticence'; cf. 83 for an instance in life of Dodds' 'diffidently expressed wisdom'.

contrast, adopted an unflinching viewpoint on his life, laying bare the full range of feelings which had lurked beneath the surface of the publicly documented career. If *Missing Persons* leaves us with a sense of someone still in search of the truth about his self (or plural 'selves', as the book's Envoi muses), *Marginal Comment* exposes its readers to the full brunt of authorial confidence in its first-person account.

In one notable respect, Dover's autobiography adopted a more artful narrative strategy than the model followed by Dodds. The latter, while reserving a freestanding central chapter for the evolution of his lifelong interest in parapsychological phenomena, for the most part synthesizes various elements of his life within a single, sequential chronological framework.[17] In the architecture of *Marginal Comment*, on the other hand, chapters are often chronologically imbricated (like roof-tiles, to use the metaphor correctly), so that what we are given is not a continuous narrative but a series of overlapping accounts of different dimensions or spheres of his life, an arrangement that he borrowed, in part at least, from Duncan Wilson's biography of Gilbert Murray.[18] This method is applied even to parts of Dover's childhood: thus Chapter 3 deals with the first twelve years of his life, up to the point of his entry into St Paul's school, focussing especially on the characters of his parents and on the 'escape routes' (from severe family tensions) provided by history, storytelling and imagination (as well as some entomology), then Chapter 4 starts again at the age of six in order to deal with matters of religion, sexual awakening and the traumatic 'discovery' of his funnel chest. Later on, this practice produces a complex construction at the heart of the book, in Chapters 12 and following, where the chronological sequence involves so many overlaps that material belonging in and around e.g. 1980 is partially covered in at least *ten* different chapters. This narrative technique is, in strictly temporal terms, a kind of artifice; it is one of the ways in which Dover enjoyed experimenting with autobiography as a genre of writing.[19] But it also reflects a realistic practice of remembering, since individuals cannot recall or reconstruct substantial tracts of their lives without to some extent splitting them into constructed segments of activity and experience; the alternative would be either a chaotic jumble or a schematic superficiality. Even so, Dover pushes this organizational principle to the point where engaged readers need to be highly alert and attentive if they are to follow the full interweaving of strands.

Matters are complicated further by a fair bit of prolepsis and analepsis (in the jargon of narrative theorists), i.e. glances forwards and backwards in time, though

---

[17]Dover just occasionally does this himself: Chapter 15 involves the thematically odd coupling of computerized stylometrics with the peculiar figure of George Devereux.

[18]We know this because Dover commented directly on the narrative arrangement of 'overlapping slabs' of Murray's life when reviewing D. Wilson, *Gilbert Murray OM 1866-1957* (Oxford, 1987) in the *Times Literary Supplement*, 24–30 June 1988, p. 700.

[19]At *MC* 27 he says that he came to realize that the pleasure of discovering the nature of autobiography as a genre was his 'prime object in writing the book'.

typically without as much signposting as some readers might expect. On p. 119, for instance, we are told about the academic work undertaken during a period which Dover spent at Harvard in 1960–1, but only on p. 137, at the end of the following chapter, are we informed about the invitation which led to that visit; moreover, the fact that his wife's ill-health meant that he initially travelled to Harvard alone is not recorded till two further chapters have passed, on p. 154. Similarly, the important Thucydidean 'turn' which Dover's career took as a result of the sudden death of A.W. Gomme in 1959 is narrated on p. 119, but in the middle of the following chapter the reader is required to wind back, so to speak, when Dover's discussion of his career options in the mid-1950s introduces reference to the possibility of succeeding Gomme in Glasgow on his forthcoming retirement in 1957 (p. 130). Or again, Dover's 1985 trip to South Africa is mentioned twice (249, 295) long before it is given its own narrative context on p. 320. As a final example, on p. 205 Dover mentions a period of sabbatical leave taken in 1973, but it is only ten pages later that he contextualizes the details of this sabbatical and its relevance to the completion of *Greek Popular Morality* (215). Perhaps unsurprisingly, even Dover's fastidious segmentation does not altogether eliminate chronological loose ends and anomalies of various kinds. The last part of Chapter 6, for instance, includes some significant memories from 1938, even though the chapter's title refers to 1935–6; the failure of Dover's application for the Regius chair of Greek in Cambridge in 1973 is tucked (p. 216) into a chapter otherwise concerned with the development of his work on and around *Greek Popular Morality*; and the Thatcher affair recounted in Chapter 30 occurred nine months earlier than the terrible dénouement of the Trevor Aston affair which occupies most of Chapter 26.

If *Marginal Comment*'s intricate pattern of chronologically overlapping chapters makes heavier demands on the reader than *Missing Persons*' more conventionally sequenced narrative, it also contributes to the impression that Dover has a more confidently analytical grasp of what particular portions of his life added up to, and felt able to discern in the overall pattern something more than the 'patchwork' of contingency which Dodds' retrospective gaze could not see beyond. This is not the result of any fundamental difference between the externals of the two lives themselves, which involved, in the broadest terms, relatively similar configurations of high-level professorial careers combined with long marriages and filled out by administrative positions held, overseas travels undertaken, and more besides. The difference in question is, rather, a matter of authorial perspective and cast of mind: the somewhat hesitant and gently ruminative persona of Dodds, on the one hand, and that of the experimentally un-self-censored Dover, on the other. It is tempting, furthermore, to link that contrast in turn to the differing focal points, as it were, of the two men's intellects. Dodds' autobiography shows us a mind committed to a tentative, contemplative mixture of poetic and philosophical 'soul-searching'. Dover's, however, is the work of 'a history man', as he titled the final chapter of *Marginal Comment*: someone who believed that the essential activity of the humanities (though not, unlike Dodds, of 'humanism') was historical enquiry and investigation, and whose autobiography is an exercise in turning the tools and methods of such enquiry on himself.[20] What's more, although Dover was aware of the possible distortions of personal memory (see p. 24), he shows little inclination to ponder its obscure and partly impenetrable workings; he has a quasi-Rousseauesque confidence in his ability to access the reality of his past experience.[21] One cannot easily imagine him agreeing with the more Augustinian reflections of another academic memoirist, the exceptional art historian Michael Baxandall, on how readily, in seeking to recall the past, one can 'find oneself incoherent'.[22] For Dover, the act of disclosing even one's previously secret thoughts and feelings is less a matter of introspective scrutiny than of making these things part of history: putting them on the record, coordinating them with other items of the past for which external evidence exists, and making them available for others to consider. In keeping with his general aversion to philosophy, or at any rate to metaphysics, and here too in contrast to Dodds, he had, it seems, no interest in problems of 'the self'.[23] In the business of the mind just as much as that of the body, Dover's conception of autobiography, as we have already seen, was that of a resolute empiricist.

* * *

Marginal Comment was controversial even before it was published. In September 1993 the book was offered to Oxford University Press, to whom Dover had promised first refusal. A total of four readers' views were solicited by the Press; correspondence about these, as well as a meeting, between Dover and Hilary O'Shea, the OUP Classics editor, took place between early January and early March 1994.[24] Although the readers diverged in their overall assessments of the book's merits (one found 'many good things' and 'ample material here for an interesting book', another thought it 'simply not interesting'), there was full

---

[20]On Dover's conception of the humanities, but his avoidance of a commitment to 'humanism', see Halliwell's epilogue in *S&C*.

[21]For a brief but nuanced account of the Rousseauesque model, and some of its problems, see the work of Dover's own former student (cf. p. 99) Bernard Williams, *Truth and Truthfulness* (Princeton, 2002) 173–85.

[22]M. Baxandall, *Episodes: A Memorybook* (London, 2010) 15, a work preoccupied with the elusive psychological processes involved in attempts to make sense of one's past life.

[23]On 'metaphysics', see the text at n. 11 above. For *MC*'s various references to philosophy, see the index; cf. Frisbee Sheffield's chapter in *S&C*.

[24]Copies of the correspondence are preserved in the Corpus Dover archive (see the Editorial Foreword); for further details of the book's rejection by OUP, see Stray's chapter in *S&C*. Possibly just a day before he received the first readers' reports (sent to him on 7 January 1994), Dover wrote to SH on 9 January, 'I await with trepidation the verdict of the Press's advisers'. One of the readers, Jasper Griffin, curiously contrived not even to mention *MC* in his obituary of Dover in the *Balliol College Annual Record 2010*, 45–7 (a piece also marred by multiple factual errors).

agreement that the work was problematic (at certain points 'embarrassing', 'indecent', 'disgusting') by reason of its outspoken criticism of individuals, its sexual explicitness, and some other aspects of its personal subject-matter. Three of the four were nonetheless open, to varying degrees, to the possibility of publication (the other was 'categorically' against), but only on condition of substantial changes and cuts. While somewhat indecisive discussion between author and editor was continuing, matters were not helped by a leak to the *Evening Standard* which produced a diary item making fun of an episode of masturbation described in the book.[25] Dover offered to make some cuts and changes but stood his ground as regards the memoir's sexual material. In early March, Hilary O'Shea apologetically informed him that OUP would not be able to publish the book. Dover then offered the book to Colin Haycraft, managing director of the publishers Duckworth, who had published Dover's *Greek Homosexuality* in 1978 and had built up an academic list which included monographs by many other distinguished classicists.[26] Haycraft accepted the book with enthusiasm, though he sadly died just a fortnight before its appearance.

Marginal Comment was eventually published in early November 1994. Within a few weeks, as we shall see, it had become headline news in the press, finding itself publicized on the front page of *The New York Times* and the subject, between late November and early February, of some thirty items – reports, reviews, comment columns, profiles, correspondence, and a *Times* leader – in the UK broadsheets. The main (and perhaps unexpected)[27] reason for this journalistic spotlight on the book was Dover's account, in Chapter 26, of his handling, when President of Corpus Christi College, Oxford, of circumstances leading up to the suicide of one of the college's fellows, Trevor Aston, in October 1985. Readers of this book can weigh for themselves the chapter in question, helped by the annotations in this edition (some of which register corrections to Dover's account), and reach their own conclusions about the various parties and points of view involved. But before considering some of the press reactions to this portion of *Marginal Comment* in late 1994 and early 1995, it is worth stating, as concisely and uncontentiously as possible, the critical factors in the Aston affair.

Trevor Aston had been a fellow of Corpus for a quarter of a century when Dover became President in 1976. Although widely recognized for his flair and passion as a historian, he had a history of grave psychological problems – probably bipolar disorder compounded by alcoholism – which had affected both his

---

[25] Dover subsequently incorporated this piece of publicity in the book itself: see 165 n. *.
[26] Cf. Hugh Lloyd-Jones, 'Publisher of the ancient classics', in Stoddard Martin, ed., *Colin Haycraft 1929–1994: Maverick Publisher* (London, 1995) 69–71.
[27] Deborah Blake, who was working at the time as an editor at Duckworth, reports (personal communication) that no one at the publisher's had seen the furore over the Aston chapter coming: the expectation was that, if anything, it would be the book's sexual passages which would attract controversy.

personal life (his first marriage has been described as 'deeply unhappy')[28] and his dealings with his colleagues. Aston's sometimes intemperate behaviour inevitably reminded Dover of his own father (see 2–3 above).[29] Nonetheless, for the first eight years or so of his presidency, Dover tried, he said, 'to do my best' for Aston, giving him 'a great deal of support and help' and continuing to be 'patient and tolerant'; another fellow of the college, the classicist Ewen Bowie, confirmed that Dover 'had enormous reserves of patience' and 'would listen to [Aston] for hours'.[30] After numerous twists and turns, some of them connected to Aston's overspending on the college library budget,[31] matters deteriorated sharply in the summer of 1985, when Aston's conduct towards his second wife led to an injunction against him and advance notice of her intention to divorce him. He attempted suicide on August 16, was compulsorily sectioned in the Warneford Hospital outside Oxford, tried to escape, and was eventually discharged though clearly far from well.[32] When further problems arose in Corpus itself in late September, some of them involving Aston's abusive treatment of college staff, Dover sent him a written warning on 30 September in what he took to be 'a frank and friendly tone' (*MC* 298). Dover also consulted several senior fellows, among whom there was agreement that Aston's resignation would be desirable, though no precise plan for how to elicit it seems to have been formulated.[33] A rancorous but inconclusive meeting took place between Dover and Aston. It evidently stretched Dover's patience to breaking point: in fateful words which the press publicity would endlessly repeat, Dover's memoir states that at this juncture he decided 'Trevor and the college must somehow be separated' and that the problem facing him as President was 'how to kill him without getting into trouble' (298).

---

[28]Quoted from the obituary of Aston's first wife, Margaret Aston (née Bridges), in *The Daily Telegraph*, 10 December 2014, p. 31.
[29]Dover admitted this consideration when it was put to him by Anthony Clare (*IPC* 99); cf. 18 below.
[30]For Dover's phrases, see *IPC* 97 and *ICNA* 104–5 (cf. n. 64 below); for Bowie's, the article by Cassandra Jardine in *The Daily Telegraph*, 25 November 1994, p. 19.
[31]See *CCH* 412–13, for further details, though their reference to the 'muzzling of [Aston's] powers as Librarian', together with their presentation of this as a 'stage' on the way to his suicide which partly reflected the 'morality' of Dover, is tendentious.
[32]For the details of this sequence of events I have taken account not only of *MC* itself but of *CCH* 409–18 and Ewen Bowie's article in *S&C*, both of which draw on an unpublished chronicle kept at the time by another Corpus fellow, James Howard-Johnston (see n. 36 below).
[33]Agreement that Aston's resignation was desirable is attested by C.C.W. Taylor, one of the senior fellows concerned, in his letter to *The Times* of 16 December 1994, p. 17, and the point was acknowledged by Dover in the addenda of the 1995 reprint of *MC* (p. 264, with an incorrect date for Taylor's letter); cf. *IPC* 101 for Dover's emphasis on having wanted to make Aston resign. However, Taylor's further claim that there was no consensus about taking action towards depriving Aston of his fellowship was not accepted by Dover (SN p. 32, with the claim that he was 'commissioned' to find out if the *History of the University* committee would 'give us a good pretext by sacking him'), and there is no way of adjudicating between their conflicting recollections: cf. *CCH* 416 n. 59.

'How to kill him', a phrase Dover came partially to regret,[34] was a sensationalized reference to the possibility of responding with inaction to a further suicide attempt, and perhaps even of helping to precipitate such an attempt. At a further meeting between the two men, Dover heightened Aston's fear that he might actually lose his fellowship, though by his own account he did so in spontaneous 'indignation', not as a calculated move.[35] In the final stages of the unfolding tragedy, a further circumstance, omitted from Dover's own narrative, played its part: a valuable book borrowed from the college library by Aston was found to be missing. That was on 14 October. Two days later, on what turned out to be the same day on which Aston received divorce papers from his wife's lawyers, Dover informed Aston that the matter of the missing book would be officially investigated.[36] Aston killed himself that night, though it was the divorce papers and a letter to his wife, not the communication about the library book, that were found next to him. It is worth adding that in the immediate aftermath of these events, little criticism of the President seems to have been voiced within Corpus, let alone outside it,[37] for his handling of the protracted problems between Aston and the college.

But that changed, to be sure, with the publication of *Marginal Comment* almost a decade later. The first newspaper column on the subject came from the *Guardian*'s literary editor, Richard Gott, who had fond memories of being taught as an Oxford history undergraduate by Trevor Aston (whose 'intemperate' and 'difficult' behaviour he conceded) and was shocked by Dover's confession that he had been willing to contemplate causing Aston's death by adding to the pressures that might push him to suicide.[38] Blurring the rather important distinction between wishing

---

[34]He told Naim Attallah that in the passage in question 'I may have made a mistake, though I'm not totally convinced of it': *ICNA* 103.

[35]The point is reinforced by Dover's description of this turn of events with a sentence that became widely quoted: Aston 'put a dagger into my hand, and I used it unthinkingly to greater effect than I could have achieved by calculation' (*MC* 299). Cf. n. 62 below for Dover's sense of how 'wounding' this meeting proved for Aston.

[36]The matter of the library book was not originally mentioned in *MC*; Dover's explanation for this omission was added to the 1995 reprint: see n. 24 to p. 300 of this edition. The subject was publicized by James Howard-Johnston, a fellow of Corpus who had long harboured reservations about Dover's presidency (see the view reported by his stepfather, Hugh Trevor-Roper, in R. Davenport-Hines and A. Sisman, eds, *One Hundred Letters from Hugh Trevor-Roper* (Oxford, 2014) 251): as well as mentioning it to two *Sunday Times* journalists (27 November 1994), he wrote an open 'letter' to Dover in *The Independent*, 29 November 1994, p. 19, and later stressed the point to Kenneth Rose, author of the 'Albany at Large' diary in *The Sunday Telegraph*, 8 January 1995, p. 27, promoting the claim that the threatened investigation of the missing book may have helped to precipitate Aston's suicide. Perhaps strangely, Howard-Johnston's suggestion was largely ignored in the widespread publicity about the Aston affair, though it was taken up by Paul Thompson in 'The life and work of Trevor Aston', *History Workshop Journal* 39 (1995) 250–69, at 266, to which Dover briefly responded in a letter, *History Workshop Journal* 41 (1996) 261–2 (points 7 and 11).

[37]The claim by Margalit Fox in the *New York Times* obituary of Dover, 14 March 2010, p. 26, that his 'moral culpability' for Aston's death was 'roundly debated' at the time 'in British academic circles', has no foundation.

[38]Richard Gott, 'Standfirst' column, *The Guardian*, 22 November 1994, p. 9.

and doing, Gott actually surmised that 'Dover seems to have killed off my tutor'. Alluding also to some of the sexual revelations in the memoir, Gott bundled these two things together in the rhetorically florid suggestion that Dover represented the 'psychic and sexual energies' which were more generally lurking in 'our ancient universities'. Gott himself, it transpired, was not unfamiliar with problematic secrets; only a fortnight after his column appeared, he resigned from his post at *The Guardian* when information emerged of his former entanglements with the KGB, including receipt of some payments from that quarter.[39] But his column had nonetheless lit, as it were, the blue touch paper as regards *Marginal Comment*, and a flurry of other pieces soon followed.

The Times, for example, published three separate items on the book in less than a week. Under the curiously binary headline of 'Oxford president plotted don's death' but also (rather clumsily) 'Classicist blames suicide on divorce', the Education Editor John O'Leary, after a telephone conversation with Dover, made some effort to give a balanced account of the competing sides of the case, though not without factual errors which Dover corrected in a letter to the paper.[40] A more outspoken column by Libby Purves moralistically reduced Dover's conviction that the interests of a community ultimately outweigh those of a (harmful) individual to the 'assumption that inconvenient people ought to die'. She supposed, moreover, on the basis of Dover's professional concern with pagan antiquity, that his mentality reflected a 'pre-Christian' ethic, though her implication that Christianity's record was more humane than 'the cruel ancient world' studied by Dover betrayed something less than an extensive knowledge of history.[41] The putative traces of a 'harsh, pre-Christian morality' were also identified by a *Times* leader of just two days later which endorsed what it regarded as the widespread 'revulsion' induced by *Marginal Comment*. Dover himself wrote to the paper to rebut the hypothesis of pagan influence, noting that his attitude to homicide was shared by many, including his own parents, who did not have 'the faintest idea of the ancient world'.[42]

The dominant tone of the newspaper reports was certainly one of shock at the ostensibly callous nature of Dover's words, with the 'how to kill him' passage

---

[39]On the extent of Gott's dealings with the KGB, see C. Andrew and V. Mitrokhin, *The Mitrokhin Archive: the KGB in Europe and the West* (Harmondsworth, 2000) 557, 869 n. 69.

[40]For O'Leary's piece, see n. 7 above; Dover's letter was printed on 3 December, p. 19.

[41]Libby Purves, 'A bizarre plot in the groves of academe: The chilling sting of a Fellow's death', *The Times*, 28 November 1994, p. 17. For Dover's own very different views, note *GPM* 133: 'it is questionable whether Christian faith has been a better moral influence in human history than pagan uncertainty', with a reference to Christian 'cruelty' in the same context; cf. ibid., xiii.

[42]The leader, 'Death in the cloister', appeared in *The Times* for 30 November 1994, p. 23; Dover's letter was the one cited in n. 40 above. Dover's denial that his moral attitudes were influenced by those of ancient Greece is made as a general observation in *MC* itself (223), though he did compare his stance on Trevor Aston to a tendency of Greek thought in his conversation with the *Telegraph* journalist Cassandra Jardine (n. 12 above). Given Dover's view of morality as unsystematic, untheoretical and non-rational (see esp. *MC* 219–20), it is worth adding that *CCH* 410–12 is philosophically confused in calling him a 'utilitarian'.

quoted again and again, if sometimes in a way which left doubt whether the chapter as a whole, including Dover's explanation of the many years spent trying to help Aston, had been read and digested. The same doubt applied even more pointedly to the terms in which Lord Monkswell, who had presumably been perusing the newspapers too quickly, raised the matter in a House of Lords question at the start of December.[43] By no means all the press publicity, however, was negative to Dover. Several pieces tried at least to strike a degree of balance, some of them citing the contrasting verdicts on Dover arrived at by different fellows of Corpus itself: this was so, for instance, with the report which appeared on the front page of *The New York Times*.[44] But a number of writers went further, committing themselves to strong sympathy for Dover's predicament in dealing with Aston. James Fenton and Laurence Marks, both in *The Independent*, and Barbara Trapido in *The Guardian*, all felt able to see things from his point of view.[45] Fenton thought, not without reason, that the 'style' in which Dover had recounted his part in the Aston affair was more shocking than its substance; he discerned Dover's underlying 'humanity' and was prepared to say, where Aston's 'utterly intolerable' and manipulative behaviour was concerned, that the 'mad' could also be 'bad'. Somewhat similarly, Marks, in a profile which reckoned with the memoir as a whole, found an 'obvious humanity' on Dover's part, despite his supposed 'profession of cold-bloodedness'; he took the latter to involve an element of melodramatic self-presentation, and concluded that Dover 'did nothing criminal or cruel', even though Aston had become 'an insufferable colleague' in his later years. Barbara Trapido was the most outspoken of the three in Dover's defence: 'my heart', she declared, 'goes out to the president'. Drawing on her own experience of struggling to help a mentally ill alcoholic academic whom she thought resembled Aston in manipulative deviousness, she said that this had 'brought home to me that everyone has a threshold': 'there will be a day when one decides to cut loose', and Dover had 'managed 10 years' before doing so. As for the impression of 'callous bravado' in the memoir's narrative, Dover was 'merely being honest enough not to pretend that he is sorry'.

Amidst all this publicity in the press, the two most important contributions came from fellows of Corpus who had lived through the whole decade of Dover's

---

[43]Lord Monkswell asked whether the government would refer to the Crown Prosecution Service 'the assertion by Sir Kenneth Dover that he was responsible [sic] for the death of Mr. Trevor Aston'; Baroness Blatch, on behalf of the government, replied that the police were looking into the details of the case: Hansard, vol. 559, for 1 December 1994.

[44]See n. 8 above: Darnton's article quotes both James Howard-Johnston and Brian Harrison, for whose views see, respectively, n. 36 above and pp. 14–15 below. The same two sources were also quoted by Mary Braid, *The Independent*, 27 November 1994, p. 9 (a piece marred by the misleading statement that Dover claimed to have 'engineered the death' of Aston).

[45]James Fenton, *The Independent*, 28 November 1994, p. 14; Barbara Trapido, *The Guardian*, 2 December 1994, p. 26; Laurence Marks, *The Independent*, 9 December 1994, p. 1.

presidency and had witnessed the evolution of Trevor Aston's relationship with the college over an even longer period. The pair of articles in question, both published in the 'Perspective' section of what was then *The Times Higher Education Supplement*, revealed how far apart were the opposite ends of the spectrum of views held on the matter by those who had been able to observe at close quarters Dover's handling of Aston's problems. The first, penned by Valentine Cunningham (who had been tutorial fellow in English since 1972), made its animus clear at the outset by speaking of Dover's thoughts of 'fixing the death' of Aston, even 'bumping [him] off'.[46] After admitting Aston's capacity for boorishness and binge-drinking, Cunningham dwelt on his countervailing qualities, 'at his best', of charisma, charm and aesthetic sensitivity, the latter qualified only by the excessively lavish expenditure on buildings and library acquisitions in which it sometimes encouraged him to indulge. The article was carefully designed to set up a stark contrast between this figure, albeit flawed, of 'creativity and sensitivity' and, on the other hand, the 'unremitting rationalism', the austere empiricism, and the quasi-Spartan *lack* of aesthetic sensibility on the part of Kenneth Dover.[47] The gravamen of Cunningham's case was that Aston was a 'poetic soul' whose life displayed and succumbed to the inevitable 'messiness' of human existence, whereas Dover represented an inhumane 'hard-mindedness' whose treatment of Aston was 'too brutal a piece of management'.

It is all the more telling, therefore, that Cunningham's piece should have been answered, a fortnight later, by the radically different views of another Corpus don, Brian Harrison (later knighted in 2005), who had been tutorial fellow in modern history and politics since 1967 and was Senior Tutor at the time of Trevor Aston's death.[48] Harrison started by describing Cunningham's portrait of Aston as 'brilliant' and true to the complexities of the man. But he strongly challenged the 'pasteboard figure' which Cunningham had constructed in his critique of Dover. Harrison admired Dover for his liberal values, his genuine liking for students, his good-humoured accessibility, and his preoccupation with the college's welfare. He disputed Cunningham's depiction of Dover as a man without emotions: 'behind the scenes', Harrison stated, he could be 'a profoundly emotional person'. At the same time he dissented from Cunningham's 'tendency to depreciate the role of reason in human affairs', defending Dover's rationalism as something hopeful, not dogmatic. Above all, in a move which puts the whole Aston affair in a different light not only from Cunningham's article but also from Dover's own account,

---

[46]Valentine Cunningham, 'Contract terminated', THES, 9 December 1994, p. 15.
[47]Dover wrote to THES on 6 January 1995, p. 10, protesting that while there was certainly a clash of character between himself and Aston, there was no clash of aesthetic culture: 'During my years of friendship with Mr Aston, which preceded the much shorter period of conflict, we constantly and strongly agreed on all matters which could be brought under the rubric "culture"'.
[48]B. Harrison, 'The Kenneth Dover I knew', THES, 23 December 1994, pp. 16–17.

Harrison insisted that the crisis had not been a 'contest between two contrasting characters', nor had Dover acted as an individual: the nub of the matter was 'the reluctant struggle by the fellows of Corpus to carry out their statutory duty' by facing up to the challenge posed by Aston's conduct.

No one who was not directly involved in the Aston affair can properly adjudicate between the different perspectives of Cunningham and Harrison. But one of Harrison's points carries special weight in relation to the nature of *Marginal Comment* itself. He hypothesizes that Dover may have retrospectively constructed a more ruthless-sounding stance on his part towards Aston than he actually took at the time, that the desire to be rid of Aston, as well as the sense of relief at his eventual death, were 'passing thoughts' rather than active motives, and that Dover's 'confessional' account, however much he convinced himself of its accuracy, had a 'self-punitive' aspect which stemmed from his humane yet unsentimental view of the world. Harrison's analysis is on a level of insight and sophistication far beyond the predominantly formulaic newspaper reactions to *Marginal Comment*.[49] And it serves to foreground the fact that part of what made the autobiography 'experimental' for its author (see 3 above) was an attempt to test not only his readers' sensibilities but also, and more far-reachingly, the limits of what he was prepared to believe about himself.

To conclude this survey of the reception of *Marginal Comment* in the few months after its publication, a glance at some formal reviews of the book is in place. Two short early reviews by writers knowledgeable about Dover's achievements as a classicist struck positive notes and succeeded in avoiding the easy moralizing that characterized the more general publicity in the press.[50] Peter Jones found the book 'extraordinary' and 'engrossing', seeing a quintessential parallel between the work's uncompromising honesty and its author's 'uncompromising scholarship'.[51] Philip Howard in *The Times* similarly thought that Dover's 'rigorous and sometimes embarrassing truth-telling' about his life (though the media had 'overblown' the treatment of the Aston affair) matched the precision of his 'scholarly footnotes'; the book displayed Dover as 'one of the sharpest, most original and most humane minds' of his generation.[52] But the verdict of Ross Leckie, a former student at Corpus during Dover's presidency (and, prior to that, a friend of Dover's son, Alan), could hardly have been more different:

---

[49] James Fenton's column in *The Independent* (n. 45 above) shares with Harrison the view that Dover was 'hard on himself' over Aston, but it does not develop the point as fully as Harrison.

[50] Another review by a classical scholar, Paul Cartledge's 'Blunt and blue', *New Statesman and Society*, 9 December 1994, p. 39, managed uniquely to praise the book's frankness without mentioning the name of Trevor Aston, though there is one faint allusion to the subject.

[51] 'A classicist's confessions', *The Sunday Telegraph*, 27 November 1994, review section, p. 12. A few days later, Jones also published a wide-ranging profile of Dover in *The Scotsman*, 30 November 1994, magazine p. 16.

[52] 'Donning the truth', *The Times*, 1 December 1994, p. 40.

unstinting though he was in his admiration for Dover the scholar ('the greatest classicist of our century') and the stylist ('beautifully written'), he nonetheless felt that he emerged from the memoir as a 'weirdo' and that the book 'advances our understanding of nothing but the strangeness of man'.[53]

Longer reviews naturally varied in what they highlighted, whether praising or finding fault with the work. Max Beloff's conservative standpoint led him to focus somewhat oddly on what he called Dover's lack of resistance to 'the impact of egalitarian and feminist ideologies' on the British educational system, a rather oblique way of alluding to his part in the reform of the Oxford admissions system (ch. 27) and his support for making Corpus a co-educational college (ch. 22); Beloff's was also the only high-profile review to complain, not without reason, about Dover's idiosyncratic invention of the graphemes 'hrm' and 'hrs' (see p. 22). Bernard Knox, a major classical scholar in his own right, admired what he saw as a lack of 'self-glorification' and acknowledged the author's 'life of devoted service to humanistic education'. By contrast, another top-flight Hellenist, Hugh Lloyd-Jones, discerned 'marked egoism' in the book, though this did not prevent him from lavishing praise on Dover as 'a scholar of prodigious powers' as well as largely siding with him over the Aston affair (as, indeed, Knox did too).[54] In another review by a professional classicist, Mary Beard, not unlike Lloyd-Jones, found an element of 'sheer exhibitionism' in the memoir (something Dover had explicitly anticipated), though she also tried to deflate the controversy over Aston by stating her impression that Dover 'admits to little more than an unwillingness to strive officiously to keep the man alive'.[55] More generally, Beard was disappointed that the book did not, in her terms, fulfil its aim of exploring the interaction between the personal and the professional, a reading not shared by other reviewers and one which is at least partly unfair to the many ways in which Dover exposes to view the entanglements between the life of the mind and the life of the body.[56] Perhaps most importantly, Beard drew a contrast with the wider array of non-academic connections attested in the autobiographies of earlier classicists such as Maurice

---

[53]'Sad chapters best forgotten', *Scotland on Sunday*, 1 January 1995.

[54]Max Beloff, 'In the margins, but from the heart', *The Times Higher Education Supplement*, 23 December 1994, p. 21; Bernard Knox, 'Habeas Corpus', *The Times Literary Supplement*, 13 January 1995, p. 22; Hugh Lloyd-Jones, 'Not always the best policy', *The Spectator*, 28 January 1995, pp. 30–2 (a review marred by a crop of incorrect dates). Lloyd-Jones may also have been the author of the obituary of Dover in *The Telegraph*, 9 March 2010, p. 31, which has the same combination of high praise for his scholarship with criticism of his 'adolescent desire to shock', the latter slur described in turn as 'bottomlessly ignorant' in the obituary by Peter Jones, *The Spectator*, 13 March 2010, p. 26.

[55]'Straight talk', *London Review of Books*, 9 February 1995, pp. 12–13. See *MC* 24 for Dover's own anticipation of the risk of being regarded as 'exhibitionist'.

[56]As well as the numerous details which actually show (without formally asserting) the entwinement of the personal and the professional, Beard seems to take no account of major statements such as p. 113 (part of the context of the notorious Matese masturbation episode, 114!) on how Dover's work on Greek homosexuality impinged on his own ideas about sex, or p. 161 on how a similar interaction occurred between his work on *GPM* and his general views on morality.

Bowra and E.R. Dodds, employing this contrast to underwrite the conclusion that Dover's life illustrated how Classics had now ceased to be at the centre of British cultural life.[57]

* * *

Marginal Comment was not exactly, or in all respects, Dover's final word on his life. For one thing, as noted in the Editorial Foreword, he left a substantial typescript (over thirty pages) of supplementary notes to his memoir, which are quoted and drawn on in some of the annotations to this edition. For another, he engaged in a good deal of correspondence with people who wrote to him about the book or, in some cases, had published reviews of it: I shall cite one of the most telling cases of such correspondence in conclusion below. He also took advantage of a few further opportunities to write or deliver talks about parts of his life. One of these was a column in the *Times Higher Education Supplement* which expanded the reference in the memoir itself to his childhood encounter with an English version of Fabre's *Book of Insects*, a work which not only turned him into an avid entomologist but, he said, 'opened up the world to me' and started to form in him a particular way of thinking about social animals.[58] Another was a talk he gave in St Andrews in March 2000 as part of a celebration of his eightieth birthday, when, among much else, he said that 'Of all the non-academic experiences in my life, I think really that five years in the Army during the War mattered most.' Finally, he gave two extended published interviews, one with the psychiatrist Anthony Clare, and one with the publisher Naim Attallah.[59]

The interviews inevitably rehearse much material from the memoir, for the most part duplicating rather than adding to what is said in the book itself. But there are certainly some significant points of illumination. Part of the interest of the Clare interview resides in the expertise of the interviewer, an experienced clinical psychiatrist who had clearly read *Marginal Comment* in detail and showed a shrewd interest in both Dover's own psychology and the mental problems of Trevor Aston.[60]

---

[57]Of later reviews, note John Gross, *The New Criterion*, March 1995, p. 64, giving a very full account of the Aston affair and judging Dover to have been under 'point-blank provocation'; Sheldon Rothblatt, *Academe*, 82.3, May-June 1996, pp. 74–5, deeming that the details of the Aston affair 'vindicate the president'; Martha Nussbaum, 'A stoic's confessions' (n. 4 above), which offers a perspective on Dover's whole *oeuvre* and ends with some acute psychological reflections on the memoir.

[58]*The Times Higher Education Supplement*, 5 May 1995, p. 23.

[59]The transcript in *IPC* of the Clare interview (first broadcast on BBC radio, 20 August 1995) contains several errors, some of them significant: on p. 85, 'Greek word order' has become 'Greek world order' (Clare's spoken error; he perhaps doubted that the former could possibly be correct!); on p. 95, 'paint' should be 'print' (not part of the broadcast version); and, most seriously, on p. 100 Dover's statement in *MC* 299 that in one of their last conversations Trevor Aston 'put a dagger into my hand' has been twice reversed as 'you put a dagger in his hand' (in the broadcast, Clare got this *right* the first time and wrong the second!).

[60]The assertion in the *Telegraph* obituary of Dover (cf. n. 54 above for its possible authorship) that 'so disoriented was Clare by the encounter that towards the end it seemed as if Dover was the one doing the interviewing' is bafflingly crass in its failure to appreciate Clare's adeptness.

This enabled Clare to probe the extent to which the impression some had of Dover's icily rational self-control was a 'mask' that concealed strong underlying emotions. In this regard, Clare teased out an admission that Aston, a 'hostile, mercurial, emotionally incontinent individual', had reminded Dover of his own father.[61] Clare himself thought that some of Dover's handling of Aston had been 'eminently reasonable, indeed quite humane and kind' (*IPC* 100), but he also extracted from Dover the revelation, *à propos* the infamous conversation with Aston reported at *MC* 300, that Dover realized at the time, possibly with a touch of pity, what an 'awful wound' it was to Aston to mention uncertainty surrounding the renewal of the latter's fellowship in 1982.[62] Clare brings his knowledge and sensitivity to bear on other matters as well, including Dover's attitudes to shame (*vis-à-vis* guilt),[63] religion, depression, and suicide. All in all, his observation that Dover 'often say[s] things that people actually do think but they don't always reveal' (*IPC* 92), and that this involves a kind of honesty (97), is stamped with Clare's professional judgement.

The interview with Naim Attallah is a little shorter but also more wide-ranging than the one with Clare. It lacks the latter's probing intelligence but is less narrowly focused on just a few central aspects of Dover's mentality. While selecting its main topics from the memoir, and inevitably revisiting the Trevor Aston affair (on which Dover strikingly claims that he knew Aston better than did some Corpus fellows who had sided with the latter during the controversy over *Marginal Comment*),[64] it succeeds in drawing out additional reflections on, for example, the nature of Dover's religious agnosticism, his 'sense of being an individual in a social species', old age (there's 'absolutely nothing' to be said for it), suicide, and his scepticism about the beneficence of nature ('Civilization consists in combating nature'). Finally, in defending some of the things he had written about the dead in his memoir, even where some of the living might 'rather not have known' those things, Dover remarks, 'But there the harsh duty of the historian comes in' (*ICNA* 95). The autobiographer, then, in the final resort, as historian: confirmation that Dover conceived of himself, more than anything else, as 'a history man' (the memoir's final chapter title).

Where autobiography is concerned, however, there is more than one kind of 'history' at issue, and more than one canon of historical truth. It is a general (if highly defeasible) expectation of the genre that it should supply not just an authentic record of what has been lived through and experienced, but something like a privileged first-person insight into the author's mind. Nobody doubts that

---

[61]See the introduction to the interview, *IPC* 84–5, with Clare's stress on the difference between rational exterior and emotional interior at 88, and the question relating to Dover's father at 99 and 107.
[62]*IPC* 100, with p. 11 above and the editorial notes on the passage of *MC* in question.
[63]There is a moment of delicious humour where Dover's statement that 'I don't really go in for guilt' elicits from Clare, in origin a Dublin-born Catholic, the riposte, 'You're not Irish!' (*IPC* 101).
[64]See *ICNA* 106, including the statement that 'Not only was I a friend of Trevor's for eight years but I was also in many respects his confidant. He told me a lot about himself that I don't think they knew …'

Marginal Comment is unsparingly candid and, to a considerable extent, quasi-documentary in what it records. But more than one judgement is possible on its status as a self-portrait. On that front, it is worth considering in conclusion the disappointed and carefully weighed verdict of one of Dover's oldest friends (they went all the way back to their Oxford undergraduate days together), the classicist Donald Russell. Unbeknownst to Dover, Russell had been one of the readers who had originally cautioned Oxford University Press against publication of the work in its submitted form (see n. 24 above). About two months after the memoir had appeared, at the point when it was receiving maximum publicity in the press, he wrote to Dover to thank him for the return of the negative from which the book's frontispiece (a photograph taken by Russell's wife, who had died in 1993) had been printed (see now Figure 13), and he took the opportunity, though clearly with painful misgivings ('it has not been easy to write this', he says towards the end), to express some of his feelings about the autobiography.[65] The letter manifests a characteristic spirit of elegiac sadness, but not without courage on Russell's part in criticizing such an old and close friend. It is a moving document, especially for anyone who knew the two men. Having said that many thought it 'cruel' as well as a 'betrayal of confidence' to have revived the tragic story of Aston's death, Russell declared: 'I understand reactions like this very well; indeed, I have to say I share them.' But appealing to the bond of friendship between them (for which he uses some Greek, as in two other parts of the letter as well) he went on to make a larger criticism: 'I should like to say that I found the book fascinating (it has made me think a lot) but not really "you", or worthy of you'; 'the qualities your friends love in you', he suggested, especially a humane and sympathetic character, were not visible in the book. 'I am sad about this', Russell admits, before adding wisely and wistfully, 'I reflect that we are all the worst possible evaluators of ourselves'.[66]

Rather startlingly, we have here a reader who tells the autobiographer that no matter how 'candid' he has been, no matter how much he purports to have removed a facade and revealed 'the truth within', he has in effect done the very opposite, actually falsifying the person that his best friends knew him to be. On this level, as opposed to that of strictly factual veracity, Russell was prepared to say, 'I do *not* believe the book' (with his emphasis). Dover, for his part, could only reply that 'others thought the opposite' and that 'different people saw different sides of him', to which he added elsewhere the striking *aperçu* that '*Everyone* is the person people

---

[65] The original of the letter, dated 7 December 1994, is preserved in the Dover papers at Corpus Christi: see the Editorial Foreword under the abbreviation SN.
[66] In correspondence with SH on 16 June 2011, Russell restated his view of 'a mismatch between Kenneth as I knew him and the persona of *MC*. It still seems to me that, by trying to be confessional, he revealed – or assumed – a remarkable degree of personal ὕβρις', the last word (Greek *hubris*) here in the sense less of pride than of harshly insistent self-assertiveness. Cf. also Russell's *Times* obituary of Dover, 9 March 2010, p. 60, and his remarks in *KJD* 172–3.

knew *plus* the person they didn't'.[67] With that double disagreement – between author and one particularly careful reader, as well as between different readers – we are left with an irresolvable enigma, if not about autobiography in general then certainly about *Marginal Comment* and its author. The book's exceptional frankness, whose partly paradoxical character was addressed at the start of this Introduction, has turned out, it seems, not to encourage convergence on the 'real' Kenneth Dover but to open up a larger space for sharply divergent viewpoints on the subject. There is no escape, after all, from the operations of perspective. And that is a consideration that will continue to impinge on readers who approach this challenging and unsettling book afresh from whatever historical distance is available to them.

---

[67]Dover's response to Russell is as reported by Russell himself in *KJD* 173 n. 25; I have not seen Dover's actual reply, though in the margin of Russell's letter in the Corpus archive he indicates that Geoffrey Rickman (see p. 183) was one of those who took the opposite view to Russell's. '*Everyone* is the person etc.' (with Dover's own emphasis) is from a letter to Ross Leckie of 19 December 1994 (also in the Corpus papers).

PREFACE

The title needs explanation, and three explanations converge.

In my professional life as a scholar I have hardly ever been a worker at the rock-face, discovering and editing inscriptions, papyri or hitherto unknown manuscripts, but rather a commentator, synthesising and interpreting what others have brought to light and, to the best of my ability, generating new ideas from old material.

In my life as a whole I feel, despite the responsibilities I have borne and the influence I have exercised, that I have nevertheless been more an observer than a participant, 'marginalised' not by any ill-will on the part of anyone else but by circumstances over which I had no control. My childhood and adolescence turned me into the kind of person to whom duty comes more easily than passion. There are many things about which I know something, but few, outside my professional work, in which I am active, and even fewer in which I can claim expert knowledge or high performance. I cannot sing in tune, or play a musical instrument faster than *maestoso*, or keep afloat in water, or stay on a horse when it canters. I have never completed a crossword, won a game of chess, or succeeded in remembering the rules of any card-game more subtle than pontoon. I know much more about plants, insects, birds and animals than the average person, but much less than a good gardener or a good naturalist. My judgement on how to get from one place to another on wild country in bad weather is better than most people's, but not comparable to a mountaineer's. And so on.

Margins have a further significance for me. Whenever I walk or drive along a country road, especially a moorland road, and come upon a stretch without fence or ditch, where I can turn off the road at will, a deep, sweet satisfaction possesses me. I thought of calling this book *Roads without Fences* (not *Unfenced Roads*, which is phonologically repellent), but decided that this struck a note of complacent libertarianism wholly out of tune with my life.

K.J.D.

St Andrews
May 1994

ACKNOWLEDGEMENTS

The whole typescript of this book was read by my wife and by Christopher and Adèle Rathbone; and certain parts of it were read by my daughter, Brian Harrison and Jay Parini.[1] All these readers drew my attention to passages which seemed to them obscure, inconsequential or misleading. In many places I changed the text to meet these criticisms, but there are many others about which I was obdurate.

I am greatly indebted for the provision of photographs to Professor D.A.F.M. Russell (Figure 13 [colour frontispiece in the 1994 edition]) and Professor L.E. Fraenkel (Figure 4). I am also indebted to the following for permission to use illustrations which I already had: St Andrews University (no. 11) and the Leverhulme Trust (no. 10). Photographs nos. 1, 2 and 5 were taken by my mother, nos. 9 and 12 by me.[2]

Linguistic Note – The grapheme 'hrm' should be pronounced 'him', 'her' or 'him or her', according to the context and the reader's predilection. So too 'hrs' is the grapheme for 'his', 'her', 'hers', 'his or her' or 'his or hers', and 's/he' for 'he', 'she' or 'he or she'.

---

[1] The last three have contributed 'memories' of Dover to *S&C*. (Eds)
[2] This paragraph of Dover's acknowledgements has been adjusted to fit the selection of photographs included in the present edition.

1 ON AUTOBIOGRAPHY

'It is often revealing to work out why something is fascinating,' he starts. *'Recently I tried to fathom why the French Revolution has stirred my interest and imagination for so long.'* No doubt, but why should we *be interested in that?*

AUBERON WAUGH[1]

Some years ago I took part, with a handful of students and lecturers, in an open-ended discussion which dug much deeper than ordinary conversation.[2] For example, the question was raised, 'Has anyone here ever seriously contemplated suicide?' Several of us said, 'Yes', though no one was willing to reveal circumstances and reasons. Then, 'What's your fundamental purpose in life?' One student said, 'To save my soul', and nobody minded. I expect I said, 'To be useful.' A bland purpose, perhaps; but it was Benjamin Britten's declared motive for composing music.[3]

What makes an autobiography useful? Affinities, I suppose, between the reader's predicaments and the writer's, and the possibility that the writer may suggest solutions which have eluded the reader. Yet I am aware of belonging to a minority in any classification of contemporary lives. For one thing, I am an intellectual;[4] that is to say, I derive intense and unfailing enjoyment from learning, analysing, investigating, reflecting and explaining, I value silence and solitude, and I am very

---

[1] From a book review in *The Independent*, 14 July 1989, p. 21, of John Haycraft, *In Search of the French Revolution* (London, 1989), by the journalist Auberon Waugh (1939–2001), son of the novelist Evelyn Waugh and known for his caustic wit (amply on display in this particular review).

[2] It is a reasonable speculation that this was the same occasion as the one referred to on p. 209.

[3] 'What matters to us now is that people want to use our music. For that, as I see it, is our job – to be useful, and to the living.' From a tribute by Britten to Michael Tippett on his sixtieth birthday in 1965: P. Kildea, ed., *Britten on Music* (Oxford, 2003) 274.

[4] In an addendum to the 1995 reprint Dover said 'People in whom the spirit of enquiry is debilitated by obsessive attachment to theory have given intellectuals a bad name.' On his negative view of 'theory', cf. p. 337.

rarely bored, except by drunks and people who talk too much about golf, dogs, or geraniums. For another thing, I have always enjoyed economic security. My father had a safe, pensionable job in the lower-middle reaches of the Civil Service. I began my professional career at 28, after five years as a student and five as a soldier, with savings of £500 and a legacy of £1,400 from my grandmother, at a salary of £700 a year, in a job which I knew I could not lose except through some gross delinquency or deficiency on my part. In worldly success I have gone far beyond the ambitions I entertained in my twenties. I have had to contend with some deep-seated and long-standing misfortunes, but I have also had some very lucky escapes from misfortune.

What interests me most when I contemplate my own life is the interaction of the personal and the professional. Biographies tend to treat one or the other perfunctorily, or, if they include both, turn them into more of a sandwich than a salad. The issue is intimately connected with the problem of selectivity. A historian has to select, because if s/he did not hrs task would never be completed; s/he has to decide what mattered, what made the difference. Since this book is autobiography and only incidentally a contribution to the history of British society, the university system and classical studies in the twentieth century, my criterion of selection is necessarily what made a difference to me. Some of those things were private, momentary, perhaps so trivial in the eyes of others that nobody noticed. This may not be everyone's experience; but how can we know, so long as people are reticent through fear of being thought vain if they speak of what is to their credit, or exhibitionists if it is discreditable, or 'unbalanced' if they reveal how little things affected them and big things did not?*

Since my subject-matter is my own experience I have a uniquely privileged access to it. Here comes danger. What I say about my own thoughts and feelings at a given time in the past, or about what was said by others during an event of which I am the sole surviving witness, cannot be checked against independent evidence. Even if my intentions are honest, it is notoriously true that one may retroject one's present views into the past, and be badly wrong. I think I can escape that danger, because although I have never kept a journal, and my engagement diaries (from 1945 onwards) serve only to provide a secure chronological framework, it has also been my custom to make an immediate note of my feelings about any good or bad event which deeply affected me. This record is sparse, but it has been invaluable in correcting distortions of memory, and that was always my purpose. What is much

---

*Early in 1994 Stephen Milligan, a Member of Parliament universally (and justly) liked and admired for his moral character, died accidentally while enacting an elaborate and perilous masturbatory fantasy. Since I found his fantasy grotesque and entirely without appeal, I wondered how many other people found it so, and this led to a question of the greatest importance: among all the people I have ever known, how many are there of whom I can say that I *know* what fantasies they entertain (and perhaps enact)? The answer was quick and firm: there are none.

more important, when my father died in 1978 he left a stack of files in a cupboard at the bottom of a bookcase and I forgot all about them until I came to empty the bookcase in pursuit of woodworm in 1990. I then found that the files contained all the letters I had written to my parents from 1938 to 1972.[5] Since these letters were mainly narrative (with a disagreeably insensitive argumentative strand in the earlier years), and I had assumed that my parents would be interested in pretty well everything that happened, this archive reminded me of much that I had forgotten, and it has left me little room for speculative reconstruction. Of course I omitted one or two things; but what a son omits in writing to his parents is the kind of thing he is in least danger of forgetting.

I accept responsibility for my actions and words, and my processes of rational thought can fairly be judged competent or incompetent. For my feelings, desires, fears and hopes I accept no responsibility at all; they simply happened to me, like health and sickness, good weather and bad. Not wanting evaluation to obtrude too much on narrative, I have only rarely drawn attention to differences between my present and past feelings. I must advise psychoanalysts, professional and amateur, that when I omit, as I usually do, to offer explanations in terms of Freudian psychodynamics, it would be imprudent to assume that the omission is caused by ignorance.[6] It's just that I wouldn't want to spoil their fun.

Some of the data which I have selected as important determinants of my life will seem to the reader ridiculous, embarrassing, contemptible or disgusting. Some readers, indeed, may decide that I am a lunatic. If so they may still find something of historical and sociological interest in the process by which a lunatic was so often invested (by election) with honours and responsibilities.

There are three determinants which affected me in childhood and have affected me ever since. I cannot hesitate in identifying the most important of all: it is my funnel chest, a grotesque and repulsive deformity which caused the centre of my sternum to recede and the bottom ribs to project. Thanks to a skotoma[7] remarkable even by my standards I was not conscious of this deformity until one afternoon in September 1932. Since then I have been oppressed by a feeling of inferiority, a feeling that I have been masquerading as a human being all my life.[8] I do not, in

---

[5] The surviving letters available to the Editors (see the Foreword) unfortunately do not extend beyond 1963.
[6] For Dover's (ambivalent) attitudes to Freudian psychoanalysis, cf. pp. 31–2 and 176–8.
[7] A blind spot (literal or metaphorical); Dover prefers a stricter Greek spelling to the more usual 'scotoma'. Cf. *IPC* 86.
[8] In his own copy of *MC* Dover sellotaped opposite this sentence a photocopied extract from an interview by Naim Attallah with the American novelist John Updike in which the latter explained how the experience of psoriasis had isolated him 'to a degree where I ... didn't feel I had hundred-per-cent credentials for being human' and had made him 'doubt my humanity': Naim Attallah, *Asking Questions: An Anthology of Encounters with Naim Attallah* (London, 1996) 489. For Dover's discovery of his funnel chest, see. p. 48, with a further reference to his resulting sense of 'inferiority' on p. 58.

this or any other connection, use 'feel' as a synonym for 'think' or 'believe', and I am aware that there are people who have far worse deformities and disabilities to cope with; but I am also aware that there are very, very many who have none. If I acquiesced in one of the more idiotic of contemporary fashions, I suppose I would call myself 'differently formed' rather than 'deformed' ('pectorally challenged'?), but I applaud Bernard Levin's dictum, 'Every euphemism is a lie', and I prefer nasty truths to silly lies.[9]

The second most important thing in my life was the bad relations between my parents, whose fundamental difference of temperament stretched beyond productive complementarity into miserable conflict. I cannot look back on a secure and happy home and childhood. This, however, had one fortunate result: since it was obvious to me that there was no unified grown-up view of the world, which I could expect to understand and accept as I matured, I had to make my own choices between contradictory values from the very beginning.

That was assisted by the third most important ingredient of my childhood, my precocity. I am told that as a baby I showed more interest in the columns of print on the front page of the newspaper than in the pictures. I certainly learned to read by the time I was three, and vividly remember my horror, on my first day at school, when I was offered what I indignantly called 'a baby's book' to read. That is one thing which, if I could have my life over again, I would certainly not want to change.

In two respects I have chosen to be guilty of falsification by omission, and in a third, omission is forced on me. First, a few experiences were so painful that I am not willing to re-live them in order to write about them. Secondly, it has been my lifelong practice not to communicate adverse criticism of any living member of my family to anyone outside the family.† This inhibition is too strong for me to break through, and for my present purpose that is a pity, because there are few things that matter to me as much as the vicissitudes of my children's lives (and lest my silence appear sinister, I must add that in my relations with my children I have been spared by great good fortune the tragic anxieties and alienation from which so many of my friends have suffered). Thirdly, although nothing but those two considerations prevents me from telling the truth about myself, telling the truth about other people incurs the risk of being sued for defamation. Evidence which in real life or historical research permits a firm conclusion is often inadmissible under the rules of evidence in a court of law, and even when it is admissible its evaluation is distorted by professional advocates whose business is not to establish the truth but

---

†But I make myself, not them, the judge of what constitutes adverse criticism.

[9] Levin (1928–2004), a *Times* columnist who was known for his trenchant opinion pieces, is quoted (presumably from memory: Levin wrote 'All euphemisms are lies') from his article 'Euphemism's new standard' in *The Times*, 17 March 1987, p. 12 (reprinted as 'An antidote to the poison of euphemism' in *The Times*, 10 August 2004, p. 16).

to win the case. Fortunately, very few of those whom I wish to defame are still alive, and nothing of great importance is lost if I express myself circumspectly about those few. I have often concealed the identities of living individuals by anonymity, and in a few cases by false names. I also have a certain revulsion against disclosure of anything said by well-known people, if they are still alive, in the course of a purely social occasion.‡ Except in two cases, where the distress caused to widows might be thought out of proportion to the importance of the data disclosed, I do not spare the dead; nor do I expect to be spared when I am dead.

It has become clear to me in writing this chapter – when I began, it was not – that my prime object in writing the book is to enjoy discovering in practice the nature and problems of one particular genre, autobiography. What I have read about the history and critical theory of the genre has not been entirely profitless, but nothing in it has induced me to change anything in the form or content of this book. I recall with mixed feelings a passage from the Introduction to William Spengemann's *The Forms of Autobiography*:

> These efforts to expand the boundaries of autobiography have split critical opinion into two schools of thought concerning its permissible methods. On the one side are those critics who continue to insist that . . . On the other side, there are those who assert the right of autobiographers to . . .[10]

Isn't it nice to know that there are people who *permit* me – by God, they give me the *right*! – to compose whatever kind of book I wish?

---

‡Quite recently a friend of mine asked the Dean of an Anglican cathedral 'Do you believe in God?' and got the answer 'No, of course not. What do you take me for?' The course of the subsequent conversation showed that the answer was not a joke. The incident is worth relating, but identification of the Dean would be an unforgivable breach of confidence.

[10]W.C. Spengemann, *The Forms of Autobiography: Episodes in the History of a Literary Genre* (New Haven, 1980) xii: a minor error in Dover's quotation has been corrected.

2 FOREBEARS

'The late lamented Patrick Morkan, our grandfather, that is,' explained Gabriel, 'commonly known in his later years as the old gentleman, was a glue-boiler.'
'O, now, Gabriel,' said Aunt Kate, laughing, 'he had a starch mill.'
JAMES JOYCE, *Dubliners*[1]

It is said that James Dover kept a pub near Birmingham early in the nineteenth century. He begot two sons, Henry and James. James eventually became a racehorse-trainer at East Ilsley, where there were some people in 1950 who still remembered him as an old man. Henry moved to London and became a foreman in the carriage-building workshop of the railway at Nine Elms.[2] He married a farmer's daughter from Somerset. I have one photograph of him with his wife; he is blond and whiskery, and looks kindly but puzzled, rather like a Tyrolean innkeeper who can't understand why his guests don't want a second helping of his soup, and she wears a sour expression which explains why she was disliked by everyone who knew her, including her children. The children were my grandfather and a girl called (I believe) Clara. My grandfather was named Henry James (Henry was not a man of bold imagination) but was always known at home as Jim.

Jim began work as a boy in the railway workshops, but got some education by attending a night-school and was taken on as a draughtsman by the Vacuum Brake Company. Having made and patented a number of inventions, he became comparatively prosperous, and after retirement about 1930 bought a house which was sold in 1945 for £6,000. He remained rather rough, occasionally uncertain of

---

[1] From 'The Dead': James Joyce, *Dubliners*, ed. Jeri Johnson (Oxford, 2000) 163.
[2] An area in the London borough of Wandsworth, formerly mostly industrial but now increasingly residential and commercial.

his initial aitches and inclined to say, 'I need a piss' rather than 'Excuse me a moment', but he was a kind and notably compassionate man; his only recorded outburst of violence was an assault on a carter who was beating an exhausted horse. He also had a great capacity for finding things interesting, a word of high commendation which he always pronounced with heavy stress on the third syllable. I was very fond of him when I was a child, because every now and then he would take me up to London for the day, or for a walk in the country, and everything we saw, everyone we encountered, attracted his attention and interest. He was also a good listener when I talked about my own enthusiasms. As a skilful but imperfectly informed gardener he distrusted all insects, and could not be persuaded that some of them are our friends; nevertheless, being as good a cabinet-maker as he was a gardener, he made me an excellent show-cabinet for the butterflies and beetles I collected.[3]

About 1890 he married Eliza, a domestic servant, daughter of Harry Gadsby. Harry's father was believed to have fought in the ranks at Waterloo, but I expect that was said of many ex-soldiers who died in the period 1830–1850. Having been orphaned at the age of eleven, Harry went to work in a factory at Spondon.[4] It was, he said, 'a hard life', and one of its rigours was to be whipped across the back by the foreman at any sign of laziness in the course of a long day. However, he was successfully apprenticed to a coppersmith, and by the time he retired he had become, like my other paternal great-grandfather, a foreman at Nine Elms. He married a Derby girl, Eliza Lloyd, who was rumoured – not an uncommon type of rumour in families like my parents' – to be the child of a coachman and the runaway daughter of landed gentry. Towards the end of his life Harry asserted that God had been good to him. My father disagreed. I would have liked to know more about the old Gadsbys, but unfortunately they often had mackerel for lunch, which my father so disliked that he ceased to visit them and so lost touch.

My grandmother Eliza[5] spoilt me when I was a child, and I was extremely fond of her. Disillusionment conquered affection when I was sixteen and we moved away from our house in Thornton Heath, a quarter of a mile from hers, to another part of London. She alternated for months between tearful self-pity and venomous sarcasm about our 'aristocratic residence' in prospect (a flat in Putney), and I gained some insight into the manipulative skill of jealous and possessive people. Some time afterwards I learned from my father that in the early years of her marriage she had secured a complete estrangement between Jim and his sister by getting up first in the morning and burning any letter addressed to Jim in the handwriting of 'that bitch'.

---

[3]For Dover's early interest in entomology, see pp. 39–40 and 51.
[4]A village near Derby which in the mid-nineteenth century became the site of several industrial enterprises. It was absorbed into the city of Derby in 1968.
[5]I.e. Eliza Gadsby, the first of the two Elizas mentioned in the previous paragraph.

Eliza had a number of brothers and sisters, but the only one of them I knew was her brother Arthur, who worked for Newnes.[6] He was a man of angelic disposition, of whom no one ever said a disapproving word: kindly, patient, generous. His wife, Kate, had white hair on her chin which made her look like a goat.

Jim and Eliza had two children, my father (born in 1892) and my aunt Lillian (born, I think, about 1897).[7] My grandmother wanted my father to be named Henry James, like his dad, but on the way to the registry my grandfather was seized with a demon of cussedness and registered him as Percy Henry James. My grandmother accepted that without demur; not so my father, after he had gone to school and discovered what other boys thought of the name 'Percy'.

Jim was blunt in speaking to Eliza, but not, during the time I knew them, ill-natured. In the last year of his life, however (he died at the end of 1940), he became impatient and contemptuous, and she complained, 'He hasn't spoken a decent word to me for months.' It was probably her disgraceful cowardice in air-raids, in which she was abetted by my aunt Lillian, which in the end turned him against her.

My father had no illusions about his mother's character, and he was irritated by her stupidity and sentimentality, but there was undoubtedly an emotional thread that connected them right up to her death in 1945, perhaps maintained by their underlying similarity of temperament. Between Jim and my father there was no such affinity. I had always imagined that they got on well, and I am sure Jim thought they did, but in 1946, when my father was going through a nervous breakdown which led to his being invalided out of the Civil Service, he talked to me more freely than he had ever done before, and on one occasion he had said, 'I hated my father, you know. He used to go into the bathroom every morning and make me *sick*.' As he said 'sick' his face was contorted with rage. Presumably Jim hawked and spat in the bathroom, thereby kindling in his son a hatred that was still aflame half a century later. This did not surprise me, because my own experience was so similar. My father never hawked – he thought it a deplorably working-class habit – but often at the end of breakfast he would cough with increasing violence, stride out of the dining-room, and spit surreptitiously down the runaway of the kitchen sink. The combination of rage, hatred and despair which overwhelmed me on every such occasion is undoubtedly the strongest emotion that I have experienced in my life. This is strange, and I have twice consulted psychiatrists about it, but they did not find the problem interesting, important or soluble.[8] When I was about fifteen and had read some Freud it occurred to me that the expectoration of mucus at the climax of a coughing-fit and the ejaculation of semen at the climax of a fuck

---

[6]George Newnes Ltd, at this date an independent and highly successful publisher of books and magazines.
[7]Lillian is mentioned again only on pp. 242–3; see also Figure 12.
[8]Dover annotated his own copy of *MC* at this point with the statement, 'Now (Nov. 2005) I understand, thanks to a *Horizon* programme on BBC2, that my reaction was "epigenetic". Neo-Lamarckism?'

are so very much alike that I must have been suffering from primal scene trauma;[9] but that postulates intuitive understanding of sexual physiology on the part of an infant, and I have never been able to take the notion of intuitive knowledge. It was some years before I thought of a more plausible hypothesis: that during my infancy my mother sometimes masturbated my father, either by reason of vaginitis or as a primitive form of contraception. One thing which has always been clear to me is that it was the embarrassed and embarrassing secretiveness of my father's action which generated my hatred and rage. If he had jumped up from the table and spat flamboyantly out of the window, like a Greek village headman by whom I was once entertained, I could have entered into the spirit of the occasion. As it was, I gained very good practice, at an early age, in concealing even the most turbulent and agonising emotion.

My parents met early in the First World War through a network of friends who devoted their spare time to music. They fell in love on very short acquaintance and became secretly engaged, but decided not to marry until the War was over, even though my father, as a Civil Servant with an unreliable knee, was exempt from conscription. My mother, Dorothy Healey, was the daughter of a couple who constituted the staff of the village school at Dawsmere, an out-of-the-way place on the Wash. Her father, Harry Healey, died five years before I was born. He had lost his parents early in life and was brought up by an uncle who paid for him to be trained as an 'elementary-school' teacher. He taught first at South Mimms, where he married one of his colleagues, Annie Millson, whose father was a forester somewhere in Berkshire. In Dawsmere Harry acted as a land surveyor in his spare time, organised and performed in all the local concerts and amateur theatricals, and was called on for advice over a wide range of practical matters (except, I presume, the growing of potatoes, on which Lincolnshire farmers did not need advice). He was also very good at hitting people; once at a political meeting, when Annie stood up to speak and was shouted down by some men who thought that women should hold their tongues, he knocked down five of them so fast that the fifth man was down before the first had got to his feet (another version says it was only three). My mother always seemed to me surprisingly cool in her attitude to him. Towards the end of her life she told me that when she became engaged she did not dare to tell him. 'Why ever not?' I asked. 'Jealousy,' said my mother crisply, and did not pursue the subject.

The Healeys had three boys and two girls. One girl died of peritonitis in childhood, and one boy was killed on the Somme. The eldest of the brood was

---

[9]'Primal scene' is a specifically psychoanalytical term, introduced by Freud himself (German *Urszene*) in 1925, for a child's witnessing (or fantasizing) of parental sexual intercourse; cf. Dover's partial endorsement of it on p. 176. In a 1995 addendum on the expectoration-ejaculation comparison, Dover cited Germaine Greer, *The Female Eunuch* (London, 1970) 254, where criticism of a man's use of a woman's body for quasi-masturbatory purposes includes the metaphor 'a human spittoon'.

FIGURE 1 Bessie Millson (great aunt), 1935.

another Harry, always called 'Shane' after he left school-teaching for journalism and adopted the pen-name 'T.N. Shane', and the youngest was Ken, after whom I was named. My mother's favourite and, I gather, everyone else's, was Gilbert, the war casualty.[10] The person who dominated their childhood and later had much to

---

[10] Gilbert John Healey, a private in the King's Own Royal Lancaster regiment, was killed in action on 23 October 1916.

do with my own and my cousins', was Annie's unmarried sister Bessie, always known as 'Miley'. She spent her life as a penniless dependent relative, neither well educated nor quick on the uptake, but devotedly busy and affectionate, and I was always very glad to see her, even though she implanted in me a lifelong nervousness about the police by threatening to tell a policeman when I was naughty. Uncle Shane and Uncle Ken contributed much more than they knew to my formation, because in different ways they provided what I could not find in my father: role-models for life as an adult male human.

3 ESCAPE ROUTES 1920–1932

As a young child I was very interested in the behaviour of my brothers and sister. It was absorbing to notice how the ideas and actions of one differed from those of another, and how different their ideas were from mine.
DOROTHY DOVER, *ined.*, 1948

Jim could sing, in a style midway between the bar-room and drawing-room, and my father was born in a household which had a piano. In his boyhood he taught himself to play, and his heart was in music for the rest of his life. His technique and memory were remarkable, ahead of any amateur I have ever known, and shortly before I was born a musical friend of his, a well-to-do solicitor who had acquired a Steinway grand, generously passed on to him a splendid Bechstein upright, which I still have. In the early nineteen-twenties, when the BBC was taking shape and assembling a small staff of regular performers, he was urged to resign from the Civil Service and make a career as a pianist.[1] I daresay he was tempted; but being as severe a critic of his own performance as he was of other people's, he knew that the spare time and energy which he had devoted to the piano was not enough to bridge the gap that separates the outstanding amateur from the competent professional. Moreover, he was never a man to take a risk, and could not seriously contemplate leaving a job which was (he professed) hateful to him but reassuringly secure. He was far too impatient to be a teacher of music, or of anything else, and he knew that. His taste had curious limitations: he was devoted to Chopin, Brahms and a gaggle of minor composers (Albeniz, Granados, Balakirev, Scriabin, Delius), but he treated Bach and Mozart with very distant respect and was totally deaf to

---

[1] The British Broadcasting Company was founded in 1922 as a commercial consortium; it became a Crown-chartered organization, the British Broadcasting Corporation, on 1 January 1927.

Beethoven. He was also moved to restless irritation by what he regarded as the melodramatic posturings of opera. He was, I think, scared of the portrayal of profound emotion; that would explain why he was intolerant of serious drama (witty farce was another matter) and greatly preferred Japanese prints to any of the European painters.

Next to music, he loved the country, and my greatest debt to him is that he implanted the same love in me on long walks, above all during holidays on Dartmoor and at weekends in the woodlands which have now largely disappeared under Crawley New Town.[2] He was often lively, witty and inventive, and versatile to the extent of making wireless-sets for our friends in the nineteen-twenties.

It may seem that I must have liked him and admired him. Unfortunately, perfect fear casteth out love (as the Epistle of Semaj observes), and I had too much reason to fear him.[3] I don't mean that he inflicted any systematic punishment on me; the occasional smack, no doubt, in circumstances in which I would have done the same, but his own schooldays had left him with a deep hatred of grown-ups who beat children (he regarded all except one of his teachers as sadists). It was simply that he had the foulest temper of anyone I knew or have known since: snarling ill-humour for days on end, for reasons which were incomprehensible to me, and unpredictable explosions of rage and hatred in which there was no limit to the violence of his words. Once, having caught me reading in bed by a very weak light, he told me that for all he cared I could go blind, and then 'we'll put you on the boiler and burn you'. He uttered the word 'burn' with frightening force. I didn't believe him, because I knew that killing people was illegal, but the underlying sentiment made a deep impression on me. The impression was reinforced, as was everything of the kind that he said when he was in a bad mood, by his massive physique; he had exceptionally broad shoulders, a deep chest, and prodigiously strong hands. Despite all his talent, all his wit and ebullience on good days, all his extravagant affection when the pendulum swung that way, I could never have felt anything but relief if he had died or vanished – unless, by some miracle (and I didn't expect miracles; I suppose, by definition, one doesn't), he could have stayed in the good phase *all* the time. It was the good phase which ensured that I never actually wanted to hurt him; never, then or subsequently, contemplated revenge.

My mother's temperament was wholly different. She was unfailingly reasonable, yet always spontaneous, humorous, and ready on occasion (as my father never was) to breach convention without fear of 'what people would think'.[4] She had

---

[2] The town of Crawley, West Sussex, designated a new town in 1947 under the New Towns Act of 1946.
[3] This inversion of 'perfect love casteth out fear' (1 John 4:18) can be found from the early 19th century; the *Oxford Dictionary of Quotations* (8th edn, 2014) cites it from a remark by Cyril Connolly in the 1940s. Dover's parallel inversion (James > Semaj) is not an actual reference to the biblical Letter of James but an ironic play on his own middle name.
[4] "When I read *The Mill on the Floss* there were things in Maggie Tulliver that reminded me vividly of my mother". (Dover SN)

none of the chilliness which sometimes marks the reasonable, and she was capable of anger against specific persons or actions, but never corroded by generalised ill-temper. If I must make a choice among all my debts to her, I would say: she sought and told the truth, whether it was welcome to her or not, and she never uttered, never could have demeaned herself to utter, such words as, 'Because I say so', or 'Oh, what a dreadful thing to say!' or 'How could you think such a thing?' She treated every opinion and argument on its merits, regardless of who said it or hrs motives for saying it. In these respects I have tried to live up to her standards.[5]

She had her limitations, most apparent in her rather naive and shallow view of the arts.[6] She also made two bad mistakes in my upbringing. One was to give me far too much help with geometrical problems in my homework during the year before I sat for a scholarship to St Paul's; her own delight in them seems to have encouraged in her an irrational faith that, given enough examples, I would in the end catch on. Her more serious mistake came much earlier in my childhood, when she was provoked by tantrums or wildly disobedient behaviour on my part into threatening that she would 'go away for ever'. A consequence of this was that for a year or two, whenever she went out shopping and I was left with the twice-weekly help, I spent the time standing at the window waiting in extreme anxiety for her reappearance at the end of the road. I would be tempted to call her mistake 'unforgivable' but for the fact that I forgave it long ago when I understood her circumstances better.

When I was a child she gave no outward sign of the unhappiness and despair that my father's bad temper inflicted on her or of the resentment she felt at the bullying and cynical way he often treated her at home when other adults were not present. Nor did she ever complain to her own family; her pride would not let her admit that she had made the age-old mistake of imagining that she could turn an emotionally unstable fiancé into a good husband. In my late teens she began to reveal a little of the past, and after the War she told me that had it not been for the sheer impracticality of earning a living with a baby to look after she would certainly have left my father during the first year of my life. She must have come nearest to leaving, even at the expense of her pride, when he was exasperated by my crying at night and shook me with a ferocity which has recently landed some fathers in the dock for murder. She told me about that a year or two before she died, in connection with the trouble that a worn vertebra in my neck was giving me, and it was the only occasion ever, in reminiscing about the past, when the steadiness of her voice failed.

---

[5]Dover had earlier (March 1973) ended the Preface to *GPM* xiii-iv, with a heartfelt tribute to his mother, whose death occurred just after the book's completion.
[6]Dover does not mention that it was music which brought his parents together, that his mother 'was, to begin with, quite a good pianist', and that his parents played piano duets in the early years of their marriage: *IPC* 92.

I doubt whether he ever struck her. For one thing, in the world as he saw it, it was only drunken navvies who hit women. For another, I think that whatever the practical difficulties, she would have left him then, believing (as I too am inclined to believe) that no marriage can reasonably be expected to survive a blow. In the nineteen-sixties, after my father had retired and they were living in a house out of earshot of neighbours, his verbal manifestations of hostility towards her were so prolonged and intense that she was afraid of being murdered by him, or at least seriously injured; but in that, I think, she was mistaken.

He would always have said that he 'really' loved her, however often his behaviour might be perverted into an appearance of the opposite by stress, anxiety, overwork, or what was then called 'neurasthenia'. My mother was sceptical, as I divined from what she said about other people in comparable situations, and even, perhaps, inclined to think that the hatred was real and the love an aberration. They were both wrong. If I love you today and hate you tomorrow, then I really love you today and really hate you tomorrow, and there is no more to it than that.

As family life was so full of tension,[7] I naturally looked for other worlds into which to insert myself. My parents' friends had either no children at all or none of my age, and the same was true of our neighbours, so that until I went to school I had very few encounters with children. Fortunately I took to reading so early in life that by the time I was five I had no difficulty at all in translating sign into sound, though the content of most of my parents' books seemed rather remote and elusive. Much more exciting were two massive sets at my grandparents' house, Arthur Mee's *Encyclopaedia* and the *Harmsworth History of the World*.[8] It was in fact in Arthur Mee that I first read about the Athenian expedition against Syracuse, an event on which I was destined one day to be regarded as an expert. The *History of the World* had abundant illustrations, evidently intended to enthral children, for they were saturated in bloodshed and cruelty: the torture of martyrs and traitors, the burning of heretics, slaughter on the battlefield. I was tempted by grisly curiosity to burn a caterpillar at the stake on a pyre of used matchsticks, but it was an experiment of a kind I never wished to repeat.

When the effect of the history of cruelty was combined with Grimm's Fairy Tales – in one tale a young man is alone in a castle and pieces of a dismembered human body fall down the chimney at night – it was not surprising that I was afraid of the dark and troubled by bad dreams. My fear of the dark began from a

---

[7]For an instance of this tension, see p. 57.
[8]Arthur Mee (1875–1943) was a journalist employed by the publisher and news magnate Alfred Harmsworth, 1st Lord Northcliffe. His *Children's Encyclopaedia* first appeared in fortnightly parts in 1908–10; later editions (the last in 1964) were published in ten volumes. The *Encyclopaedia* was very popular: it was written in an accessible and straightforward style, and as it was not in alphabetic sequence, was very good for browsing. The *Harmsworth History of the World*, edited by Mee, J.A. Hammerton and A.D. Innes, was published in eight volumes, 1907–9.

story[9] about a man stalked by hyenas at night; from then on, an imaginary hyena lurked on the stairs of my home. One dream, in which an old woman in Elizabethan dress, her face parchment-white, glided into my bedroom and dug her nails into my hand, while some of my school-friends sat round the room chatting as if they saw nothing of what was happening, has lodged into my memory more vividly than any waking event of that year.

Occasionally I crossed the boundary between dream and hallucination. A white rough-haired terrier materialised under my window in the halflight of dawn, trotted briskly towards my bed and vanished. I began to sort this out one day when my father asked me to fetch something from the drawing-room, which was at the other end of the house, and I shrank back from the passage, saying (and believing) that a chimney-sweep with his black brushes was peering round the corner. My parents looked, saw nothing, and said so; and I realised that the experience which we call 'seeing a ghost' is not evidence for the existence of something there to be seen. All the same, my fear of ghosts took a long time to fade. My friends at school loved stories of haunted houses, and the rumour spread that there was a ghost in a house under construction on an estate adjoining the school. We crept up to the window to explore it during the lunch-hour, but a succession of trumpeting farts, much louder than any ghost could produce, persuaded us that the only inhabitant of the house was a tramp.

For all the fears that it engendered, my reading opened up to me the vast and varied history of the world, and Arthur Mee made one other contribution of lasting value. Every dozen pages or so there was one of Aesop's fables, and since the moral of the fable made sense in terms of my own experience I began to reflect on human relationships and to articulate elementary moral principles. Not all of these principles came from Aesop; I formed some of my own which rather surprised my parents by their intensity. One expressed itself in a vehement revulsion against the destruction of usable objects or the waste of consumable food and drink; to this day, while I can tolerate the throwing of bad eggs in a political demonstration, I cannot forgive the throwing of edible eggs or flour. My other moral oddity was the elevation of ingratitude to the pinnacle of vice; I remember an occasion at school when we were required to write an essay on whatever each of us considered to be the worst delinquency, and I wrote in strong terms on ingratitude. This is probably why I never wanted revenge on my father; I recognised how much I owed him, and how good his intentions were much of the time.

With one important exception, it was always history and human experience, not science, which engaged my interest and enthusiasm. The exception was the world of insects. Such insects as were to be seen in our garden (twenty feet by fourteen) attracted me by the time I was three; I was willing to follow them and

---

[9]Recounted by his grandfather 'Jim' (SN), perhaps as some sort of intimidation (cf. p. 31).

observe them patiently as they made their way through the wild hills and jungles which to a creature of my size were only clods and weeds. I read, and re-read, until I almost knew it by heart, an English abridgement of Fabre's *Souvenirs entomologiques*.[10] By eight I had become an avid collector, and at twelve I wanted to be an entomologist when I grew up. At fourteen I gave up collecting, partly because linguistic interests were taking over but also because I came to feel that the triumph of securing a specimen could not outweigh the shame of making the species rarer by the act of securing a specimen. I remain tied to insects by a (one-sided) bond of affection. This does not extend to spiders, which I hate and fear, as my mother did.[11]

Some boys form gangs, and sometimes a boy's gang is his own creation, recognising him as its leader. My relationship to my own gang represented the extreme of domination, because its members were my own soft toys, invested with personalities by Miley, who drew on her long experience of village life, and by my mother, whose skill in making up complicated stories was a product of her upbringing in a village teacher's family dependent for its entertainment on its own resources and imagination. The toys, Big Creatures and Little Creatures constituting a minute but elaborately organised city-state ('Gangtown'), were tyrannised and manipulated by a certain Wimpee (so spelt, but pronounced 'Wimpy'), a tailless primate, female, resolute, charming and unscrupulous. Teddy was a good-natured but slow-witted yokel, Jacko a fastidious *bon viveur* with intellectual pretensions; Felix embarrassed the others by drunken misbehaviour and frequent vomiting, while Edwin (unmistakably a gibbon) was a cool operator who patiently climbed to power over the years and eventually displaced even Wimpee. My father once tore off Wimpee's head when I was exceptionally naughty (but what did I *do*? What exactly was naughtiness?), and my mother sewed it on again.[12]

My mother's skill in story-telling was equalled, even surpassed, by Uncle Ken's. I always welcomed his visits, because he was vigorous, cheerful, tolerant and unfailingly good-tempered. He and I went for walks on which he told me wonderful stories, full of dynastic rivalries in Ruritanian countries, intrigue, conspiracies, spying, treason, and coded messages, and he had an enviable ability to feed in complications as the story took shape and resolve them all tidily in the last half-

---

[10]Mrs Rodolph Stawell, *Fabre's Book of Insects* (1921): cf. the further reference on p. 51. In *The Times Higher Education Supplement* for 5 May 1995, p. 23, Dover wrote an article in a series of pieces entitled 'Speaking Volumes' in which he recalls this book (he read the complete French original at a later date) as the one 'which opened up the world to me'; he also states that he ultimately owes it to Fabre 'that I explain morality in biological rather than religious terms'.

[11]Dover SN traces his arachnophobia to an incident at the age of three when he unknowingly brought a spider into the house in a bucket and his mother shrieked with horror at the sight of it.

[12]On Wimpee, see Stray's chapter on Dover's schooling in *S&C*. Cf. p. 59 below for Wimpee's development in 1935 into a quasi-fascist dictator.

mile of the walk. These stories were valuable to me not just as entertainment but as a means of enlarging my circle of friends at school, because I recalled them in every detail and re-told them in instalments to other boys on the way home.

My first school was a local private day-school which took boys from five to sixteen. As I could read easily when I started there and had no difficulty with the early stages of any subject, I found myself at six and a half in a class of which the average age was nine. I did not realise that disparity until, years later, I came across a file of my old school reports. It was a long time before I became aware that there existed schools in which children were grouped together solely in accordance with the number of years that had elapsed since their birth, and that seemed to be a daft idea.

I doubt whether the staff of the school had any professional qualifications, but with the exception of the headmaster they were remarkably good. The most impressive was the deputy headmaster, whose personality commanded attention for every moment that he was in a classroom. He had another attribute unusual in private school masters at that time: he was black. Though we occasionally discussed whether he came from Africa or the Caribbean, I never heard any boy make even the faintest adverse comment on his colour. At that time black people were rare in London suburbs, and those who assimilated themselves earned the same degree of respect as people who had overcome serious physical handicaps. Among the other teachers there was one, a lame, stumpy man of unimpressive appearance but delightful personality, who captured our imagination when he introduced us to social history; and another, Maurice Brown, who in English lessons encouraged me to write as much as I liked about anything I liked, and always had good constructive criticism to offer. Unfortunately, the syllabus of the school was determined by the College of Preceptors examinations, and the textbooks were chosen by the headmaster.[13] These books were educationally incompetent to a degree which a modern teacher of history, geography or languages would find hard to believe.

If I had put into improving my Latin and French a fraction of the enterprise I devoted to the study of beetles and dragonflies and to the imaginary politics of Gangtown, I could easily have remedied the defects of my schooling. The available fraction, however, was claimed by another topic, language-related and eventually useful to me. This came from the influence of Uncle Shane, whose character and temperament I admired almost as much as Ken's (not quite as much, though, because Shane's life in Fleet Street predisposed him to a cynicism not always compatible with rationality). Shane was interested in many things, and one of his hobbies was the study of Egyptian hieroglyphics and Akkadian cuneiform. That

---

[13] The College of Preceptors was founded in 1846 to certify schoolteachers. Its examinations were widely used by private schools. The College was absorbed by the (UCL) Institute of Education in 2003.

inspired in me a passion for the history of writing-systems, and just as I had collected stamps and insects I began to collect scripts.

When I sat for a scholarship to St Paul's in the summer of 1932 my Latin and French were deplorable – my translation from English into Latin earned no marks at all – and it was not surprising that I was unsuccessful. However, my English paper must have made a strong impression, because when a successful competitor withdrew at the end of summer his place was offered to me and I began life at St Paul's in September. As I still rated entomology as my central interest, I wanted to go on the Science side, but I was firmly directed into Classics. I spent the first six weeks of the term in a form designed for people like me, who had no Greek and little Latin; we did nothing but Latin and Greek all day, every day, I became competent in Latin, and I fell in love with Greek. I was now on course.

4 BODY AND SOUL
1926–1934

Because you are not sheep of my flock, you do not believe.

JOHN 10.26

One day my mother gave me some surprising news. Uncle Ken had decided to give up bulb-farming and train for ordination as an Anglican clergyman. How he came to that decision, I shall never know for sure; years later he referred in an article to 'an encounter with Jesus Christ which could not be denied', but he never explained himself to his brother and sister. He was ordained in 1932, and after three Lincolnshire rural parishes in succession became Archdeacon of Lincoln and eventually Bishop of Grimsby.[1] I could observe no change at all, for better or worse, in his personality. Much as I admired him, I admired the character of my irreligious mother a fraction more; so I had no reason to think that commitment to Christian belief wrought a transformation in the outward person, whatever it might do to the language of one's inner dialogue with oneself.

My father's parents, although they had sent my father to Sunday-school, did not otherwise acknowledge the existence of religion, and my father was not baptised. He himself was irreconcilably hostile to Christianity, and most of his friends, none of whom ever went to church if s/he could help it, were more amused than offended when he referred to Christianity as 'God-slobber'. My mother's parents had been to church when they taught at Dawsmere, because it would have been hard for them, in that place at that time, to have done otherwise; the vicar's family and the schoolmaster's family were closer to each other than either of them was to any professional family in the nearest market-town or to the farmers' families. When

---

[1] He was Bishop Suffragan of Grimsby 1958–65: there was a brief obituary in *The Times*, 27 February 1985, p. 12.

FIGURE 2 Kenneth Healey (uncle), 1935.

my grandmother retired, there was no religion among the Healeys until Ken's conversion in 1930. My mother found all creeds and ritual ridiculous and repellent. By the time I went to school I was aware that there were buildings called 'churches' scattered around, and that men wearing their collars backwards had something to do with churches, but these data did not arouse my curiosity. I was baptised because a close friend of my parents, Francis Davidson (the friendship was founded, as always, on music), wanted to be my godfather, but he died when I was a baby.

When I was six my mother thought it was time I made the acquaintance of the Bible, and she provided me with children's books of Bible stories. I found a strong undertone of menace in these books; expulsion from the Garden of Eden seemed an outrageously severe punishment for eating the forbidden fruit (why was it forbidden anyway?), and the cruel practical joke played by God on Abraham and Isaac did not endear him to me. In any case, such stories could not compete in interest and excitement with the Wimpee stories which my mother's inventive talent supplied, or indeed with the behaviour of the beetles which I watched in the garden.

Things changed when I was eight. Most of my friends at school came from homes no more geared to religion than mine. From two of these friends, John and Alec, who were both very nice, good-natured, straightforward boys (my mother was particularly fond of those two) I learned the elements of sexual differentiation. I needed to learn that; as an infant I had surprised my mother naked and 'saw' what I expected to see: genitals exactly like mine, only bigger, and no pubic hair. I also learned a graded list of swear-words, from 'damn' upwards, with 'sod' a special word so potent that it had to be communicated in a hushed voice. There were other boys, not always of comparable appeal, whose teaching was of a different kind. They wore Crusader badges in their lapels, and one of them, Martin, became my closest friend for many years.[2] It was he who first persuaded me of the reality of God. He came from an evangelical home, in most ways cheerful, relaxed and down-to-earth, but a home in which visits to the cinema and theatre were forbidden and secular music and painting regarded with suspicion, on the grounds that the Gospels offered no reason for thinking that Jesus cared about the arts. Martin's elder brother became a missionary, and Martin himself has spent most of his own life as a missionary in Brazil before moving to Canada.

He visualised God as an old man in the sky with a mane of white hair and blazing red eyes. God ruled and legislated for all creation. One day, which might arrive at any moment, he would raise the dead, judge everyone according to the faith they had shown on earth, and consign sinners to Hell, where they (that is, most of us) would be tortured by demons forever. This was not good news. I found no difficulty in believing that the universe, like the home, was ruled by a dangerous male in a bad temper; the real problem was one of practical self-interest: how to escape Hell.

The rules of some religions (e.g. 'Don't eat pigs') are clear and precise, and we know whether we have broken them or not. Others, such as the injunction to have faith, are such that we have no sure means of deciding whether we pass or fail. We

---

[2] The Crusaders' Union, founded in 1906 to bring the teachings of the Bible to young people who did not attend church, had over 250 local groups by 1939. At its centenary in 2006 it was renamed Urban Saints. On his friend Martin, Dover wrote in the 1995 addenda: 'After 48 years' silence, he reappeared in my life in 1986, and we corresponded regularly after that, until a letter he wrote in November 1994 told me that it would be his last. He died of liver cancer two weeks later, having prayed for me every day. It hurt me sorely to hurt him by my unbelief, but I couldn't pretend.'

can only guess at the standards which the rule-maker, in his role as judge, will adopt. God demanded not simply that we should fear him and, so far as his rules were intelligible, obey him, as we fear and obey the police, but also that we should *love* him. How was that possible? The Christian's answer was that he had sacrificed his Son as an atonement for our sins. Now, if God had saved us by sacrificing himself in combat against an external force stronger than himself and all of us, that would indeed be a claim on our gratitude and love. But the scenario[3] was set up by God in the first place; he created everything, he defined sin, and then he expected us to love him if he arbitrarily refrained from punishing some breaches of the rules which he need not have made. For me there was a further, very painful, problem: what should I do about my parents' disbelief? Clearly they were destined for damnation, which would be monstrously unjust to my mother, and even at my most vehement moments of hostility to my father I could not bear the notion that he would suffer eternal punishment.* If I could forgive him, why couldn't God? More to the point, how would God deal with me on the Day of Judgement if I had not even tried to save two souls when it lay in my power at least to make the attempt? Fear of embarrassment prevailed over awareness of duty, and my parents never knew that between the ages of eight and thirteen I had believed in God.[4]

I was saved from internal conflict by reading the Bible from beginning to end in the course of 1933. As I came to it free of the preconceptions implanted in some children by assurances that Jesus is a loving friend, it was not the goodness of Jesus that impressed me when I came to the Gospels but his tone of menace and vindictiveness. I could (and do) admire his courage, some (not all) of his moral precepts, and some (not all) of his extravagant but illuminating thrusts at human pretensions. I perceived that some of his injunctions are so enigmatic or ambiguous that pacifists and warriors, hanging judges and poor friars, can all find there justification for whatever they want to justify. As I had by this time embarked at school on Euripides and Virgil, the Pauline Epistles struck me as mumbo-jumbo from which we can extract sense (given ingenuity on our part) only on the initial assumption that there is sense to be made of it. Revelation I thought the ravings of a disagreeable witch-doctor. Many years later I heard about a young American Bible Belt salesman who said to himself, on finishing the last page, 'No Sir! That ain't likely!', and that is a fair description of my own state of mind at the end of 1933.

---

*On this matter, I have been astonished at the complacency of friends who say of their fathers 'I guess he got what was coming to him', or sentiments to that effect.

[3]'I originally wrote "the whole crackpot scenario", but toned it down in order not to be thought merely rude about religion.' (Dover SN)

[4]For a lingering trace of religious sensibility, finally dispelled at a decisive moment in 1961, see pp. 158–9.

However hard it might be to estimate one's own holiness, at least there was no doubt in the minds of Christian boys that masturbation was a sin; indeed, because of its ease of definition and the lack of opportunity or temptation to commit more spectacular and bloodthirsty sins, it was virtually equated with sin. As my first school took boys well beyond puberty, younger boys learned about masturbation from their seniors, and many of us looked forward to it. I expect other boys' fathers told them, as mine told me, that they would fall gravely ill if they 'played with themselves', but we recognised that although some statements made by grown-ups conveyed scientifically validated information, others were intended simply as deterrents and could well be false. Martin, despite his inexhaustible appetite for conversation about genitals and his readiness to take out a ruler and measure his erections competitively against mine, resisted temptation by prayer and thanked God for saving him from 'so many foul sins'. Alec, untroubled by religious scruples, was a cheerful, tireless wanker, and one evening when we were alone in his house I asked him to give me a demonstration. He was glad to do so, and raised an erection in no time, but then found himself inhibited by the presence of a patient observer, and asked me to wait in the kitchen until he called me back. The moment I was exiled, I became furious with him and vowed to God that I would never masturbate. After a while he pleaded with me to give him a 'nance' ('Oh, come on! I haven't had a decent nance for *ages!*'), but I refused.[5] Eventually he called me in, just in time for the eruption. He immediately jumped up, stuffed away his cock, rubbed the semen into the rug with one stroke of his shoe, and that was that. As he had already gone on to another school and his parents soon moved house to be nearer to it, I saw him only rarely from then on. He remained a very good-natured person, and evidently had a tough core, because he won a DFC[6] in the War. I have dwelt on the incident at his house not just because it has remained so vividly in my mind, but because it gave rise to very far-reaching reflections on morality. I had asked him to put on a show for me, and he had complied. He had asked for something in return, and I had refused. Since I wanted to witness an ejaculation, there was plainly no point in allowing him contact which would actually frustrate that (I wasn't sure what 'nance' meant, but imagined it must be sodomy), but why couldn't I promise him 'Next time' and keep my promise? And why did I become so angry when I was sent out of the room? Primal scene trauma? It cannot have been disgust, because I had no adverse aesthetic reaction to genitals and their products. The power of convention? Reflection left me in no doubt that whereas my request and his compliance had no *moral* significance at all, and whatever we had done next time would have been equally devoid of moral significance, my

---

[5] The *OED* recognizes 'nance' only in the sense of a homosexual or effeminate man; this is clearly a derived usage.
[6] Distinguished Flying Cross.

failure to do him one morally indifferent favour in return for another *was* a serious delinquency. As for my vow, I suppose that many of us in our childhood have made such vows, but in sexual matters our resolve does not usually survive the discovery that the orgasm is the purest and most powerful – with sporadic competition from Bach, victory, love, Wester Ross, rare birds and the relief of despair – of all the good emotional experiences available to humankind.[7]

A year before my anxiety about the fate of my soul was allayed by my unfavourable response to the Bible, a far greater anxiety about my body, unconnected with sex, seized me like a beast in ambush and has never let go. On my first Monday at St Paul's Martin and I were having showers after physical training when his eyes widened and he exclaimed, 'Man! Your *chest*!' I looked down, expecting to see that I had broken out in a rash, and then, in a terrifying second, realised that among all those boys running round naked I alone had a funnel chest. How could I not have known? Photographs taken on the beach when I was about eight show that the deformity was evident by then. No one had commented on it at the local swimming-baths when I was trying to learn to swim. Anyway, there I was now, separated from all my contemporaries by an irreversible deformity. It was no fault of mine; but what difference did that make? I developed techniques of concealment with all the cunning of an alcoholic concealing his addiction: showering with my back to the crowd, contriving to dry myself in such a way that the towel hid my chest, and fixing a pad of folded cloth inside my rugger-vest to fill out the hollow. It also meant that I took no more part in sport than the minimum required of a day-boy at St Paul's, and that is something which I regretted at the time and ever after. I was not physically weak, I enjoyed stretching my body in violent exercise, and at my first school I had been a fast runner and a good jumper. It was the changing-room I feared, not the sports-field. The trouble was that I had no support; our boxing instructor once said, in a voice trembling with emotion, 'My boy! Never let a St Paul's boy get into that shape!', and it was hopeless to tell him that I hadn't 'got into it'. My parents had no conception of how much my life was affected, and I didn't feel able to explain that in a way which would really sink in. I was twenty-one before I heard the first word of spontaneous, compassionate acceptance, and that was from a Turkish girl in Cairo who played to perfection the corny but endearing role of the prostitute with the heart of gold.[8]

Obsessive awareness of my deformity was the chief contribution that the history of my body made to the destruction of my self-esteem, but not the only

---

[7] In his interview with Naim Attallah, Dover said that this remark about orgasms 'was meant to be slightly jocular' (*ICNA* 100).
[8] See p. 93 for a further reference to the Turkish prostitute in question. Dover later learned that some of his mother's side of the family also suffered from funnel chest.

one. I was born at a time when the craze for circumcision, which infected England in the latter part of the nineteenth century, was reaching its peak, and I was one of its millions of victims.[9] Of the dozen boys I knew best at my first school, at least five were circumcised; but at least five were not, and these included Alec and Martin, to whom I was closest. Each of us naturally championed his own kind of cock. One night, however, just before I went to sleep, a message which seemed to come from outside myself told me, with magisterial finality, that foreskins are good and circumcision bad.[10] This message was not articulated in words, but invaded me in two shock-waves about a second apart: whoof! ... whoof! I felt that my whole system of values had been turned upside-down, and from that moment I have never been reconciled to my mutilation. This was the first of three occasions in my life on which a 'voice' has communicated with me; the second (in 1946) told me to marry Audrey Latimer, and the third (in 1961) assured me that I had no need of a God.[11] If such messages are of divine origin, the third is hard to explain, and so, I suppose, is the first; if diabolical, the second is equally hard to explain. It seems more reasonable to believe that we experience some messages from our internal computer as if they came from outside ourselves.

I am cheered now by learning that it has become difficult to find a doctor in Britain who can be induced by money to mutilate babies unnecessarily. That, however, is feeling, not thought.[12] If it is really true that smegma is a cause of uterine cancer,[13] we shall have to circumcise every male within reach, and never mind. My dislike of circumcision did nothing to make me anti-Jewish, partly because I don't think anything could have done, and partly because I knew from my reading in anthropology and ancient history that it wasn't the fault of the Jews; it began independently in ancient Egypt, from which it has spread into central and eastern Africa and over the whole Islamic world, and in some areas of the south-western Pacific. I am pretty sure, however, that it turned me off Semitic† languages, in which I was beginning to be interested, and reinforced my loyalty to the Greeks and Romans, who rejected and ridiculed circumcision.

To return, however, to my body; it was not through with me yet. In the spring of 1934 I fell seriously ill with scarlet fever and spent six weeks in the local isolation

---

†My linguistic orientation makes it impossible for me to use 'anti-Semitic' in the sense 'anti-Jewish', since the Semitic language-family includes Arabic and some languages of Ethiopia as well as Hebrew and Aramaic.

[9]For the historico-medical background, see D.L. Gollaher, *Circumcision: A History of the World's Most Controversial Surgery* (New York, 2000) 73–108.

[10]In his own copy of *MC* Dover added: 'I think I was prejudiced by a friend who told me his girl-friend liked to play with his foreskin.'

[11]For further references to the second and third of these 'voices', see respectively pp. 102 (with the same 'internal computer' metaphor as here) and 158. One might compare Dover's 'voices' with E.R. Dodds' 'daemon': see the Introduction at n. 16.

[12]For Dover's somewhat idiosyncratic application of this distinction, see p. 25.

[13]An idea which more recent scientific research has debunked.

hospital, the first week in a delirious condition with a very high temperature and agonising earache, and two weeks after that in slowly regaining the strength to stand up and walk. Scarlet fever seems to have been a worse disease then than it is now; the boy in the next bed to me died. This was the first time I had been away from home, except for the odd night or two with grandparents or other relatives, and my first close acquaintance with working-class children; I found that I could cope, not brilliantly, but adequately. Just before I was due to go back to school, two months after the onset of the illness, the abscess in my ear flared up again and resisted treatment, and in consequence I missed the whole term. During the year that followed I often felt deplorably weak and tired for days on end, and since then I have suffered from the same weakness and fatigue whenever I have pushed myself physically past a certain limit.[14] In the War I was passed 'A2' (i.e. fit, but with glasses) and served for five years without collapsing, and I am still, in my early seventies, regarded as fit by anyone who compares me superficially with fat men who take no exercise, but I know, in a way that the outside observer cannot know, how low my reserves are. Curiously, this weakness, even in the immediate aftermath of scarlet fever, never (until 1983) reduced my appetite for intellectual work or my capacity to get on with it.

---

[14]For Dover's experience of acute fatigue much later in his life, including the significance of 1983 (two sentences below) as a turning-point, see pp. 311–12.

5 **EXOTICA 1933–**

Also spoken in Tadzhikistan are Yagnob and the various languages of the Pamir group: Shugn, Rushan, Bartang, Oroshor, Yazgulyam, Ishkashim, and Vakh.

BERNARD COMRIE[1]

At some time – I can't be precise – my interest in alphabets, writing-systems and codes (I did not draw any significant distinction between an evolving script and an invented code) made a decisive and enduring shift from symbol to substance: I became interested in languages. This was no doubt accelerated by the intensive and highly professional teaching of Greek and Latin which I underwent during my first six weeks at St Paul's, and it must have been far advanced by the end of 1932, because my thirteenth-birthday present from my parents in March 1933 was Alice Werner's little book *The Language-Families of Africa*, and I don't think they can have been guessing.[2] I read it and re-read it, as I had done with *Fabre's Book of Insects*; it opened a magic casement, and I have exulted ever since in the view which it revealed. It introduced me to the concept of linguistic change and the reconstruction of hypothetical past languages from their differentiated descendants. I was now no longer a collector, but a historian, enthralled by the challenge of analysis, taxonomy and reconstruction. Almost at once thereafter I came upon Dorothea Bleek's *Bushman Folklore* in the Croydon public library and put together a rudimentary Bushman grammar from its texts and literal translations.[3]

---

[1] B. Comrie, *The Languages of the Soviet Union* (Cambridge, 1981) 159.
[2] Alice Werner (1859–1935) was one of the first teachers at the School of Oriental Studies (subsequently Oriental and African Studies) at its foundation as part of London University in 1917; she eventually held a chair there in Swahili and Bantu languages. The book Dover refers to was published in 1915.
[3] Dover's reference here is slightly inaccurate: the work in question, which contains original texts with facing translations, must be *Specimens of Bushman Folklore*, collected by Dorothea Bleek's father and aunt, W.H.I. Bleek and L.C. Lloyd, and edited by the latter (London, 1911), but in which Dorothea herself had no part, though she did edit a separate work by the same relatives and containing only translations, *The Mantis and his Friends: Bushman Folkore* (Capetown, 1924).

Codrington's *Melanesian Languages*[4] followed as a Christmas present. From that moment, with an abruptness rather like Toad's conversion from caravans to cars in *The Wind in the Willows*, I was hooked on the Western Pacific, and dropped Africa. By 1938 I had collected over thirty grammars, dictionaries and comparative studies of the languages of Indonesia, New Guinea and the Pacific islands. It sounds an expensive hobby, but it was not, because second-hand books were so cheap, even by the standards of that time. My pocket-money was two shillings a week, rising after a while to half-a-crown, and in addition I could accumulate two or three pounds a year in Christmas and birthday presents from aunts and uncles. I seldom had any inclination to spend this money on anything except books. Many translations of portions of the Bible into languages of New Guinea and the Pacific islands were obtainable from the British and Foreign Bible Society and the Melanesian Mission for as little as sixpence apiece. For a nominal subscription as a student associate I was able to use the libraries of the Royal African Society and the Royal Asiatic Society on Saturday mornings, where I had access to foreign periodicals, including the marvellous *Anthropos*. The biblical translations and texts published in *Anthropos* enabled me to get the hang of the working of many languages, especially in New Guinea, about which there was no information in Codrington or in Ray's *Melanesian Island Languages*.[5] This activity was concentrated in the holidays and some parts of some weekends, so there was no direct conflict with schoolwork. If it had been possible for me to take a first degree in linguistics at Oxford or Cambridge (as a Pauline, I didn't contemplate any other university), that would have been my aim. It would have been a bad mistake. I would not have been much good at fieldwork, because my ear is not discriminating enough, nor would I have enjoyed the physical conditions in which fieldwork is conducted. Theoretical linguistics has never interested me much except in so far as it impinges on comparative and historical linguistics; my attempts to read Chomsky are enfeebled by the rapid onset of boredom, because for me constant change and the instability of rules are the essential features of language.[6]

Apart from one brief meeting with Walter Ivens[7] and one exchange of letters with Ray (he didn't grasp, I'm afraid, the point of the enquiry I addressed to him),

---

[4]R.H. Codrington, *The Melanesian Languages* (Oxford, 1885), a large and technical work of grammatical analysis; the thought of it as serious reading for a young teenager is mind-boggling. Dover was still making use of this book at least as late as 1977: he cites it several times in his Oxford Maurice Bowra Memorial Lecture, 'Song-language in preliterate cultures' (*G&G* 1–15).

[5]Sidney Ray (1858–1939) was a linguist who specialized in Melanesian languages. Despite being employed as a primary school teacher throughout his working life, he established an academic reputation, and was part of A.C. Haddon's expedition to the Torres Strait in 1898. See R. Wells, 'Sidney Herbert Ray: linguist and educationalist', *Cambridge Journal of Anthropology* 21 (1999) 79–99.

[6]For this important conviction of Dover's, compare e.g. *G&G* 94: in the continuous process of linguistic change, 'rules contract and extend their domains, some perish and others are born'.

[7]Walter George Ivens (1871–1939) was a missionary who translated the Bible into several Melanesian languages and published grammars of a number of them.

I was entirely on my own in my study of Pacific languages, and although this isolation must have sent me from time to time up alleys which others had already found to be blind, it also afforded me the constant joy of discovery – illusory, no doubt, on many occasions, but not always. Each of the languages of New Guinea and Melanesia is either 'Papuan' or 'Austronesian'. The Austronesian family, which includes the languages of Indonesia, the Philippines and Madagascar, shares a core vocabulary which permits the reconstruction of a proto-Austronesian parent language, and many grammatical features are also shared. The Papuan languages comprise a large number of families which diverge very greatly in vocabulary but to a large extent share grammatical systems which differentiate them very strongly from Austronesian. If you draw a line on the map separating Papuan from Austronesian, and then draw a line separating languages which permit closed syllables from those which have only open syllables, you find that the two boundary-lines cut right across each other; that is to say, the conventional 'genealogical' model of linguistic classification breaks down at the phonological level. Moreover, a few Austronesian languages which are out on a limb surrounded by Papuan-speaking communities have case-endings, like their neighbours, whereas case-endings are quite alien to the Austronesian family as a whole. And a few Papuan languages in continuous contact with Austronesian-speaking communities have the highly distinctive Austronesian way of indicating the genitive relationship. A few years later, when I heard Robert Browning read a paper to the Junior Philological Society at Oxford on 'Balkan' phenomena shared by the rather distantly interrelated languages Albanian, Bulgarian and Modern Greek, the notion of 'areal' linguistics took shape in my mind, and I began to entertain serious doubts about the adequacy of genealogical models.[8]

Although I would reckon Fabre's book and Werner's as the two most exciting books I read in the first fifteen years of my life, the most influential in the long run was G.C. Wheeler's *Mono-Alu Folklore*,[9] which I picked up second-hand for six shillings in a bookshop opposite the British Museum. The book contained stories and songs in the language (Mono) of two islands in the Bougainville Strait in Melanesia, with a literal translation, abundant linguistic notes, a vocabulary and a

---

[8]The talk Dover recalls is likely to have been given in 1946–7, when Browning was Harmsworth Senior Scholar at Merton College, Oxford. Robert Browning (1914–97) subsequently became a leading specialist in Byzantine Greek and Professor of Classics at Birkbeck College, London, 1965–81; though Balliol-educated, it was held against him, when he was considered for a tutorial fellowship at Balliol in 1953 (see p. 128 for Gordon Williams' appointment), that he was a member of the Communist Party (Dover's letter home, 10 March 1953). But Dover had a high regard for Browning's linguistic abilities. See the British Academy memoir by Averil Cameron, *PBA* 105 (2000) 289–306, and the *ODNB* article by N.G. Wilson.

[9]Published by Routledge in 1926, the book was the London DSc thesis of the anthropologist Gerald Clair Wheeler (1872–1943); Dover cited the book in his 1977 Maurice Bowra Memorial Lecture in Oxford (*G&G* 1–15, with material related to this paragraph on pp. 7 and 9). Alu was an older dialect eventually replaced by Mono.

page of grammatical guidance. Here was a challenge: by analysing this finite corpus of texts, to write a descriptive grammar of the language. Although I had attempted that sort of thing in a very rudimentary way with Bushman texts, it took a year of browsing in Wheeler before I felt confident enough to tackle the job. I started by taking as a model the grammars which made up the greater part of the books by Codrington and Ray, and they adhered, with a minimum of inescapable adjustments, to the Graeco-Latin framework which it had long been the practice to impose on description of African and Pacific languages. But it was better sense to begin by classifying every word in a Mono text as either a 'verb', if it had prefixes which signify subject-person and tense, or as a 'non-verb' if it had not. This would take care of such utterances as *o-i-afa-ua ga too-ŋ i-masimasini*, 'you-PAST-what-with *ga* head-your it(PAST)-red', i.e. 'Why has your head become red?' But the distinction between verb and non-verb is undermined by a phenomenon peculiar to Mono. It is generally characteristic of Melanesian languages to express possession in different ways according to the degree of alienability of what is possessed; thus for 'my arm' or 'my mother' the possessive pronoun would be suffixed directly to the noun (in Mono, *ime-gu, nka-gu*), but for (e.g.) 'my house' the pronoun is suffixed to one or other of a set of 'possessives' in apposition to the object possessed; in Mono, 'my house' is *numa sa-gu*, 'house *sa*-my'. But this construction is used, with partial reduplication of the verb-stem, also to express sustained action, thus: *i-lofo*, 'he flew', but *lolofo sa-na*, 'he kept on flying'. In other words, a 'non-verb' word-group, often constituting a complete sentence, corresponds to an English verb.

A further problem was raised by the very common word *ga*. We might well conclude on first acquaintance that *ga* is a definite article. But this analysis cannot be sustained in the face of *e-na-afa ga fealo*, 'the sun was shining', *fealo ga e-na-afa*, 'the sun shines', *ea ga rekona*, 'this is good', *rekona ga ea*, 'this is good', *natu-gu maraka ga*, 'my child is a bird', *natu-na ga iri-fati*, 'they took out her child', and very many others. I found a clue in Ray's grammar of Roviana, a language not far distant from the Bougainville Strait and in many ways closely akin to Mono. Under the rubric 'Article' he lists a word *si*, of which he says, 'Its exact use is difficult to define. It is almost an expletive, and Mr Leembruggen' (the missionary whom Ray consulted) 'regards it as regulating and balancing a sentence.' It seemed to me that Mono *ga* was also a 'balancer', its presence or absence being determined by the speaker's rhythmical preferences.*

I never completed my Mono grammar, because by the time I was sixteen too many other things, of which Greek was not the least, were competing for my enthusiasm, but I learned enduring lessons from the attempt. Most obviously, if I

---

*Although I would still not be prepared to discard that consideration, there are, of course, other approaches of which I was ignorant in 1936.

was right about *ga* (with acknowledgements to Mr Leembruggen), aesthetic caprice must be included among the determinants of linguistic form; and even if I was wrong, it was still apparent that categories designed for the description of one language could well be unhelpful, and might be positively misleading, if they were employed for the description of another. I remembered those lessons when I came to write about Greek word order in 1959, and again in the nineteen-sixties when I devised a beginner's course in Greek for my Department.[10] What was more important, I began to wonder (long before Foucault): do these considerations apply only to language? Do not comparable problems of classification and categorisation arise in many fields of human behaviour?[11]

The indirect effect of my absorbing hobby on my work in Classics has been deep and pervasive, although I made no explicit use of it until 1963.[12] Essentially, it means that I look at the Greeks and the Pacific islanders without changing my spectacles. From the start, the hobby was a very powerful inoculation against racism. If naked savages who lived in mud huts and were ignorant of writing nevertheless spoke languages which were not only charged with subtle allusiveness and imagery but often endowed (or burdened, according to one's viewpoint) with systems of inflection as complex as Greek or Russian, it seemed that prevalent assumptions about the limited mental capacity of 'natives' were rather wide of the mark. What was even more interesting was the absence of correlation between the complexity of a language and the technology, culture or administrative organisation of the people who speak it. The Pacific affords an excellent illustration, because in many areas Papuan speech-communities manipulating an enormous battery of inflections are at exactly the same cultural level as adjacent Austronesian speech-communities whose grammatical armoury is very simple. Language seems to go its own way, neither reflecting nor affecting other aspects of cultural or social behaviour. This provokes thought on the autonomy of art-forms in general and the lack of clear correlations – even, in some cases, the presence of strong disparities – between the technical level of one art in a given culture and the low level of another art in the same culture.[13]

Part of the time in vacations during my first two years at Oxford I entertained the possibility of writing a monograph on the semantics of reduplication in

---

[10]On Dover's own Greek coursebook, and its exaggerated faith that students would share his own ability to reconstruct grammatical principles from specimens of a language, see p. 182 with note.

[11]In *G&G* 94, Dover compares the lack of systematic coherence in the rules of a living language to the unsystematic nature of a culture's moral attitudes (cf. *MC* 220): 'The determinants of linguistic change, as of morality, are heterogeneous'. He thought the same about both religious and sexual attitudes; it was perhaps the latter which prompted his allusion to Michel Foucault (1926–84), whose own work on the history of sexuality was influenced by Dover's *GH*: see Atack's chapter in *S&C*.

[12]The 1963 allusion is to the article on 'The poetry of Archilochos': see p. 123 for the link with Dover's interest in Pacific languages.

[13]'I have in mind especially the gulf between Homeric poetry and the visual arts in early archaic Greece: if we had only the latter to go by, would we imagine anything of the former?' (Dover SN)

Austronesian languages, but it ran into the sand. On two months' leave from the Army after the end of the War I looked into the possibility of separating word-base from 'root' in languages of Melanesia in the way successfully pioneered for Indonesia by a Swiss scholar many years earlier, but this project foundered on a technical difficulty which threatened to make any prima facie results far too speculative and open to too many alternative interpretations.[14] I turned instead to writing an essay on *The Translation of Greek Poetry*, which I submitted with success for the Cromer Prize offered by the British Academy.[15] Since that time (for I have only one lifetime at my disposal) I have not attempted to keep up with Pacific linguistics. Occasionally I look through a new book on the subject, and I recognise easily enough what it is talking about; but I could not put it more strongly than that.

The subject afforded me, all through my adolescence, a richly rewarding escape from the tensions and frustrations of life at home and at school. My choice of the word 'escape' sounds a note which could be taken as regret or repentance, but that would be an unwise interpretation. I would have liked to be different physically and temperamentally. I would have liked to live in a home where I could feel emotionally secure and relaxed. If those conditions had been met, it is possible that my inclinations and ambitions would have taken a different turn. Whether in consequence I would have been happier at, say, twenty-eight than I actually was, I greatly doubt.

---

[14] The Swiss scholar was 'Brandstetter, whose major essays, combined and translated as *An Introduction to Indonesian Linguistics*, are a masterpiece of clear exposition and have served me as model throughout my academic life.' (Dover SN) *An Introduction to Indonesian Linguistics* was published by the Royal Asiatic Society in 1916.

[15] The Cromer Prize was established in 1916 for an essay on any aspect of ancient Greek culture written by someone under the age of twenty-six. Dover won the prize in 1946, though we know from his letters that he had started drafting his essay (which seems not to have survived) as early as January-February 1944 while still serving in Italy.

6 RECONSTITUTION 1935–1936

Felices los amados y los amantes y los que pueden prescindir del amor. Felices los felices.

BORGES[1]

One day when we were on holiday in September 1935 my father cut up a sticky bar of pressed dates and offered me a slice. I put out my hand to take it, and he snarled, 'Open your mouth!' My mother, reproaching him in my presence for the first time that I can recall, exclaimed, 'Oh, for goodness' sake, can't you just *say*, "Open your mouth"?' 'I did,' he snapped. 'No, you didn't,' I said, half crying, 'you snarled, as you always do.' He moved towards me as if to strike me, I picked up my camera by the sling of its case to defend myself, and my mother calmed us both down. For the rest of the day we treated each other with wary courtesy. The next day, when my father and I were walking on the moor, he said that he was puzzled by my saying 'as you always do', because he had 'never regarded [himself] as a particularly foul-tempered man'. There was nothing I could say. If he believed his own words, he was encased in an illusion which rational communication could not penetrate; if he did not, he was deceiving me. The whole thing was deeply disturbing. It was the first time that my mother's self-control had broken, and the first time since infancy that I had made a gesture of fighting back and simultaneously betrayed my emotion in my voice. I reflected on the tension with which I lived all the time. My circumstances were not unlike those in which some adolescents nowadays run away from home, but no such absurd idea occurred to me, because I depended on my parents for realisation of my ambition to enjoy an interesting professional career; for that, the completion of my schooling, and then university, were necessary.

---

[1]'Happy are the loved and the lovers and those who can do without love. Happy are the happy.' From Borges' poem, 'Fragments from an Apocryphal Gospel', nos. 50–1: A. Coleman, ed., *Jorge Luis Borges: Selected Poems* (London, 1999) 294–5.

One complication was that things were not going as well at school as I would have wished. I had been due to take School Certificate in the summer of 1934 – it was the policy of St Paul's to push boys through their miscellaneous subjects at the earliest possible age – but because of scarlet fever and its complications I had to put it off until December. The results were highly satisfactory (though I find it hard to believe that I deserved my Credit in History), and in January 1935 I went into the Lower Eighth,* where I had not only to cope with a form full of boys I did not know but also to catch up at mid-point with its concentrated Classical curriculum. I was relieved and surprised when I gained a Senior Scholarship in June 1935 and so ensured my free tuition for the rest of my time at school. I was not yet really confident about my own academic ability, and in other respects my confidence was negligible. If I say that I was unhappy at school, I must add at once that this was in no way the fault of the school. St Paul's was tolerant and civilised.[2] As a day-boy, I never encountered any bullying (and I don't know whether the boarders did or not). A few of those who taught us were a little dreary and unbending, one was scatty, one culpably lazy, and one unattractive character automatically gave two blows of the cane to anyone who made two bad mistakes in French in the same week (I learned my French verbs more thoroughly than I would have done without the threat of pain);† but the great majority were not only lucid, painstaking and efficient, but kindly, reasonable and perceptive. My trouble was the deep sense of inferiority generated by my chest,[3] which made it hard for me to believe in my own reality. I felt that there was *nothing there* between my neck and my midriff, and longed to feel top-heavy, as I imagined normal people felt. I was wary of meeting half-way the good friendship which was abundantly on offer. In later years, when I met my former teachers and contemporaries, I was taken aback to find how friendly they were, and I must assume that I had been less withdrawn and churlish than I thought I was. Perhaps I have tended to see my schooldays as a whole in the dark shade of 1935.

In order to counteract my vulnerability I set about becoming a different kind of person. This sounds unrealistically ambitious; but if your relationship with your circumstances is hard to bear, and there is no conceivable way of changing your circumstances, it is yourself that you must change. My first and easiest step was to change my handwriting, dropping the spiky style which I had used until then and adopting the limpid flow of Uncle Ken's style. The second step was to cultivate stoicism, to make myself live within a shell impermeable both to my emotions on

---

*In most other schools the 'Eighth' form would be the 'Sixth'.
†In the whole of my six years at St Paul's there were only two occasions on which I saw a boy beaten, and one on which I knew that someone was beaten behind closed doors.

[2]'St Paul's had a high proportion of London Jews . . . and they had a very civilizing effect on the ethos of the school.' (Dover SN)
[3]Cf. the earlier reference to Dover's funnel chest on p. 25.

the way out and to other people's on the way in.‡ In this I was a little too successful and to this day, despite my unqualified love of my wife and children, if I call someone 'emotional', I imply: unreasonable, impatient, bad-tempered, unreliable, to be avoided if possible. Fond though I was of my mother, I know that to the end of her life I did not make my affection as explicit and demonstrative as would have been welcome and reassuring to her, and my regret for that is anguished. I have found sociability easy enough, but firm friendship – until fairly recently – difficult, because I have always put work first and friends second. I have never yet experienced what could properly be called grief at anybody's death.[4] At their suffering, yes; I can be torn to pieces by other people's suffering; but death has always seemed like the return of a book to the stack.

For many years I believed that I had methodically, single-handedly changed my own character in the course of 1935. Later I realised that fifteen is an age at which people often change a lot anyway, so that my experience was perhaps more an event than an action. So far as concerns my intentions, what I have said above is true, but it makes sense to believe at least that my rejection (towards the end of 1935) of my father's political and social attitudes was created not by a cool decision on my part but by Hitler, the Italian invasion of Abyssinia, and the political awareness of my friends at school. Certainly until the end of 1934 I held no political opinions which were not an echo of my father's. I can date my reorientation with some precision from my memory of the imaginary politics of Gangtown.[5] In January 1935 the Gang elected Wimpee as Leader (they must have been in a bad way to do that, but I have forgotten the nature of the crisis). Wimpee instituted a ruthlessly dictatorial style of government, which I found gratifying, but by the end of the year it sickened me.[6] In January 1936 they elected Felix, who was an amiable egalitarian but an easy victim of a coup by Edwin, who mysteriously but characteristically escaped the odium of having been Wimpee's hatchet-man. After that the Gang faded into the shadows, and their place was taken by the politics of the late Roman Republic.

My father's parents undoubtedly voted Conservative, but they were not rabid Conservatives, for they were willing to respect (as some of my current Conservative acquaintances cannot) some individual politicians of other parties. (I have said

---

‡About that time I coined the dictum, 'Instinct is the force that makes us repeat our mistakes', and was rather proud of it.

[4]Dover subsequently qualified this statement: he told both Naim Attallah and Anthony Clare that by 1994 it had not been true for some years; he had first felt grief for a friend's death in 1984 (*ICNA* 102, *IPC* 102).

[5]See the earlier reference on p. 40 to this imaginary world of his childhood. In his own copy of *MC*, Dover references Salman Rushdie's novel *Fury*, whose protagonist, a former academic, makes miniature dolls (eventually for TV) whose imagined lives 'were as real to him as anyone else he knew': *Fury* (London, 2001) 95.

[6]'At some time in 1934/5 I was briefly attracted by Mosley's Fascist movement.' (Dover SN)

'they', but I doubt whether my grandmother arrived at political opinions of her own.) I know nothing about the politics of my mother's parents. She herself would not have admitted, at any rate at home, to voting anything but Conservative, but I suspect that the voting-booth afforded her a delectable moment of rebellion. Both my parents, however, together with most of our friends and relations, took it for granted that the British middle class of the early twentieth century was the triumphant end-product of human evolution. They would never turn on a light without first drawing the curtain, they did not readily forgive or forget ignorant mistakes in spelling or pronunciation, and my mother's family at any rate (to use a criterion of gentility which I have heard invoked in Devon) farted only in solitude.[7] Encountering anyone of noble family or great inherited wealth who dressed inconspicuously and spoke quietly and courteously, we rolled over with our paws in the air, but we were quick to snarl at the sight of ostentatious behaviour or the sound of a loud, arrogant voice. We took capitalism for granted (without being completely reconciled to its logical consequences), although we had no more respect for the major predator than for the navvy. Capitalism was, after all, the alternative to socialism, and in our eyes socialism meant drunken scum destroying things and proclaiming that they were as good as everyone else while demonstrating by their behaviour that they were not.

Even in my late teens I did not wholly reject my parents' values, and there are some of which I am still tenacious. We had a meal in a restaurant only two or three times a year, and although a pint in a pub during a country walk was acceptable, we never went into a town pub or bar. I have inherited a hatred of drunks, contempt for gluttons, and rather less respect for connoisseurs of food and drink than they like to receive.§ My parents took it for granted, as my grandparents had done, that no sane person incurs a debt that cannot be discharged by return of post. I take that for granted, too; it has meant going without a lot of things, but the resultant feeling of freedom and security has been worth it. On one occasion during the first year of marriage I inadvertently ran an overdraft of seven pounds; that scared me to death, and I have never had an overdraft since (though I must admit to borrowing half the price of our house in 1967, giving priority to the principle of not allowing savings to fall below the level of a year's nett income). All those inhibitions are my father in me.[8]

Until the emergence of the Nazis, foreign affairs were not particularly interesting to the adults I knew. The generation which remembered the disaster of Caporetto but knew nothing about the battles on the Isonzo was inclined to think that

---

§But I cherish Egon Ronay's insistence that good cooking 'comes from the heart' and is performed 'lovingly'.

[7]'My father overheard a conversation in a pub at Ivybridge: "No, no, e an't stuck-up at all. E varts at supper and calls ee 'bugger' just like you and I."' (Dover SN)

[8]Cf. pp. 107–8, 'there is a bit more of my father in me than I could bring myself to acknowledge'.

Mussolini's dictatorship was good for the undisciplined Italians; they forgave, in a patronising way, his arrogant theatricality, and they were ignorant of his crimes.⁹ They regarded Russia, where the imperial family had been murdered and many 'decent people' driven into exile, as governed by evil thugs but so deeply mired in incompetence that it could not be taken seriously as a great power, only as a generator of malevolent conspiracies in other countries. When the Nazis came to power in Germany, many different sentiments conflicted in the minds of the British suburban middle class. Hostility to the Jews was unquestionably one element; I recall hearing, 'My dad says, you've got to hand it to Hitler for one thing, he's smashed the bloody Jews.' My parents' generation never doubted that Germany bore the responsibility for the First World War, and there were some for whom the Hun would always be the enemy. Yet British men who had fought on the Western Front often felt greater ill-will towards the French. They knew about the French mutinies of 1917 and the temporary incapacitation of the French army which was one strategic reason for the fearful Passchendaele offensive. Add to this that the British soldier in France was dependent on the French for wine, women and other amenities; the buyer is often prompt to accuse the seller of profiteering, and when s/he can also accuse the seller of ingratitude hrs animus is increased. The courage and endurance of the Germans, by contrast, had made a deep impression, and by 1930 there was a widespread feeling that Clemenceau and Lloyd George had been cruel and unreasonable in the peace terms they had imposed on Germany. This feeling was reinforced progressively as more Britons went on holiday to France and Germany. It was observed that many Germans have blue eyes and fair hair, attributes which in this country have traditionally been associated with virtue and honesty. They were certainly cleaner and tidier than the French (or ourselves), and agreeably efficient. Their young people in particular were cheerful, friendly, outgoing, disciplined and musical, whereas the French appeared to be surly and mean. This pro-German and anti-French sentiment was a strand in British society between the Wars which should never be underrated. The notion that Hitler was 'a bulwark against Bolshevism' seeped down from higher political levels, but it was not, in my recollection, of much importance. At my first school, when we organised mass fighting games in the playground, the two sides were French and English, not German and English. (Folk-memory of Napoleon?)‖

My own detestation of the Nazis was created not by their cruelty and violence *per se*, but by their war against reason. If they had decreed strangulation as the penalty for embezzlement of public funds, I would have thought their penal code

---

‖My mother-in-law, as a child in south Devon, knew a children's song which began 'Bonaparte/Let a fartie/ …'

⁹Caporetto, then in Austria (and now Kobarid in Slovenia), was the site of a battle in autumn 1917 in which Italian troops were massively defeated by Austro-German forces. This was the last of twelve battles near the Isonzo river, 1915–17.

rather severe but no business of mine. If they had declared infant circumcision illegal, brushing aside 'religious reasons' as a contradiction in terms, I would have thought them truly civilised. But they persecuted people whose parents had adhered to the Jewish religion, and it seemed to me irrational to the point of insanity to hurt any individual for somebody else's choices. They justified this outrageous behaviour by theories about 'Jewish blood' and 'Aryan blood', and although my education in science had not been as good as it might have been, it was enough for me to recognise drivel of this kind for what it was. The fact that the government of a powerful nation openly adopted the opinions of ignorant or paranoid street-corner gossips on questions of scientific and historical fact was frightening, and portended armageddon between reason and unreason. What is more, the Nazis burned books and punished people for speaking out. In other words, they would not listen; and though I had not formulated my subsequent belief that civilisation is a state of affairs in which people listen to each other and take criticism seriously, I was at least groping after it.

The Italian invasion of Abyssinia followed, and the Spanish Civil War, and the Japanese invasion of China. In all three cases I greatly overrated the prospects of successful resistance by the victims, but I knew which side I was on. The Italians and the Japanese made silly excuses for their aggression, and Franco was the champion of a dogmatic religion which was Antichrist to my evangelical friends and evidence of mental instability in the eyes of my parents' circle. As each year passed, one had the feeling that Britain and France were being forced into a corner from which they would one day have to fight their way out at considerable disadvantage, and the firm acquisition of Russia as an ally would be a great help. Moreover, I was now inclined to regard socialism as the expression of law and of reason in human affairs and therefore as an indispensable ally against the menacing forces of unreason: Mussolini's glorification of war for its own sake, Hitler's Aryan blood and German destiny, Franco's Catholic faith, Japanese emperor-worship. A brief incident in my childhood, stowed away in my mind for years, reasserted itself. During the great depression in 1930 my father and I, out for a walk, met a middle-aged man, respectably dressed and quiet-spoken, whom my father evidently knew. This man said that his firm had had to sack half its employees, and he was now out of a job; 'I don't know,' he said, 'where my bread and butter is coming from next week.' A fortnight later I heard that he had killed himself. Now I wondered: what is a slump? If a great chain of earthquakes or a worldwide plague of locusts had suddenly reduced the productive capacity of the human race, one could see why there should be a great increase of hunger and suffering. But nothing of the kind had happened; the world's productive capacity had not changed overnight. What had gone wrong was something in the financial and commercial system which governed the realisation of productive capacity and the distribution of its products. If a system breaks down and patently lacks a self-correcting mechanism, one tries a different system. The Russians' boast that they were 'the first society in history to break the power of money' needed to be taken seriously. I did indeed take it seriously, because I was aware that 'mine', 'yours' and 'theirs' are not defined by God or by nature, but by law, which a nation can alter when it wishes. I have never experienced any ill-feeling towards tax-collectors, and I can feel nothing but contempt for rich people who whine about 'penal' taxation, because it is reasonable that the rest of us should protect ourselves against those whose primary aim is to acquire an exceptionally large share of the total resources and services available to the community.¶

Many people well knew that Stalin, as the Russians themselves have been saying for a long time now, was a tyrant in process of committing monstrous crimes against his own people. Some understood that a one-party state is necessarily corrupt from the moment of its inception, whatever the intentions and principles of its creators, because it elevates loyalty to the party – that is to say, to the gang at the top of the party – above loyalty to the community. Many of my generation did not understand that; has there ever been a generation of which that could not be said? Few Westerners spoke Russian, and hardly any could go where they wished in the Soviet Union and talk freely to the people, so that it was easy for the official organs of communication between Russia and the West to give the impression that most Russians were less impoverished, oppressed and insecure in 1936 than in 1906. Whether less so than they would have been by 1936 if the October Revolution had never happened, hardly anyone asked, and Communists, if they considered the question at all, dismissed it contemptuously as hypothetical (though every revolution, in so far as it contains an element of foresight and planning, is an answer to a hypothetical question, and before killing a lot of people it is desirable to think quite hard about alternative answers). Hitler and the Depression between them encouraged great numbers to disregard as capitalist propaganda what enemies of the Soviet Union said. That disregard was sometimes right, but the series of trials in which Stalin eliminated all those of whose sycophancy he did not feel assured was not so easy to stomach. I heard much ingenious argument in its defence, but my nose told me that the whole thing, the grovelling confessions, Vishinsky's callous rhetoric, the bloodthirsty Soviet press, simply stank.[10] For once, I trusted my nose, and however close I came to the Communists on the need for a planned and centralised economy, I could never identify with them – a predicament for which Vishinsky, who boasted of his own keen nose for class enemies, would have produced a fluent explanation.

¶Adam Smith observed that manufacturers and dealers in commodities are 'an order of men ... who have generally an interest to deceive and even to oppress the public, and who accordingly have, upon many occasions, both deceived and oppressed it.' [EDS The Wealth of Nations, *Book I, chapter 11.*] Nowadays they stigmatise measures for the restraint of deceit and oppression as 'petty bureaucratic regulations'.

[10]Andrei Vyshinsky (1883–1954) was a state prosecutor in Stalin's purge trials.

My father, as a Civil Servant with an unreliable knee, had been exempt from military service, but my uncles and most of my father's friends had served in France or Mesopotamia. Some men of that generation, though surprisingly few, even among those who had been through many horrible experiences, were so sickened by the war that they favoured peace at any price. That is to say, they believed that the consequences of armed resistance were always and necessarily worse than the consequences of yielding to whatever threats and demands another nation might make. There was something to be said for that view. Seen from the standpoint of the nineteen-twenties, the rulers of Europe seemed to have caused vast suffering recklessly, even frivolously, for what they conceived as national honour. They and their advisers stood to lose face if the fortunes of war went against them but not, like some of those whom they commanded, their faces. But what was beginning to take shape in the nineteen-thirties was a throwback to war as most of the human race had known it in earlier times. The persecution of the Jews in Germany was a foretaste of what was later to befall Poland and Russia, because it showed that if the holders of power wish to destroy all members of a particular category – for example, former trade union officials, or inhabitants of Nanking – there is no salvation in a refusal to resist by force. That was, I suppose, irrelevant in the eyes of true pacifists, who believe that God forbids the taking of human life in all circumstances, but I had no contact with that degree of pacifism, which has never presented me with even a second's temptation. It is one of the things, like sadism, ski-jumping and Christian Science, of which I can honestly say that I cannot imagine what it would feel like.

I knew boys at school who believed that one state attacks another only when it feels threatened, and they concluded that attack can be averted by disarmament; or that war is made by old men, whose crafty and callous designs can be frustrated if the young, whom they manipulate, refuse to fight. These boys did not confront the fact that many men enjoy attacking someone else if they think that they will win quickly and easily. Readiness to take that risk, each individual confidently believing that he personally will survive, is much more conspicuous in the young than in the old.[11] That was recognised by the ancient world throughout its history; but it was also apparent at the time of the Munich Pact in 1938, when Britain and France put extreme pressure on Czechoslovakia to cede its German-speaking border area to Hitler. I knew no one at school, and very few at Oxford when I went up to Balliol a fortnight later, who supported the pact. We, the young, the 'cannon-fodder', thought it would have been right to risk war in defence of Czechoslovakia, and regarded Chamberlain and his government as craven dodderers. I wept, for the first time

---

[11] The last two sentences have a markedly Thucydidean resonance – not the only place in Dover's writing where his voice recalls that of the historian to whom he devoted much of his scholarly energies (see esp. pp. 118–20).

since childhood, at the news of Munich, because I had no doubts about the magnitude of the issue. By then I had been briefly in Italy[12] and had seen how walls in every Italian town were covered with stencils of Mussolini in profile and the slogans 'The Leader is always right' and 'Believe, obey, fight', an experience which inclines me to laugh wryly when I hear the term 'fascist' used in political discourse nowadays as a synonym for 'somewhat authoritarian'. I had also been on holiday in Germany in 1936, and having by that time learned a fair amount of German I could read both on and between the lines of the *Völkischer Beobachter*.[13] I had seen brass plates advertising 'Aryan doctor' and 'Aryan dentist', and I had noticed that in the agreeable little Black Forest town of Furtwangen one page of the local paper, posted conspicuously outside the town hall, named and pilloried individuals who had been denounced by neighbours because they had been seen entering Jewish-owned shops. All of us, though, in 1938 overrated the Czechoslovak frontier fortifications, with no inkling of the German military expertise which only a year later would break Poland to pieces in ten days. We overrated also the capacity of Britain and the willingness of France to attack Germany. Illusions were nourished by the fact that Germany had been defeated in 1918 and we had been on the winning side; few of us understood what it had taken to achieve that result.

One little incident in 1936 disturbed my confidence and came back to trouble me in 1938. I was on a walk with my parents on a steep slope through woods in the Black Forest, when there was a noise of machines and voices on a nearby track, and down came German soldiers on motorcycles with sidecars, wearing steel helmets and very modern-looking open-necked uniforms, jolting and swaying wildly over the rough ground and shouting with laughter at the most violent bumps. I had always thought of Germans as rigid, stern, unimaginative, gratifyingly outwitted by the spontaneous and light-hearted inventiveness of the British. German soldiers *laughing*? It didn't fit, and it gave me a shock, as reality does when it intrudes upon schematic illusion. Evil and high spirits make a formidable team.

---

[12]This was in March 1938, when he and his companions travelled through parts of Italy, including Turin and Rome, en route to Greece (see p. 69).
[13]The newspaper of the Nazi Party.

7 TRANSITION 1936–1940

Leo used to say: 'If you emend a text, you should do so as if the fate of your immortal soul depended on the rightness of your emendation.'
EDUARD FRAENKEL[1]

My last three years at St Paul's, in the Middle Eighth and Upper Eighth, were spent almost entirely on Greek, Latin and Ancient History; there were eight of us in our batch, and about the same number in each of the batches junior and senior to mine. Other boys were at the same time going through equally specialised programmes in history, mathematics, modern languages or science, all aiming at the best possible performance in Higher Certificate (which carried the promise of State Scholarships) and at winning open scholarships or exhibitions at Oxford or Cambridge colleges. This policy was very successful, inasmuch as thirty of us got open awards in 1938. It was also, in the eyes of believers in breadth, wicked, because the soupçon of English, French, German, New Testament and Current Affairs which occupied a small corner of our time as classicists could hardly be regarded as a broad education; but I found those three years extremely enjoyable and cannot say that I regret them.

I was taught Greek by George Bean, Latin by Robert James, and Ancient History by Philip Whitting.[2] Whitting, for whom the subject was a sideline – as form-

---

[1] Dover had previously quoted this passage in his 1976 Presidential address to the Classical Association (*G&L* 307). On Eduard Fraenkel, see p. 72 with note; Friedrich Leo (1851-1914) had been Fraenkel's doctoral supervisor in Göttingen. 'Of course, neither Leo nor Fraenkel believed that the fate of their souls *actually* depended on their emendations. People have sometimes referred to the dictum without taking account of the crucial "as if"'. (Dover SN)

[2] There were photographs of Bean and Whitting in the group of plates, nos. 6–7, after p. 120 in the first edition of *MC*. George Bean (1903–77) taught Greek at St Paul's 1926–43; for his post-war career in Turkey, see pp. 70–1. Robert James (1905–82) taught Classics at St Paul's 1928–39 and later returned as High Master 1946–53. Philip Whitting (1903–88) was form-master in history at St Paul's 1929–63 and became an expert numismatist of Byzantine coinage; he was also awarded a George Medal in the Second World War. On Whitting, Dover wrote in the 1995 addenda: 'He often gave us a salutary jolt. Once, when we admitted we hadn't observed a news item about the drowning of a million Chinese by the Yellow River floods, he growled, 'Well, *I* care, because they're so much better people than *you* are.'

master of the History Eighth he had to spend most of his teaching-time on medieval and modern history, and his own special interest was Byzantium – was the most memorable teacher I have ever known. He had a natural talent for clarity of exposition and explanation and the simplification of complex issues, and his analogies, comparisons and generalisations, all presented (without notes, of course) vigorously and fluently in a powerful and mobile voice, opened our eyes to human history as a whole. George Bean had an extraordinary understanding of the Greek language. He was finicky and pedantic, delighting in abnormal uses of the subjunctive and always deducting a full mark for a wrong accent, but at the same time subtle and imaginative when it came to deciding just how a Greek would have expressed something which in English sounded hopelessly un-Greek. Curiously, he did not seem to have much idea of what it was like to be a Greek engaged in any activity other than the use of language, and the occasional notes he dictated to us on historical topics, with a lack of enthusiasm that aroused our compassion, were puerile. Nevertheless his teaching was what I wanted and needed, because it built me a firm foundation of linguistic expertise, a foundation which could support a great variety of enterprises, and I was never for a moment bored.[3]

James was more lively, less stolid, less predictable, but not so good a teacher, because his Latin lacked the finesse of George's Greek. His heart was in Roman history, and he overloaded us with details of the forties BC without contriving to make them real. That may be why I have never felt myself to be ambidextrous in Greek and Latin. If so, it is the only time that my interest and enthusiasm for a subject have been affected more by the teacher than by the subject itself; my normal reaction to unsatisfactory teaching has always been to think of ways in which the material could be presented better. But I may be mistaken about the relative effects of George's and Robert's teaching, because there was a strong tendency among classicists of my generation to go for Greek in preference to Latin. We were all the grandchildren of Gilbert Murray.[4]

A very important ingredient of our work was composition, which meant the translation of sophisticated literary English into Greek or Latin prose and of passages of English poetry into Greek or Latin verse. The rest of our time went on the preparation of texts for translation in class (with rather limited time for

---

[3] Bean's teaching was also fondly remembered by Dover's contemporaries John Chadwick and Geoffrey Woodhead: see J.T. Killen and Anna Morpurgo Davies, 'John Chadwick 1920–1998', in *PBA* 115 (2003) 135–65, at 135–6.
[4] Gilbert Murray (1866–1957), Regius Professor of Greek at Oxford 1908–36 and a leading advocate of the humanistic importance of Greek literature and culture: see Duncan Wilson, *Gilbert Murray OM 1866–1957* (Oxford, 1987), C. Stray, ed., *Gilbert Murray Reassessed* (Oxford, 2007), and the shorter account by Robert Fowler in *CSBE* 321–34. Dover (first?) heard Murray lecture in May 1940 and told his parents that he had 'a unique style which paralyses criticism' (letter of 16 May 1940); for the flavour of his mature views on Murray, see his review of Wilson's biography in the *Times Literary Supplement*, 24–30 June 1988, p. 700, with further discussion in Rood's contribution to *S&C*.

discussion). By the time I left school I had read, with close attention to exactitude in translation, three plays of Aeschylus, three of Sophokles, two books of Thucydides, two of Plato's *Republic* (including the daunting Book VII), most of Theokritos, much of Pindar, and so on, adding up to rather more than some university students nowadays will have read in the course of three years' work for a degree in Classics. We also learned by heart half of Euripides' *Hecuba* and most of Vergil's first and fourth *Georgics*. It is perhaps significant that I cannot now remember which Latin texts (apart from Vergil) I read at school and which later. St Paul's was well endowed with prizes, and I won those for which I competed in my last two years. In March 1938 I won the top open scholarship at Balliol; some years later I saw the marksheet and was a little surprised that I was preferred to Robin Barbour, but apparently it was my non-Classical General Paper which, even if minutely, tipped the scale.[5] One or two of us at school may have had parents or other relatives at some particular Oxford or Cambridge college, and consequently a wish to put that college at the top of their list of preferences, but in general we were 'placed' by Robert James, who knew the scene well and considered not only which pupil would be best suited by which tutor but also how best to distribute candidates of comparable ability in order to maximise the number of top awards for the glory of the school. Having no ties with any college, I was simply told 'Balliol', and said yes.

Prize-money ensured that I could build up a good library before I arrived in Oxford and it also made possible a memorable trip to Greece in 1938. I had been there once already, with a school-friend in 1937, on an educational cruise which cost nearly thirty pounds from my mother's savings. It was a rough sort of cruise – ten of us slept on bunks in a compartment over the propeller – and not very smoothly organised, but it had revealed the unforgettable Greek landscape to me. Of the three high points in my memory, one was the temple sculptures at Olympia and the second a thunderstorm at Delphi, which occurred after my friend and I had set out light-heartedly to cut across country down to the ship at Itea. The third was an attempt to reach the ancient fort of Phyle in the Parnes range, starting from the village of Khasia; the guide of our group – Andrew Burn, who should have known better – somehow lost the way, and after an exhausting clamber up to the wrong summit we had to stumble down an endless valley, while darkness fell, to our rendezvous in a village on the north edge of the Eleusinian plain.[6] Now in the spring of 1938 George Bean proposed a five-week trip with me and another

---

[5] The Scotsman Robert ('Robin') Barbour (1921–2014) went up to Balliol from Rugby. He graduated with a double first in Greats (cf. n. 22 below) and later became Professor of New Testament Exegesis at Aberdeen University 1971–82.
[6] Andrew Robert Burn (1902–91) was at this date senior Classics master at Uppingham School; he later served in the Intelligence Corps and at the British Embassy in Athens, and subsequently taught ancient history at the University of Glasgow 1946–69: see D.W. Baronowski in *DBC*, i 121–3.

school-friend Alistair Matthews, in which we would travel around the mainland by mule and car and look at many out-of-the-way sites. The whole trip was going to cost about £50 each, and my parents made no objection to my using a massive school prize of £40 as the main contribution to the cost. So it was that I saw the old Greece as it was when most travel between villages was by horse or mule. The weather was mainly bad, and snow prevented us from going over the Metsovo Pass from Ioannina to Kalambaka, so that we had to fly back from Ioannina to Athens; the fare was less than £1 each. I was taken aback by the dirtiness of the Greeks. They hawked and spat incessantly, sometimes exploding in your face in mid-sentence; they shat anywhere, sometimes ignoring in hotels the management's plea that used toilet-paper should be put in the bowl and not discarded on the floor; they washed so little that old women often had black lines of dirt embedded in the wrinkles of their faces (I last observed this on Chios in 1984);[7] and herdsmen gave off a stench of rancid fat and old sweat which one could almost visualise as a fine putty-coloured mist around them. Middle-class city-dwellers were different, but we didn't see much of them, and it was the difference between the country people and the stereotype of a dignified ancient Greek in flowing white robes which made the impression. These people were very tough, violent, quarrelsome, vivacious, generous, candid, hospitable and pious; I was not surprised when their army smashed through the Italian front in Albania in 1940, wolves against house-trained dogs.[8]

George, Alistair and I were all, each in his own way, loners, but the ways were very different. Alistair was my close rival at school, and I had a great regard for him. I don't think it was reciprocated, and I can see why; we both had high academic ability, but he was self-reliant, ambitious, resolute and mature.[9] Legends gathered around him, one of them (which may be true, for all I know) saying that while still at school he had organised and led a tour of older people round Greece. He won a major award at Christ Church, but did not return to Oxford after war service. George never came back to St Paul's after the War, but became Professor of Greek at Istanbul.[10] Having a strong interest in archaeological problems, he was able to devote much time to exploration of sites in the interior of Turkey, some of it in

---

[7] For the Chios trip in question, see p. 277.
[8] Later in 1938 Dover had copies of his letters home from this trip to Greece bound into a booklet entitled *A Journey on the Mainland of Greece*. This was acquired after his death by a Dutch book dealer; the editors are grateful to Dr Frederick Naerebout of Leiden University for sharing further information about the contents of the booklet.
[9] In his own copy of *MC*, Dover added here, 'I was vividly reminded of him when I saw Goya's portrait of Wellington.'
[10] Bean's battered suitcase, containing over 3,000 photos of Turkey, was deposited in Cambridge in 1990, unearthed in 2014, and then catalogued: see https://www.classics.cam.ac.uk/museum/collections/collection-videos-1/the-bean-archive-1.

FIGURE 3 Near Khasia, Attica, with Alistair Matthews, March 1938. *Photo: George Bean*.

company with a man who later became a good friend of mine at St Andrews, Terence Mitford.[11]

Work at Oxford was essentially similar to work at school. I was required to produce two compositions a week for my tutors and to attend a dozen lectures a week on prescribed texts and a Special Subject. I had already studied most of the texts at school, but now had to think about them harder and learn much more about textual criticism and the reconstruction of relationships between manuscripts. I found all this entirely congenial and sometimes exciting, just as genetic relationships between languages were. I was never required to write an essay on any Classical subject for my tutors, but in our first year we were all expected, in accordance with a long-standing Balliol custom, to read essays on general topics to the Master and miscellaneous tutors.

What mattered most at Oxford was Eduard Fraenkel's seminar on the *Agamemnon* of Aeschylus, which was attended by some dons and a select number

---

[11]Bean collaborated with Mitford on *Journeys in Rough Cilicia 1964–1968* (Vienna, 1970), one of several volumes of Greek inscriptions from Asia Minor produced by Bean. On Mitford see p. 134.

of undergraduates recommended by their tutors.[12] We took turns at presenting our expositions of successive portions of the play. My portion was part of the Kassandra scene, which I treated as if it were a newly discovered text and we were looking at it with innocent eyes. Fraenkel had an immense influence on me (too much; it was twenty years before I came to acknowledge his limitations), but it was hard to explain the nature of the spell which he cast. Not long ago I put the question to a friend who had attended his seminars some years after me, and on reflection she said, 'It was his *seriousness*.' She didn't mean that he was gloomy or portentous, but that he acknowledged the Greeks and Romans as real people, who did not write *for* us, but for and within a culture which we can come to understand if we work at it. I felt that the older generation of Oxford scholars, for the most part, had not worked at it hard enough, but thought of the Classical poets as interesting neighbours who called in at the vicarage for tea and entertained the company by quoting from their poems. This is an arrogant judgement, and if I had been called on to justify it I don't think I could have done so, but, looking back, I can see what provoked it; Fraenkel understood and explained to us the constants and the variables in Greek and Latin literature, the interplay of tradition and innovation, and that was an aspect of literature which did not seem to interest many British scholars. The younger generation – notably Bill Watt, Spencer Barrett and Frederick Wells[13] – understood it well, and cared about it; so, among their elders, did Dodds, who had succeeded Gilbert Murray as Regius Professor of Greek in 1936.[14] Dodds was ill received by some Oxford dons, a matter to which he has alluded with characteristic charity and reticence in his autobiography. Maurice Bowra had wanted the Chair, and others had hoped that Denniston would get it.[15] Denniston

---

[12]Eduard Fraenkel (1888–1970), who left Germany in 1934 after being stripped of his chair at Freiburg in 1933 under the Nazis' anti-semitic legislation, was Corpus Professor of Latin at Oxford 1935–53: for accounts of his career see G. Williams, *PBA* 56 (1970) 415–42, Lloyd-Jones, *BG*, 251–60, and N. Horsfall, *CSBE* 61–7. For his *Agamemnon* seminar (which Dover started to attend in October 1939, i.e. in his second year), see Stephanie West, 'Eduard Fraenkel recalled', in *OC* 203–18, C. Stray, 'Eduard Fraenkel: an exploration', *Syllecta Classica* 25 (2014) 113–72, at 141–4, P.J. Conradi, *Iris Murdoch: A Life* (London, 2001) 115–22.

[13]Bill (W.S.) Watt (1913–2002) was a tutorial fellow at Balliol 1938–52 (hence, briefly, a later colleague of Dover's: see p. 127 below) and Professor of Humanity (Latin) at Aberdeen University 1952–79 (see the obituary by Donald Russell in *The Independent*, 4 January 2003, p. 20); Spencer (W.S.) Barrett (1914–2001) was Classics tutor at Keble College 1939–81 (see the obituary by Adrian Hollis, *The Guardian*, 17 October 2001, p. 22); Arthur Frederick Wells (1912–66) was fellow of University College 1936–66.

[14]On Murray, see n. 4 above. E.R. Dodds (1893–1979) was Regius Professor of Greek at Oxford 1936–60; he became widely known for his influential book *The Greeks and the Irrational* (Berkeley, 1951): see C. Stray, C. Pelling, S. Harrison, eds, *Rediscovering E. R. Dodds* (Oxford, 2019). The reference to Dodds' autobiography in the next sentence is to *MP* 125–6; cf. the Introduction, 4–8.

[15]Sir Maurice Bowra (1898–1971, Kt 1951) was Warden of Wadham College, Oxford, 1938–70; opinions are divided on his calibre as a classical scholar: see Lloyd-Jones, *BG*, 271–86 (~ *PBA* 58 (1972) 393–408). On his reaction to Dodds' appointment, see Leslie Mitchell, *Maurice Bowra: A Life* (Oxford, 2010) 84–8. John Dewar Denniston (1887–1949) was a tutorial fellow of Hertford College, Oxford, from 1913: see the article on him by Dover himself in *DBC*, i 238–9.

FIGURE 4 Eduard Fraenkel, with young Italian classicists.

himself, who would indeed have made an admirable Regius Professor, was not a man to harbour malice, but that did not save Dodds from being treated with unfailing discourtesy by some of his colleagues, most notoriously by Denys Page.[16] The root of the trouble was not just academic jealousies, but the fact that as an Irishman who felt that he owed no allegiance to the British crown Dodds had not fought in the First World War, while Bowra and Denniston had been in the trenches.

That war had created an antipathy to Germans, and Fraenkel, who was a German refugee and had been a pupil of Wilamowitz,[17] was a target for the parochial jibes and facetiousness commonly directed against German scholars by their British inferiors. Even people of the stature of W.M. Lindsay, whom Fraenkel venerated for his scholarly work on Plautus and early Latin, was tainted by this prejudice; he

---

*When Fraenkel visited St Andrews in 1966 I took the book out of the Library and hid it at home. It was on the same occasion that he would not come to a reception at my house if I invited Douglas Young (who, fortunately, was in America). [EDS *Eduard Fraenkel* (n. 12 above) received an honorary D.Litt. from St Andrews in 1964; it is not impossible that 1966 is a mistake for that date. On Douglas Young, see note on p. 132.]

[16]Sir Denys Page (1908–78, Kt 1971), Regius Professor of Greek at Cambridge 1950–73, was an acute philologist not incapable of malice: see Lloyd-Jones, *BG*, 295–304 (~ *PBA* 65 (1979) 759–69).

[17]Ulrich von Wilamowitz-Moellendorff (1848–1931), a Greek scholar of prodigious powers, was the most influential classical philologist of the late nineteenth and early twentieth century: see the account of his career by Robert Fowler in *CSBE* 489–522.

received, in homage, a copy (now in the University Library at St Andrews)* of Fraenkel's early book on the metre of Plautus, and wrote on the flyleaf, 'Where in the world, except in Germany, would three hundred pages of this rubbish find a publisher?'[18] When I knew him, Fraenkel had repudiated what he acknowledged to be the extravagances of that book; and long before that, Lindsay had recognised his true quality.

Fraenkel never had the tact to overcome the mistrust with which the older generation regarded German authoritarianism. He tended to revere the opinions of his teachers, above all Wilamowitz and Leo, because they were who they were, but he also told me that the essential qualification for admission to Wilamowitz's seminar was not how learned you were but how much you cared about the subject and how hard you were prepared to work. Once (about 1958) I had dinner with Andrew Gow in Trinity College, Cambridge, and he expressed with great assurance the opinion that Wilamowitz was a Prussian autocrat who would never brook disagreement from a student.[19] It so happened that Kurt Latte, himself a pupil of Wilamowitz, was another guest on that occasion, and contradicted Gow vigorously, asserting that Wilamowitz always respected intelligent criticism, no matter who made it; and I heard the same from Paul Maas.[20] None the less, Fraenkel himself undeniably inherited and displayed an autocratic streak, and I suspected at times that his seminars were designed not really to discover what we thought but to cause us to arrive at conclusions at which he had arrived long before. All the same, in setting me the task, within a few months of my arrival in Oxford, of expounding the Kassandra scene to the seminar, he was saying in effect, 'Go away on your own,

---

[18]Wallace Martin Lindsay (1858–1937) was Professor of Humanity (Latin) at St Andrews 1899–1937: the inscription Dover recalls, at the top of p. 1 of Fraenkel's *Iktus und Akzent im lateinischen Sprechvers* (Berlin, 1928), actually reads: 'Really, one asks, is there a nation in the world where 400 pages of this stuff would be written, printed[?] & published, except Germany? (China? Well, perhaps China)'. Lindsay's view may have been coloured by the fact that Fraenkel made no mention of his own *Early Latin Verse* (Oxford, 1922). By 1934, however, Lindsay was prepared to call Fraenkel 'the greatest Latin scholar ... in the whole world' (quoted by G. Williams, *PBA* 56 (1970) 422). On Lindsay, see H.J. Rose's British Academy memoir, *PBA* 23 (1937) 487–512, and the articles by C.J. Fordyce, rev. R.T. Stearn, in *ODNB* and by M. Deufert in *DBC*, ii 583–5.

[19]Andrew Sydenham Farrar Gow (1886–1978), fellow of Trinity 1925–51: see F.H. Sandbach, *PBA* 64 (1978) 427–41. The occasion was the Triennial (classical) Conference, which had alternated between Oxford and Cambridge since its first meeting in Oxford in 1942. Dover told his parents on 16 August 1958 that he and Hugh Lloyd-Jones had gone to Cambridge on the 7th: 'Latte, the German for whom I took the chair, was almost inaudible, & spoke for only 45 minutes, so that in making my closing remarks I had to guess at what he had said; as he quoted abundantly from Archilochus, it was hard to tell what was Archilochus & what was Latte – on hearing "I know how to requite my enemies with terrible evils" I thought for a moment he was talking about his Göttingen colleagues.' Kurt Latte (1891–1964), a specialist in Roman religion, succeeded Eduard Fraenkel in the chair of classical philology at Göttingen in 1931.

[20]On Paul Maas, see p. 116 with note.

compose *a good commentary* on this portion of the play, and come back and tell us all about it.' In saying that he was starting me on my professional career.

Everything went well for me at Oxford. I won the Gaisford Prize for Greek verse in my first year, translating a scene from Racine's *Phèdre*, and came *proxime* in the Hertford and De Paravicini prize scholarship examination.[21] This was followed in March 1940 by a good First in Mods[22] (though I lapsed to an alpha-beta in one paper, where a startling memory-blank caused me to answer a question about Aristotle's definition of tragedy without ever mentioning pity and fear). My call-up was due in July 1940, so that I had one term of Greats work (Philosophy and Ancient History) before going into the army. This gave me a wholly misleading impression of Greats and the amount of work it would entail, because the tutors to whom I was farmed out (the Balliol Greats tutors being already in warwork) were not exacting. I recall writing a couple of essays on Hegel in enviable ignorance of his reputation as a very obscure author.[23] I suppose I was simply playing a terminological game without knowing what it was all about.

In the early nineteen-eighties, when I was handling admissions to Corpus, some applicants were put off by the impression of Oxford which they received from the television version of Evelyn Waugh's *Brideshead Revisited*.[24] Admissions Tutors called this the 'Brideshead Syndrome'. I was able to tell such applicants that even in the late nineteen-thirties I had not encountered any wealthy, idle drunkards in Oxford. They must have existed, even at Balliol, but their existence did not impinge on my world. Oxford was full of people I had known at St Paul's, and I tended to stick to them, prolonging my ingrained wariness towards new friends; all my friendships, therefore, were with people who were frugal and hard-working, and I had little or nothing to do with what the public imagined to be the 'social life' of Oxford. My excursions outside my work were not into dining-clubs and parties (difficult on the one pound a week which I had available after paying fees, board and lodging) but into the arts and politics.

---

[21] The Racine translation (covering the first 113 lines of the play) technically became Dover's first publication; it was printed as a pamphlet by Blackwell in 1939 and received two positive reviews in classical journals. The Hertford and De Paravicini scholarship exam involved a set of six papers in Latin language and literature.

[22] Mods (i.e., Classical Honour Moderations) is the first part of the Oxford Classics degree, with exams taken after five terms and followed by seven terms of 'Greats' or Literae Humaniores, the whole degree lasting four years. For Dover's later concerns over the structure of the degree, see pp. 128 and 137.

[23] 'For my first term of Greats philosophy I was sent to a man called Beck...I can't think what he thought he was doing, giving me essays on Hegel to write. He taught me some elementary psychology – classification of personality-types – from which I derived no lasting benefit.' (Dover SN) For Maximilian Beck, see Stray's chapter on Dover at school and university in *S&C*. Dover had been excited by his first taste of philosophy: on 4 May 1940 he wrote home, 'I have really fallen in love with philosophy; after only two essays I find it has induced a staggering increase in clarity of thinking.' But see pp. 95–9 for his subsequent disillusionment with the subject.

[24] First broadcast on ITV between October and December 1981.

Up to that time my interests and enthusiasms had been, in the broad sense of the word, scientific, and the stimulus of Classics, in which I rejoiced, was more intellectual than aesthetic. In spite of the importance of music in my home, music had meant little to me until, one evening in September 1936, I overheard an enthralling sequence of sounds which turned out to be the second[25] movement of Sibelius's Fourth Symphony, and music has been important to me ever since. I don't think that until after I was eighteen I read any English poetry except in the school-room for examination purposes. The fiction which I had read and re-read with enjoyment amounted to no more than A.A. Milne's two books of stories about Winnie the Pooh, Kipling's *Jungle Book*, the collected short stories of H.G. Wells and Wells's novels *The War of the Worlds* and *The First Men in the Moon*. I had managed, with some tenacity and with relief when the job was done, to get through *Westward Ho*, *Hereward the Wake* and (skipping some bits) *Pickwick Papers*, but could not get as far as halfway through *David Copperfield*, *Kenilworth* and *Quentin Durward*. Comparative linguistics was so much more enthralling. Since, however, my mother was an enthusiastic theatre-goer, I had seen quite a number of plays, and at Oxford I got into the habit of going to the Playhouse every week (at a cost of one-and-threepence); I also managed to see almost every film that was worth seeing, together with some which were not. In my second year, having broken out of my comparatively small circle of Pauline friends – with the help of one of them, my future brother-in-law, Hugh Latimer – I was one of a small team producing an amateur fortnightly magazine of stories, poems and reviews. On occasion, when copy was scarce, I wrote much of it myself under a variety of pseudonyms. The editor-in-chief was a wholly imaginary person called 'Tancred Paul', and I was amused, years later, to meet someone who claimed to have known him.

I also wrote the film critiques for the *Labour Club Bulletin*, slanting them sometimes awkwardly and insincerely to suit the medium. The Labour Club had split by then, and the preponderant left wing kept the name. I was a fellow-traveller, *spiacente a Dio ed ai nemici suoi*,[26] because I said all the right things but could not believe all that I said, and the obvious limitations on my commitment irritated those of my friends who were members of the Communist party. The nights of my first few weeks at Oxford, in the immediate aftermath of Munich, had been consumed in political conversation, and I doubt if there was ever a time during those first two years at Oxford when I spent less than ten hours a week talking about politics, almost entirely with like-minded people. Munich was the topic that kept us going for some months; after that, the predicted German take-over of

---

[25]Dover originally wrote 'third' but changed this in the margin of his own copy and in SN. Sibelius remained one of his favourite composers throughout his life; see the allusion to *Finlandia* on p. 129, and cf. n. † to p. 268.
[26]'Hateful to God as well as to his enemies': an approximate version of Dante, *Inferno*, Canto III 63, where the Italian reads 'a Dio spiacenti e a' nemici sui', a condemnation of cowards.

Czechoslovakia and the lackadaisical approaches of Britain and France to the Soviet Union over the possibility of an alliance against further German aggression. It seemed pretty obvious that our government did not want a Soviet alliance, and post-War memoirs have confirmed that. For all our exasperation, we did not waver in our confident belief that the Soviet Union was always and in all circumstances the enemy of Nazi Germany. We were therefore thunderstruck by the Nazi-Soviet nonaggression pact of August 1939; I called it at the time 'the worst news of my lifetime', and I cannot unsay that now. The ingenuity with which my Communist friends defended it, justified the subsequent seizure of eastern Poland by the Soviet Union, and made excuses for the disastrous showing of the Red Army in its invasion of Finland, was remarkable. Some of what they said was true, and I believed some additional propositions which were not; but the Soviet-inspired (and grotesquely short-sighted) slogan 'Stop the imperialist war!' went beyond anything that I could accept, because even if the motives of our own government had been, in some way or other, 'imperialistic', there were other good reasons, including mine, for fighting the war, and no course of action can be condemned simply because some of those performing it are improperly motivated.

As soon as I went back to Oxford after the outbreak of war I joined the OTC[27] with a view to obtaining Certificate B and increasing my chances of acceptance for training as an officer when I was called up. I had no idea whether or not I would be any good as an officer, but as a matter of self-respect I did not want to settle for less responsibility without even an attempt to see if I could take more. I considered that I did not have the dash and vigour desirable in infantry or tanks, but I knew that I could be reasonably stoical, so I chose the artillery. I hope that other former members of the Royal Regiment will forgive me the implications of that disclosure – and of the further disclosure that since as a child I had never been allowed to make a loud noise the prospect of being not merely allowed but actually required to make very loud noises was entrancing. Conscience made it impossible for me even to consider trying for any kind of safe job; after all, I believed in the war, I had wanted it as the only alternative to the lasting establishment of Nazi power throughout Europe, and the shame of evading the personal consequences would have been unbearable.

Why, then, was it bearable to be in the company of people who fervently believed in the need to 'stop the imperialist war'? Partly, I think, because I find it hard, when there are alternative strategies for the achievement of the same ultimate purpose, to take a firm stand; partly also from a temperamental reluctance (largely outgrown by now) to cut myself off from friends who turn out to be stupid or dishonest. I shared lodgings in 1940 with Michael Samuels (eventually Professor of English Language at Glasgow) and another friend. Mike had no strong political

---

[27]Officers' Training Corps.

views, but the other man was a committed and extremely articulate Communist with a great grasp of detail. Largely agreeing with his standpoint (I have not personally known a Communist who was not motivated by compassion and indignation), I could not face a show-down on its practical implications. I only once dug in my heels, when he incorporated in an article a statement that Chamberlain had promised never to introduce conscription in peacetime; I pointed out that this was untrue, and he said, 'Never mind, any stick's good enough to beat Chamberlain with.' This turned me against the Cause – though Conservatives also lie, the stock of lies in circulation should never be increased knowingly – and later in the term I had reason to doubt, or more than doubt, its proponents' grasp on reality. When the news of the German breakthrough to Amiens and Abbeville came out, there were three Party members in our room. They laughed exultantly and ran down the stairs singing the Marseillaise. That was not because they liked Hitler, but because they truly believed, having learned something about the Paris Commune of 1871, that defeat in the West would necessarily bring about a patriotic anti-fascist workers' revolt in France, whereupon the Soviet Union would attack Germany (and, of course, win). Even after Abbeville, they did not grasp that war moved faster in 1940 than in 1871, and their trust in Stalin's high principles was absolute.[28]

My mother's reaction to the fall of France was, 'Well . . ., thank goodness, now we don't have to rely on anyone else.'

---

[28]'Dodds in his autobiography (*Missing Persons*, p. 137) relates that the Oxford psychologist William Brown believed that if he could only get an introduction to Hitler . . . he could initiate a psychoanalytic relationship with the Führer and so avert war. Preposterous though this story may seem, it is quite true. Karl Stein, a school-friend of mine, introduced me to Brown, and in a (very) small seminar Brown really did enlarge on his hope of psychoanalysing Hitler. In the summer of 1939 Karl told me the project was hopeless, because he (Karl) became convinced that the 'Hitler' who was seen in public and heard on the radio was actually a look-alike puppet of the General Staff (which presumably had disposed of Mr Schickelgrüber's son).' (Dover SN)

8 INTERMISSION 1940–1945

Heavy artillery is a marvellous sound; there is nothing quite like it.
WITTGENSTEIN[1]

In July 1940 I was called up and posted to a Royal Artillery Field Training Regiment on the south coast. By October the threat of cross-Channel invasion had receded, while German air attacks on British cities by night had increased. There was therefore a great enlargement of the anti-aircraft component of the artillery at the expense of field regiments, and those of us who had been identified as potential officers (I was one of them, thanks to my Certificate B at Oxford) were invited to apply for commissions in anti-aircraft. I was accepted on interview and went to the anti-aircraft officer cadet training unit ('OCTU') at Llandrindod Wells. Having survived a severe Welsh winter and a training course less exacting than its counterpart in Shrivenham, I was commissioned in March 1941.[2] After a few days leave at home, which by chance covered my twenty-first birthday, I was sent out to the Middle East, at the end of nearly six weeks at sea arrived at the R.A. Base Depot at Almaza (near Cairo) and was eventually posted to a Light A.A. regiment protecting some sites in Egypt against potential air attacks which were never realised. In March 1942 we became part of the Eighth Army, and I spent the next year and a half in the Desert. On the retreat from Gazala to Alamein I and the troop I commanded[3] had the good fortune to be attached to raiding columns, so that we escaped, by the narrowest of margins, being sent into Tobruk, and soon after that another stroke of luck attached us to a formation retreating far inland,

---

[1] The remark was recalled by Wittgenstein's friend Martin Drury: M. O'C. Drury, 'Conversations with Wittgenstein', in R. Rhees, ed., *Recollections of Wittgenstein*, 2nd edn (Oxford, 1984) 149. Wittgenstein had served (and won bravery medals) as an Austrian artillery spotter or observer, directing fire against enemy targets, for part of the First World War.
[2] Shrivenham in Oxfordshire was the site of what is now known as the Defence Academy.
[3] 'From March 1942 to July 1943 I commanded a four-gun troop, then from August 1943 to the end of the war I was second-in-command of a six-gun troop.' (Dover SN)

while the rest of my battery was cut off in Mersa Matruh and suffered heavy losses (mostly taken prisoner) in the break-out. After Alamein, Benghazi and Tripoli, when the scene of action shifted to Tunisia and then to Sicily, we spent a dreary time in eastern Libya, 'protecting' the dummy tanks and landing-craft of the imaginary 'Twelfth Army', invented to make the Germans think that an invasion of Greece was intended. That period of slothful reflection, which ought to have been spent in hard training, ended when we were assigned to the Fifth Army's invasion of Italy at Salerno.[4] For the rest of the War I was in Italy. I recall standing on the bank of the Adige near Rovigo at the end of April 1945 when for the first time in two years the night fell properly black and silent, and there were no more thumps and flashes.

Although I was one of only four selected for OCTU out of thirteen applicants interviewed in my batch, passed out of OCTU with a grade B ('above average') and ended the War with a Mention in Despatches, I do not consider that I was a good officer, nor did I imagine so at the time. At OCTU I profited from my skills in written examinations and oral exposition; I learned the language (e.g. 'clean' = 'highly polished'), and evidently I put on an adequate act in respect of other soldierly virtues. In 1942 I gathered from a drunken sergeant at a party that I had a good reputation for coolness in unpleasant and difficult situations. This basic talent, an extension of the stoicism I had begun to cultivate at fifteen,[5] was rarely put to a severe test. The most severe, to my mind, was the spell of nightly air-attacks on Benghazi harbour at the end of 1942, when my command-post was among the stacks of bombs and petrol which the ships were unloading. During that time I had also to combat jaundice – it would have been very tactless to report sick – and I often felt so ill that being bombed was almost a welcome distraction. As an individual I was never, so far as I know, in an enemy's sights, and I doubt if there were more than fifty occasions during my five years in the army on which I was an ingredient of a larger target for bombing, shelling or machine-gunning. On seven of those occasions I considered that I had a very lucky escape; but, come to think of it, most active participants in a war must be able to say the same, or casualties would be so high that wars would soon stop for lack of manpower, and there have been more than seven occasions in peacetime on which I have had equally lucky escapes from serious road-accidents. I never saw a live enemy except as a prisoner of war or, in brief glimpses, the pilots of low-flying aircraft. From April 1944 onwards I did not even see an enemy aircraft, because the resources of the German air force were so strained in Russia and the West that the German armies in Italy virtually had to manage without. Many of our Heavy A.A. batteries were brought forward and used as artillery against targets on the ground. This

---

[4]September 1943; the US Fifth Army led the invasion.
[5]See p. 58 above.

needed more mathematics and therefore more officers in the command-posts. I was glad to be seconded to Heavy batteries for long periods in the first half of 1944,[6] because the routine of Light A.A. was stultifying; when enemy aircraft are active, a gun-crew can justify its existence by firing the first shot within ten seconds of the air-sentry's cry of 'Plane!', but as one quiet month succeeds another the destructive thought, 'What are we *for*?' gains in strength. In the last stages of the Italian campaign, however, Light A.A. batteries, including my own, were moved up close to the infantry to lay down harassing fire by night on German supply-routes, and occasionally to take on selected targets by day, a role for which their flat-trajectory, high-velocity shells were very suitable. This required a completely new fire-control system, and I devised one which worked.

That was the kind of thing I could do well; in other respects I constantly found that I knew what should be done but lacked the self-confidence, physical energy and management skill actually to get it done. Things might have been different if I had been posted in 1941 to a newly-formed battery, but I came into one made up of the survivors of three batteries; all three had been at Dunkirk, two of them also in Greece and Crete, a combination of demoralising defeats and evacuations leavened only (for a minority) by an exhilarating victory over the Italians in Libya in December 1940. Many men were already war-weary at a time when the War plainly had a long time still to run, and they were all inclined to believe themselves so experienced that no one could teach them anything. The depth of their experience certainly could not be questioned – at one time I had under my command four sergeants who had won the Military Medal in Greece or Crete – and I was intimidated by that. Although we had never been told at OCTU that an officer should be able to do every job better than the men whom he commanded, it was a principle in which I believed (taking the relationship between teacher and pupil as an obvious analogy), and I was abashed to find that 'keenness' in a new officer was regarded rather as 'swots' are regarded in a third-rate school. The training given me by my first troop commander amounted to a single glum sentence, 'There isn't much to do, really.' My knowledge of the maintenance and repair of vehicles was rudimentary, and I had hoped to increase it by spending part of every day in the repair-shop, but this was as unwelcome to the mechanics as it was incomprehensible to my colleagues, and I gave up. When we went to the Desert in 1942 we were provided with a new type of gun-tractor which overheated and constantly needed to have its radiator topped up. This was not a good prospect for mobile warfare in a hot desert but I found it impossible to make any of my seniors

---

[6]It was during this period, by a remarkable coincidence identified only many years later, that Dover and his future St Andrews colleague Ian Kidd (see p. 132 with note) were in close proximity, after Kidd had been taken prisoner by the Germans at the river Garigliano, not far from Cassino, in January 1944.

take the problem seriously and turn their minds to devising remedies. In the end it was I and my troop, detached on column work, who suffered the worst consequences of the drain on our always inadequate and often irregular supply of water. Some of my most experienced NCOs, including two of my decorated sergeants, were morally crushed by the time we got back to Alamein. It was just one retreat too many, and greatly aggravated by thirst and constipation. Access to regular water (though it sometimes tasted of diesel) and the daily extrusion of a massive turd raised morale several degrees, but the initiative and resilience which had served them so well in the past had gone for good. I realised then that experience in itself means very little; what matters is energetic reflection on experience and readiness to imagine circumstances which may require reappraisal of what we think we have learned. A doorstep has seen life, but its opinions are not interesting.

I have not said all this as an excuse for the fact that I was still a lieutenant* at the end of the War, when a third pip on my shoulder would have been nicer for my self-esteem. A.A. casualties in the Mediterranean were so low after the autumn of 1943 that there were virtually no promotions, and I was demobilised in the company of many lieutenants senior to me in date of commission. When the structure of Light A.A. batteries was changed in 1943 and commanders of six-gun troops became captains, I was passed over, probably because I was expecting a summons to Cairo for a job ostensibly connected with Greece. As it turned out, there was no such job, and I assume it was all part of the 'Twelfth Army' deception plan. My Battery Commander professed to be certain that I would get the job, and assured me that this was his only reason for passing me over. I never learned whether he was telling the truth (and he's dead now). If he was not, I give him low marks for candour but quite high for intuitive judgement.

There is little doubt that I would have been of more use to my country as a backroom boy,[7] but it would not have been of so much use to me. Generally speaking, any tourist who has seen the Grand Canyon and Pyramids is glad to have seen them. It is even more satisfying to look back on personal participation in historical events which really mattered: the Blitz, Alamein, the Salerno landings, the final battle at Cassino.

No one now could pretend that the situation at any time between May 1940 and December 1941 offered us a prospect of victory, and even after America's entry into the war it was not until the Russian counter-offensive at Stalingrad that a

---

*'Major' according to the Master's Letter in the Balliol College Annual Record for 1955, but I don't know where he got that from; certainly not from me.

[7] Dover has in mind the wartime work in military intelligence, especially at Bletchley Park, which so many academics, not least classicists, undertook: for a useful list (including several people mentioned in *MC*), with links to Bletchley Park records, see https://www.thebritishacademy.ac.uk/publishing/memoirs/humanities-scholars-who-worked-military-intelligence-second-world-war/

rational person could feel confidence in the practicability of a cross-Channel invasion of France. Irrational hope sustains resistance at least as well as rational calculation, often better.[8] In our case, having emerged from the First World War on the winning side, we had a deep-seated belief in our own superiority, and people with an inadequate knowledge of history tended also to believe that God ensures, after a ration of tribulations, the triumph of righteousness. This self-confidence distorted our sense of proportion, generating ready acceptance of agreeable rumours, and it encouraged us to draw grand conclusions from trivial successes.

The tradition of victory sporadically infected the highest levels in the direction of the war. For example, the belief that the Germans could be deprived of their will to win by massive air-raids on their city-centres violated a fundamental axiom of war, the axiom that your enemy is at least as brave, intelligent, resourceful and energetic as you are, and may well be more so. The landing at Anzio in January 1944 was expected to 'cut the enemy lines of communication and threaten the rear of the German 14th Corps',† although everyone knew by then that if you threaten Germans they react with remarkable speed and ferocity. I do not mean that the Anzio operation was wrong, only that the hopes invested in it were unrealistic, and I cite it because it exemplifies a conflict within myself which I took a long time to resolve. As I was steeped in historical reading and also addicted to fantasy, I found it possible much of the time to treat the war as a spectacular drama, intricate and absorbing, from which I could and would return to ordinary life when the lights went up and I was allowed to leave the theatre. Every now and then this persistent state of illusion was brutally dispelled by events which growled, 'This is *real*, this is happening *now*, and it's happening to *you*.' The first such occasion – I recall it as possibly the blackest moment of my life – was when I heard in Alexandria the whispered rumour (it was true) that *Prince of Wales* and *Repulse* had been sunk off Malaya by Japanese aircraft.[9] A second occasion was the sight of the immense curtain of black smoke, filling half the northern horizon, which rose from the great supply-dumps at Misheifa, abandoned and burned as we were chased back from Libya into Egypt. In Italy we were long past fearing defeat, but when I heard about Anzio I was split, and consciously aware of being split, between common sense and naive trust in happy endings. There was one later time at which I succumbed to the theatrical illusion; that was when I had a grandstand view of the final battle for Cassino from an artillery observation-post on Monte Trocchio. For the rest of the war the question '*How long* is it going to last?' extinguished all residual illusion and fantasy.

---

†Alexander's Operation Instruction of 2 January 1944, quoted in the British official history (*Mediterranean and Middle East*, vol. v, p. 645).

[8]For the quasi-Thucydidean ethos of this sentence, cf. p. 64 n. 16.
[9]On 10 December 1941 the Royal Navy battleship HMS *Prince of Wales* and battlecruiser HMS *Repulse* were sunk by land-based bombers and torpedo bombers of the Imperial Japanese Navy.

People have taken a long time to face the unwelcome fact that, by and large, the Germans were better soldiers than the British and Americans. Simple assertion of this fact provokes indignant response: 'What about Arnhem? Bastogne? Kidney Ridge?' and so on, because it is always hard to accept that no statement about 'most' can be invalidated by a statement about 'some'. Press handling of events in wartime does not help; whereas a stubborn defence of a position by one's own troops is 'resolute' and 'tenacious', a similar defence by the enemy is 'fanatical' – a rhetorical trick which imputes mental instability to the defenders and excuses the failure of the nice, normal attackers. I can hardly have been the only British soldier in Italy who, as the campaign went into its second year, felt an ever-increasing admiration for the skill, resilience and courage of the Germans, an admiration which has never had any bearing on my attitude to the cause for which they fought.

Not long after the end of the war in Italy my battery was divided into small cadres and given control of German transport companies which had fled westwards from the Russians in search of kindlier captivity. They were organised by us for getting food supplies to the population of southern Austria; my own cadre was based originally at Osoppo, but later moved to Villach.[10] Since I spoke the language, I had more direct access than my colleagues to the sentiments of these German soldiers. They had been thrown back hundreds of miles and they had lost the war utterly, yet their energy, morale and discipline were strikingly superior to ours. Some of their officers looked forward to an Anglo-American-German alliance which after a few months' rest would resume the war and invade the Soviet Union afresh. The men they commanded were less enthusiastic about the prospect of another interminable war, but at least they were indomitably cheerful and resourceful, even under the constant need to improvise running repairs, often in pouring rain, to their decrepit collection of Russian, Czech, Hungarian and Rumanian vehicles.

Infantry and tank-men, accustomed to be at the sharp end of attack and defence, usually had opinions about their generals. Light A.A. soldiers, normally cast in a defensive role and often a long way behind the front line, knew little about generals except through scraps of mainly improbable gossip, and I cannot recall anyone above the rank of brigadier whose name meant anything to me – except, of course, Montgomery. There has been plenty of controversy about the respective contributions of Auchinleck (who took over personal command of Eighth Army and stopped the Germans on the Alamein Line in July 1942) and Montgomery (who became Eighth Army commander in August) to the turn of our fortunes in Africa. Auchinleck undeniably did stop Rommel, and the sight of a lot of exhausted Germans taken prisoner on July 3rd-4th raised our spirits; but there was widespread

---

[10]Cf. p. 90.

talk among my superiors about the likelihood of our having to give up Egypt, and no real confidence that when Rommel next launched a properly prepared offensive he could be stopped. Montgomery's achievement in revivifying Eighth Army should never be underestimated. It was not simply that he impressed his reassuring personality even on people (me for example) who never set eyes on him; he actually won a crucial battle within three weeks of taking over. On the last night of August Rommel opened a conventional Rommelish attack towards Alam Halfa, suffered a serious defeat, and after a week of heavy losses withdrew to dig in. We all felt sure that this must be, as indeed it was, the turning-point of the war in Africa. I retained unlimited confidence in Montgomery for more than a year after Alam Halfa. I shed some of it on reading his absurdly optimistic Order of the Day before the battle of the Sangro in November 1943. All the same, I have never lost my admiration for his professionalism, his devotion to planning and training, his understanding of the need for a touch of showmanship (a sure understanding at one time, but later increasingly ill-judged as it became tainted by megalomania), and above all his insistence on precise definition of the end before consideration is given to the means. All these things are as important in the teaching of Greek as they are in the conduct of war.

In the training regiment in which I spent my first four months of service I soon learned what hard monotonous manual work is like, and I learned to value sleep, tea and cigarettes. A few of the sergeants and bombardiers were fierce, most were strict, and some had a very limited range of responses; but none was unjust, and neither I nor anyone I knew was bullied. Among the officers, there was one who attracted devotion because people know pure gold when they see it, one was obviously useless, one was nasty but very competent and a man to be trusted in an emergency, and the rest were as unobjectionable as they were unimpressive. In the course of time I came to feel considerable respect for the professionals. Intellectuals are apt to make fun of what they call the 'military mentality', and it is true that professional soldiers can sometimes make naive assessments of civilian issues; not as naive, though, as civilian assessments of issues which soldiers have to resolve while an enemy is doing his utmost to ensure their failure.

After the first month those of us who were classified as likely candidates for commissions were all put together in the same troop. This was a mistake, because we were mostly students and ex-students and immediately formed an academic clique just at the time when we should have been forced to cut loose from our previous lives as cleanly as possible. Much the same was true at OCTU, on the troopship (I was one of a batch of new officers with no responsibilities during the voyage), and at the base depot at Almaza. I could hardly have had a worse preparation for arrival, twelve months after being called up, in a unit where only a couple of men had ever attended a university. In my battery the Major and Battery Captain and two of the Troop Commanders were Territorials who had known each other in peacetime; the Commanding Officer of the regiment came from that milieu too. Their courage was exemplary, and fraud and corruption were entirely alien to them; but although courage is indispensable, and integrity desirable, for the conduct of war, victory demands other virtues and skills in addition. These men's judgement of people and situations was shrewd in the context of the sports-club and the small traditional business, but once off that ground they were lost. Their education had taught them to read and write, to perform simple arithmetical calculations, to communicate with French-speakers at an elementary level, and to play cricket and football. To this they added competence in golf, tennis and billiards. They admired (but did not seek to acquire) skill in representational drawing and painting, they liked (but could not play) music as an accompaniment to dancing, and they read thrillers, the occasional best-seller (if not too long), and what were then regarded as salacious novels. Otherwise the arts meant absolutely nothing to them. Their ignorance of the world and of human history was almost total; my Battery Captain, for example, did not know there was a Polish language, for he thought that Poland was 'all horrible Jews and people'. I was unprepared for the company of men who could not conceive what it would be like to find a historical or scientific subject interesting and study it for its own sake.

I was mistrusted as an intellectual, and perhaps mistrusted even more deeply because of my deformed chest, which was assumed to be the consequence of crouching over books and eschewing manly sports. My Commanding Officer and Battery Commander made one or two efforts to get rid of me, but did not succeed. They had more success with two other new officers who were perfectly competent but for various bad reasons were regarded as not 'one of us'; one of those two later attracted attention as an outstandingly courageous Troop Commander in another battery. My uncomfortable relations with my superiors did not change until in January 1942 I acquired sudden merit by a meticulous report on an exercise which required me to discover the suitability of the ground, a hundred miles into the desert from Cairo, for vehicles of different weights and types. By the time we arrived in Libya in the spring of 1942 I was a full member of the club and had no further experience of marginalisation. It is understandable that a unit often subjected to extreme stress and the demand for self-sacrifice should generate a group loyalty which discriminates intuitively between 'one of us' and 'outsiders', and I daresay the social and local solidarity of the typical Territorial unit proved valuable in Greece and Crete. It was less appropriate to the Territorial ingredient in a reconstituted unit, yet it never wholly withered. One of its worst consequences was manifested at the end of 1944, when Light A.A. batteries were cut down from three troops each to two, so that thirty per cent of their men could be retrained as infantry. It seems obvious now, in retrospect, that it was our duty to release those men who, in our judgement, would make the best infantry soldiers. In fact, we treated it as an opportunity to get rid of the junior officers who were least liked and the laziest, stupidest and most recalcitrant of the NCOs and gunners. I don't think I offered any objection to that. This conflict between the conception of a unit as a clan, gang or club and the alternative conception of it as an instrument for the achievement of an end far transcending its own satisfaction made a deep impression on me – once I reflected in tranquillity on what we had done – and affected my attitude to colleges when I came to preside over an Oxford college thirty-two years later.[11]

I was naturally prepared to find that middle-class political opinion outside the universities was predominantly Conservative, but I underestimated the residual strength of pro-German and anti-Bolshevik sentiment. When Molotov's indignant condemnation of Germany's invasion of the Soviet Union was reported on the radio there was a shout of laughter in the officers' mess at Almaza, and an officer sitting next to me asked me, in genuine perplexity, 'What do we do now? Join up with Germany against Russia?' We suffered a bit from pilfering from our tents by Egyptians, and one of my colleagues spoke enviously of German ruthlessness: 'They wouldn't stand for this nonsense. They'd just shoot a hundred Wogs, and the pilfering would stop.' Such a measure might well have found widespread support; some officers felt a surge of anger at the mere sight of a 'filthy Wog' passing by. More sinister, to my mind, was the reaction of one officer to the pictures of the dead and dying at Belsen at the end of the war: 'Well, you have to remember that a lot of these people were pretty ropy physical specimens to start with.' These anecdotal scraps should not be taken to mean that a significant number of officers – that is to say, of bank clerks, shop assistants, insurance salesmen, and so on – had their hearts on the wrong side; I cite them because they help to remind us of the very wide range of attitudes and opinions to be found in a nation at war. There were five officers at Almaza who to my certain knowledge (thanks to indiscretion, after long acquaintance, on the part of two of them, combined with the sharp ear for conversational clues which I had developed at Oxford) were members of the Communist Party; the number of potential Nazi collaborators was probably no greater. Most officers would have agreed with one whom I knew very well: 'I'm fighting this war because I don't want a lot of bloody Huns telling me what to do.'

The middle class was deeply attached to preservation of 'the traditional fabric of British life' (they usually said 'English'), and, like my father's generation, they took it for granted that British is always best. The 'fabric' included the social and economic structure of the country, not exactly as it was in 1938, but as it had been just the other side of the hill when one looked back, before it began to be eroded by 'agitators' and 'socialist schoolteachers'. There were Conservatives among working-class soldiers: some who accepted existing structures as dictated by the law of nature, and others, competitive by temperament, even predatory, who thought they would do better for themselves in civilian life after the War if other

---

[11]This anticipates Dover's account in ch. 26 of how in dealing with Trevor Aston at Corpus in 1985 he saw the college's interests as outweighing those of a problematic individual.

people were not protected by officious legislation. The majority, however, were traditional Labour voters, and a few (one of them a very bad advertisement for the Party) were Communists.

Whereas a Light A.A. troop after the summer of 1943 usually had three officers, the maximum before that was two, and for several months I was the only officer in the troop which (from March 1942) I commanded. As troops were commonly deployed at some distance from each other, for the greater part of the war in the Desert and Italy I never had a meal in an officers' mess. In those circumstances an officer and his men come to know each other's values, attitudes and weaknesses very well. I certainly knew my driver-mechanic, Jimmy Brown, better than I had known anyone up to that time (and I owed my liberty, possibly my life, to his ingenuity in fashioning a temporary carburettor gasket from my shirt-collar).‡ Through him the ethos of working-class Burnley became more familiar to me than that of Oxford undergraduates from the home counties. I learned from direct acquaintance what I had previously assumed in theory: that among people who had left school at fourteen and gone straight into manual jobs there were very many who had been living far below their potential, while among those who had stayed on at public school until seventeen or eighteen there were too many accustomed to be given privileges and responsibilities at a higher level than they deserved. Within the working-class, individuals were spread along a very wide scale between the extremes of security and deprivation, and there was no clear correlation between their intelligence and the point on the scale at which they had been brought up. One or two were halfwits and one or two had been through an unimaginably horrible childhood, but they were not the same ones. One or two were criminals, cruel and selfish people, and violent when they felt safe enough, but they had not had as bad a time as some others whose humanity and integrity were irreproachable. It looked as if the variables in the interaction between heredity and environment were rather numerous.

What I learned from my fellow-humans during those years was always in my mind thirty years later when I came to write *Greek Popular Morality*. The ancient world spent a very high proportion of its time and energy on war, and it was useful to me, as a student of ancient history, to discover by participation something of what war is like. In studying *Lysistrata* I have recalled the effect of encouraging rumours and exaggerated news of localised successes in 1940. Reading Thucydides' account of the Athenian retreat from Syracuse, I was vividly reminded of an irrational feeling which affected some men on the retreat from Libya, the feeling

---

‡ I ought to have sought him out after the War, but I felt in 1945/6 – rightly or wrongly (if I may be permitted an occasional foolish cliché) – that I wanted a complete break with the past. [EDS *In his 1995 addenda Dover wrote of JB, 'In some ways, I suppose, he was my Platon Karataev, but much more ruthless', a reference to the warm-hearted peasant character who restores Pierre Bezukhov's faith in life in Tolstoy's* War and Peace, *Book IV, part 1, chs. 12–13.*]

that if only we could get to Fuka or Daba a supernatural referee would blow the whistle and we would be given time to prepare for a return match.[12]

Nothing, however, was of such importance for my professional life as the discovery that I could teach and that I loved teaching. The Army set quite a good example, because it was obvious to me from my first day as a gunner that a remarkable amount of careful thought had gone into methods of instruction and training. Our Physical Training instructors, for example, were in a completely different class from the obtuse creature under whose unfriendly eye I had failed to acquire any gymnastic skills at school,[13] and I have met a disappointingly large number of university lecturers whose clarity of exposition fell far short of the standard expected in gunnery schools. I had many opportunities to explain the essentials of ballistics, explosives and anti-aircraft predictors to NCOs who had left school at fourteen with no more than a basic knowledge of arithmetic.[14] In the last weeks of the War I had to teach them how to use trigonometrical log-tables, and having successfully met the challenge of finding some way to make the nature of logarithms and trigonometrical ratios intelligible to them I have never despaired of explaining anything to anyone who is prepared to listen. Nor have I ever been able to resist tinkering with whatever methods of exposition I inherit and trying to improve on them, sometimes by a radical shift of starting-point.

The War probably accentuated my natural streak of coarseness, so that I still feel, when I am constrained by the delicacy of the company to call shit 'faeces' or fucking 'sexual intercourse', as if I were wearing a funny hat at an uncongenial party.[15] After moving so often with no more personal possessions than I could carry, and sleeping under the protection of earth and canvas (or none at all), sustained by a diet of extreme monotony and wretched quality, I know the difference between necessities and luxuries, and for many years after the War (unlike some of my friends in the army, who vowed they would never again dispense with clean sheets) I got

---

[12]The Athenian retreat from Syracuse in 413 BC is recounted in harrowing detail at Thucydides 7.75–84; the irrational element of hope is especially prominent in Nicias' words at 7.77.1–6: cf. Dover's comment in *Historical Commentary on Thucydides*, vol. iv, p. 454, 'logic is a bleak consolation to a demoralized army'. Note the related passage in *The Greeks*, 2nd edn (Oxford, 1982) 45: 'I have gained a great deal in understanding Thucydides from having been a participant in a demoralised retreat 2354 years after the Athenian retreat from Syracuse.'

[13]Conceivably the same person as the 'boxing instructor' at St Paul's whose crushing comment on Dover's funnel chest was mentioned on p. 48.

[14]In a talk at an 80th birthday celebration in St Andrews in 2000, Dover said, *à propos* this teaching: 'This was *not*, as one rather obtuse reviewer of my autobiography seemed to think, a matter of *drilling* people; it was all a matter of explaining theory.'

[15]Although Dover here accepts that the register of 'fuck' is 'coarse' (cf. *GH* 123), he elsewhere purports to use the word as a neutral term: see esp. pp. 31, 94, 164, 316. Contrary to what is sometimes suggested, even in his work on Aristophanes and homosexuality Dover restricts such language to contexts where Greek vocabulary of an equivalently coarse register is concerned.

immense pleasure from living and sleeping rough – once or twice a year, and for a few days; the rest of the year, of course, my basic needs include an affectionate wife, pupils, a teaching programme, antibiotics and a very large university library. Whether the War brutalised me, in the sense of making me more callous or bellicose than I was to start with, I can hardly say; it is the kind of question on which deference to the judgement of others is more profitable than self-assessment.[16] I was not upset by blood or dismembered bodies, and no more upset than any other reasonable person by the smell of decomposing human flesh; that at least should save me from unhelpful emotions if I were ever required to clear up after accidents and disasters. I committed a minor atrocity when I compelled a weeping old couple in Rimini to get out of an abandoned house which my Troop Commander wanted as our headquarters (his view was that Italians should be thankful to have *anything*).§ I came very close at that point to disobeying a direct order; but I did not disobey. If anything, I was more disturbed at the end of the War by the pain and suffering of others than I had been previously. A few weeks from the end an artillery observer amused himself by directing the fire of my troop on to enemy-occupied houses beyond the Senio. 'Bloody good!' he exclaimed. 'There's a bloody great red cross on the roof, and you've put a shell smack through the middle of it!' 'Oh God!' I said. 'Has it got wounded men in it?' 'I hope so!' he replied with gusto, and I was at least as shocked at that as I would have been five years earlier. Maybe that just shows what a soft war I had had since 1943. Only one man in my battery was killed in Italy, so that I could not feel the fervent hatred of the enemy which is generated by heavy losses.

Indifference on the strategic and political plane is another matter. When I read Nikolai Tolstoy's *Victims of Yalta* in 1978 I recalled that I bad been at Villach, from which thousands of hapless East Europeans were returned indiscriminately to Tito and Stalin for massacre, during June and July 1945, when all that was going on. Did I know about it at the time? The plain truth is that I cannot remember whether I

---

§It must be remembered that Mussolini's entry into the War at a moment when he thought he would share in the spoils without incurring any serious risk generated great bitterness against the Italians.

[16]'It dawned on me, three years after this book was published, that the war had a considerable effect on my attitude and behaviour towards Trevor Aston (see chapter 26). Our job in anti-aircraft was to prevent enemy aircraft from damaging what they wished to damage. The only way to do that was to shoot the planes down, and if that involved death, incineration or mutilation for the pilots, well and good; we didn't feel any personal hatred for them, and if any of them had baled out and landed among us with serious wounds or burns we would have looked after them in accordance with the rules of war. Paul Thompson and others who have said that I "hated" Trevor have gone badly astray. If hatred is the desire that someone else should *suffer*, I don't hate anyone below the level of the top international villains, I simply wish that their character would change for the better; and if it doesn't, I don't feel any compunction about causing their death in order to reduce the damage that they do.' (Dover SN). The reference to Paul Thompson is to 'The life and death of Trevor Aston', *History Workshop Journal* 39 (1995) 250–69; Dover replied with a letter in the same journal, 41 (1996) 261–2.

knew or not. If I had known, I might well have felt: Tito and Stalin are our allies, they've helped us to win, give them what they want, get on with it, and let's go home.

I went home on August 1st with six weeks leave in prospect. We flew from Naples to Peterborough in Lancaster bombers, twenty other ranks and one officer in each aircraft. My 'seat' was in the perspex nose, which was uncomfortable all the way and scary on take-off and landing but afforded a wonderful view of France from the air and proved to me that England really does look a strikingly 'green and pleasant land'. When we came down to breakfast next morning, the papers carried the news of the nuclear bomb dropped on Hiroshima.[17] A flood of pure joy possessed us. It meant that the War was as good as over.[18] Not only would the British and Indians and Americans be spared the dreadful casualties entailed by an assault on Malaya and the Japanese mainland; we – that man, and that one over there, and me too – would not be sent out to the Far East when our leave was over. Demobilisation and return to our previous way of life suddenly became real and assured. During the next few months I sometimes met people who regretted that the Japanese had surrendered so promptly after Hiroshima and Nagasaki, thereby depriving us of any justification for killing a lot more of them. It was not until late October that I met someone who had moral misgivings about the bomb and thought that we ought to have given the Japanese a demonstration on an uninhabited island. I did not agree.[19]

---

[17]The bomb was dropped on Hiroshima on 6 August 1945, so there is a slight chronological discrepancy with the start of this paragraph.
[18]Such feelings were not untypical at the time; compare e.g. Mary Warnock (twenty-one in 1945), *A Memoir: People and Places* (London, 2000) 14: 'Hiroshima, though almost incredible when we first heard of it, did not, I am a bit ashamed to say, cause half such horror [sc. as the Holocaust]. It was difficult not to think simply that the war in Japan was over, and be thankful for that.'
[19]Cf. Dover's later reference (p. 275) to visiting Hiroshima in 1982.

9 WOMEN, CHILDREN AND WORK 1940–1951

If I had had any sexual experience, even no more than deep petting, before I went into the Army at the age of twenty, I would have considered that I had fared well, because among the middle-class young of my time the distinction between those who did and those who didn't was sharper, and the second category much larger, than in my children's generation. Many of the young officers with whom I went out to the Middle East admitted, when one got to know them well enough and the conversation turned to sex, that they were virgins, and even one or two of those with whom I was demobilised four years later made the same admission at twenty-five or so. On the other hand, I learned from four different friends (all straightforward and trustworthy men) something of the free-for-all sexual weekend parties in which, as white-collar suburban employees in peacetime, they had taken a joyful part; but they were clearly a minority.

The quickest way to shed virginity was to visit one of the officers' brothels (the class distinction was unofficial) in Cairo or Alexandria. I was prompt to do so, and was fortunate to get a girl with an agreeable, relaxed expression and no obtrusive make-up, but I was over-anxious (should I apologise to the other girls for not choosing any of them, and, if so, in what terms?) and she had to work hard to bring me to a half-hearted orgasm. I was ashamed of my poor performance, but not of anything else. The girl seemed to me a very nice person, whom I would have been glad to know (with a view eventually to carnal knowledge) in more leisurely circumstances.[1] I could see that the ethos of prostitution, its curious blend of brisk and coy, was not what I looked for in sex. I have never been to a brothel since, except once in Haifa for bacon and eggs at two o'clock in the morning (our gunnery

---

[1] For an earlier reference to this woman, see p. 48.

instructor, one of the best teachers I have ever known, amused us by his persistent attempt to seduce the stern middle-aged lady who cooked the breakfast).

In the Desert I saw no women and had no leave. Italy was a different matter. The sexuality of the invading armies was explosive, and the population of the south was demoralised by defeat and privation. I knew of one instance in which a girl accepted twelve ounces of corned beef as a fair price for taking eight men one after another. The immediate consequence of this promiscuity was widespread venereal disease. Becoming infected was treated as a punishable offence, and good men had bad luck; our Battery Sergeant-Major was reduced to the ranks when he became infected from a single fuck, whereas a sergeant who never had the same woman two days running escaped entirely (the same man boasted later that he had never taken anti-malaria pills; perhaps a Christian Scientist would call him *anima naturaliter Christiana*).[2] Officers tended to be favoured by discriminating middle-class women whose husbands and lovers had been carried off to forced labour in Germany or had simply vanished when the Italian Eighth Army was swept away by the Russians on the Don. Even so, I knew one officer who became infected, and fear of punishment often deterred us from following up attractive opportunities. My only emotional commitment during 1944 was to a young woman in Perugia who was already happily married, so the commitment remained silent and hopeless.

At the beginning of 1945, in a small town in the north of Italy, the woman who owned the house in which I had billeted myself made a very obvious play for me, but I was put off by her flat breasts and snub nose, and there was nothing in her shallow and coquettish personality to make her physical shortcomings irrelevant. Disappointed in me, she transferred herself to my Troop Commander. He was a good-looking man, with a smile which attracted many women, but he once confessed to me that he found twice a night hard to manage. He was scared by the frequency and intensity of our landlady's orgasms; 'six times,' he told me, awestruck, 'before I'd even got it in.' Eventually she was fucked by our batman, a Fifer brought up with horses, who had strong balls and invincible self-respect.

By that time a girl just under sixteen, who lived in a nearby house, had been impressed by stories of my fluency in Italian and sent a message to ask if I could help her with her English. Without knowing anything about her, I agreed with enthusiasm, because I could guess the kind of academic school-book she was using, and I was sure that I could do better than that in explaining how spoken English really works; also because teaching a girl anything was likely to be nicer than teaching gunnery to soldiers. Maria, as I will call her,[3] had short legs and a dumpy figure, but neat features

---

[2] Dover toys ironically with a phrase, 'a naturally Christian soul', originally used by the theologian Tertullian (*c.* 160–240 AD) to denote pagans who unwittingly manifested a sort of innate awareness of the one true god.
[3] Her actual name was Wilma: Dover mentioned the liaison in a letter to his parents of 22 February 1945. He later told Audrey about the matter when they were courting.

and the hair, skin, eyes and teeth of an adolescent girl in perfect health. Above all, she had a lively, radiant integrity which made people feel good when they met her. After she had been coming for lessons ten evenings in succession, I gained courage, and thereafter we spent more time in exploration of each other than of English syntax. We never went all the way. This was not because of her youth, a consideration which hardly entered my head ('age of consent' is a rather artificial concept,* and anyway, what was the age of consent in Italy in 1945?). Nor were her feelings undeveloped; I was taken aback (maybe she was, too) when my hand on her midriff gave her an orgasm. It was simply that she obeyed the rules of her own culture. For my part, I could not bring myself, then or ever, to beg, nor could I countenance the idea that she had the slightest obligation to satisfy the desire which I had chosen to allow her to arouse in me. I was sharply and sadly aware that I was going through an experience far more appropriate to her age than to mine; but a late start is better than an even later start, and meantime each of us rejoiced in the existence of the other.

After I had moved on from that part of Italy I knew no more of Maria until she wrote to me just before Christmas 1945, by which time I had been back at Oxford for a term, and sent me photographs of herself. At that time I had attracted a beautiful English girl, whom I promptly lost through a characteristic failure of self-confidence. The photographs of Maria showed a girl notably slimmer and taller than she had been when I last saw her, and her smile was as I remembered it. We began a happily passionate correspondence, until in November 1946 I had to tell her that I was engaged. She replied with a chilly dignity which showed the depth of her hurt more vividly than an outburst would have done, and that was that. I realised that I had, in the weighty old-fashioned phrase, 'trifled with her affections' out of pride, for the sake of escaping from the despised category of young men who have no girl-friends. I ought to have responded to her first letter in cooler terms and devoted some thought to weaning her off me, because I knew intuitively that I wasn't going to marry her. She deserved a very good husband, and if I knew that she found one I would be a little happier than I am.

That first term back at Oxford was desperately hard work. At one time during the War, during the summer of 1943, I had had doubts about the morality of continuing with Classics, and I wrote to Sandy Lindsay, then Master of Balliol, to suggest that on my return I might be allowed to change to PPE.[4] He sent a brief but wise reply

---

*A view held, I learn, by the late Dame Margaret Miles, who was not an apologist for paedophilia. [EDS *Margaret Miles (1911–94, DBE 1970) was a prominent headmistress and campaigner for comprehensive education.*]

[4] The Oxford degree Philosophy, Politics and Economics, first set up in 1920 as a form of 'modern humanities' (see R. Currie in *HUO* 113–15); it would have been an unlikely choice for Dover to make. Alexander (Sandie/Sandy) Dunlop Lindsay (1879–1952, 1st Baron Lindsay of Birker 1945), a philosopher, was Master of Balliol 1924–49; see p. 127 for a further, unflattering reference.

which amounted to 'wait and see'. Having waited, I saw in 1945 that Classics was what I loved, and I judged that I might be more useful as a good classicist than as a mediocre economist. The rightness of my decision was confirmed by the rapid discovery that I disliked that half of the Greats course which was devoted to ancient and modern philosophy. My tutor in ancient history was Russell Meiggs,† who made no allowance at all for the fact that we had all been away from academic work for several years. In that he was right, for once excuses are allowed they begin to breed. His comments on our essays were always penetrating, sometimes brutal; it was several weeks before I wrung a word of praise from him, and the end of term before I discovered that he regarded me highly. This would have been a pleasing recompense for working a seventy-hour week, if recompense had been needed, but the intellectual excitement of immersion in the history of fifth-century Athens – the first volume of Gomme's *Historical Commentary on Thucydides*[5] had just been published – was its own reward. Meiggs combined an expertise in documentary inscriptions with a down-to-earth curiosity about how things really worked, and how people really felt, in the ancient world. He had no time for the kind of solution of historical problems which shuffles the ingredients of a problem into an ingenious pattern and turns history into an intellectual game. The seed of two habits was planted in me by Meiggs more firmly than either of us realised at the time. One was: on any question in Greek history or the Greek language, go first to inscriptions and only after that to literature. The general practice among ancient historians in the English-speaking world had been to treat Herodotus, Thucydides and Xenophon as 'authorities' and inscriptions as an optional side-dish. I preferred to begin with the inscriptions, construct historical hypotheses to account for *this* stone, bearing *these* words, found *here*, and then to see how the historiography of the time fitted. Students of the Greek language mostly ignored the existence of inscriptions, and even in my own time good scholars have made untrue statements through failure to look in the right places. The second thing I learned from Meiggs was never for a moment to forget that the people whose activities I was studying were *real*, and that I must make every possible effort to put myself into their place. This I have found an invaluable principle in textual criticism.

In my second term a change came over Meiggs. His eyes were downcast, his movements slow, his responses dull and vague. At the beginning of the third term he perked up and apologised to me for having been a useless tutor because of 'a

---

†I use his surname throughout in order to avoid confusion with Donald Russell. [EDS *For Donald Russell, see the note on p. 106 below. Russell Meiggs (1902–89) was tutorial fellow in ancient history at Balliol, 1939–70: see Dover's own British Academy memoir of him, PBA 80 (1993) 361-70, and the article by M.H. Chambers in DBC, ii 640-2.*]

[5] Arnold Wycombe Gomme (1886–1959) was Professor of Greek at Glasgow 1946–57: see the article by M.H. Chambers in *DBC*, ii 381-4. For his Thucydides commentary, a work which was to play an important part in the development of Dover's career, see pp. 118–19.

particularly foul illness'. It was in fact the first attack of a cyclic depression which continued to afflict him for many years. He had several doses of electro-convulsive therapy, and a couple of days after each treatment he would suddenly resume a vigorous, cheerful personality, effervescing with good ideas and practical plans – until, six months or so later, an internal switch was turned and he was plunged back into darkness. It is a matter for astonishment and admiration that he achieved so much good work of permanent value during the bright phases. In those days the pharmacological treatment of psychoneurotic illness was in its infancy, and the illness itself was widely regarded as discreditable.‡ Meiggs's depression could not be talked about openly as one would have talked about arthritis or cataract; David Keir (Master from 1949) persisted in saying that Meiggs was simply overworked and 'needed a good holiday'. I myself knew nothing at all about depression. I was destined to learn more.

Three other people influenced me deeply by their style of teaching. Wade-Gery was a charismatic lecturer who attracted large and loyal audiences.[6] The structure he gave to a sixteen-lecture course, leading off in the first two with a perfectly lucid exposition of the issues and bringing all the strands together in the last two, was an impressive work of art; but he did not like to leave a datum lying around unused, and his inclination to treat everything we know about the fifth century BC as relevant to the topic under discussion sometimes betrayed him into over-ingenuity. Hugh Last, who lectured on Roman inscriptions, was dry but methodologically a good model. Faced with a mutilated, complex and obscure document, he began with those elements in it, however few, which were absolutely clear and certain, progressed from there to what was rather less certain, and so on until we felt confident about the context in which the really tricky issue remained to be resolved. (He shocked me, though, by beginning a lecture on the newly-discovered *Tabula Hebana* by saying, 'The first question a historian should ask is, "What would Mommsen have said about this?".')[7] Ben Meritt from Princeton, who was Eastman Visiting Professor that year, held a seminar, of which I was a devoted member, on

---

‡At a meeting of heads of colleges with psychiatrists to discuss undergraduate mental illness, Geoffrey Mure, Warden of Merton and author of *Retreat from Truth*, said that he would prefer the student to see a priest, who would 'at least tell him that he is a miserable sinner'.

[6]Henry Theodore Wade-Gery (1888–1972) was Wykeham Professor of Ancient History at Oxford 1939–53 and a leading scholar of Greek epigraphy, one of Dover's burgeoning interests after the war (see p. 96). See M. Chambers in *DBC*, iii 1009–12, and the British Academy memoir by Antony Andrewes, *PBA* 59 (1973) 419–26. Dover attended a small class of Wade-Gery's on Hesiod as an undergraduate in autumn 1946 and reported on it in several letters to his parents.

[7]Hugh Last (1894–1957) was Camden Professor of Roman History at Oxford 1936–49. The *Tabula Hebana*, an important Roman bronze inscription, attracted much attention on its discovery in 1947. Theodor Mommsen (1817–1903) is widely regarded as the greatest ancient historian of the nineteenth century: for an account of his career, see the article by Alexander Demandt in *CSBE* 285–309.

Attic inscriptions, and delighted me by his relaxed, humorous, unpretentious approach to epigraphic problems.

By the end of my first year back at Oxford I felt sure that I wanted to be a Greek historian, but I did not draw any sharp distinction in my mind between different kinds of history: of politics, of society, of literature, of language. I was encouraged by Bill Watt, the Mods tutor at Balliol, to compete for the Ireland prize scholarship, the examination for which comprised only papers in composition, translation and Greek and Latin language and literature. Bill, a superb Latinist, gave me some teaching to this end, and I won the Ireland in December 1946.[8]

Philosophy was a different matter, because I heard no lectures which aroused my interest in the subject. H.J. Paton, Professor of Moral Philosophy, read his script at a pace too fast for dictation but too slowly for it to be acceptable as oral exposition; those lectures nowadays would earn a probationary lecturer the sack.[9] Price was lucid and methodical, but did not convince me that perception is a suitable subject for philosophical discourse.[10] Ayer also lectured on perception, but I found his style irritatingly jerky, casual and peevish.[11] My tutor was Donald Allan, certainly a first-rate Platonic and Aristotelian scholar (he soon left Balliol to become Reader in Ancient Philosophy at Edinburgh, and eventually Professor of Greek at Glasgow), but useless (to me, anyway) in tutorials, because he was a shy and silent man who fired arrows at the target from different angles in an unpredictable order and lacked the ability to sustain a continuous thread of critical comment on a pupil's essay.[12] When I look back on my encounter with philosophy that year, it seems to me that my difficulty lay in coming to terms with the assumption that it is actually about something. I could well appreciate the importance of logic, but could see no point in attempting to construct a logical validation of inductive reasoning, because it seemed to me obvious that we have no alternative to treating its validity as a working hypothesis. I felt the same about the unsolved and (for reasons which, again, I thought obvious) insoluble 'problem of free will'. However, the question 'Is the question, "Is the question of free will a

---

[8]Dover had previously entered for the Ireland in his first year at Oxford. On Bill Watt, see p. 72.
[9]H.J. Paton (1887–1969) was White's Professor of Moral Philosophy at Oxford 1937–52 and a Kant scholar of note; see the British Academy memoir by W.H. Walsh, *PBA* 56 (1970) 293–308.
[10]H.H. Price (1899–1984) was Wykeham Professor of Logic at Oxford 1935–59; his interests included parapsychology as well as epistemology: see the British Academy memoir by Jonathan Harrison, *PBA* 80 (1993) 473–91.
[11]Sir Alfred ('Freddie') Ayer (1910–89, Kt 1970) was at this stage a fellow of Wadham College, Oxford (1944–6) and known for his *Language, Truth and Logic* (1936), a statement of so-called 'logical positivism', an extreme form of empiricism: see the further reference to him on p. 228, and note Dover's reference to Ayer's book on p. 104 when characterizing his wife's reductionist cast of mind. In his talk at an 80th birthday celebration in St Andrews in 2000, Dover said 'I belong to the generation that was brought up on logical positivism.'
[12]Donald James Allan (1907–78) was tutorial fellow in Classics at Balliol 1931–47 and Professor of Greek at Glasgow 1957–71; see the British Academy memoir by Donald Russell, *PBA* 65 (1979) 565–71.

scientific question?" itself a scientific question?' is not idle; there seems to be room for philosophical questions after all. I wish my teachers had come clean. Before I was launched into Plato, Aristotle, Descartes and Kant I should have been encouraged to come up with some answer to the question 'On what grounds can a proposition, problem or question justifiably be called "philosophical"?' The kind of linguistic analysis associated with the name of Oxford was not much in evidence when I was an undergraduate, though its great days were not far off. In 1951 I asked my pupil Bernard Williams, the day after he had taken Greats, whether he would agree that philosophy was a branch of English lexicography.[13] He did agree (but I wouldn't hold him to that now). Perhaps I wouldn't have taken to the new philosophy any better than I did to the old. I love semantics, but precise definition is an activity that rarely affects anything beyond itself.[14]

Life at Oxford was absorbingly interesting, but life at home in vacations was strange and horrible; and although I was less vulnerable in my twenties than in my teens, wider acquaintance with ordinary people had made me less tolerant of much that I had previously accepted as unalterable. My parents had come through the War well. My mother had found satisfaction as a volunteer clerical worker for the Red Cross, and my father, despite his lifelong fear of some kinds of physical peril (he would never eat mushrooms, in case the picker had made a mistake), took air-raids very calmly. Once the War was over he had a nervous breakdown which he attributed to overwork – although his colleagues, as I learned later, thought him rather lazy – and his ambition now was to be invalided out of the Civil Service. He achieved this in 1946 after a further series of nervous breakdowns. In that period he talked to me with greater candour about himself than at any time before or after, and it seemed to me that he was making a pre-emptive strike against what he mistakenly believed would be attempts by my mother to enlist my sympathy against him. He told me, for example, that she was 'going to pieces', which was plainly not so. He told me too that when he brought work home and had his supper on a tray in the study, ostensibly because he had too much to do and could not finish it in the office, the real reason was that he could not bear to sit at the table with my mother and see her putting too much in her mouth (she didn't, actually).

---

[13]Bernard Williams (1929–2003, Kt 1999) became one of the most distinguished of twentieth-century English philosophers, holding chairs successively at London, Cambridge, Berkeley and Oxford; see the further references to him on pp. 109 and 211, with the British Academy memoir by Simon Blackburn, *PBA* 150 (2008) 335–48, and the website dedicated to him at https://sites.google.com/site/bernardwilliamsphilosopher/home

[14]'Bertrand Russell in his autobiography says that he spent a sleepless night puzzling over the statement "George III asked if Sir Walter Scott was the author of *Waverley*". If he had reflected for a moment on the circumstances in which the King could have displayed his uncertainty (e.g. "Who wrote *Waverley*?" or "Is that fellow over there called Scott the chap who wrote *Waverley*?", etc.) he could have slept sound. This kind of nonsense is still with us.' (Dover SN)

My ignorance of the sexuality of men in their fifties prevented me from giving him sympathy and support. The fact is that my mother at 55, with varicose veins in both legs and an excess of wrinkles, looked 75. I realised that one day in 1950, when she came up to Oxford unexpectedly and knocked at the door of my room in College. As she entered, I thought for a moment, 'Who on earth is this old, old woman?', and only then realised that it was my own mother, at whom I was looking for the first time unencumbered by the misperceptions which memory imposes. It was obtuse of me in 1946 not to understand how desperately my father wished for a younger, sleeker woman; all the more obtuse, because I could see that his sidelong glances at attractive young women glimpsed in the street through the bus window were just as hungry as mine. It is hard to say, though, what advice I could have given him; and once, when he confided to me that he would like to set fire to the hair of a

FIGURE 5 Percy Dover (father), 1943.

FIGURE 6 Dorothy Dover, née Healey (mother), 1941.

noisy blonde three seats ahead of us on the bus, I realised that there must be alarming complications in his sexuality.

In the spring of 1946 Hugh Latimer, whom I had known ever since our first day at St Paul's, re-introduced me to his sister Audrey, whom I had met once or twice before the War.[15] She was now planning a fortnight of youth-hostelling in the

---

[15]They first met, so Dover SN records, as members of a group that sometimes queued for gallery seats at Covent Garden. The Latimer family owned a Plymouth printing firm, Latimer Trend (used by Oxford University Press for, among much else, the revised supplement to the Liddell and Scott Greek lexicon in 1996); it ceased trading in 2019.

Lakes with another girl, and they thought it would be a good idea to have a man with them. I agreed to go. On our first day in the open she produced a massive pasty from her rucksack and ate her way through it. I thought, 'This woman has the right ideas.' As it turned out, the other girl had to go home before the fortnight was up, so that Audrey and I had the last few days to ourselves. The weather was atrocious most of the time, which may have accelerated our discovery that we understood each other very well. We were both lovers of rocks and moors and the smell of grass, both sceptical and unconventional beneath a top-dressing of inoffensive conformity. We agreed about what was funny and what was dispensable. Neither of us had ever regarded sex as holy or as dirty. I did not hear her once utter a cliché, and I don't think I've heard her utter one since. It has been said that if two people can bear each other for a fortnight of rain in the Lakes, they can bear each other for life, and it is not surprising that my internal computer, disguising itself as a magisterial external voice, told me to ask Audrey to marry me.[16] She was very prompt to agree. We got engaged in November 1946 and were married in March 1947. Audrey's mother Cicely was insistent on a church wedding, and the obvious place for that was the chapel in Balliol. Unfortunately, it was not licensed for marriages, so we had to be married in the Oxford Registry at the end of the morning, part for lunch, and meet again for the religious ceremony in the afternoon. It was a couple of days after the interminable frost of that winter was dissolved in a monstrous gale, which blocked the Banbury Road with fallen trees and flooded the railway line between Oxford and London, so that the wedding was not as well attended as it might have been. We spent our honeymoon in Locarno, very cheaply, because the Swiss after the War were desperate to recapture visitors. The weather which had tested our endurance in the Lakes returned to batter us in the Ticino and I found also that I had underestimated the problems of cross-country walking in those parts, despite my experience in Italy. I learned my lesson when we had to wade twice through an icy river because footbridges had disappeared. However, we took a daily walk to a café in Ascona where there was a pingpong table and lavish mugs of *caffè latte*. On our last day we found that we were packed and ready to leave our hotel forty minutes before our taxi was due to arrive. What should one do with forty spare minutes? Audrey made a brisk monosyllabic suggestion, and I thought for the second time, 'This woman has the right ideas.'

We were fortunate in securing a pair of furnished rooms in Oxford, with use of the landlady's kitchen, in a house near the northern by-pass. Audrey's upbringing had been even more frugal than mine, with good reason; her father had been killed in an accident when she was eleven, and her mother Cicely, with three children to bring up, had been largely dependent on better-off relations, assisted by the

---

[16]For an earlier reference to this experience of a quasi-external 'voice' produced by the 'internal computer', see p. 49.

FIGURE 7 Wedding of Hugh Latimer (brother-in-law) and Moira Sketch, 1949. Kenneth and Audrey at far right, Cicely (Audrey's mother) next to them, Helen (Audrey's sister) next to Moira.

children's talent for winning scholarships. Consequently Audrey was well accustomed to counting the pence and to relying (like my mother) more on the family and its circle of like-minded friends than on any kind of social life which costs money. Her ready acceptance of my very long working hours astonished the neighbours. Sexual contentment had an immensely beneficial effect on my academic work during the summer of 1947. I had been inclined earlier to spend far too long on the organisation of an essay, going round in circles before I could decide on the most appropriate sequence, but now I moved directly into the structure which arose of its own accord from the data, and consequently I got through much more.

Philosophy, though, was still something of a problem; my tutor now was Donald MacKinnon,[17] a man of great good will, but not really the right tutor for me, because he sustained a discussion by feeding in discrete ideas which were often

---

[17]Donald MacKinnon (1913–94) was both philosopher and theologian; at this date he was a tutorial fellow at Keble College, Oxford: for a flavour of his unusual character, see P.J. Conradi, *Iris Murdoch: A Life* (London, 2001) 123–8 (with incorrect date of birth), and see the British Academy memoir by Stewart Sutherland, *PBA* 97 (1998) 381–9.

stimulating in isolation but not spread out and systematically followed up in the way I would have wished.

I was allowed to choose between July and December for my final 'Schools' (examination) – in those immediate post-War years there were a great number of special regulations designed to accommodate people who had come back from war service at various times during 1945 and 1946 – and I chose December. I had, after all, missed the long vacation which in peacetime would have intervened between my first and second term of Greats, and I needed that amount of free time to sort everything out.

Audrey's education (at University College London) had been in mathematics and physics, and at the time of our engagement she was a research assistant in the Building Research Station at Watford. By nature she was strongly reductionist, and when I tried to explain philosophical problems to her she was apt to take the view that a philosophical statement is either uninformed science or ritual verbiage. (She had never read Ayer's *Language, Truth and Logic*, but the spirit of the age works in many people at many levels.)[18] Naturally I found this at first very threatening, but in the long vacation of 1947 it had a very good effect on me, because it compelled me to go back to the beginning and re-work my two years of philosophy in quite a different way. I put all my material, both historical and philosophical, in a very condensed form, into six large hard-cover notebooks, and in the course of my last term I found it possible to imprint practically every page on to my memory. I sat Greats in December; I was despondent after the first paper, Moral Philosophy, and much more confident about Logic and Metaphysics later in the examination, but in fact I got a first-class mark on the former and only an alpha-beta on the latter. My ancient history marks were all high alphas, so that I ended up with one of the best Firsts of that year. James Holladay, I believe, got the best.[19]

By that time I had been elected to a Harmsworth Senior Scholarship at Merton and had been awarded two University post-graduate scholarships. We were also offered a flat in the top floor of 2 Rawlinson Road, a Balliol house of which the greater part housed Thomas Balogh and his family, and we moved in just before Christmas. Three newly married fellows – we, the Hares and the Strettons – were given the opportunity to buy furniture and carpets at probate valuation from a house which Ernest Walker had bequeathed to the College, and we did extremely well out of that. Three years later, when Bill Williams left Balliol to become Warden

---

[18]On Ayer's book, cf. n. 11 above.
[19]James Holladay (1921–89) subsequently became a prize fellow at All Souls, 1947–9, and then tutorial fellow in ancient history at Trinity College, Oxford, 1949–82; see the introduction by Fergus Millar to A.J. Podlecki, ed., *Athens in the Fifth Century and Other Studies in Greek History: the Collected Papers of A. James Holladay* (Chicago, 2002) ix-xi.

of Rhodes House, we were allocated the College-owned house which he had occupied in Woodstock Road.[20]

As a would-be professional scholar, what I needed after Greats was at least a year in which to fill in the gaps which Greats had left: reading texts attentively, remedying my ignorance of some ancillary disciplines, attending seminars on specialised areas, and gradually formulating a topic on which to write a doctoral thesis in the course of the following two or three years. All that was just what a graduate student at Oxford in 1948 was not allowed to do. I was required to state at the beginning my proposed topic of research, and then, in effect, to start writing a good book. Fraenkel, among others, recognised that this was nonsense. Fortunately, since then much hard thinking has gone into the structure of postgraduate work in Oxford, and the modern system is a vast improvement on the old; but the improvement came far too late for me. I chose to work on Athens in the two decades immediately after the Peloponnesian War, because I wanted to understand how the Athenians recovered as quickly as they did from total defeat and loss of wealth, how they came to perceive their own experience of war, and why they were so prompt to involve themselves in future warfare. At my own request, I was allowed to have Arnaldo Momigliano as my supervisor; although he had by then been appointed to a professorial chair at Bristol, he still lived in Oxford and it was easy for us to meet.[21] For learning, accuracy of recall, speed of absorption and breadth of historical interests he was a man whose like I have not known. He agreed that I should begin by tackling the dating of forensic speeches (mainly Lysias, but also early Isocrates) and of the very numerous lost comedies of which we have only the titles and some citations (normally, but rather misleadingly, called 'fragments'). 'After all,' he said, 'if we could get absolutely *everything* in *exactly* the right order, all historical questions would solve themselves.'[22]

It did not take me long to discover that if I wanted to do the job properly, I had not one D.Phil. thesis on my hands, but half a dozen. Interpretation of the comic fragments, last edited by Kock in 1880–1884, was a deep drift of assumptions which had not been blown away since Kock's time. Fragments had been assigned to plays, and plays to dates, on what were often very flimsy grounds, and attempts to reconstruct a dramatically plausible context for an isolated passage of dialogue

---

[20] On Thomas Balogh, see 127, on Bill Williams, p. 130. The other Balliol fellows referred to here are the moral philosopher R.M. Hare (1919–2002) and the modern historian Hugh Stretton (1924–2015). Ernest Walker (1870–1949) was a musicologist and composer who had been director of music at Balliol 1901–25.

[21] Arnaldo Momigliano (1908–87), an intellectual historian of huge range and sophistication, had arrived in Oxford in 1939 as a Jewish refugee from Mussolini's Italy. His initial appointment at Bristol was strictly speaking a lectureship. See the British Academy memoir by Peter Brown, *PBA* 74 (1988) 405–42, and the articles by Oswyn Murray in *ODNB* and Karl Christ in *CSBE* 277–84.

[22] As Dover pointed out in the book's original addenda, cross-referencing what he says on pp. 336–7, he did not himself share this view of historical questions.

had seldom been thought through adequately. For prose works – a question largely of relative, not absolute, dating – a number of scholars had nibbled at dating by stylistic change, but no one had properly explored, except for Plato, the shifts in genuine lexical and syntactical alternatives within an author's work. I allowed myself to be side-tracked into establishing relative dates, by a study of shifts of that kind, for the speeches ascribed to Antiphon, only one of which is securely datable on external grounds. I began from the observation that certain generalising passages are present in two speeches, those traditionally numbered 'V' and 'VI', in almost identical form, but with minor differences of language, and that where they differ the versions in V are consistently in accord with the language of the fragments of the speech which Antiphon delivered in his own defence before his execution at the end of 411. The order thus indicated, VI before V, is confirmed by many parameters drawn from passages other than those which the two speeches have in common, and the speech traditionally numbered 'I' falls neatly between them. Moreover, three hypothetical model speeches (studies in argument from probability) attributed to Antiphon can be shown on those same parameters impossible to accommodate anywhere in the sequence or before it, and must§ therefore be presumed to be by someone else.

My awareness that I had embarked on a D.Phil. thesis which was going to interest me much less than some of its side-products increased my anxiety abut my future employment. I applied for the vacant Mods fellowship at St John's, but they wisely preferred Donald Russell.[23] This was my second defeat within a year at Donald's hands, because a few months earlier he had secured a fixed-term lectureship at Christ Church for which I had competed. Which of us was the right person for that lectureship might be hard for either of us to decide, but he was certainly right for St John's, and perhaps it was unwise on my part to try there. They wanted someone whose teaching would be mostly on the Latin side of Mods, and certainly not someone easily seduced by Greek history. In any case, Donald's judgement and sensitivity on literature have always been better than mine, and Meiggs had warned me, with characteristic bluntness, that Donald had 'a better brain' than I had, although he would 'never be as good a historian'. It did not enter my head to put in for jobs outside Oxford and Cambridge. I would have been a strong candidate for a lectureship in any Classics department anywhere, but at that time other universities simply did not exist for me.

---

§Or so I thought; recognition of the different styles adopted by a Greek prose author for different kinds of subject-matter now makes me far less sure. [EDS *For some of Dover's technical investigations of this point, see* EGPS, *46–56.*]

[23]Donald Russell (1920–2020) was tutorial fellow in Classics at St John's College, Oxford, 1948–88, and Professor of Classical Literature at Oxford 1985–8: see the British Academy memoir by C. Pelling and M. Winterbottom in *BMF* XIX. On Russell's reactions to *MC* itself, see the Introduction, 19–20.

All apprehensions about the future were dispelled when I was elected in the summer of 1948 to a Balliol fellowship. The job was tailor-made for me; I was to teach the Greek side of Mods and some of the Greek history for Greats, and at the same time I would hold, at least for the first three years, a lectureship at Wadham, teaching both Greek and Latin. Donald would also combine his fellowship at St John's with a lectureship at Wadham. I abandoned my D.Phil. with relief, and in the course of the next two years produced a substantial article on the chronology of Antiphon's speeches and another short piece in which I took a fresh look at some comic fragments. To go without a doctorate was no disadvantage at Oxford; there was even a tendency to look askance at people who completed doctorates, because it meant that they had not been snapped up for tutorial fellowships and had stayed on the shelf for three years.

Our son Alan was conceived as soon as we moved into the Rawlinson Road flat, and was born in September 1948, just before I began my work as a tutor. Audrey and I had always taken it for granted that we would have children, and would have felt our life mutilated without them. Alan, unfortunately, was reluctant to be born and in the end had to be delivered by Caesarean section. Having been jammed head-first in the exit for several days, he had a severe headache for the first two days of his life and was kept in a baby-room, not next to Audrey in the ward. Afterwards I realised that the guarded words and looks of the ward sister were taking account of the possibility that his brain might be permanently damaged, but at the time I was slow on the uptake. I do not know if either of us could ever have felt affection for a child with capacities far below the human norm, especially if his behaviour were aggressive.

Audrey felt physically weak for a long time after Alan's birth, and he was a baby with an insatiable appetite, a crying voice of extraordinary volume and persistence, a precocious alertness to sights and sounds, a tendency to take fright at dogs or butterflies, and a reluctance to calm down after being frustrated or scared. The first two years were difficult for us, because we got so little sleep; in his second year, when he was old enough to substitute syllables for yells, he developed the habit of cot-rocking in the early hours of the morning, imitating a cockerel or a steam-engine while lurching, or rather whizzing, back and forth a couple of thousand times (one night, I counted), and this habit lasted for about nine months. All the same, we survived, and we looked forward to the birth of our second child in 1950. Catherine turned out to be an extraordinarily peaceful baby, needing to be woken for feeds. After she learned to walk, some oddities in her behaviour worried us, not least her tendency to walk smack into obstacles, and when she could talk it became increasingly clear that she saw virtually nothing close at hand, and more distant things in two dimensions. At four and a half she got her first pair of glasses, and life expanded for her.

My chief ambition in my relations with the children was to get right what my father had got wrong. In this I was not wholly successful, because there is a bit more of my father in me than I could bring myself to acknowledge and there were one or two occasions when I reacted too strongly against ingredients in Alan's own temperament which reminded me too much of my father. Alan was jealous of Catherine, and that was a problem which I should have handled with more patience and thoughtfulness. However, Audrey's superior sense of proportion limited the damage I might have done, and things came right in the end. I had wanted three children, and Audrey, herself the middle one of three, had originally agreed that it would be a good idea. But in spite of having approached the day of Catherine's birth in high confidence, cheerfully encouraged by her sister Helen who was at that time a midwife, she found the experience of normal birth so appalling by comparison with a Caesarean under anaesthetic that she was reluctant to face it again, and the long period of physical weakness entailed in carrying babies around took too big a slice out of her available energy. We settled for two.

My tutorial work in the first two terms of the year was much the kind of thing I had experienced as an undergraduate in Mods: translation from sophisticated English, prose and verse, into Greek and Latin. Some of us were coming to doubt whether the dominance of 'composition' was a good thing for the subject, but we were caught up in a system from which no individual tutor could break away. University prizes and scholarships in Classics were mostly awarded for composition, and success in that area was both a necessity for the prospects of those who aimed at a professional career and a major contribution to the prestige of their colleges. In Mods itself composition amounted only to four papers out of fourteen; the teaching for the rest was done by means of lectures on a university basis, the tutor's role being as a rule confined to setting test papers at the end of term. I was not strongly inclined to rebel against this system, because I myself had always found that six hours or more spent on a composition (and I sometimes spent twelve) taught me more about the language than the same amount of time spent on reading texts. People in non-linguistic subjects imagined that when a pupil had submitted his composition and I had corrected it I produced the 'right answer' and gave him a copy of it; they found it hard to understand that when one is translating from a modern language into the language of an alien culture there is no 'right answer', but as many good answers as there are good translators, and translation calls for argument and discussion, not bare assertion by the teacher. I always wrote my own translations, never putting less than a day's work into each one, and so built up a stock of about a hundred pieces, which was adequate for teaching purposes. My Wadham pupils cost me more time and trouble than those at Balliol, because my Latin had become rusty in the last nine months, and I found it advisable to devote part of each day to attentive re-reading of Cicero and Ovid. To vary the diet of composition I organised a seminar for my Wadham pupils on the funeral speech ascribed to Lysias, a peg on which I could hang many different explorations of Greek literary form and ethos. This, however, was extremely unpopular, because the text was not among the texts prescribed for Mods; and a wholly recalcitrant seminar is not a practical proposition.

One pupil sent to me by Wadham was the holder of a scholarship in English who was required to pass Latin in the Preliminary Examination and had failed it in the first attempt. If he failed again, three months later, he would at least lose his scholarship and might be sent down for good. Confronted with a Latin text, he shook, and could make no sense even of the simplest passage. I taught him to home in on the main verb and to identify its subject and object before worrying about what any of the words meant. At our second meeting he stopped shaking, and after eight meetings he passed the examination. The moment at which I noticed he had stopped shaking gave me a stronger charge of pride than the day, two years later, when eight of my Balliol pupils got Firsts in Mods. Maybe my sense of proportion is slightly askew, but, of course, those eight who got Firsts were people I could not easily have prevented from doing so; most of the Balliol men were formidably bright – my second-year group included Robin Nisbet and Bernard Williams[24] – and there was not much I could explain to them which they did not already understand. Weak students are easily frightened, and it is a tutor's job to put hrmself in their place, feel their fear, and then set about allaying it. I learned that early on when one such pupil turned round at the door as he was going out after his first tutorial and said, 'Tell me – is there any hope?' I had played the perfectionist, niggling over almost every word in his Greek prose, and had marked it beta minus. So I brought him back, told him that beta minus is a second class mark, not third class, and went over the prose with him again, explaining how the red ink I had used on it so lavishly was not occasioned by gross errors but by insufficient precision and subtlety. He seemed reassured, and subsequently got a good Second; thank goodness he had plucked up the courage to ask me that dramatic question. I had some failures in those early years, through immaturity in my understanding of people fundamentally unlike myself; four failures, anyway, that I can recall (maybe one of them was not my fault), though some of my former pupils may tell you that I had more than I knew.

I was astonished to discover from my pupils that hardly any of them spent any time at all in political discussions. I should have guessed as much from my own experience as an undergraduate in 1945–7, but I was thinking back to the political fervours of 1938–40. I suppose that politics after the War did not present issues comparable in stark drama or exciting enough to first-year students. In recent years I have sometimes been asked by Americans what it was like to live through the time at which the British Empire was broken up, and my candid answer is that I don't remember. Perhaps I took for granted the independence of India and Pakistan and one former possession after another. At any rate, after going through

---

[24] On Nisbet and Williams, see the notes on, respectively, pp. 115 and 99.

a six-year war I would have been exceedingly unwilling to be recalled to service and risk my life in an attempt to sustain British rule in Asia or Africa; and if I'm not willing to risk my own life, I don't like to ask others to risk theirs. I was also influenced by the argument of Leonard Barnes' *Soviet Light on the Colonies* (which I had read during the War) that the potential of the individual subject is inadequately realised under an alien ruler, even though I was pretty sure that the rule of a native political elite anywhere in Asia or Africa was likely to be more cruel, corrupt and oppressive than rule by any colonial power. Generally speaking, my mind was not on politics in the nineteen-fifties. I fell in with the prevalent sloppy use of labels such as 'progressive' and 'reactionary', but I was shocked by the sinister imbecility of G.D.H. Cole when he declared at a dinner of the Leonardo Society in 1948, 'Well, if there is a war between Russia and America, I hope the Russians win it.'[25]

During the dull periods in the War I had written one and a half novels, which I put aside for a year or two; when I read them over I decided that I was not cut out for fiction.[26] I also wrote some poems, a few of which were published,[27] but entirely lost the inclination when a wife and children became the focus of my emotions and my appetite for creative work was fully satisfied by historical exposition. At the same time, I filled a gap in my education by reading books which I would have read in my early twenties if I had not been on service abroad: *War and Peace*, *Crime and Punishment* and Boswell's *Life of Johnson* all in the first three months of 1947. It was the best part of another twenty years before I got round to Balzac, Flaubert, Stendhal, Zola, Trollope, Dickens and George Eliot. Except for *Buddenbrooks* (in translation) Thomas Mann did not attract me, and I have never taken to Proust.

My ambition in 1945 had been: to marry a congenial wife,[28] and with her to bring up children who would become good people; to get a tutorial fellowship at an Oxford or Cambridge college, preferably Balliol; and to write at least one book

---

[25]The Leonardo Society was a Balliol College society, first formed in the 1920s, for the promotion of socialist values. G.D.H. Cole (1889–1959), educated like Dover himself at St Paul's and Balliol, was a political theorist of a strongly socialist stamp; in 1948 he was Chichele Professor of Social and Political Theory at Oxford.

[26]From September 1941 onwards Dover had sent his parents instalments of a novel entitled *Paul's Rock*; his letter home of 31 January 1946 refers to it as something he still hoped to complete, but no more is heard of it after that.

[27]No published poems have been identified. Dover's letter home of 22 November 1939 tells his parents he had written perhaps twenty complete poems, in a variety of metrical forms, over the previous three years, and was (cautiously) willing to consider having them 'printed'. In early April 1941 he sent them one entitled 'The Wicked Man'. On 28 April 1942 he sent a thirty-line poem, 'An In Memoriam for a man killed in Libya', in the form of a Greek choral ode. These two poems are printed in an appendix to Stray's chapter in *S&C* on Dover at school and university.

[28]'Because of my deformity, I did not dare to hope for beauty as well.' (Dover SN)

which would be well regarded by people in my own subject and would be of lasting value to them. I felt by 1950 that I had not done too badly so far. I leave aside wilder ambitions, such as writing a good novel or becoming Regius Professor of Greek at Oxford, and fantasies, such as growing a prehensile tail covered with dense fur. The acquisition of wealth has never played any part in my ambitions, or in Audrey's. When I was elected to a fellowship at Balliol no one told me what my salary would be, and I thought it would be rude to ask. Maybe £500 a year, I thought, and was delighted to find it was actually £700. The second year gave me even greater pleasure, because I discovered that there was an annual increment. The creation of the National Health Service liberated us from the fear of medical expenses which had cast so deep a shadow over our parents' lives. We did not think that we would ever be rich enough to own a car, but we both agreed that it would have been crazy to let anything like that affect my choice of career. Whether we would have thought it crazy if my grandmother had not left me £1,400 in her will when she died in 1945 is hard to say with certainty; even quite a modest fence to keep the wolf from the door allows a nicer view over the landscape than most people can enjoy. And actually, we did get a car in 1951 – a superannuated London taxi which I bought in Hackney for £100. Not long afterwards we replaced it (everything about it except the engine was in a sorry state, and we were glad to dispose of it to some students for £30) with a brand-new Jowett Bradford, designed for itinerant bakers and fishmongers in the Dales and astonishingly uncomfortable, but reliable, simple, and so accessible that its maintenance and repair presented no problems.

This made holiday visits to our parents much easier, but also imposed on us (or so we felt) an obligation to visit them more often, and that was not an unmixed blessing. With Cicely, a very good granny when the children were small, there was no problem. She had moved away from St Albans and bought a house at Hartfield which had once been the lodge at the drive-entrance of a mansion. It had an immense pond, virtually a lochan, surrounded by woods, and there was never any lack of things for the children to do; there we could relax and enjoy ourselves. My own parents had moved into one wing of the early nineteenth-century rectory at Algarkirk, in the Lincolnshire fens, where Uncle Ken was rector. The garden was enchanting, and to everyone's surprise my father who had never stirred a finger in the garden when we had one in Thornton Heath took to gardening with great enthusiasm and did much to awaken a similar enthusiasm in me. Even more surprisingly, he found the parish records, which were continuous from the late sixteenth century onwards, absorbingly interesting, and for some years immersed himself in the historical problems raised by 'culyer rent' and the accounts of the 'dyke-reeves'. This was fine for me, and the garden was splendid for the children, but the surrounding countryside was rather lacking in bite by comparison with the Ashdown Forest so easily accessible from Hartfield. My father was fond of the children so long as they were amusing, charming and compliant, but as they grew older their potential for sometimes being otherwise increased and this, combined with my father's bad moods and hostility to my mother, ensured tension. When we went there for two weeks I thought of the time as divided into 42 units, three to each day, and ticked off each one mentally as we survived it, until the glorious last day arrived. This was hard on my mother, with whom we had no granny-problems which could not be amicably resolved.

10 HISTORY, COMEDY AND OTHER THINGS 1949–

Books VI and VII of Thucydides were one of the prescribed texts for Mods.[1] For some years Dorothea Gray[2] had lectured on them, but now wanted a change, and since I was known to combine a passion for Greek history with a high degree of competence in the Greek language I was invited by the Sub-faculty to take over.

A few years ago I read a strange article in *The Daily Telegraph* written by a lawyer who said that he had been a lecturer in law for a short period and had come to the conclusion that university lecturers have a peculiarly undemanding job. He himself had delivered a hundred lectures in the course of a year, and 'allow, say, 100 hours for administration and preparation...'. I thought at first that the printer had accidentally omitted a nought, but decided that the author probably meant what was printed, and I felt like congratulating the institution concerned on its good fortune in losing the services of so lazy and irresponsible an employee. My sequence of forty-eight lectures on Thucydides entailed nearly a thousand hours of preparation, i.e. roughly twenty hours of preparation for every hour of delivery, and I have found that to be a consistent ratio in any lecture-course which I am giving for the first time. When one gives the same course for a second time, the twenty hours can be cut to eight, but certainly not to less than that, because any lecturer capable of self-criticism knows that during the first time round one observes any number of things which need to be re-cast in the light of the audience's reactions, to say nothing of fresh evidence and new publications. If the course is given more than twice, an average of four hours preparation per lecture should suffice from the third time onwards. People who believe (as no doubt some readers of *The Daily Telegraph* do) that university teachers work only half the year, or that giving a lecture is a matter of improvisation or of simple recall, have much to learn

---

[1] For the term Mods, see note 22 to p. 75.
[2] Dorothea H.F. Gray (1905–83) was tutorial fellow in Classics at St Hugh's College, Oxford, 1935–73.

about real life. Preparation for tutorials is, on the whole, simpler; in my first three years at Balliol it meant something like a thousand hours of preparation altogether, but after the third year I could live off my fat much of the time in tutorials.

Lectures were of vital importance for Mods, because there existed so few adequate commentaries even on texts of central importance. In the case of Thucydides VI–VII the only commentaries available in English were those of E.C. Marchant,[3] published before the end of the last century, and the study of Greek history, particularly the study of the documentary sources, had moved up on to a different plane since then. Classen's commentary, revised by Steup, was quite good on textual and linguistic problems, but curiously deficient in historical curiosity; it was written in German, which most Oxford students could not read, and unobtainable anyway. The essence of my job in lecturing on those two books of Thucydides was to produce a better commentary on them than anyone had done hitherto. Other lecturers on other texts had the same obligation.

Although I published five articles during 1952–5 which were a spin-off from my lectures,[4] I had no intention at that time of writing anything about Thucydides on a larger scale. I wasn't at all sure what my first major work was going to be, though I was confident by 1950 that it would be literary or linguistic rather than historical in the narrow sense of the word. One idea was an Oxford Classical Text of the orators Antiphon and Andocides, for which I made fresh collations of the manuscripts; a second was a grammar of Attic inscriptions (there had been none since Meisterhans in 1900, and the number of inscriptions discovered had doubled), and I made some headway in indexing the phonological and morphological features of the inscriptions which pre-dated the mid-fifth century. Both these projects were held up while I prepared a revised edition of Denniston's *Greek Particles*, putting in the additions and corrections that were in his own interleaved copy at the time of his death, and re-wording or abbreviating in order to cause the least possible disturbance to the lineation.* Once having dealt with *Greek Particles* I found that my enthusiasm for my two main projects had waned: for Antiphon and Andocides, because I doubted whether a new edition was really needed; and for 'the new Meisterhans' because I felt I should await publication of

---

*This edition is sometimes listed as 'revised by K.J. Dover', but I very deliberately left my name off the title page, because the revision was Denniston's own. Apart from a few notes which I added at the end, my task was essentially editorial. [EDS *On Denniston, see p. 72 with note. He died in May 1949; Dover completed his work in 1950 but the revised edition did not appear until 1954. When a reprint of the second edition was issued in 1996 by two different publishers, they neglected Dover's wishes and put 'revised by K.J. Dover' on the title page.*]

[3]Edgar Cardew Marchant (1864–1960) had two stints teaching at St Paul's and was later Sub-Rector of Lincoln College, Oxford.
[4]There were in fact six of them in 1953–5; one was omitted from the (defective) bibliography in *OA* 401–2.

the great number of ostraka excavated in the Athenian Agora and the corpus of vase-inscriptions which Immerwahr had it in mind to compile.†

Meanwhile two fresh lines of research took shape, one of which was an attempt to explain the principles underlying the order of words in Greek. In English, where all the case-endings of nouns except the genitive -*'s* have perished, the order of words is determined by their syntactical function; we cannot play about with the order of ingredients in 'Jimmy kicked Willie' without risking communication of the opposite of what we intended to communicate, and in both English and German the place of the verb is governed by strict rules. In a highly inflected language such as Greek the speaker and writer have much greater freedom. Sometimes we can see how this freedom is exploited in order to give a high emotive charge to the opening or closing word of a sentence, but there is a great deal of utterance which carries no emotive charge, and it is the apparently arbitrary exercise of freedom in that which constitutes the problem. One of my first pupils at Balliol was Robin Nisbet, and on one occasion when I changed the order of words in a passage of a Greek prose composition which he had written he asked me for my reason. I couldn't give him any better reason than my own *Sprachgefühl*, and afterwards I thought, 'My God, this won't do!'[5] I also found in my initial work on Antiphon, whose text is transmitted in two medieval manuscripts of the same age and of equal claim on our consideration as evidence, I had no rational grounds for decision between them in many passages where they differ in word order. This suggested to me that I should begin my enquiry with documentary inscriptions, where the chances of transcriptional error are virtually nil. My reward was immediate. Such inscriptions (e.g. boundary-stones) often use formulae which are identical in content but different in word order. We sometimes find that whereas the composer's choice between the orders ABC, ACB, CAB and CBA is indifferent, the orders BAC and BCA do not occur. Why not? What is it about ingredient B that debars it from first place? It did not take me long to see the reason: B conveys no new information; it could be omitted without loss of intelligibility, and would indeed be omitted if the text had to be cut down in an expensive telegram. The proof that it could be omitted is that sometimes it is; thus, if Kallias dedicates a helmet to Zeus, the inscription on it may say either 'Kallias dedicated this to Zeus' or 'Kallias to Zeus', because the material context – the presence of a helmet in a

---

†Beazley told me that to his very great regret he had not made a complete record of all the dipinti and incisi on the tens of thousands of vases which he had examined in the course of his lifelong work on the history of Attic vase-painting. [EDS *Sir John Beazley (1885–1970, Kt 1949), was Lincoln and Merton Professor of Classical Archaeology and Art in Oxford 1925–56. See the British Academy memoir by Bernard Ashmole*, PBA 56 (1970) 443–61, *and the articles by D. von Bothmer in* CSBE 1–6, *and D. Gill in* DBC, *i 60–3.*]

[5]There is another reference to the present incident in Dover's *Greek Word Order*, v. Robin Nisbet (1925–2013) would eventually become Corpus Professor of Latin at Oxford, 1970–92; see the British Academy memoir by S.J. Harrison in *BMF* XIII.

sanctuary of Zeus – suffices to tell the reader that the helmet is a dedication. Once this principle is established from inscriptions, its operation in literary prose can be followed up. I called the ingredients which are indispensable because they contribute new information 'nuclear' and the dispensable ingredients 'concomitant'.

Greek contains a number of little words (e.g. 'and', 'if') which are now called 'prepositives', because they are normally preceded by some degree of pause and must be followed without pause by another word, and it contains many more (e.g. 'him', 'something') which are 'postpositives' and cannot be preceded by pause but 'gravitate' to a place immediately after another word (often a word following pause). I adopted this terminology and added the term 'mobile' to cover all words which were neither prepositive nor postpositive. Wackernagel in 1892 had analysed the role of postpositives in Indo-European languages generally, and Eduard Fraenkel in two seminal articles (1932–3) showed how application of the principle that postpositives tend to follow the leading word of a sentence illuminates also the phrasing within a sentence.[6] It seemed to me that there was a close analogy between the relation of postpositives to mobiles and the relation of concomitants to nuclei; using the abbreviations M(obile), N(ucleus) and C(oncomitant), and symbolising 'postpositive' as q, I could offer the formula $NC(C)N \sim Mq(q)M$. Working through all the material needed for its demonstration took quite a while, but when I was invited to give the J.H. Gray Lectures in Cambridge in 1959 I took Greek word order as my subject and turned my lectures into a book the following year.[7] It was a very short book, in emulation of Paul Maas, who said more in fewer words (and with greater clarity) than anyone I have known.‡

The anonymous reviewer of my book in the *TLS* found that my answer to the question, 'What determines Greek word order?' was 'meagre and gritty'; no doubt s/he wanted aesthetics but got mere linguistics.[8] If I were to be remembered for

---

‡A Professor at Königsberg before the War, he was an adviser to the Oxford University Press. He lived austerely. The positivism of his scholarship verged on the narrow-minded, but I learned much from him. I once asked him if *historia* could mean 'explanation' in Byzantine Greek, and his answer, 'If you have found it in that sense, yes', nicely reflected the state of our knowledge of Byzantine Greek. [EDS For further information about Maas (1880–1964), a Jewish refugee from Nazi Germany who lived in Oxford from 1939, see Lloyd-Jones, BG, 215–18, and K.B. Bär in DBC, ii 599–602.]

[6]Jacob Wackernagel (1853–1938) was a comparative philologist of prodigious linguistic abilities. He was Professor of Greek for many years in Basel, where he had actually been a student of Friedrich Nietzsche (whom he later remembered with some warmth, though not for his philological teaching). For an account of his career, see the article by Rüdiger Schmitt in *CSBE* 379–88. On Fraenkel, see p. 72 with note.

[7]Dover gave his three Gray lectures in February 1959 and had completed preparation of the typescript for publication, with characteristic efficiency, by May.

[8]A strangely garbled memory: there never was, in fact, a *TLS* review of the book. In his SN, Dover identifies the putative reviewer as Bedell Stanford (1910–84, Regius Professor of Greek at Trinity College Dublin, 1940–80, and mentioned in the following paragraph; Dover was not an admirer of his), but Stanford actually reviewed the book, not unfavourably, in the journal *Hermathena*, where the phrase in question does not appear. We have not been able to find any other source for the putative comment on the book.

just one contribution to the subject, I would rather be remembered for *Greek Word Order* than for anything else. Or so I thought until very recently (April 1994); I now realise, in the light of discussion with an admirable young Dutch scholar, Helma Dik, that if I had been in less of a hurry to publish I would have reflected longer on the work published by Loepfe and Frisk, and might even have anticipated her own work by re-casting the problem in terms of 'topic' and 'focus'.⁹ But I do not repent of starting from inscriptions rather than literature.

But for the invitation to lecture at Cambridge, I might well have put off the publication of anything on Greek word order for a long time, perhaps until retirement. It actually interrupted work on a major project which took shape early in the nineteen-fifties. The Clarendon Press wanted to produce a new Oxford Classical Text of Aristophanes, and it was proposed that each of the eleven plays should be entrusted to a different scholar, who would re-edit the text and write a full up-to-date commentary. That process completed, the new texts of the plays would be combined to make an Oxford Classical Text. The joint General Editors of the series would be Robert Levens and I;¹⁰ our responsibility would be to enforce a common format and satisfy ourselves that each edition of an individual play submitted was of a satisfactory scholarly standard (Maurice Platnauer's *Peace*, the first to be published, was not, but none of us had the nerve to say so).¹¹ Robert himself did not want to contribute a play to the series, but I had it in mind to take on *Frogs*. Denniston had lectured on the play, and when he died his very full lecture-notes were given to me by Denys Page for future use. I learned, however, that in some way which was mysterious to me Bedell Stanford at Trinity College, Dublin, had another copy of the (hand-written) lecture-notes and with that encouragement was getting on fast with an edition and commentary of his own (for Macmillan, not the Clarendon Press).¹² I then decided to do *Clouds* instead, but did not start on it until 1955, because early in 1954 I was asked to contribute the chapter on Greek Comedy to a book being organised by Maurice Platnauer under the title *Fifty Years of Classical Scholarship*, and also to write an analytical bibliographical survey, for the German periodical *Lustrum*, of all the work done on Aristophanes from 1938 to 1955. These two tasks fitted together very well, consolidated my own status in Aristophanic studies, and filled in the background I needed before embarking on a particular play. I wanted somehow to bring

---

⁹See Helma Dik, *Word Order in Ancient Greek* (Amsterdam, 1995), where the work of Frisk and Loepfe is cited.
¹⁰Robert Levens (1901–76), a specialist in fact in Latin literature, was tutorial fellow in Classics at Merton College, Oxford, 1927–68.
¹¹Maurice Platnauer (1887–1974) was a fellow of Brasenose College, Oxford, from 1922 and later its Principal (1956–60); his unsatisfactory edition of *Peace* appeared in 1964.
¹²'Stanford ... had more charisma than intelligence, and was a great success as Sather Lecturer at Berkeley, but the book of the lectures is third-rate'. (Dover SN) The book in question is *The Sound of Greek* (Berkeley, 1967).

Aristophanes to life. I can't explain in what way I felt that previous commentators had failed to do so, and I can't say how far I succeeded; you must ask other people. His work has been well called 'a synthesis of levity and gravity' (Edith Hall), by turns coarse and subtle, brutal and sensitive, superficial and penetrating, combining ingredients which we would nowadays classify as sitcom, variety turn and political satire, and I just felt that I understood him.

I was particularly keen (see p. 105) that if the Clarendon Press's project was realised, I myself should take on the fragments of Aristophanes (there are about a thousand, including the one-word citations). The brief article which I published on two fragments of the comic poet Plato (a very different person from the philosopher of the same name) gave rise to a correspondence with J.M. Edmonds, an old Cambridge don who had himself prepared an edition of all the fragments of Greek comedy and was seeking a publisher. His difficulty in finding one was understandable, not just because so much of his work was slipshod and wayward, but because he had persuaded himself that the Cairo codex of Menander contained an interlinear paraphrase from which it was possible not only to fill in the lacunae of the text but to work out what must have happened in the missing portions of the plays originally contained in the codex. The trouble was, apart from the intrinsic improbability of an interlinear paraphrase of Menander, that Edmonds was the only person who could see it. Experienced papyrologists could not. He wrote despairingly to Gilbert Murray, who reasonably cried off on the grounds that his eyesight was no longer sharp but added 'There's a young man here called Dover who is interested in comedy...'. So the infra-red photographs of the Cairo codex came to me, and I was satisfied beyond doubt that Edmonds' alleged paraphrase was the most remarkable systematic delusion that I was ever likely to encounter. I pleaded inexperience in papyrology, and remained on good terms with Edmonds, whom I visited once in Cambridge. He found a publisher – Brill of Leyden – and his four massive volumes appeared in 1957–61. Reviewers were naturally wary of saying, 'This man is insane', but it became possible to say so after his death.[13] At the same time, large portions of the lacunose plays became available from other sources, and it could be seen that the reconstructions of plots which he had inferred from his imaginary paraphrases were quite wrong.

However, my work on Aristophanes was stopped dead by an unforeseen event at the beginning of 1959. In the late nineteen-thirties Gomme began a massive *Historical Commentary on Thucydides*, of which the first volume appeared in 1945. Four years after that he completed his work on Books II, III, IV and V.1–25, but on

---

[13]In fact, Edmonds was already dead (1958) when reviews, uniform in their dismay at his fantasies over the Cairo codex, started to appear; some criticism was directed at Edmonds' literary executors for allowing the most egregious of his views to reach print. For further information on Edmonds, see the article by D.A. Campbell in *DBC*, i 272–3.

his journey to Oxford to hand his material over to the Press his suitcase was stolen, and he had no carbon copy.[14] He thus had to start again, and his second and third volumes did not appear until 1956. When he retired from Glasgow in 1957 at the age of seventy he was very fit and youthful (he almost beat me in running for a bus the year before), and in the belief that he had plenty of time he turned aside to work on a commentary on Menander. His belief was mistaken, for within a year he was mortally stricken by cancer and died in January 1959. The Press were anxious that the *Historical Commentary* should be completed, and proposed that Tony Andrewes and I should take it on.[15] We agreed at once and in the summer of 1959 I went down to stay with Tony for a few days and see what draft material Gomme had left in his house in Long Crendon. It was clear that I ought to take on Books VI and VII, since I had done so much on them for my lecture-course at Oxford, while Tony should look after Books V.25–116 and VIII. We found that Gomme's draft on Book V was inadequate, and there were only some skimpy notes on the early chapters of Book VI; nothing on the rest of VI, and nothing on VII and VIII. I came back with a gift from Phyllis Gomme, a bit of honeysuckle from the garden at Long Crendon, which now reaches the top of our house and overhangs my study window.

I was able to devote all my research time for the rest of 1959 and 1960 to my part of the job, making particularly good progress during my time at Harvard (September 1960 to January 1961), thanks to the resources of the Widener Library.[16] I held a seminar there on problems in Thucydides, and profited from the contributions made to it by (among others) Adam Parry.[17] During this time Tony's work was held up by his commitment to completion of another book, and it was not until 1970 that the first volume of the two which we planned appeared in print.[18] The second, which covered Book VIII and included a couple of appendixes on the composition of Thucydides' work, was published in 1981. The pace may seem slow, but the time we took was worth taking, for the longer we worked, the better able we became to raise questions which previous commentators had not even considered, let alone answered. Each of us read and criticised every word that

---

[14]Gomme's typescript, as well as many valuable notes, was in a case stolen on a train from Glasgow to London; others have dated the incident to 1945 or 1946 rather than 1949. Cf. the earlier reference to Gomme on p. 96.

[15]Antony Andrewes (1910–90) was Wykeham Professor of Ancient History at Oxford 1953–77: see the British Academy memoir by D.M. Lewis, *PBA* 80 (1993) 221–31.

[16]For Dover's invitation to Harvard, see pp. 137 and 154.

[17]Adam Milman Parry (1928–71), son of the Homeric scholar Milman Parry famous for his work on oral poetry. Adam, whose Harvard PhD thesis had been on Thucydides, was an assistant professor there at the time of Dover's visit; he later taught at Yale up to the date of his early death in a motorcycle accident.

[18]In the meantime (1965) Dover had published two shorter 'school' editions of Thucydides Books 6 and 7; cf. later references to these on pp. 184, 191.

the other drafted, and we met regularly to resolve disagreements (they were never serious) by discussion. Tony was the perfect collaborator: sharp, meticulous and pertinacious, but infinitely patient and unfailingly good-humoured. I only wished, at times, that I was quicker to understand the more allusive and quirky of his comments. I'm not quite sure why, but the Appendix that I wrote (in the course of 1974–5) on the 'strata of composition' in Thucydides gave me more lasting satisfaction than anything else that I had written.§ I didn't think I would ever come back to Thucydides and find anything more to say about him, but of course I was wrong; he is an inexhaustibly interesting author who can still spring surprises after forty years of careful re-reading.[19]

Once I had got through 1961 I was able to come back to Aristophanes, and sent my edition of *Clouds* to press in 1966. For this I re-examined the manuscript tradition, fully collating forty-one manuscripts, and it was as well that I did; since the nineteen-twenties Victor Coulon's text of Aristophanes had achieved canonical status and was assumed to give us adequate and accurate information about the manuscript readings, but in fact his choice of manuscripts was in part an arbitrary inheritance from one of his predecessors, and he also inherited some misreported readings. One consequence of his procedure was concealment of the fact that some good emendations attributed by him to editors of the modern era were actually made by Byzantine scholars before 1350, and when the attributions have been corrected we get a much better idea of Byzantine scholarship. As for the content of the play, *Clouds* is exceptional in two respects. Its main target of ridicule is Socrates, a real person whose personality and philosophical activity are presented to us in vivid detail by Plato and Xenophon; and since the play was not well received at its performance in 423 BC, Aristophanes set about rewriting it, but never completed the revision, so that the text we have is the text of a play half revised but not sufficiently revised for performance. These facts create major problems, to which I devoted a hundred pages of introductory chapters. In my commentary I tried throughout to produce the play in my mind's eye, never being content with vagueness and uncertainty about the position and movements of any character on stage at any moment of the action. The spirit of the nineteen-sixties also allowed me to explain in plain terms the sexual humour of some of the dialogue, and new material from different areas of the Classical field contributed to the interpretation of details.

People accustomed to disciplines in which the pace of discovery is breathless, such as entomology and pharmacology, sometimes imagine that classicists mis-

---

§A very able historian of the younger generation tells me that it is 'radically question-begging', but I am still waiting to hear what question(s) it begs. [EDS Dover SN identifies the scholar as John Moles (1949–2015).]

[19] In the margin of his own copy, Dover tagged Thucydides here with the German 'den man nie auslesen kann' (whom one can never finish reading), which he recalled hearing an unidentified scholar utter.

spend their time on forming subjective differences of opinion on material wholly contained within a boundary drawn long ago. Even if the boundary had been drawn, this view would still be wrong, because it is possible to ask new questions about what has been under our noses for centuries, and 'opinions' backed by evidence differ in 'competitive probability' (the phrase is Martin Bernal's)[20] as much in historical studies as in science. In fact, fragmentary new texts – papyri and inscriptions – accumulate continuously, and their repercussions on our interpretation of long-familiar data are sometimes spectacular.[21] Moreover, no one concerned with literary texts can afford to disregard the 'silent' evidence of buildings and artefacts which excavation produces. For these reasons alone there can never be a 'definitive' commentary on a Greek text, but there are additional reasons: when the available evidence is not conclusive, individuals are very likely to disagree over the relative importance to be assigned to different considerations – a situation not unknown in (e.g.) cosmology and palaeontology. I could have spent the rest of my life in an attempt to make my *Clouds* decreasingly imperfect, but I decided, as I said in the preface, to 'raise the drawbridge' in 1966.

After *Clouds* appeared, I did not at once drop Aristophanes, but wrote a book for the general reader, *Aristophanic Comedy*, which has, I think, served a useful purpose.[22] Then other things took over, and it was not until after 1980 that I began serious work on *Frogs*. On retirement in 1986 I gave it the highest priority, and it was published in 1993. At present I do not envisage further original work on Aristophanes, though I hope to be allowed (as in the past) to read and comment on the first draft of other scholars' commentaries on other plays.

One sideline, with an easily defined beginning and end, should be mentioned. In 1952 and 1954 I had given a short lecture-course at Oxford on the iambic and elegiac poets of the archaic period. That is no doubt why, when the edition of the fragments of Archilochos by Lasserre and Bonnard was published, *Classical Review* asked me to review it.[23] I gave it a very unfavourable review on two grounds: first, it assigned one-word or one-phrase citations to particular poems, and constructed contexts for them in a way which Lasserre may have thought demonstrated

---

[20]Bernal's phrase was actually 'competitive plausibility'. Martin Bernal (1937–2013) is best known for his controversial trilogy *Black Athena* (1987–2006), which maintained that ancient Greek culture was far more indebted to Egyptian and other near-eastern cultures than modern classical scholarship, partly for reasons of racism and cultural arrogance, was willing to accept. This appears to be Dover's only reference to Bernal anywhere in print.

[21]With a characteristic liking for quantification, Dover SN observes that the 1996 revised Supplement to the standard Liddell and Scott Greek lexicon contained 'well over 5000 lexemes' not known at the time of the 9th edition of 1940.

[22]*Aristophanic Comedy*, published in 1972, grew from a general class which Dover gave at Berkeley in 1967 during his occupancy of the Sather chair (see pp. 185 and 191–4).

[23]The review was reprinted in *G&G* 122–6.

historical imagination but actually demonstrated nothing but lack of discipline; and secondly, it followed a current fashion, popularised by Bruno Snell[1] and Hermann Fränkel, in supposing that the contrast between Homeric epic and the (slightly later) songs of Archilochos was evidence for the emergence of a new, self-conscious, anti-heroic ethos, whereas in fact it is simply a reminder that we know

FIGURE 8 Entretien on Archilochus, Vandoeuvres, 1963. Denys Page second from left, Bruno Snell centre in bow-tie. *Photo: Mary Rochat.*

---

[1] Snell was one of the best people it has been my privilege to know, and I regret the necessity of criticising his book *The Discovery of the Mind* for the bad influence it has had in the study of the Greeks.

nothing at all about songs and non-epic poetry in the period of the epic.[24] It was perhaps because of this review that I was invited to take part in a small international symposium on Archilochos, to be held at the Fondation Hardt, near Geneva, in 1963. I was asked if I would give a paper on 'The Poetry of Archilochos'; and having promptly agreed to do so I wondered what on earth I was going to say. But I spent my spare time for a few months in 1963 working up a paper, and found that in fact I had a good deal new to say; among other things, I drew on the songs of preliterate cultures in the Pacific to show how unsafe it is to take the first person singular in an Archilochean poem to refer to the poet himself rather than to an imaginary persona adopted for the purposes of the poem.[25] The happy *entretien* in August 1963 – two Britons, four Germans, a Frenchman, a Greek and a Swede, devoting a week to one Greek author – was my first such experience and gave me an appetite for more, an appetite satisfied in 1979 and 1991.

In this chapter I have spoken almost exclusively about research and publication. The researcher who resents the duty of teaching and the devoted teacher who has no taste for research are familiar stereotypes in any discussion of university life. Neither is typical, but both exist; I have met them. Research and teaching are alternative ways of spending time and therefore necessarily in potential conflict, like any two ways of spending time. It is, however, a disastrous mistake to speak of the researcher and the teacher as if they were two genetically distinct sub-species of the human race; many of those who are outstanding in research are stimulated by explaining things to pupils (the zoologist Mick Callan[26] at St Andrews set a wonderful example), and many outstanding teachers put into their preparation a great deal of what can properly be called research but is not easily cast in the form of publishable papers. A researcher may be good or bad at teaching, just as s/he may be good or bad at swimming, sexual seduction, playing the clarinet, or anything else which is not research. It is possible to learn how to do better what one does badly to start with, and a researcher, however talented, who is paid to

---

[24]Bruno Snell (1896–1986), who taught at Hamburg for most of his career, associated Archilochus with archaic Greece's supposed 'discovery' of the psychology of the individual: *The Discovery of the Mind in Greek Philosophy and Literature*, trans. T.G. Rosenmeyer (Oxford, 1953) 46–56. Hermann Fränkel (1888–1977), a Jewish refugee from Germany in 1933 who subsequently held a professorship at Stanford University, had briefly taught Snell at Göttingen in the early 1920s; his similar views on Archilochus are most easily found in *Early Greek Poetry and Philosophy*, trans. M. Hadas and J. Willis (Oxford, 1975) 132–51.

[25]In drawing on his knowledge of preliterate Pacific cultures, Dover was of course exploiting a longstanding interest: see pp. 52–6. The Archilochus paper was reprinted in *G&G* 97–121. The further Fondation Hardt seminars alluded to at the end of the paragraph were on modern classical scholarship (1979: Dover gave a paper on the expurgation of Greek literature, reprinted in *G&L* 270–91: cf. p. 162 n. 5) and Aristophanes (1991).

[26]Harold Garnet ('Mick') Callan FRS (1917–93), mentioned again on p. 134, was Professor of Natural History at St Andrews 1950–82 and a distinguished geneticist: see the obituary by H.C. Macgregor in *The Independent*, 12 November 1993, p. 16.

teach and fails to do the job properly should not expect to be treated leniently. To be a good teacher without ever spending time on research is, by definition, impossible, no matter how great the affection and esteem in which one is held by one's pupils (remember, they don't know any better), because the spirit of enquiry is an absolutely essential ingredient of good teaching; goodness is not all charisma. Moreover, the teacher who abjures research should reflect that it is only because other people in the past have engaged in research that there is anything at all to teach. At certain points in my career I have been sharply aware that the claims of teaching and research on my time were in direct competition, putting me into the situation (since I love them both) of Captain Macheath, and at one such point I gave precedence to research. That has not been a common situation, though, because so much of my research was generated by my interest in what I was teaching, and so much of it could be put back into my teaching. I have not had to confront the problems of the researcher whose main interest lies in topics which are remote from hrs teaching programme and cannot be fed into it – a problem more often encountered in the sciences than in the humanities. My contract of employment at St Andrews in 1955 required me 'to do all in [my] power to promote and advance the knowledge of [my] subject', a most heartening job-description, and I never forgot that the 'knowledge' to which it refers was not just mine, but other people's too.

11 MIGRATION 1951–1960

Although I have often felt, and sometimes said, that my debt to Balliol is immeasurable, not least for providing me with a tailor-made academic job, I am conscious of a strand of uneasiness running through my years as tutorial fellow of the College. In part, no doubt, this was caused by dissatisfaction with the structure and ethos of the Classics syllabus at Oxford (cf. p. 108), but a more important cause was my awareness of tensions within the fellowship and my inability – a product of my upbringing in a home so rarely free of tension – to shrug off or laugh off the things that made me uncomfortable. I could not describe Balliol of the nineteen-fifties as a happy college; but the reader is warned that my colleagues of those years, for most of whom (most, not all) I retain great affection and respect, might be very surprised at my adverse judgement.

In 1951 I was appointed Senior Tutor. At Balliol the duties of Senior Tutor were combined with those of Tutor for Admissions, and virtually all the work of my office was concerned with applications for admission. On the other side, I had to deal with the financial problems of undergraduates whose grants were delayed or inadequate (my recollection is that there were very few such problems), and the farming-out of undergraduates when their tutors were on leave (but the tutors themselves usually arranged that). For a year or two I was secretary of the intercollegiate Senior Tutors' Committee, but I cannot now recall any issue that was discussed by that committee.

As Tutor for Admissions I was responsible for all correspondence with applicants up to the time of their final acceptance or rejection. I did not have the power to admit anyone myself; that rested, rightly, with the tutors in the subject concerned. An applicant to Balliol had three hurdles to get over, if he was a candidate for a scholarship or exhibition, or four, if he was aiming only at a commoner's place. The first was the minimum formal entrance requirements for admission to Oxford University, and that was a straightforward enough issue; a college was not allowed to present for matriculation anyone who did not satisfy those requirements, and in cases of disagreement over the status of unusual qualifications the University won. An applicant who hoped to be awarded a scholarship or exhibition had to take a competitive examination which was run, for each subject, by the tutors of the subject in a group of colleges. A candidate who did not get an award might none the less be admitted as a commoner on the strength of his performance in the examination. Those who did not wish to try for an award at all had to take an Entrance Examination, and each college ran its own, the dates being spread over the winter; hence the applicant unsuccessful at the college of his first choice would normally try for a second and, if resolute, a third, even a fourth. This situation generated a quite misleading impression of the ratio of applicants to places at Oxford, because there was at that time no central Admissions Office to keep track of individual applicants. All candidates for awards, however weak their performance on paper, were interviewed during the scholarship examination. Of those who took the Entrance Examination, anyone whose written papers were hopeless was rejected without interview (unless his teacher's recommendation contained some unusually interesting and encouraging ingredient), and the final selection was made after interviewing the rest.

Thus there were three tests common to all applicants: formal requirements, competitive performance on paper, and performance in interview. For those who took only the Entrance Examination, however, there was a fourth, intervening between the first and second: once I had satisfied myself that an applicant was formally eligible, I had to send his dossier to the Master, for his opinion on whether the applicant should be allowed to take the examination at all or be eliminated straight away. Quite often Keir and I agreed that the applicant's academic record was so weak that it would be a hopeless struggle for him to get through an Oxford degree course and a kindness to prevent him from trying (we never took anyone for a Pass Degree, though there were one or two who lapsed to that level after floundering in Honours). Yet there were some occasions on which it seemed to me that Keir was asking himself not, 'Does this applicant deserve the chance?' but 'Is he the sort of chap we want in the College?', and when it came to sorts of chap Keir's criteria and mine were not always the same. It was widely believed – and the belief has still not lost its hold – that in the process of selection Oxford colleges attached less importance to academic promise than to parentage, friendships, connections with trusted schoolmasters,* and the 'character' manifested on the sports fields of public schools. I cannot speak for other colleges, but I can say with assurance that at Balliol in the nineteen-fifties the Master was the only person in whom I ever detected even a glimmer of such a preference.† No more than a

---

*Often rightly trusted; at Balliol in 1951–5, just as at Corpus in 1976–86, I was aware that there were certain teachers whose assessment of high potential in their pupils was extremely perceptive.
†Theo Tylor, the Law tutor, was one of the most conservative fellows. People were nice to him because he was blind, but I found the snobbery and philistinism which he occasionally expressed in conversation almost beyond belief. [EDS *Sir Theodore Tylor (1900–68, Kt 1965) was tutorial fellow in jurisprudence at Balliol 1929–67.*]

glimmer, but it was enough to antagonise some tutors, notably the economist Thomas Balogh and the philosopher Patrick Corbett.¹ In a sense, it was our own fault. When we elected Keir in 1949 (he had a very narrow victory over Roger Mynors)‡ we knew that we wanted a Master who would secure the goodwill of old members of the College and break decisively with Lindsay's habit of ignoring and insulting them.§ In that respect, Keir fulfilled our expectations magnificently, but in his social, political and moral attitudes he was more profoundly conservative and conventional than any of us had realised. It would have been better if he had expressed and defended his own predilections more robustly, but he went to great lengths to avoid any confrontation with a tutor, and the transparency of his occasional subterfuges invited disrespect.

Balogh and Corbett saw no value in the study of the ancient world (Marcus Dick, on the other hand, whose education had been in the sciences before he became a philosopher, told me that he thought Aristotle's *Nicomachean Ethics* 'by far the best book on moral philosophy ever written'). War broke out in 1951–2, when the PPE tutors, with some backing from the modem historians, called in question the inordinately high proportion of our entrance awards which were allocated in advance to Classics. Bill Watt fought hard and straight in the interests of Classics, defending the high academic status which the College owed in such large measure to the outstanding classicists attracted by its array of awards. I found it hard to give him the forthright support he would have liked, because I could not help seeing the situation as the PPE tutors saw it, and knew what line I would have taken if I had been one of them. As it was, we got off very lightly in the redistribution of awards, more by luck than by force of argument; Balogh was often right on all kinds of issues, but rarely got his way, because his cynical and suspicious interpretation of other people's motives engendered in his colleagues equal suspicion of his own. The right answer (eventually adopted by most colleges) would have been to throw all awards open to all subjects, without any earmarking. I would like to believe that I thought of that at the time, but I have no recollection of doing so.

---

‡Since there were no internal candidates, the process of election, which lasted two years, bore no resemblance at all to Snow's *The Masters*. [EDS *Sir Roger Mynors (1903–89, Kt 1963) had been tutorial fellow in Classics at Balliol 1926–44 and therefore one of Dover's Mods tutors. He had gone on to be Kennedy Professor of Latin at Cambridge 1944–53. For C.P. Snow, cf. p. 232 with note.*]

§When Lindsay died I was editor of the *Balliol College Record*, and I had the utmost difficulty in finding anyone willing to write his obituary. In the end I twisted John Fulton's arm almost to dislocation. [EDS *On Lindsay, see note to p. 95. Some Balliol students, at least, had a more favourable opinion of him: see Denis Healey, The Time of My Life (London, 1989) 28–30; cf. MC 256 for a reference to Healey.*]

¹Thomas Balogh (1905–85, Kt 1968) was a Hungarian-British economist, a fellow of Balliol 1945–73, and an advisor to governments. Patrick Corbett (1916–99) was fellow of Balliol 1945–61 and subsequently Professor of Philosophy at Sussex and Bradford.

Bill Watt left in 1952 for the Chair of Latin ('Humanity') at Aberdeen, and with the arrival of Gordon Williams as his successor in 1953 I turned my mind again to the possibility of initiating thoroughgoing reform of the Classics syllabus at Oxford.[2] Gordon was not a product of the Oxford system, for he had graduated from Trinity College, Dublin, and held a lectureship at Cardiff. He and I agreed that the systematic study of ancient literature ought to be available to Greats students as an optional alternative either (in accordance with individual preference) to philosophy or to ancient history. In this we were strongly supported by Fraenkel, Dodds and Spencer Barrett, and between us we drafted a syllabus. Fraenkel's support was the kiss of death, because so many of the older members of the Sub-faculty (notably Maurice Bowra) resented any criticisms that came from him, and huddling together to protect themselves against interference by professors was second nature to Mods tutors (the Sub-faculty was devilish democratic), so that no one took any notice of the diffidently expressed wisdom of Dodds.[3] This was disappointing, and the reactions of the Sub-faculties of Philosophy and Ancient History were worse than that. The philosophers seemed to think that all subjects other than philosophy were at best propaedeutic to theirs, and those of them who had come into philosophy through PPE and not through Mods and Greats had not the remotest idea of the kinds of work involved in the study of ancient literature. The ancient historians betrayed an astonishing lack of confidence in their own subject by taking the line that no one would study ancient history unless it were compulsory.

Eventually, ten years after I had left Oxford for St Andrews, the three Sub-faculties agreed on a reform which brought 'tripartite' Greats into being, at the price (fair enough) of introducing philosophical and historical ingredients into Mods (so that students beginning Greats would be able to choose with the experience of all three options behind them), but in 1954 I felt that there would never be agreement on reform; and that was one thing, though by no means the only thing, which made me ready to contemplate leaving Oxford.

It must have been early in 1953 that Robert Cross, my near neighbour in the Woodstock Road, told me that H.J. Rose would be retiring from the Chair of Greek at St Andrews in September, and that he had been asked to discover if I would be

---

[2]Gordon Willis Williams (1926–2010) was a tutorial fellow at Balliol 1953–63; he was later a colleague of Dover's for a second time as Professor of Humanity at St Andrews 1963–73 (see pp. 209, 222), and eventually became Thacher Professor of Latin Literature at Yale 1974–2004. He made his name with a big book, *Tradition and Originality in Roman Poetry* (1968).
[3]On Dodds' support for reform of Greats, see *MP* 177–8; cf. the later reference to this issue on pp. 137–8, with C. Stray, 'An Irishman abroad', in C. Stray et al., eds, *Rediscovering E. R. Dodds* (Oxford, 1990), at 28–31.

interested.⁴ Soon afterwards he arranged for me to meet Malcolm Knox, who was at that time Acting Principal of St Andrews.⁵ Knox explained to me that there was a body of opinion in St Andrews which held that since W.L. Lorimer, now in charge of Latin at Queen's College,⁶ Dundee, ought (in their view) to have been elected to the chair of Greek in St Andrews when Rose got it in 1927, it would be rather nice if Lorimer could have it from 1953 until he reached retiring age in 1955.⁷ Knox himself preferred to bring in new blood right away (I discovered later that he took an unfriendly view of Lorimer's personality; he could hardly have faulted his scholarship). I had to tell him that we were still looking for someone to succeed Bill Watt by October 1953, and it would be a serious blow for Classics at Balliol if I too left at the same time; I could not think of moving until 1955. We left it at that.

The idea of living and working in Scotland greatly attracted me for reasons which were not academic. In the spring of 1950, while Audrey and Alan were staying with Cicely, I had hitchhiked from Oxford to Scotland with the intention of spending a week walking in the Highlands. When I got there, after spending one night sleeping under a hedge in the Forest of Bowland and a second night under another hedge near Falkirk, I discovered how cold it can be in the Highlands at night in the last week of March. I had a 'commando' down-filled sleeping-bag, but even so, trying to sleep under some scattered trees between Loch Tummel and Loch Kinardochy, I found it advisable to ward off hypothermia by shovelling together a layer of deer-dung as insulation between my sleeping-bag and the frozen ground. Next morning I moved on southward at first light and thawed under the morning sun while eating my breakfast below Schiehallion. From there, Aberfeldy and a massive pot of coffee, then Killin and Crianlarich with diversions one way and another. It was a perfect week, sunny and windless with a plastering of snow on the heights. At Crianlarich, where I slept in a pine-wood, there was a moment of magic when I heard a strange cry, like the recurrent shuddering motif on the brass in *Finlandia*,⁸ uttered by an invisible bird flying very swiftly along the river at dusk. I knew then for sure that this was a country in which I would be happy. Later that year I brought Audrey up to Killin for a week's holiday; cataclysms of rain thwarted our attempts on Ben More, Tarmacban and Ben Lawers, but there

---

⁴It was in fact, as Dover's letters home show, as early as November 1952 that he was alerted to the situation in St Andrews. Herbert Jennings Rose (1883–1961) was Professor of Greek at St Andrews 1927–53: see the article by E.M. Craik in *DBC*, iii 834–6, and the British Academy memoir by W.L. Lorimer, *PBA* 48 (1962) 397–410.
⁵Thomas Malcolm Knox (1900–80, Kt 1961) was Professor of Moral Philosophy at St Andrews 1936–53; after being the university's Acting Principal 1952–3 he served as Principal 1953–66.
⁶Strictly speaking, at this date, University College, Dundee, which officially became Queen's College only in April 1954.
⁷William Laughton Lorimer (1885–1967) did indeed occupy the chair of Greek for those two years: Dover himself wrote Lorimer's British Academy memoir, *PBA* 53 (1967) 437–48.
⁸For Dover's love of Sibelius, one of his favourite composers to the end of his life, cf. p. 76.

were just enough fine spells for her to see that I had not exaggerated the beauty of the country.

As 1955 approached, I took some advice. St Andrews was reputed to be a quarrelsome place. Sir James Irvine, who had become Principal in 1920, had enthusiastic supporters in his successful efforts to turn it into a residential university, but he also made enemies of those who called that 'anglification' (in some quarters he was referred to as 'the little beast'). University College, Dundee, which had been put under the control of the St Andrews Senate and Court at the end of the last century, resented its subordinate status. However, Irvine died in 1952, and in the same year a Royal Commission chaired by Lord Tedder created a new set-up in which St Andrews (i.e. 'the United College of St Salvator and St Leonard')‖ and Dundee (from then on, 'Queen's College') would be equal partners. David Keir had been a member of the Commission, and I sounded him on the problems and personalities concerned. Knox he told me was 'resolute'; and 'the people of Dundee', he added sadly, 'are as God made them, and it can't be helped'. Others were more discouraging. 'Can't think why you should want to go to St Andrews', said Russell Meiggs. 'Their standards are no better than Aberdeen's.' And Bill Williams: 'The only thing I know about St Andrews is that it has the worst Professor of History in the United Kingdom' (he meant his namesake, J.W. Williams, who in fact retired in 1955). The most interesting and helpful talk I had was with Christian Fordyce, the Professor of Humanity (= Latin) at Glasgow.[9] He wanted me to succeed Gomme there in 1957, and told me, with the self-confidence of a man long accustomed to getting his own way (he was Clerk of Senate at Glasgow, and everyone was afraid of him) that if I wanted Gomme's chair I could have it. I explained that Dodds would be retiring from the Regius Chair at Oxford in 1960, and that Fraenkel had told me I was virtually certain to succeed him; if I took Glasgow in 1957, I could not decently leave after three years, whereas after five years at St Andrews it would be reasonable for me to return to Oxford. There was a long silence while Fordyce puffed at his pipe, and eventually he said, 'You might not want to, of course.' I agreed that I *might* not want to. It was an idea that had not previously occurred to me, but I didn't tell Fordyce that. Another long pause, until he said, 'What I couldn't stand about St Andrews would be having a colleague who wasn't interested in his subject.' He was thinking of Erskine Wright, the Professor of Humanity at St Andrews, a nice man and sound Latinist, with quite a sharp mind, but whatever academic fire there had been in him had sputtered out during his years as a Mods tutor at Queen's College, Oxford, where he abandoned research in favour of correspondence with former pupils (who thought

---

‖St Mary's College, situated in St Andrews, is the Faculty of Divinity.

[9] C.J. Fordyce (1901–74) was Professor of Humanity at Glasgow 1934–71; see the further reference to him on p. 181, with the article by C. Panayotakis in *DBC*, i 326–7. He had personal knowledge of St Andrews, having been a lecturer in Greek there in 1925–6.

highly of him).[10] Well, yes; but at least I could be sure that he would not actively oppose anything that I wanted to do in my own Department. Fordyce went further: 'The place is hopeless. You may think you can put your shoulder to the wheel to get it out of the rut – but there isn't a wheel to put your shoulder to.' That was all very well, but Erskine Wright sent me (without comment) a set of annual reports of the Carnegie Trust, and I observed that the number of St Andrews graduates who went on with Carnegie grants to the successful completion of doctorates at Oxford, Cambridge and elsewhere was out of all proportion to the small size of the university.[11] This showed that whatever Fordyce or anyone else might think of its academic standards, St Andrews got a lot of very bright students.

In 1954 Audrey and I went up to St Andrews for a couple of days, staying with the Knoxes, and were promised the lease of a roomy, four-storey terrace house, five minutes' walk from my future Department, at a rent which could fairly be called nominal by comparison with what we were paying Balliol for our house in Woodstock Road. It was obvious to us that St Andrews with its combination of long sandy beaches, rocky shores and immediate access to an enchanting countryside, would be an ideal place for the children, and we made up our minds to take the opportunity to move.

I was appointed to the Chair of Greek early in 1955, and we moved in August. It was a lovely late summer, and as we drove across Fife through Milnathort, Auchtermuchty and Cupar the subtle colours of sky, fields and hills delighted us, as they have done ever since. Just for a moment, when the grey cluster of St Andrews came into view, I felt a stab of misgiving, 'My God, what have I done?', but this passed and never returned.

The house should have been ready for us, but it was badly behind schedule; most of the painting had still to be done, and my books stayed in packing-cases while I waited for shelves to be fitted in the study. As the weather was continuously fine, we spent many days on the beach or up in the highlands of Perthshire and Angus. Just before term began I drove up to the north-west on my own and came back stupefied by what I had seen of Glen Garry and Glen Torridon. (This was in late September, and I did not know then what we all learned when we went on a camping holiday in the north-west a couple of years later: that a little earlier in the year the midges in those parts can make life unbearable.) The following September we all stayed for a fortnight in a farmhouse near Grantown-on-Spey. I went up Cairn Gorm from Loch Morlich – long before the car-park, ski-lift and café which now disfigure it were more than a gleam in a developer's eye – and one day Audrey and I tackled Braeriach from the corrie at the top of Glen Einich, leaving the

---

[10]Erskine Wright (1902–86) was Professor of Humanity at St Andrews 1948–62; he had been tutorial fellow in Classics at Queen's College, Oxford, 1928–48.
[11]In 1955 St Andrews had approximately 1,200 students (cf. p. 139), with a further 800 attached to Queen's College, Dundee.

children with the farmer's wife. We had intended to return over Sron na Lairig, but on top of Braeriach, where there is a fearful drop on the south side, the weather turned nasty and I found I had forgotten to bring a compass, so we took advantage of a break in the cloud to head straight down to the Lairig Ghru. Two miles of slow going over boulders and four more miles of slush under relentless rain brought us back to the car in the dark, and after that we never forgot that a day's round walk in the Highlands is not the same sort of thing as in the Lakes. That day in the Cairngorms did not diminish Audrey's appetite for the country, but it restricted her ambitions, because it started up a recurrent backache which was not finally dispelled until she had a hysterectomy in 1967.

During my first term Ian Kidd was my only colleague in the Department but we were joined in January by Douglas Young, who had previously dealt with Latin in Dundee.[12] There were five classes to teach, including the beginners, though Junior and Senior Honours were combined for a two-year cycle of lectures. This meant nineteen lecture-hours a week, largely on texts which previously I had never taught or even read with close attention. I now had to forget about the standard of preparation which I had thought necessary for lecturing at Oxford[13] and adopt a journalistic approach, digesting material quickly with a view to expounding its essentials a few hours later; there were in fact some occasions in that first term when I finished putting together at two in the morning a lecture which I would give at nine the same morning. With Ian's agreement I also restored individual tutorials for students in the Honours classes which Lorimer, despite the friendly, unassuming respect with which he treated his pupils, had eschewed as a degenerate English practice. I also judged it advisable that I should teach the beginners, to remind myself of the difficulties encountered at that stage of teaching Greek; at the same time I joined the beginners' class in Russian, to share the experience of learners coming to grips with a highly inflected language.

Ian Kidd was with me all through my time at St Andrews; not long before I left he was awarded a personal chair in ancient philosophy, and he was my successor in the chair of Greek. I count it my exceptional good fortune to have worked so long with a colleague of absolute integrity and unfailing goodwill. Ian does not fizz with immediate reactions to every topic that comes up (nor do I), and for that reason he has been underrated by some of those who fizz more readily, but what

---

[12]On Ian Kidd (1922-2011), see the British Academy memoir by A.A. Long in *BMF* XIV; on Douglas Young (1913-73), whose nationalist politics saw him serve as Chairman of the Scottish National Party 1942-5, see Ward Briggs, 'Douglas Young, Hellenist', *Studies in Scottish Literature* 47 (2021) 115-34, and the memoir by C. Young and D. Murison in *A Clear Voice: Douglas Young, Poet and Polymath* (Loanhead, 1977) 9-34, though on p. 22 the latter misdates to 1953 (as do other printed sources, including the *ODNB*) Young's move from Dundee to St Andrews, which is correctly placed in the academic year 1955-6 by Dover.

[13]For Dover's hours of lecture preparation in Oxford, see p. 113.

emerges from his deliberation is always formidable, and I was very happy last year (1993) when his edition and discussion of the fragments of Posidonius earned him election to the British Academy. About Douglas Young I always had some reservations. He was certainly magnanimous, because although as a candidate for the chair and a Scot of strongly nationalist sentiment he cannot have failed to feel disappointment at being set aside in favour of an Englishman, in his personal dealings with me he was always friendly, generous and helpful. I enjoyed his charm, wit and flamboyant eccentricities, and there was no denying his expertise in palaeography and codicology; yet it never seemed to me that he really understood the attitudes and presuppositions of an alien culture to the extent required in studying the ancient Greeks.[14] As a textual critic he inherited from one of his Oxford mentors, T.W. Allen, a propensity to defend at any price the readings of the oldest manuscripts,¶ as if textual criticism were a game won by whoever could think of the minimum visual error needing correction in order to restore some kind of sense. For these reasons, much as I liked him as a person, I was rather relieved when he moved to Canada in 1968.

Greek flourished. The idea got around in the schools that St Andrews was a good place in which to study the subject, and by my third year I had a first-year class of over forty. Outstanding students came not only from our own catchment area but from other areas of Scotland. I was particularly pleased to be teaching so many women, because I was aware of something in myself which I called the 'peacock syndrome', a stronger desire to arouse interest in women than in men.[15] I would be surprised if I were the only male teacher of which that is true. Now and again I had recourse to calculated showmanship; in an effort to persuade the first-year class to tackle a Greek unseen by deciding on the grammatical relations between words before they thought about what the words meant, I got them to procure a simple Arabic unseen from the Department of Oriental Languages and translated it (correctly) in their presence by combining my fairly sound knowledge of Arabic grammar with my exiguous Arabic vocabulary.

My expectation that Erskine Wright would raise no objection to anything that I did in the Greek Department proved correct, and, for my part, I made no criticism of the way he handled Latin, although his first-year class ('General Humanity'),

---

¶Allen, embittered by the First World War, hated German scholars. After his death I bought some of his texts and noticed that he had heavily scored out emendations, even the most obvious, if they had been made by Germans, and had underlined the manuscripts' reading in the apparatus criticus, even if it was nonsense. Douglas was incapable of hatred, and transmuted Allen's prejudice from passion into jocularity. [EDS *T.W. Allen (1862–1950) was for most of his career a fellow of Queen's College, Oxford; see the British Academy memoir by N.G. Wilson, PBA 76 (1990) 311–19.*]

[14]For Dover's qualified view of ancient Greek culture as 'alien', see p. 180 with his note there.
[15]For the recollections of one of Dover's female students in this period (as an undergraduate 1956–60), see Elizabeth Craik's chapter in *S&C*.

overflowing with students who were virtually forced by the Arts regulations to take Latin but did not like it and did it very badly, damaged the reputation of the subject. From a loyalty which I now think misplaced (as loyalty commonly is; there are few more potent generators of crime), I supported Erskine against the modern linguists and historians when they wished to alter the regulations. The weakest students, who failed first-year Latin repeatedly, were coached in a group ('the Gamma Club') under a strangely anomalous figure in that Department, Terence Mitford.[16] Terence was an archaeologist of distinction, an expert explorer of Greek sites in Cyprus and Turkey. Despite our difference in political outlook – he gave up *The Times* 'because of its extreme left-wing opinions' – he and I got on very well right from the start. It was largely through the Archaeological Society, of which he was the permanent Secretary, that Audrey and I very quickly came to be friends with many people of the town. This made quite a change from Oxford, because during the years when we lived in Woodstock Road we knew no one, except the people in the next door house either side, who was not in the University. In Queen's Gardens, the short street in which we now lived, we counted as friends seven families who were 'town' and not 'gown'. The characteristically Scottish spirit of courteous and humorous egalitarianism dissolved the glue which at Oxford had kept class boundaries in place.

In the social life of the academic community a surprisingly old-fashioned formality prevailed. At the wedding of a professor's daughter in St Salvator's College Chapel Mick Callan.and I were the only two males not wearing morning dress.[17] I had never imagined that I could have any need of such an outfit; I had not worn it for my own wedding, and at the last two weddings I had attended before that only the principals wore it. Attendance at church in St Andrews was high, and between half-past ten and eleven on Sunday mornings the town was crowded with cars and people on their way to one or other of the six main churches. Agnostic academics observed discretion, and their true views were not widely known.**

**John Wright, Professor of Logic and Metaphysics, was alleged by his obituarist in 1983 to have been sustained by 'his deep Christian faith', but that cannot be true. One day in the 1970s, when he and I had taken part the previous evening in a discussion group weighing the arguments for and against the existence of God, he crossed the street to greet me, said, 'How *can* the Christians go on talking the way they do? It's such *nonsense!*', and laughed gleefully. [EDS *1983 may be a slip for 1982: the* Times' *obituary for John Nicholson Wright (1896–1982), the only one we have seen, does not mention religious faith. For Dover's own agnosticism, see esp. pp. 159, 221.*]

[16]Mitford (1905–78) spent his whole career in the Department of Humanity (Latin) at St Andrews but developed remarkable expertise, as indicated, in the archaeology of Cyprus and Turkey: cf. the references to him on pp. 71 and 159, and see the British Academy memoir by F.G. Maier, *PBA* 67 (1981) 433–42, and Dover's own obituary of him in *The Times* for 25 November 1978, p. 14. A cartoon image of Mitford, drawn by the student Fred Hepburn (see p. 326), appeared as plate 15, after p. 120, in the first edition of *MC*.

[17]On Callan, cf. p. 123.

We soon came to realise that there were things we had missed in Oxford without properly perceiving that we were missing them, and other things which we were now well content to have left behind. Until the last quarter of the nineteenth century every Oxford don, except for some heads of colleges, was a bachelor, and the college was his home. By the nineteen-fifties most dons had real homes. Lunch in the Senior Common Room served a good practical purpose, just as a works canteen does, and I was glad of it. Dinner at High Table was a different matter; it was rather like dining at a club, which is a valuable facility for bachelors, widowers and misogynists, but many of us felt that it would be an odd sort of man who, with a wife and children at home, wanted at the end of a long working day to dine at a club with his colleagues.

Fellows invited guests to dine, from other colleges or from outside the University, and it was assumed, in default of evidence to the contrary (though this was sometimes abundant) that these guests would be interesting and agreeable people. Unfortunately, they were all male, for until the nineteen-seventies there was no men's college which admitted women either as members or as guests.[18] The exclusion of female guests originated in the Victorian belief that any attempt to talk to women on a serious subject was socially objectionable and in any case intellectually impracticable. Conservatives such as Thomas Case, who was President of Corpus from 1904 to 1924 and an assiduous writer of letters to *The Times* on education matters, continued to voice that belief half a century after the first President of Cornell had discovered and proclaimed its falsity.[19] At Balliol no female could eat a meal in Hall or in the Senior Common Room. When Agnes Headlam-Morley was appointed Professor of International Relations in 1948 the professorial fellowship which went with the Chair had to be transferred from Balliol to St Hugh's.[20] We honoured her with a dinner, but not in the Hall, and then saw no more of her. This sort of foolery was tolerated by most fellows' wives with surprising equanimity. They recognised the complex of conventions focused on High Table as an obtrusive archaism which owed its endurance to a failure of the spirit of enquiry, but acknowledged that if one's husband has secured a rewarding and interesting job there is a price to be paid. The odd thing is that there is nothing so very special about conversations at High Table; I cannot recall any which could

---

[18] An addendum to the 1995 reprint states: 'On women guests in men's colleges, I learn now that the first exceptions were earlier than 1970.'
[19] For various aspects of Case's presidency, including his reactionary views on the education of women, see *CCH* 336–65. Cornell University, with whose history Dover will have become familiar during his visits of 1984–9 (see pp. 319–22), had admitted women from its first enrolment of students in 1868.
[20] Agnes Headlam-Morley (1902–86) was already a fellow of St Hugh's College, Oxford, when she was appointed Montague Burton Professor of International Relations in 1948, a position she held till 1970; she was the first woman to hold a professorship in any subject at Oxford: see the *ODNB* article on her by Adam Roberts.

not just as well have been carried on round my own dining-table at home. At St Andrews the nearest thing to a Senior Common Room was the Staff Club, of which not only university staff but also their spouses were members on an equal footing. Families also entertained families as a matter of course, and conversation was not inhibited.

On average – and I must emphasise, on average – neither the staff nor the students at St Andrews were of the high calibre to which I had been accustomed at Oxford. A few of the older staff were deplorably weak, more through inertia and complacency than stupidity, and the weakest students would not have lasted long at Oxford, even if they had managed to get there in the first place. However, it did me good to have some of the presuppositions of Oxford academic life shaken out of me. One of these was the notion that the 'first-class man' and the 'second-class man' are different species of *homo sapiens*, distinguishable by intuition on very short acquaintance. Of course one can tell the difference between the outstanding and the incompetent, but most people do some things well and some things badly, and the teacher's job is to enable them to do more things better. Among Oxford dons mistakes were not readily forgotten or forgiven, and in my own subject the dominance of composition ensured that a linguistic mistake weighed more heavily in the scale than any amount of historical acumen. Edgar Lobel†† was the most sinister offender in this respect; he was a superb papyrologist, well served by a faultless memory and a gift for meticulous accuracy, but his derogatory comments on Fraenkel's *Agamemnon*, designed to cut as deep and painfully as possible – and relished by Denys Page, Hugh Lloyd-Jones and me (I can't pretend I didn't enjoy beautifully expressed malevolence) – sound unimpressive in retrospect.[21] The most dangerous aspect of donnish cattiness‡‡ is that it engenders the notion, often disastrously wrong, that an idea merits no serious consideration if it is put forward by someone who has made a mistake about something else. The notion dies hard. When Gordon Williams's book *Tradition and Originality in Roman Poetry*

---

††It is sometimes assumed that I must have known Lobel well, but in fact I didn't know him at all. I set eyes on him just once, at the far end of the High Table, but would not have recognised him if I had met him again. [EDS *Edgar Lobel (1888–1982), born in Romania but educated in England (including Balliol), spent most of his career in Oxford: see the article by H. Lloyd-Jones in the* ODNB. *Examples of his cutting comments on Fraenkel's* Agamemnon *are quoted by C. Stray in C.S. Kraus and C. Stray, eds,* Classical Commentaries (Oxford, 2015) 44.]

‡‡Zaehner, the only time I encountered him, seemed to me an extreme example. After his death, Hans Schenk, while praising his generosity in bequeathing his books to Wolfson, added, with awe in his voice, 'Of course, he was a *horrible* man! Oh, *horrible!*' [EDS *R.C. Zaehner (1913–74) was Spalding Professor of Eastern Religions and Ethics at Oxford from 1952 to 1974. Hans Schenk (1912–79) was a Prague-born modern historian and a fellow of Wolfson College, Oxford, 1966–79.*]

[21]On Denys Page, see note on p. 73. Hugh Lloyd-Jones (1922–2009, Kt 1989) and Dover first encountered one another when they overlapped as Oxford undergraduates after the war; thereafter, there was a thinly veiled history of rivalry between them, despite their public friendship: see further in the notes on pp. 138 and 217.

appeared in 1968 one don[22] spotted what seemed to her an error of translation in one passage and remarked, 'If he can't even translate the stuff correctly, why should I bother to read what he has to say about it?' Fifteen years earlier I would have sympathised with her, but in 1968 the rhetorical question seemed to me rather silly, for its answer was so obvious: 'Because people who make some mistakes often get other things right.'

My change of heart may have been generated by the more relaxed ambience (and lower standards, if you will) of St Andrews, but what influenced me more was the consideration that in classical scholarship one has just as great a duty to exploit the virtues of others as to correct their errors. And I had a salutary shock when I was joint examiner of a thesis with an Oxford colleague of whom I had once been openly contemptuous.[23] We wrote our reports on the thesis independently, and when I read his I found that his criticisms were all the same as mine and founded on the same evidence and arguments. I thought that if he was a slob who didn't publish enough, maybe I was a slob who published too much.

One morning in March 1960 a letter and a telegram arrived simultaneously; the telegram was from Harvard, inviting me there as a visiting lecturer from the following September to January, and the letter was from the Prime Minister (Harold Macmillan), telling me that he wished to recommend me to the Queen for appointment to the Regius Chair of Greek at Oxford. The invitation to Harvard was irresistible; I had only to find a benevolent colleague to stand in for me as Dean of Arts for four months (and Tony Woozley agreed to do so).[24] The offer of the Regius Chair at Oxford was the fulfilment of the highest professional ambition that I had ever entertained. When I came to St Andrews five years earlier the possibility of declining the offer would have seemed to me incredible; and yet, for academic and personal reasons, I did decline it. I told the Prime Minister the chief academic reason: my dissatisfaction with the structure of Classics at Oxford and my view that its reform was unlikely in the foreseeable future.[25] The second choice of the Prime Minister's advisers was, inevitably,[26] Hugh Lloyd-Jones, who is not

---

[22]Dover confirmed orally that this was Margaret Hubbard (1924–2011), tutorial fellow of St Anne's College, Oxford, 1957–86. For Dover's further thoughts on the implications of linguistic errors, cf. p. 323.

[23]Dover SN identifies him as R.W.B. ('Reggie') Burton, tutorial fellow in Classics at Oriel College, Oxford, 1932–76.

[24]A.D. Woozley was Professor of Moral Philosophy at St Andrews 1954–66; for Dover's Deanship in 1960-3, see pp. 146–50.

[25]Cf. the earlier reference to this issue on p. 128.

[26]'When I declined the offer of the Regius Chair I told the Prime Minister's secretary I recommended Spencer Barrett for the job. Bowra learned that Barrett had come into the running, "recommended from a very respectable source", and worked on the secretary to rule him out. Hugh professed (to me) that he assumed Fraenkel was the "respectable source", and I have never known whether he knew that it was I.' (Dover SN) Lloyd-Jones held the Regius chair 1960–89.

only a scholar of formidable talent but proved far more energetic than Dodds had been (and more, I think, than I would have been) in organising graduate seminars on newly discovered texts and bringing foreign scholars to Oxford. Years before, I had bet Hugh that he would be the next Regius Professor and he had bet me that I would be. Now that one of us had been invited and the other appointed, neither of us thought it appropriate to recall the bet. Confidentiality at Oxford is seldom respected, and my rejection of the Chair was immediately known. Dodds implored me to reconsider, on the grounds that my perception of what was wrong with Oxford was what the Faculty needed.[27] Fraenkel, who always underrated Hugh, said sadly that I might have told my friends that I wasn't going to come; but, of course, I couldn't tell them until I knew my own mind, and I didn't finally make up my mind before the invitation came. Later in the year I picked up a rumour (circulating, I gather, in the University Press) that my judgement had been impaired by a severe nervous breakdown. At Harvard, Ved Mehta[28] told me he understood that I had of course wanted to return to Oxford but Audrey had refused; this hurt me, because it was so unjust to her. Evidently people at Oxford could not take seriously the possibility that anyone would rather be somewhere else. Perhaps I contributed to setting a fashion; in the course of 1993 three professors at St Andrews declined invitations to chairs at Oxford.

---

[27] Although Dodds' letter seems not to survive, Dover's reply (of 24 March 1960) does (in the Bodleian's Dodds archive): it includes the statement 'Greek studies have a higher claim on me than any one university, and I am bound to say that I can't agree with you on the decisive importance of Oxford for the future of Greek'. Dover also calls his own recommendation of Barrett 'treacherous' but remarks that 'Barrett's complete integrity as a scholar would be a better thing for Oxford than Lloyd-Jones's philotimia [i.e., competitiveness – Eds]'.

[28] Dover's encounter with Ved Mehta (1934–2021), later to become a highly successful writer, will not have been accidental. The two had communicated in 1955 when Mehta, a blind Indian-born student, wrote to Balliol enquiring about admission; Dover replied in his capacity as Senior Tutor and was later visited by Mehta's father: Ved Mehta, *Up at Oxford* (London, 1993) 4–5; the book recounts in detail his subsequent experiences as a Balliol history undergraduate 1956–9. In 1960–1 Mehta was studying at Harvard for a (subsequently abandoned) PhD.

12 PEOPLE AND POWER 1955–1966

Never ascribe to an opponent motives meaner than your own.

J.M. BARRIE[1]

No academic building had been put up in St Andrews since 1932, when the student population was less than 600. Now it was nearly 1,200, and the shortage of space was very severe. Our thoughts turned to new buildings. The Town Council of St Andrews enjoyed the privilege of being its own Planning Authority, responsible directly to the Secretary of State for Scotland, and in 1950 it engaged Thomas Sharp as its consultant. It happened that in South Street there was a row of splendid town houses adjoining the southern block of University buildings and divided from them only by a narrow thoroughfare called West Burn Lane. These houses had gardens nearly two hundred yards long, known as the Long Riggs. Sharp recommended that a large part of the gardens should be zoned for University development. The Town Council did not like this advice, and did not take it, objecting that the University had quite enough land of its own already. That objection was valid (though only just) if one added up all the bits and pieces that could be built over in and around the northern block, and overwhelmingly valid if one took into account all the land in University ownership within a mile and a half southwards and westwards from the West Port at the end of South Street. The University, however, long accustomed to all the conveniences of concentration, did not want to become a 'split site' university, even if that was the only way to avoid spoiling the amenity of the northern block. West Burn Lane would form a continuum with the southern block; and if Physics and Chemistry and Biochemistry were put there, they would not only join with the existing biological and medical

---

[1] The epigraph is from the Rectorial address, 'Courage', delivered to St Andrews students by Barrie on 3 May 1922; Dover is likely to have read a number of such rectorial addresses after he moved to St Andrews. For the position of Rector in Scottish universities, see p. 232.

buildings to form a single science precinct but also vacate in the northern block buildings into which Arts could expand.

The University commissioned Sir William Holford and Partners to draw up the main lines of a plan for the future development of the University as a whole. Their report arrived in March 1956 and was very strongly in favour of West Burn Lane. The Secretary of State had already (January 1956) commanded the Town Council to alter its development plan, within three months, in a way which would provide the University with land adequate for foreseeable requirements, in the central part of the Burgh and 'in reasonable proximity to the existing buildings of the University'. The Town Council protested, a public enquiry was set up, and in the light of its findings the Secretary of State ruled in favour of the University. The objectors, however, did not give up. The Town Council itself was fiercely divided, and after deciding on a Compulsory Purchase Order in February 1958 it rescinded the Order in May. There was then a second public enquiry, in order to decide whether the circumstances justified the Secretary of State in overruling the Town Council. This was held by J.O.M. Hunter at the end of September 1958, and it went against the University.

The cosy relationship between town and gown which had impressed us in St Andrews was deeply eroded by the West Burn Lane affair. Apart from people of strongly Conservative sentiment, to whom compulsory purchase was Stalinism, there was much resentment at the upsetting of what had come to be regarded as a comfortable 'balance' between town and gown. It was said that the University was 'eating the heart out of the town', to which Knox retorted that the University was putting heart into it. Most of the retailers and skilled tradesmen agreed with him. Once upon a time well-to-do people had come to St Andrews for long holidays, bringing their retainers with them (my mother-in-law first saw St Andrews as a nanny/governess/companion in the Boothby family), but now golfers drove in for the day and away in the evening. Many hotels came on the market, and the University was the only bidder for them; its critics imagined that it had a bottomless purse, but in fact it was not allowed by the UGC (University Grants Committee) to pay above the price set by the district valuer.

From the beginning there were three deadly weaknesses in our case. One was that the Holford report in March 1956 had recommended us to keep in mind, as a 'second reserve', Queen's Gardens, a street of some twenty houses, with their front gardens on the opposite side of the road, which ran from the Town Hall in South Street down the western[2] side of the southern University block. This recommendation had not been concealed from the Town Council (whose reaction to it was extremely unfriendly), and the University had quite explicitly forsworn it in May, but nothing could remove from the minds of our adversaries the suspicion

---

[2] In the first edition, Dover wrongly wrote 'eastern'.

that one day, pleading 'changed circumstances', we would demand Queen's Gardens after all, and that there must be an item somewhere in Court minutes which would give the game away. For some legal reason that I do not understand, our counsel (Graham Guest) resisted the request that the minutes should be made available to the objectors, and the Commissioner agreed with him. I have now read all the minutes, and can find nothing which justifies the objectors' suspicions.

The second weakness was a mistrust of Knox arising from a conversation he was alleged to have had with a certain Dr McKerrow, who owned one of the South Street houses. Dr McKerrow built a house on his Long Rigg (to the embarrassment of the planners and conservationists brought in by the objectors to give evidence), intending to live in it on retirement and leave his son to carry on the practice from the main house. He asserted that in July 1954 Knox had told him in conversation at a party that the University was not interested in West Burn Lane. Knox could not recall that, but claimed that in March 1955 he had told McKerrow that the University *was* interested. McKerrow could not recall *that* conversation. In the light of my own experiences, I find it easy to forgive everyone concerned for not remembering conversations, but the disagreement started us round the parish pump on the wrong foot.

The third weakness in our case was a heavy incubus: widespread knowledge of the fact that neither John Read, the Professor of Chemistry, nor Jack Allen, the Professor of Physics, was really satisfied that West Burn Lane would be an adequate site for more than twenty years. Nor was Holford, and he had told us so; but the Court had persuaded itself that there would never be, must never be, more than 1,700 students in St Andrews, although the Senate, in discussing a total of 1,700 as desirable, had not expressed itself so uncompromisingly. Neither Read nor Allen was called on to give evidence at either Enquiry. From a legalistic standpoint, this was probably correct, for the Court was the body which took decisions on policy, and it is never for the Professor of X to decide how large Department X should be; but that was not appreciated by the public. The Silence of the Professors[3] was ominously emphasised in a House of Lords debate in December 1957. John Read let that pass; finding himself in a minority, he had gone back on the estimate he had made early in 1955 of the space needed for Chemistry. Jack Allen, however, wrote to the *Scotsman* to clarify his position, which was simply that in the second half of the twentieth century it seemed short-sighted to plan a science precinct on so limited a site. That was exactly the point which many of the objectors made repeatedly, and the profession of some of them that they were thinking only of the

---

[3] In an addendum to the first edition, regarding 'the silence of the Professors', Dover said that the University's counsel deliberately misled the enquiry in a way which 'had an enduring effect on my attitude to lawyers'.

interests of the University was sincere, even though there were others who readily used any argument to save their friends' gardens from compulsory purchase. The *Glasgow Herald* picked up a rumour that there were people in the University who favoured West Burn Lane precisely because it would limit expansion in science. There was a time, before the *Glasgow Herald* brought it half into the open, when I entertained an intuitive suspicion that Knox himself saw the project in that light.*

In the summer of 1958 the University took one step which further alienated public opinion. In a letter authorised by the committee which the Court had set up to deal with planning matters between the monthly Court meetings, Knox told the Town Council that since the University would not countenance a peripheral site and our advisers regarded all other central sites as unsuitable, 'If the development projected for the West Burn Lane site cannot take place there, it cannot take place in St Andrews at all.' It was a very Knoxian letter, in which he said exactly what he meant (that the capital grant for 1960–3 could not be spent in St Andrews) without stopping to reflect on what other people would think it meant, which was 'If the University doesn't get West Burn Lane, there will never be any expansion of science at St Andrews.' The misunderstanding was cleared up, but not before resentment at what was called an 'ultimatum' and widely believed to be designed to frighten the Town Council was firmly consolidated.

One way and another, it did not surprise me that the outcome of the Hunter Enquiry was unfavourable to the University.

Although we were advised by counsel not to give up, realism prevailed. None of us wanted a continuing fight in which we would be armed only with the letter of the law against adversaries whose armoury was stocked with all the weapons which cross-examination of witnesses at both enquiries had provided. Serious moral damage had been done to the University by Hunter's observation on the May 'ultimatum': 'It seems inconceivable to me that the University Court would make such an announcement unless the Grants Committee had made their position very plain at an earlier stage.' Sir Keith Murray, Chairman of the UGC, had testified to the contrary, but Hunter observed, 'I am afraid that this evidence did not impress me favourably', and he returned to this theme towards the end of the report: 'If these extreme statements had not been made it would have been much

---

*Knox was regarded by the UGC as an 'academic dinosaur', and some of his views were undeniably primitive. He derided social history on the grounds that 'squalor is the same in all ages'. I learn from Fay Weldon, who was a student of his, that he professed to regard women as incapable of sustained rationality, and I can testify that he expressed regret when a female candidate for a lectureship was obviously better than the male candidates. Still, he agreed that she *was* better, and put no obstacle in the way of her appointment; and I had several occasions, when matters of academic standards were at issue, to welcome his ability to deflate pretentiousness with a question of deadly simplicity. [EDS *The writer Fay Weldon (1931–) read economics and psychology at St Andrews 1949–52; her recollections of Knox's gross sexism are recorded in* Auto da Fay *(London, 2002) 218.*]

easier to place full reliance on the evidence given by Sir Keith Murray and Principal Knox.' This was a silky way of accusing both Murray and Knox of being (to use a disgusting expression recently popularised)[4] 'economical with the truth' under oath. It delighted Knox's enemies in the town. 'He'll go to Hell, of course,' said Rose complacently, adjusting his eschatology to the requirements of polemic. Yet the charge against Murray was untrue. I happened to know that, because a nephew of his, one of my students, had told me before the Hunter Enquiry that his uncle, so far from conniving at the May ultimatum, had been taken aback by it. I infer from Murray's letter to Knox on 22 May, containing the first hint that the money for science expansion in 1960–3 might be allocated to Dundee (the dread name of Dundee was not mentioned, but 're-shaping the expansion of the programme of the University as a whole' could hardly mean anything else), that the UGC already accepted our view that we should not build on a peripheral site and that no central site except West Burn Lane was adequate. That was certainly the UGC's view at its meeting on 12 June, and Murray's subsequent letter to Knox, on 13 June, spelled out the consequences plainly: the money would go to Dundee unless we could be sure of West Burn Lane, and the decision could not be delayed beyond 'later in the summer'. That wasn't very helpful, because the Hunter Enquiry obviously could not complete its work and report before the beginning of winter. Knox told the Enquiry that Murray's letter of 22 May was 'a staggering blow', and the Commissioner was not the only person to raise his eyebrows at that. I did, for one, because we had already tried the patience of the UGC considerably, at a time when Dundee could have got on with the job straight away. Moreover, I had learned from John Wright that Knox himself had envisaged in private conversation the allocation of the money to Dundee. It is fair to remember that in his testimony Knox was speaking of the Court as a whole, not just of himself. I can understand, though, why the Commissioner felt uneasy. The harsh treatment of Murray's evidence is a different matter, and there was a lesson in it for historians. Something may seem 'inconceivable' to a very experienced and intelligent judge, and yet there may be someone somewhere who knows – as I knew in this case, through a chance conversation with Murray's nephew – that so far from being inconceivable, it was the plain truth.†

Queen's College rejoiced, and depression enfolded St Salvator's. We had to consider now building on all the usable bits of land in the northern block. Holford worked out for us what could be done, but made it plain that the actual doing of it would be so contrary to his own principles that we would have to employ someone

---

†I am glad to say that Lord Murray was able to read my draft of this chapter a few months before his death in 1993.

[4] It was 'popularised', and much ridiculed, in 1986 when the UK cabinet secretary Sir Robert Armstrong used it at the 'Spycatcher' trial in Australia as an evasive euphemism for lying.

else. Since the 1960–3 buildings grant was going to Dundee, we had time to think about what could be done in St Andrews in 1964 and after. We didn't get very far; but at the very end of 1959 the prospects were suddenly, unexpectedly and radically transformed. In a friendly conversation with John Wright in the bar of the Royal and Ancient,[5] Alexander Cheape, the biggest individual landowner in the town, impulsively agreed to sell us a tract of 67 acres of agricultural land (the North Haugh) on the western edge of town. It was big enough to take Mathematics, Physics and Chemistry, at least two major student residences, and such other buildings as academic developments then unforeseen might require. Hardly a 'central' site, because its eastern edge is the best part of a kilometre by road and path from the northern block of the University; but as universities go, that is not bad, and we simply had to adjust our conceptions of centrality and peripherality. All kinds of thing could now go ahead; old science accommodation could be taken over by Arts, and a new Arts building[6] could go up on one central site (Union Street) which we had not dared to earmark for Arts until the location of new science buildings could be settled. One other conceptual adjustment had to be made, and most of us made it effortlessly and painlessly: the notion that St Andrews could not possibly go beyond the limit of 1,700 students without irreparable damage to the ethos of the University was slain by a letter from the UGC (January 1960) in which it was admitted that the number of sixth-form pupils aiming at university entry had increased beyond the Committee's expectations. Now, therefore, we were told that we should aim at 2,000 at the very least, preferably 2,300, or even 2,500. Those were the days when money was being lavished on the universities, and we could be pretty sure of getting grants both for the erection of new buildings and for the purchase of buildings and land offered to us at valuer's prices.

Although Lord Robbins' report on the expansion of university education in Britain was not published until 1963, the census data which made the question urgent were known before then, and it was not hard to foresee that the UGC, which in 1957 had accepted 1,700 as the limit for St Andrews, would by 1967 be regarding 2,700 as an unhelpfully low figure. The Robbins report provoked some disturbingly mindless criticisms. 'More means worse' is an uninteresting truism if it is simply saying that the average ability of a thousand applicants is likely to be lower than the average ability of the best hundred among them; we didn't need to be told that. If the slogan means that the abilities of the best hundred are diminished by the presence of the next best nine hundred, it is false. Or maybe the idea was that

---

[5]The Royal and Ancient Golf Club of St Andrews.
[6]The Buchanan Building, named after the great Renaissance humanist George Buchanan (1506–82, a St Andrews student and later the Principal of St Leonard's College), was completed in 1964 to house the university's Modern Languages.

academics ought not to be expected to teach any but the brightest and best prepared, although not a few dim and lazy young men had been taught uncomplainingly by Oxford and Cambridge dons between the Wars. Some dons, I suppose, were unacquainted with the joy of promoting intellectual development in students who have serious intentions but a low starting-point; or bad students made a deeper impression on them than good; or they dismissed as insoluble the problem of teaching together students who are very unequally prepared for a course. Elements of class conflict were conspicuous in public and private debate. I was asked by Lady Victoria Wemyss,[7] 'But if everyone goes to a university, who's going to sweep the roads?', a question of the same rhetorical mould as cries which greeted Lloyd George's Insurance Act, 'I shall spend all my time licking stamps!'[8] If I had had wider experience of America at that time I might have replied that there was no good reason why a graduate should not, for some of hrs life at least, sweep roads. The truth was that because of the very high birth-rate in the years immediately after the War the percentage of school-leavers admitted to university in the mid-1960s would fall extraordinarily unless a great many more university places were created. That fact alone sufficed to justify Robbins' recommendations. Moreover, even if we could keep a constant percentage, it was still lower than was acceptable in most other civilised countries, even making allowance for our much higher ratio of completed to uncompleted courses. We did not know, no one knew, when 'the bottom of the barrel' would be reached, but my acquaintance with the men I had commanded during the War left me in no doubt at all that there was plenty left in the top half of the barrel, and I have yet to be persuaded that anyone is any the worse for increased knowledge, understanding and skill.

The implementation of Robbins was in many ways misdirected and extravagant. I don't think it was only my membership of a small university which persuaded me that by far the quickest and most efficient way of increasing university places was to start by bringing all universities which had less than 5,000 students up to the 5,000 level. Many localities in Britain treated possession of a university of their very own as a matter of prestige and status. In Scotland four towns competed jealously, the partisans of each site organising campaigns, and Stirling incurred some odium by winning.[9] None of that had much to do with education.

---

[7] 1890–1994, for many years a lady-in-waiting to Queen Elizabeth the Queen Mother: her home at Wemyss was not far from St Andrews and during the 1960s she served on the board of governors of St Leonards [sic] School, St Andrews; it may have been in this last context that Dover encountered her, since he was a governor himself for some years.
[8] The Insurance Act of 1911, when Lloyd George was Chancellor of the Exchequer, set up an early form of social security system (relating to health and unemployment) for the poor; it was ridiculed by some for requiring employers to paste stamps into their records for each of their employees.
[9] Stirling University was founded by Royal Charter in 1967.

During my first year at St Andrews I was hardly more than a spectator of events which had to do with planning, except that as the holder of an established chair I was a permanent voting member of the Senate. In 1956, however, I was appointed to St Salvator's College Council, and soon found myself in the chair of its Committee on New Residences, whose first job was to plan for the doubling in size of University Hall. In that role I went to look at new residences in Hull, Leicester, Newcastle and Southampton, accumulated ideas about what could be done within the stringent cost limits imposed by the UGC, and stored in my mind for future exploitation Aberdeen's experiment (it seemed at that time impossibly daring for St Andrews) in accommodating males and females in the same residence. Throughout the building on the University Hall site I was on the best of terms with the architect, Sinclair Gauldie, and when I met him thirty years later he pleased me immensely by introducing me to a friend as 'the best chairman I've ever known'. I'm sorry he has not had better fortune in his encounters with committees, but his words confirmed my feeling that in meeting, with every appearance of patience and good humour, sometimes for hours on end, objections (on occasion waspish) from members of the College Council I was being put through a much more advanced course in chairmanship than at any time in my life up to then. In 1963, when we were authorised to put up a new residence on the North Haugh (Andrew Melville Hall), to be shared by students of both sexes, I was made a member of the planning committee, under Lionel Butler's chairmanship. Urged by the students not to be parochial but to look for a big name and ensure that we got a residence which would be a notable work of art, we picked James Stirling. He was a designer of very large building-like objects which elicited admiring cries from those (including me) who did not have to work in them and cries of another kind from those who did. Our experience was not happy; there were exasperating differences of opinion between Stirling's quantity surveyor and the UGC's, and after Andrew Melville Hall was occupied matters disputed between architect, contractor and University dragged on for some years.[10]

In 1959 I was elected Dean by the Faculty of Arts, and I held that office from the beginning of 1960 to the end of 1963. This was a taste of power, because although I could not overrule a majority vote of the Faculty on any academic question, the application of regulations to individual cases was often up to me. I discovered that while I had the power to make students cry, I also had the power to stop them crying, and it gave me much pleasure to manipulate or circumvent regulations in order to rescue people from predicaments not altogether of their own making. Moreover, I was solely responsible for the selection of candidates for admission to

---

[10]Andrew Melville Hall, built 1964–8, has nonetheless continued to attract interest from aficionados of the renowned architect James Stirling (1926–92) and the so-called New Brutalist style.

the Arts Faculty, both in St Andrews and in Dundee; the buck, in the form of despairing or menacing parents, stopped in my office.[11] Fortunately I inherited from my predecessor a secretary, Rhoda Cleghorn, who combined efficiency, discretion and humanity to a degree unequalled among secretaries in my experience up to now (when Classics was allowed a secretary in 1964, she moved to Classics, I am glad to say).

The admissions procedure was crude, perfunctory and arbitrary; selection depended on the candidate's examination record at school and the head teacher's testimonial, which in the case of some Scottish schools was so laconic as to be useless. Interviews, except in the case of candidates for the Scholarship and Bursary examination, were out of the question on grounds of time alone, because my duties as Dean entitled me to no remission of my duties as Professor of Greek. Interviewing by members of Departments was not judged to be useful, because in Scotland an applicant is admitted to a Faculty, not to a Department. This was, and still is, one of the great strengths of the Scottish universities. Except in the main languages, sciences and mathematics, first-year courses do not have admission requirements, and I discovered that between the time of their admission in December or January and their arrival the following October thirty per cent of the students in the Faculty of Arts had changed their minds about their proposed subjects of study. Further changes of mind came in the first or second year in consequence of their sampling of courses, and in the year for which I went through the records there was not one student in the Honours Classes in philosophy or economics who had originally intended to study that subject. In the English universities at that time departmental quotas made this healthy elasticity impossible. They evidently thought that Departments had a right to know in advance how many students they would have to teach in a year's time. We had no such right, and did not ask for it.

My most intractable problem as Dean was created by the very strong tendency in Scottish schools to steer boys into science and girls into languages. If we wanted a balance of the sexes in Arts, we could not get it except by turning away Scottish girls of high achievement in favour of English boys of the same calibre or Scottish boys of lower. This became a political issue. St Andrews had for many years attracted English applicants because it had student residences; some parents of English boys thought that for that reason it was the next best thing after Oxford and Cambridge, and many parents of English girls thought that their daughters were less likely to be seduced in a residence than in lodgings. In consequence, the University was often derided elsewhere in Scotland as 'an English university'. A few brassy southern accents gave our Scottish students the impression that the Faculty

---

[11] This system has since changed: individual departments now have their own admissions officers with responsibility for the selection of applicants; but it remains the case, as the next paragraph states, that students are technically admitted to a faculty, not to a department.

of Arts was overrun by English girls, although in fact we had as high a percentage of women of Scottish parentage or education (or both) as the Faculty of Arts in Edinburgh. If our critics had had nothing in their armoury except prejudice and misapprehension, we could have weathered that and admitted students solely on the strength of their academic achievement, regardless of sex or nationality, which is what many voices on College Council and in the Senate urged me to do. But there was more to it than that. Scottish applicants normally left school after spending one year on the Higher Scottish Certificate of Education in five subjects, but English applicants after two years on three A-levels. A Scottish applicant therefore had little chance of admission to an English university, whereas an English applicant turned down by St Andrews still had plenty of other chances. It seemed to me that on those grounds we had an obligation to the Scots, and I slanted my admissions policy in their favour, rejecting only those whose record suggested to me that they would have difficulty in surviving the first year, and making up the shortfall with the best English applicants I could get. So Arts remained predominantly female and Science predominantly male. In one respect, though, all Faculties underwent a gradual process of anglicisation. An ever-increasing proportion of students opted for the four-year Honours course, not resting content with the three-year Ordinary degree which had long been a distinctive feature of the Scottish system. They could not be kept out of Honours except by raising the standard of examination at the end of Special (second-year) courses, and there was no enthusiasm for that; on the contrary, Departments wanted bigger Honours classes, and those which had one-year Honours courses wanted to enlarge them to two-year courses. Breadth was everywhere sacrificed to depth, a development not invariably advantageous to minority subjects. Scottish degrees began to look more like English degrees, and eventually graduation with an Ordinary degree came to mean much what a Pass degree (where it still exists) means in England.[12]

It did not take me long to discover that among the professors in the Faculty of Arts there were three who should not have been there. One was J.W. Nisbet (Political Economy), a cheerful rogue comically unaware of his own transparency, and a second was Alec Falconer (English), more devious and malevolent.[13] There was also the mulish A.M. Honeyman, who was Professor of Hebrew and Oriental Languages in the Faculty of Divinity and responsible for Hebrew and Arabic in Arts; having lost interest in Hebrew, he devoted his time to teaching Arabic and

---

[12]The Ordinary degree in St Andrews is now called the General degree, though some other Scottish universities retain the term 'Ordinary'.
[13]James Wilkie Nisbet (1903–74) was Professor of Political Economy 1947–70, Alexander Frederick Falconer (1908–87) was Berry Professor of English 1955–78.

devising elaborate excuses for not doing the rest of the job he was paid to do.[14] I tried, with the Dean of Divinity, to sort him out, in the interests of such Arts students as might wish to learn Hebrew, but could not defend him when the Court demoted him from Professor to Research Lecturer.

I first came up against Nisbet when he thought he could secure the compliance of a new, innocent Dean in the setting up of a 'Single Honours' course in Political Economy (i.e. Economics), which hitherto could be taken for Honours only in conjunction with another subject. This proposal was quite contrary to the guidelines laid down by the 1951 Commission for the different development of Dundee and St Andrews, but he assured me that Archie Campbell, the Professor of Economics in Dundee, had no objection. This assurance was wholly untrue, and Campbell, whom I greatly liked and respected, blew up when he heard about it. Nisbet's proposal was firmly stopped by Knox, invoking the Commission. Later that summer all the lecturers in Nisbet's Department presented themselves in my office and told me that Nisbet had divulged to his students the questions set by the external examiner for the Honours examination in May. Apparently he had given them advice on the topics which they should revise carefully, and one student, more mature morally than the others, became suspicious and showed the list of topics to one of his lecturers. The lecturer immediately recognised the external examiner's questions – even the order was the same – and now he and his colleagues wanted to know, what was I going to do about it? I told them that they must inform the external examiner, tell Nisbet they had done so, and give me the student's notes, with the student's own affidavit about the occasion on which they had been taken. All this was done, and I then wrote to Nisbet to tell him my part in the business and express my feelings about it. He blustered elaborately, but was not in a position to deny the facts. I hope he never tried the same trick again, which would have devalued a St Andrews degree in Political Economy considerably if it became known outside the university.

My breach with Falconer was more serious. In 1960 Norton Smith was appointed as a lecturer in English. At the end of his probationary year Falconer recommended that the appointment should not be confirmed, and this was such an unusual event that an ad hoc committee, consisting of Knox, me, Falconer, John Wright (Logic and Metaphysics) and Carr (German, ex-Dean), was formed to interview Norton Smith. The interview left me uneasy, because there was no charge either of neglect of duty or of inadequate scholarship; the trouble seemed to be that his severe assessments of his students' performance upset their morale – and upset Falconer, whose own

---

[14]Alexander Mackie Honeyman (1907–88) was Professor of Hebrew and Oriental Languages 1936–67; his *Times* obituary, 29 August 1988, p. 12, stated that he resigned his post 'because his interpretation of his professorial duties varied from that of the university'. There is no record in the St Andrews university *Calendar* of the demotion mentioned by Dover: Honeyman's resignation presumably forestalled it.

assessments were much more favourable. I would have hoped that the views of someone who had come fresh from teaching first-year undergraduates at Oxford might be of some interest to the Department, even if they were sometimes expressed rather brashly, but apparently not. Falconer implied that Oakden, a senior lecturer in the Department, had complained; and when Norton Smith said, 'I wasn't aware that Dr Oakden had complained about me', Falconer replied, 'People sometimes write letters'. True, they do; but was it an answer? It fooled me at the time. We decided not to confirm Norton Smith's appointment, on the grounds that in a small department (and all departments at St Andrews were small) it just doesn't do to have one member at odds with the rest; and at that time a lecturer's contract made him totally subordinate to the professor. As we came away from the interview, Carr said with a faint smile, 'Falconer will never get away with this again.' That was all very well, but in the meantime Norton Smith had lost his job. In the course of the next few days I learned that he had approached the Association of University Teachers for help in fighting his case; and, no less important, Oakden and another lecturer in the English Department, Tony Ladd, told me that neither of them had written any letter of complaint about Norton Smith and neither of them thought that termination of his employment was justified. I took these facts to Knox, and the University Court gave Norton Smith a second probationary year. That would not have been a particularly happy year for him, and fortunately he was able, with Knox's backing, to get a lectureship at Hull straight away (some years later he became Professor of English at Dundee, an appointment which cannot have given Falconer any pleasure). After the matter was settled, I wrote to Falconer to tell him what part I had taken in it, and why. He was enraged, and demanded of Knox that I should be censured by the University Court. Finding that Knox, who remembered 'People sometimes write letters' as well as I did, was unsympathetic, he had recourse to law, and at the end of the summer I received a menacing three-page letter from his solicitor. My own solicitor made light of this, on the grounds that since I had not communicated the content of my letter to any third party I could not be sued for libel. Having already consulted the relevant law books, I knew that he was wrong, for under Scots law (at that time, though not now) the recipient of a letter could sue for injury to his feelings, but I thought it would be polite to let him discover that for himself, as indeed he did before I next saw him. Although I could be sure of winning, having the other members of the committee as witnesses, I was extremely unwilling to risk heavy expenditure on legal fees, and the University would suffer from the publicity given to litigation between two of its professors. To be on the safe side, therefore, I apologised for my letter with an adequate degree of grovelling, and there was no further threat of litigation, but Falconer never spoke to me again and naturally did not attend any further Faculty meetings while I was Dean.

One predictable consequence of the Robbins Report was that Queen's College turned into the University of Dundee. This was a right decision, because the mere holding of alternate Court and Senate meetings in Dundee and St Andrews was nothing like enough to unify two half-universities fifteen miles apart; Durham and Newcastle had discovered that already. The issue was settled by 1964 and took effect in the autumn of 1967. Knox, who had worked very hard, faithful to the spirit of the 1951 Commission, to treat the two halves of the University with impartiality – and had inevitably been regarded by some people in St Andrews as favouring Dundee – decided that it would be appropriate for him to retire then. An informal gathering of St Andrews professors met several times to draw up a short list of names which we might submit to the Secretary of State (the University did not at that time have what it has now, the right to elect its own Principal) but none of them was approved – or maybe none of them wanted the job. One day in the Easter Vacation of 1966 I happened to be in North Street and saw Knox come out of College Gate, heading for University House, in the company of an unmistakable figure, Steven Watson. It is the only time I have ever been first in St Andrews with a piece of gossip, and it was true gossip at that. Knox, I believe, did not approve of his successor; at any rate, he made no reference to him, even though Steven was in the audience, in his address to the last graduation over which he presided. Perhaps Steven's appearances on television in *That Was The Week That Was*, which in the eyes of many of us, including me, did him credit, seemed to Knox incompatible with the dignity of high office.[15]

---

[15]John Steven Watson (1916–86), an English historian who had taught at Christ Church, Oxford, 1945–66, served as Principal of St Andrews 1966–86. *That Was the Week That Was* was a BBC TV programme of topical satire, featuring a variety of guests, which ran for two series in 1962–3.

13 MIND AND BODY 1958–

Life is what happens to you when you're busy making other plans.
JOHN LENNON[1]

One Sunday morning in November 1958 Audrey called me down from the study and asked me if I could find a chemist's shop (they took it in turns to open for emergencies on Sunday) where I could buy a clinical thermometer, because she 'felt extremely odd' and thought she might have a high temperature. I got one all right, and her temperature was a bit high, but not monstrously so. She took to her bed, and was all right after a few days. It seemed to be a typical attack of flu, but at the back of my mind her uncharacteristic reaction troubled me; I would have expected her to say, 'I think I'm getting flu, so I'd better go to bed', and to wait until next day for the thermometer. Early in December I had to drive down to England to pick up from Alison Duke at Girton the files and card-indexes which Sophie Trenkner, who died the previous winter, had compiled with a view to writing a history of early Greek prose style.[2] It was bitter weather, and my Jowett Bradford was unheated. On the second day of my journey back (I stayed the night with my parents at Algarkirk) the north-east of England was gripped by freezing fog. Between Sleaford and Lincoln I bought a pint of anti-freeze, and after that stopped every few miles to slosh it over my windscreen when a sudden icing-over made it impossible to peer through the fog. At Selby I detected a faint but glorious hint of a blue smile in the sky, and by York I was clear of the fog. I stayed that night with

---

[1] From his song 'Beautiful Boy (Darling Boy)' (with 'while' for 'when').
[2] Dover took possession of the card-indexes compiled by Sophie (Zofia) Trenkner (1908–58), a Polish classical scholar with a doctorate from Brussels who had spent periods working in both Cambridge (Girton College) and Oxford; he had at one time considered collaborating with her. When he came to start work in the late 1980s on his own book *The Evolution of Greek Prose Style* (1997), he could no longer locate the card-indexes, which remain lost: some idea of their content was given by D. Fehling, 'Nachlass Sophie Trenkner', *Gnomon* 44 (1972) 320.

Grigor McClelland at Gateshead, where a meal and good company restored my confidence for what proved in fact to be a trouble-free journey home next day. Yet I could not shake off a feeling that those long and dangerous hours between Algarkirk and York had somehow drained me of an energy *which would never be replaced*. No doubt this was biologically nonsensical, but if one subsumes the psychosomatic under the biological it possibly makes better sense.

I had a dose of flu later that month, which cleared up before Christmas, but then a second dose, together with Alan, in January. Alan didn't seem to recover properly; all through that term he had recurrent spells of fever, looked a pale bluish colour, and spent a lot of time in bed, which did wonders for his progress in reading. Eventually a specialist prescribed phenobarbitone, which had the effect, more amusing than alarming, of relaxing some of his social inhibitions, and at the same time quickly restored him to vigorous health. I was less fortunate. The fourth day of my flu was the day on which St Salvator's College Council was due to take its final decision on a long list of issues in the building of the new wing of University Hall.[3] As chairman of the project committee I could not possibly miss that meeting, no other date for a whole month was practicable for the architect, and that much delay in the building stage would mean a year's delay in the opening, as it makes no sense to open a new student residence at any time other than the start of an academic year. I went to the meeting, felt progressively worse for the next three months – no fever, but weakness in the arms and legs, irregular heart-beats, vague pains in the torso – and ended up in the Royal Infirmary in Dundee after what I thought of, rather unscientifically, as a 'heart attack'. I was examined by Sir Ian Hill (professors look after their own), who found that my heart was perfectly sound; I was suffering from a form of exhaustion. I slowly got better during the summer, and in September kept pace with Gordon Williams on a walk up to an unexacting summit at the head of Glen Clova.

But while I was getting better, things were not going well with Audrey. Every mid-month her temperature went above normal – sometimes with great suddenness, as I could tell simply from her face – and she was overcome by lethargy and sleepiness. No diagnostic tests revealed anything wrong. Disagreeable and inconvenient though this recurrent illness was, it was not entirely disabling, and neither of us saw it as a deterrent to my acceptance of the invitation to Harvard.[4] To avoid interruption to the children's education, we agreed that I should go there alone for the first three months, and Audrey and the children should join me shortly before Christmas. Our correspondence during my three months on my own was uniformly cheerful on both sides, and when we were re-united we had a wonderful time in Boston, New York (two operas at the Met), Philadelphia,

---

[3]Cf. p. 146.
[4]For Dover's time at Harvard, cf. pp. 119, 137.

Swarthmore and Washington, seeing all the sights that one sees on those occasions. The voyage home, on a 20,000-tonner in a prolonged and ferocious Atlantic gale, also had its memorable moments, not least when furniture in the lounge broke loose from its moorings and scooped passengers into a screaming heap. Of all my memories of those four months in America, the vividest is (as usual) the worst: very heavy snowfalls throughout the north-east delayed the trains between Boston and New York on the day I went to meet my family off the ship, and I was frantic with anxiety that they might come ashore before I got there and wonder what had happened to me. As it happened, I was on time, but it was an experience of a kind that I have in bad dreams, and it reinforced the resentment of snow which I had harboured ever since the winter of 1944 in Italy.

It was only after we got home that Audrey told me that our doctor (George Caithness, the best G.P. it has been my good fortune to know) had put it to her that her trouble might be psychotic and that she should see a psychiatrist. She was not indignant about that, but deeply sceptical. Neither of us knew anything like enough about the different forms depression can take; it had afflicted some of my students, but associated in them with feelings of guilt, worthlessness and the futility of living (feelings not apparent in Audrey), without physical symptoms (so far as I knew), and I had not thought of my father's behaviour as the manifestation of illness. However, in the spring Audrey started crying more and more, sometimes for hours on end, often on waking up during the night, though she retained enough self-control never to cry in front of the children. She believed that her unhappiness was caused by a physical condition which medical science had so far failed to diagnose, and even after seeing David Ross, the very shrewd medical superintendent of the mental hospital near Cupar,[5] she turned for a few days obstinate and hostile to doctors. However, Ross told me that all her symptoms were 'absolutely, one hundred per cent, characteristic of severe depression', and I persuaded her to go into the hospital for electro-convulsive therapy. ECT had a marvellous effect; the first treatment stopped her crying and brought her back out of hell, and after the sixth and last she was able to come home and pick up the threads of her life in the first optimistic frame of mind she had experienced for many months.

Since those days psychopharmacology has made extraordinary progress, and recourse to ECT is now less frequent. It has its disadvantages, notably in impairment of memory, but anything is better than severe depression. A student of mine once became passionate on the subject of ECT and described it as 'absolutely evil' because it 'alters your fundamental personality'. I could only say that if my personality had a propensity to depression I would like nothing better than to alter it fundamentally. The dogma that mental illnesses are social rather than medical phenomena was popular among students in the nineteen-seventies, and it derived

---

[5] Stratheden hospital.

support from the writings of Thomas Szasz, who regarded 'mental illness' as an inappropriate term and asserted that 'repressed people are simply unhappy', a fatuous statement easily refuted by anyone who has experienced both unhappiness and depression and knows the difference. The 'anti-psychiatric' approach of Laing and Cooper was also fashionable at that time, founded on a psychodynamic which explained persuasively why people feel like committing very cruel and destructive acts but did not attempt to explain what makes some of them cross the immense gulf which separates feeling like doing something from actually doing it. We had no temptation whatever to subject Audrey's depression to any kind of psychotherapy in preference to orthodox medical psychiatry. Of the only three people I knew who had undergone psychoanalysis, one had committed suicide after spending all his money on an analyst over a two-year period, and the other two gave no sign of benefiting from analysis; in any case, I learned a few years later from George Devereux[6] that Freudian analysis does not even profess to treat depression. The opponents of psychiatry did not seem to understand – perhaps they just didn't know – how pills and talk work together to achieve a result which pills would be slow, and talk unable, to achieve by themselves. For the lay person, parent or spouse or friend, what matters is to avoid saying things that make the situation worse and impede cure; to imagine that saying the right things will by itself effect a cure is a delusion persistently entertained by people who have not the faintest idea of what a real depression is like.

The rest of 1961 was a good time, but in 1962 Audrey again became sluggish, sleepy and rather morose, and it was discovered that her thyroid had packed in. A daily dose of thyroid extract remedied this part of the time, but during the first three months of 1963 she slid inexorably into depression again. This time she was sent to a day-hospital, and as she had passed her driving-test in 1962 she was able to drive there and back. Three things worked together for good. One was a switch from the thyroid of oxen, which fluctuates considerably in strength, to synthetic thyroid, which does not. The second was a prescription of desipramine, which proved to be the right pharmacological answer. The third was the friendship of the occupational therapist at the hospital, Pat Simpson, who had infinite patience and a genius for putting the right casual question at the right moment. She was robustly irreligious, telling me once, 'I just *couldn't* believe in God. Even if he leaned down from the sky and shook me by the hand, I still wouldn't believe in him!' As Audrey is equally irreligious, Pat's skilful psychotherapy was not obstructed by a complication common in depressives, anxiety over loss of faith.

A small daily dose of desipramine served excellently for nine years. In 1972 we both had a severe attack of flu, and a few months after that Audrey began to have spells of lethargy, inaugurated by silent clicks in the head. A shift to aventil sorted

---

[6]On Devereux, see pp. 174–7.

that out for another nine years; when aventil seemed to be losing its grip a little an experiment was tried with the rather inappropriate flupenthixol, and then from 1984 trazodone held the fort until the arrival of paroxetine in 1992. There are no doubt people who would shrink from 'living on pills', but I don't think they would greatly enjoy the alternative, which is much worse than the side-effects of the pills. Fortunately I have no prejudice on doctrinaire or 'philosophical' grounds against any treatment which works well and quickly; if I had, and if I were induced by that to resist curtailment of the suffering of someone else, let alone my own wife, I would be a contemptible creature.

While the children were small Audrey neither had nor wanted any other job than looking after a family, but it was by no means out of the question that she might seek a job when they were older. Depression ruled that out, because it left its mark in various forms of disorientation, forgetfulness (especially of names) and dilatoriness; ever since 1961 we have had to recognise that there are some kinds of thing that she can't do, so we concentrate on what she can. That has included, from 1963 onwards, both at St Andrews and at Oxford, much voluntary work with people who are mentally ill – not necessarily within the framework of any recognised organisation, but none the less useful for that, and not less demanding.

I myself was very fit during 1961–3, and therefore able to cope with the situation. There was just one moment in 1961 when I received an offer of a very well-paid chair in an American university and allowed my mind to dwell briefly on the possibility of cutting completely adrift, going to America, living frugally there, and remitting half my salary to my family.[7] The mental picture of a family deserted just when they needed me most was too horrible to contemplate; it has returned now and again to haunt me, and it is my fault that I ever let it in. Late in 1962 I had an episode of self-pity, and one day in the spring of 1963, when I was travelling alone in Greece, a cruel dream submerged me in misery for thirty-six hours. This misery suddenly lifted, within a few seconds, while I was on the train from Olympia to Patras, and both its disproportionate intensity and its unexpected disappearance at a moment when nothing was happening to make it disappear gave me a certain insight into the nature of depression. It was only in 1964 that I began to suffer from the wear and tear to which the three-year crisis in our lives had subjected me. The doctor gave me valium, which is now regarded as addictive, but I didn't find it so; as soon as it made me feel better, I forgot to take it. In 1965 we went on a camping holiday across France, but I became so tired and felt so ill that we cut it short and came home. Some of the time we were at Berkeley in 1967, I felt more dead than alive (excessive coffee?), and flu in 1972 gave me a short spell of depression. Summer 1975, summer 1977, autumn 1977, summer 1978; on the last three of those four occasions the onset of exhaustion, with irregular heart and sinking

---

[7]The offer came from Pittsburgh University (Dover SN).

feelings, was inexplicable. Cardiograms, encephalograms, blood tests, urine tests, X-rays, all represented me as thoroughly fit. At any rate I didn't miss a day's work, scarcely even an hour's, because I had learned to put on an act, but I could have done without the need to put it on so often. Did I really use up something irreplaceable on that day's drive in December 1958?

When Audrey was first in hospital I was fortified by the intuitive tact and humour of the children, and even at the worst period of her depression she never became suspicious, hostile or petulant towards me or towards them. Nevertheless, there is no denying that mental illness in one's partner imposes a barrier to empathy and creates in oneself a dreadful feeling of loneliness. Katharine Curtis, one of Catherine's teachers and a devout Baptist, advocated 'casting one's troubles upon One Above', and I was not entirely ill-disposed to the idea. During our first few years at St Andrews I had occasionally attended St Salvator's Chapel and found attractive features in the service; it seemed a good idea that principals and professors should sometimes declare publicly that they are miserable sinners. In 1960, filling in a publisher's questionnaire, I put down 'non-denominational Christian' as my religious affiliation. Then one day, while I was driving to see Audrey in hospital and mulling over the idea of One Above, I had what I can only describe as a spiritual experience in reverse: the heavens opened, and a voice declared 'You have no need of a God.' I felt as if I had crashed right *through* religion and come out on the other side on to a calm sea under a blue sky. Many years later I learned that A.J.P. Taylor had had a similar experience as a boy, when he was sitting at a window and a 'voice' informed him 'There is no God' – since when, he said, religion had never been one of his 'many troubles in life'.[8] I would describe my own experience as somewhat mystical in type, because I had an exultant feeling of *understanding* something and yet found it impossible subsequently to recall, let alone communicate, what clinched the understanding. It has commonly been believed that I am hostile to religion, but I would not describe my own sentiment as hostility. I have read (and re-read attentively) Bernanos' *Journal d'un curé de campagne* with what I conceive to be sympathetic understanding, and I purr over Cyril Alington's assurance to the parents of boys at Eton that the purpose of the school was not to prepare boys for life, but to prepare them for death.[9] But

---

[8] A.J.P. Taylor, *A Personal History* (London, 1983) 47. Taylor (1906–90) became a high-profile modern historian and was a fellow of Magdalen College, Oxford, 1938–76; cf. pp. 282–8 for his prominent role in the Blunt controversy at the British Academy in 1980.

[9] Georges Bernanos (1888–1948), a Catholic, was author of numerous novels with strongly religious and ethical themes, this one published in 1936; it is a curious work for Dover to have read more than once. Cyril Alington (1872–1955) was headmaster of Eton 1916–33: the sentiment cited was an echo of a Platonic definition of philosophy (Plato, *Phaedo* 64a), though Dover is unlikely to have admired it so much in that context.

sympathetic understanding of a belief does not necessarily entail sharing it in the absence of good evidence, let alone condoning it as an excuse for inflicting harm on others; if I am regarded as hostile to religion, it is because I judge it by criteria which are not themselves religious.*

I have never been much impressed by the assertion, not uncommon among lay Catholics, that the existence of God is demonstrable with certainty. Aquinas, after all, said that it isn't. When an ex-Jesuit[10] tells me (I seem to know many more ex-Jesuits than Jesuits) that 'Christianity is absolute nonsense', and I know that he has plenty of sense as well as a sharp intellect, I don't think I need spend much time on what one distinguished Protestant divine calls 'Theological Science'. As for feelings of conviction, however overwhelming they are, they tell us much about the person who experiences them, but nothing about their truth-value. Dodds,[11] resolutely agnostic all his life, told me that the nearest he came to religious experience was in contemplating wild and beautiful scenery. I can well understand his emotion, but I was surprised that he associated it with religion. One of the most intense emotional experiences of my life was contemplation of Lochan Fada (in Wester Ross) on a midsummer night, but the power of the scene lay in its wonderful impersonality, which would have been spoilt by the intrusion of God. I would be inclined to dismiss the vague feeling that there is Someone There as a symptom of non-specific psychitis;[12] no doubt my own concentration on Something Here would be dismissed by many as a product of tunnel vision.

My colleagues were sympathetic during Audrey's depression, but I observed that I myself was the object of their sympathy. On one and the same day in 1963, when I had to tell various people about Audrey's treatment at the day-hospital, Terence Mitford looked very shocked and said, 'How awful for *you!*'; Ian

---

*Tolstoy, who spoke much of God, asked himself in 1906 'Does God exist?', and his answer was 'I don't know'. He went on to say what he meant by the word 'God', in terms which seem to me entirely incompatible with 'faith' and very hard to reconcile with what a Christian, Muslim or Jew would call 'religion', but easily translatable into moral terms (*Tolstoy's Diaries*, ed. R.F. Christian, p. 399). [EDS *The page reference is not to the two-volume 1985 edition but the 1996 one-volume paperback: the diary entry is for 30 July 1906; Tolstoy's definition of God is 'a law governing my spiritual being'. For R.F. Christian himself, see p. 205.*]

[10]Anthony Levi (1929–2004), a distinguished scholar of early-modern French whom Dover knew as Buchanan Professor of French at St Andrews 1971–87. Levi had been a Jesuit priest 1962–71. Dover SN adds three more putative 'ex-Jesuits' whom he had known, but only one of the three, Levi's brother, the poet and translator Peter Levi (1931–2000), was actually so. Of the other two, the American classicist Jack Winkler (1943–90), whom Dover encountered at Stanford University when a visiting professor there (cf. p. 321), had been a Benedictine monk, while the philosopher Sir Anthony Kenny (1931-, Master of Balliol 1978–89, Kt 1992), though ordained as a catholic priest, was not a Jesuit either.
[11]See note on p. 72.
[12]Psychitis is not a generally recognized term; did Dover intend it to be a coinage?

McFarlane[13] gave a wry smile and said, '*You* must be having a difficult time'; Gordon Williams' face contracted in pain and he said, 'Oh, poor Audrey!' I was relieved that one of them got it right. During the crises both my mother and Cicely came up to St Andrews in turn to help keep house, and this was immeasurably helpful. My father understandably kept out of the way, and I must say that, to my surprise, I heard no word from him of criticism, even oblique criticism, of Audrey. Although he was not normally tolerant of anybody's shortcomings except his own, and especially inclined to stand up for 'overworked' men who were 'let down' by their wives (it seems to have been customary in his time for colleagues at work to complain to one another about their wives, a habit which I find intolerable), I think his own experience gave him some understanding of what Audrey was going through, difficult though he would have found it to say as much. My mother was compassionate by nature, distressed by Audrey's condition, and well aware that I was not the patient, but I thought I detected in her a residual trace of the Victorian concept of 'will-power' and therefore an incomplete understanding of the fact that whatever else will-power may be it is that which is attacked by depression and consequently does not function (we don't upbraid a sufferer from leukaemia for weakness of blood). With Cicely it was not so easy, because her feeling that Audrey was culpable was not consistently suppressed or concealed. I was aware by now that relations between Audrey and her mother had never been as good, at any rate since Audrey was sixteen or so, as I had imagined when I first knew them, and I observed some of the things that went wrong; for instance, Cicely would ask for Audrey's opinion, reject it with, 'Well, I don't know why you think that!', and then give serious attention to exactly the same opinion when it was expressed by me. I now found myself in the unusual position of a man whose mother-in-law thinks that her son-in-law has had a raw deal from her daughter. For different reasons Audrey and I had long felt an underlying urge to cut adrift from our pre-existing families and start life afresh with our own; but where would we have been without grandmothers who came to the rescue in a crisis?

---

[13]Ian McFarlane (1915–2002) was Buchanan Professor of French at St Andrews 1961–70: see the British Academy memoir by Terence Cave, *PBA* 124 (2004) 183–203 (available at https://www.thebritishacademy.ac.uk/publishing/memoirs/3/).

14 PLATO AND AFTER 1962–1989

One should often ask oneself: such a measure may be just, but is it useful?
CATHERINE THE GREAT[1]

We always included a major Platonic text in our Honours syllabus, and for some years Ian Kidd lectured on *Phaedrus*. In 1962 we thought it would be a good idea if he had a rest from that and I took on Plato for a year, although I had never previously tackled any philosophical text more advanced than the *Apology*. I did not imagine that I could compete with Ian on *Phaedrus*, to which he had devoted much time and thought, and it would have been wasteful if we both prepared Honours lectures on the same text. Some of the major Platonic texts *(Phaedo*, for example, and portions of the *Republic)* played a part in courses run by the philosophy departments,[2] and in any case needed treatment by someone who was more of a philosopher than I am. I was strongly attracted to the *Symposium*; initially, I think, by the fact that it is devoted to a series of encomia, delivered at an imaginary party, in honour of Eros, the god who is the personification of sexual love. Some work which I had done in 1948 had aroused my interest in oratorical genres, notably the funeral speech and the encomium. The encomia in the *Symposium* are extremely diverse; they include at least two parodies, one satirising the dextrous, sportive style of Gorgias and the other satirising pretentious medical theory, while a third speech, put into the mouth of Aristophanes, is (in my view) a very sophisticated folk-tale of the 'how the leopard got his spots' type.

---

[1] *The Memoirs of Catherine the Great*, ed. D. Maroger, trans. M. Budberg (London, 1955) 366. Cf. Dover's earlier reference (p. 23) to Benjamin Britten's desire to be 'useful'.
[2] The plural is correct: St Andrews had at that time two departments of philosophy, one of moral philosophy and the other of logic and metaphysics.

Moreover, all the speakers except Aristophanes treat homosexual eros as eros *par excellence*. The work I did for a lecture-course at Oxford in 1954[3] on the elegiac poets, combined with the implications of some passages of comedy, had left me in no doubt that practically everything said during the last few centuries about the psychology, ethics and sociology of Greek homosexuality was confused and misleading.[4] The root of the confusion was the failure to understand how quite different attitudes to the 'active' and the 'passive' role coexist, and extreme reluctance to admit that the Greeks regarded homosexual arousal as natural and normal. If an Athenian adult male fell in love with a handsome boy or still-beardless youth, no inhibition restrained him from saying so; but the 'quarry' was expected to rebuff the 'pursuer', a boy who actually sought to arouse older males was condemned, and so were homosexual relationships between two bearded males. Within the *Symposium*, to say nothing of abundant evidence from other sources, the situation is clearly discernible from the speech put into the mouth of a certain Pausanias, who complains of the 'complexity' of Athenian attitudes: the man who tries to make the boy say 'yes' receives sympathy and encouragement, but the boy is invariably under pressure to say 'no'. It happened that I had recently read a survey of contemporary sexual attitudes among the young, and had taken the point that a father who is by no means unsympathetic to his son's seduction of the neighbour's daughter is nevertheless enraged at the seduction of his own daughter by the neighbour's son. Get to the heart of the feelings, attitudes and traditions which underlie this illogicality, change the gender of some of the pronouns in Pausanias' speech (as indeed a prudish English translation in the eighteenth century did),[5] and that portion of the *Symposium* turns into a startlingly familiar description of a heterosexual ethos which many of us are old enough to remember: good girls say 'no', but a boy who doesn't try to make them say 'yes' is a wimp.

Soon after my course on the *Symposium,* I was invited to give a set of three lectures in University College, London. One of them, on Pausanias' speech, appeared as an article under the title 'Eros and Nomos', and to judge by references to it in subsequent literature it seems to have been a 'foundation document' of what has been published since 1964 on the subject of Greek homosexuality. The other two were on the date of the *Symposium*, which I believe can be firmly located between 385 and 378, and on the generic affinities of Aristophanes' speech; the

---

[3]Cf. p. 121 for an earlier reference to this course.
[4]On the professional development of Dover's interest in Greek homosexuality, see Halliwell's Foreword, 'The book and its author', to the 2016 reprint of *GH*, vii-xiv.
[5]The reference is to Floyer Sydenham's version, first published in 1761: Dover discussed this and other translations of the *Symposium* in his essay on 'Expurgation of Greek Literature', reprinted in *G&L* 270–91.

former was published in 1965, the latter in 1966. Both involved me in the consideration of philosophical points. Socrates' long speech in the *Symposium*, which purports to be his reproduction of metaphysical doctrine received by him from a priestess called Diotima, contains passages which suggest that Plato did not at the time of writing the *Symposium* believe in the immortality of the soul; and if that were so, the relation of the work to *Phaedo*, in which Socrates seeks to demonstrate immortality, would be a major problem. It seemed to me to be a pseudo-problem, because the doctrine of immortality can be expressed either as '*There is in me* something which will live when *I* am dead' or as '*I* shall live when *my body* is dead', and Plato could adopt either formulation according to the context: 'There is in me ...' is entirely reconcilable with the *Symposium*, but in *Phaedo*, where Socrates is consoling his grieving friends, '*I* shall live ...' is more appropriate. Since Plato's Socrates explicitly leaves open the question, '*How* do particulars "participate" in universals?', it would not be surprising if Plato for some years left open also the machinery of immortality.

'Aristophanes' differs from the other speakers in *Symposium* in declining to treat eros as a response to beauty. In the fairy-tale which he tells, human beings were once double: male-male, male-female and female-female. Zeus split them down the middle, and ever since then each of us has sought hrs own 'other half'. The real Aristophanes would not have been so foolish as to deny that we fall in love with beautiful people, but he would also have been aware that if we never fell in love with anyone else most of us would be doomed to loveless lives. The story told by the fictitious Aristophanes is vigorously rejected by Plato's Diotima. Why did Plato make Aristophanes the mouthpiece of the 'other half' doctrine? My own answer was (and is) that Plato recognised it as a vulgar, uneducated idea, and therefore appropriate to a writer of comedies which are undeniably vulgar and populist. Those of us who are happily married are aware that one falls in love with someone who is, or comes near to being, the right 'recipe' for oneself. Diotima's doctrine is, by contrast, unattractive, even repulsive. For her, erotic response to the beauty of an individual is only the first step on an intellectual ascent which leads, through awareness of the beauty present in two or more individuals, towards apprehension by 'the eye of the soul' of eternal, immutable Beauty. The ascent is a dialectical process in which the older and younger male co-operate intellectually, fiercely assailed by bodily desire but struggling to repel it. Together they procreate hypotheses and conclusions which in Diotima's eyes, and no doubt in Plato's, are greatly to be preferred to the mortal children produced by mere mating. There is something extraordinarily impersonal – one might say, anti-personal – in all this, for it seems to follow necessarily that if after embarking on the ascent with A I meet B, who appears to me a more promising partner in the enterprise, I simply drop A and continue the ascent with B.

The need to expound the *Symposium* in lectures and in print made me sort out my own ideas on sexual love, and thinking about it in Greek rather than English was a great help. Our use of the word 'love' has got us into a mess: 'love thy neighbour', 'I love making love (= 'fucking') on the carpet', and so on. In Greek the verb *philein* and the noun *philia* denote the affection, ranging from intense to mild, which one may feel for a sexual partner, a parent, a child, a friend, a colleague, a nation or a place. The verb *erân* and the noun *erōs* denote 'love' in the sense which it has in the English phrases 'to be in love (with ...)' and 'fall in love (with ...)', not just simple lust (for which Greek has other words) but the exclusive and obsessive lust which one feels for a particular person.[6] Most of us are so constituted that we necessarily desire the satisfaction of lust by orgasm. Most of us also are capable of affection, and beauty is one (but only one) of the stimuli which evoke it. Affection sometimes generates eros, especially when consummation is physiologically easy and socially tolerated. Conversely, lust commonly generates affection, and its satisfaction may generate eros. It seems to me, therefore, that eros is not like a chemical compound, possessing properties which differ from the properties of any of its constituents, but like a chemical mixture, in which the constituents may be put together in any ratios and retain their own properties.

Plato (unlike Socrates) did not marry, and there is nothing in the biographical tradition to suggest that he begot any children. His inclination may have been exclusively homosexual, an uncommon phenomenon in the Greek world;[7] the probability is relevant to the formation of the metaphysical axioms in which his philosophy is rooted, and to assumptions, priorities and blind spots which we may observe in all that he has to say about Eros, but there are large areas in which it has no relevance at all. The *Symposium* and *Phaedrus*, taken together, leave us in no doubt that our response to the stimulus afforded by the sight of a beautiful human seemed to Plato the strongest hint we have of the existence of abstract immutable Beauty. It is not thoughtless reductionism on our part, but Plato's own (sometimes startling) choice of words, which identifies the first intimation of Beauty with the sensation in the genitals which heralds arousal.[8] At one point in lecturing on the *Symposium* I remembered a strange occasion in 1944 when I had gone to the top of a hill a few miles south of Mignano. It was an absolutely still day, with a blue sky from one horizon to the other, and the Matese massif was covered from end to end with snow. The scene struck directly at my penis, so I sat down on a log and

---

[6]Dover SN explains: 'I consistently use "lust" in the morally neutral sense "sexual desire", and never *contrast* it with love.'

[7]As Dover SN stresses, 'uncommon' here refers specifically to the idea of an *exclusively* homosexual orientation.

[8]Dover is thinking here of *Phaedrus* 251a-e, where Socrates describes the soul's response to beauty (most directly, a male lover's response to a beautiful boy) in quasi-physical imagery of shuddering, sweating, melting, swelling, gushing, and throbbing.

masturbated; it seemed the appropriate response.* The explanation of such events is scientific rather than philosophical.⁹

The favourable reception of my article 'Eros and Nomos' encouraged me to think that there was a need for a whole book on the history of homosexuality in the Greek world. Scholarly qualifications aside, I felt that I had one other qualification for writing the book, which I eventually expressed in the Preface in these words: 'I am fortunate in not experiencing moral shock or disgust at any genital act whatsoever, provided that it is welcome and agreeable to all the participants (whether they number one, two, or more than two)', and I made it plain that no biological, medical, legal or religious categorisations of homosexuality could affect my *moral* judgement of any particular homosexual act. Paul Cartledge called this 'an extreme, perhaps the ultimate, expression of scholarly amoralism';¹⁰ but, of course, I was not (for once) trying to be scholarly, let alone (heaven forfend) amoral, but telling the plain truth about my own feelings, which in this respect have not changed since puberty. Naturally, aesthetic reactions are not precluded, though they are not violent; while I have never had any inclination to put my penis into anyone else's anus (or vice versa), I would rather do it (or vice versa) than take melted mutton fat into my mouth. From a moral standpoint, I abhor the cynical popular dictum, 'All's fair in love (i.e. sexual pursuit) and war.' In war, as in dealings with criminals, deception is necessary; otherwise, no attempt to realise one's own purpose by lies, pretence or false promises should be tolerated; and if the purpose is sexual, that is no extenuation but an aggravation. Rape I find inconceivable; for me, as a male, being welcomed in is one of the essential ingredients of sex, and even in fantasy I have never entertained the idea of sex with a hostile partner.

Since my intention to write the book on Greek homosexuality took shape at the beginning of the 1970s, I was able to make notes on all relevant passages in the course of the very extensive re-reading of Greek texts which I had to do for *Greek Popular Morality*.¹¹ Literary texts, however, tell only half the story. The other half is

---

*Someone in Oxford who had read the typescript of my book (which was originally submitted to the Oxford University Press) communicated this incident to a journalist, and the *Evening Standard* (21 February 1994), under the headline 'Oxford Don Takes Memoirs In Hand', conveyed the impression that I had written a sort of *Confessions of a Wanker*. Thanks to the international academic grapevine, I think I know now who blabbed (it was not, of course, Hilary O'Shea, nor did I ever imagine that it was). Alan Bennett has justly remarked, 'All you need to do, if you want the nation's press camped on your doorstep, is to say that you once had a wank in 1947.' [EDS *The most likely source of the leak, as Dover himself later believed, was Jasper Griffin: see the Introduction, p. 8 n. 24. Alan Bennett's remark, with minor differences from Dover's version, appeared first in his diary, 'Where I was in 1993', in the London Review of Books 16 December 1993.*]

⁹Contrast the statement on p. 177 that all questions about human 'feeling' are 'necessarily historical'.
¹⁰P. Cartledge, 'The politics of Spartan pederasty', *Proceedings of the Cambridge Philological Society* [subsequently *The Cambridge Classical Journal*] 27 (1981) 17–36, at 30 n. 9.
¹¹See pp. 214–20 for Dover's main discussion of *GPM*.

to be sought in the many hundreds of painted vases, from the early sixth century to the late fifth, which depict *all* stages of homosexual activity, from eye-catching to consummation, via a courtship which may include the fingering of the young male's genitals by the older. There are tens of thousands of fragmentary Greek vases, and there is no comprehensive index of subjects; one cannot key in (e.g.) 'bracelet' or 'cabbage' and get a print-out of the data needed to track down all the relevant vases.[12] Moreover, many of the vases most needed for my project were discreetly tucked away in museum basements, and even when they were published it was not unknown for some portion of the picture to be blacked out. However, the *Corpus Vasorum Antiquorum* (an international publication which goes rather slowly, but will, I hope, go on forever) escapes censorship; and an illustrated article published in 1969 by Emily Vermeule achieved a breakthrough comparable to the liberation of the printed word which followed the unsuccessful prosecution of *Lady Chatterley's Lover* earlier in the decade.[13] In the course of 1973–5 I worked my way through the *Corpus* and all the collection-catalogues and illustrated histories of vase-painting that I could find. This in itself would have provided me with ample material for a history of representation of homosexual activity in the visual arts. Then the really interesting job started: relating the visual representation to the literary representation. I was able to put together a coherent history which made sense of a complex of Greek moral, social and political attitudes to sexual behaviour, while noting that Aristophanic comedy, which may normally be expected to take a cynical view of most human transactions, offers a picture in many ways at odds with that presented by serious literature.

The book, which appeared in 1978, was well received by classicists, while Roger Scruton dismissed it as 'trivialising',† and some homosexuals did not like to be told that much of their wishful idealisation of 'Greek love' was wide of the mark. A Californian gay periodical began its very favourable review by saying that I was 'President of Christ Church and a practising homosexual'.[14] I contemplated profitable litigation, but was advised by a wise American lawyer that (a) the case would have to be tried before a Californian jury, who might not consider that I had been defamed, (b) as a public figure, I could not claim damages for defamation unless I could prove malicious intent, which plainly I could not, and (c) the periodical in question had no money. 'A lawyer's dream,' he said, 'and a client's

---

†In *Sexual Desire,* p. 308. I think I can see what he meant; but I am not abashed, because despite profound agreement with part of his analysis of sexual emotion, I attach importance to some phenomena which he ignores.

[12] This has now to some extent been remedied by online databases, especially that of the Beazley Archive in Oxford.
[13] Emily Vermeule, 'Some erotica in Boston', *Antike Kunst* 12 (1969) 9–15.
[14] Although this anecdote was repeated in several later sources, including obituaries of Dover, we have been unable to identify the publication in question.

nightmare.' I learned my lesson, and simply wrote a letter to the reviewer, asking him to correct the error of fact about my orientation (and, for good measure, assigning me to the right college); I don't know if he ever did. Some years later I learned that there are indeed people who think I am homosexual, a notion apparently founded on the assumption that otherwise I wouldn't have wanted to write a book on the subject.

It was clear from some reviews that I was thought not to have understood (but I did understand, and fancied that I had said so) how greatly the way Greeks actually behaved may have differed from the way their behaviour was conventionally represented in the arts.[15] I also disappointed readers who were hungry for a satisfying explanation of the fact of Greek homosexuality, and I must continue to disappoint them.[16] In recent years it has been suggested (following up a hypothesis first formulated in 1907) that the characteristic Greek homosexual relationship was the descendant of prehistoric rituals in which young males underwent an initiation similar to that which is common in some other parts of the world. The anthropological parallels are indeed provocative, but the fact remains that it was not until the end of the seventh century BC – later than Homer, Hesiod and the earliest poets – that homosexuality became *overt,* described in straightforward erotic language and adopted as a subject of myth and drama. This overtness is the feature which above all distinguishes the Greeks from other peoples of the ancient eastern Mediterranean, and it is hard to see how overt homosexuality could have emerged at a certain point in time as a consequence of prehistoric rituals which by that time were lost to view. Proponents of the initiation hypothesis seem to me to have misinterpreted, even sometimes misrepresented, many of the passages on which they rely. I could not resist writing a rather polemical article about all that for the second volume of my Collected Papers in 1988, years after I had dropped sex for syntax in the belief that I had no more to say about sex.[17]

While I was awaiting the publication of *Greek Homosexuality,* in which I had devoted a section to what I called the 'philosophical exploitation' of homosexuality, I was invited to contribute a text and exegesis of the *Symposium* to the series 'Cambridge Greek and Latin Classics', and I took that on readily.[18] I was able to start from the work I had done in 1962–4, but naturally I needed to reflect much further on the philosophical argument in order to explain to sixth-formers and

---

[15]For a critique of Dover's use of visual evidence in *GH*, see Elsner's chapter in *S&C*.
[16]Dover SN says that after reading Bruce Bagemihl, *Biological Exuberance: Animal Homosexuality and Natural Diversity* (London, 1999), 'I no longer trouble myself with questions about the "cause" of homosexuality', only with differences in attitudes to it across cultures.
[17]See 'Greek homosexuality and initiation', in *G&L* 115–34.
[18]For a critical analysis of this book, see Frisbee Sheffield's chapter in *S&C*; for its successful sales, see Roy Gibson's chapter, 'Fifty years of green and yellow', in S. Harrison and C. Pelling, eds, *Classical Scholarship and its History* (Berlin, 2021), at 205–6.

undergraduates exactly what Plato's reasoning is and how far it is valid. It seemed to me that his metaphysical arguments make sense only if one adopts, with the fervent faith patently characteristic of his Socrates, three axioms. First, that since what we perceive of the world is subject to change and decay, *there must be something which is eternal and immutable*. Secondly, that since opinions and inferences founded on our experience of the world are corrigible, *there must be something which is understandable by incorrigible reasoning*. And thirdly, that if we follow the path of reason to the end, *we must perceive that ultimate reality is good*, and since love is necessarily our reaction to good, reason and love converge and fuse in the experience of that perception. Plato does not offer us adequate reasons for accepting his theory of eternal and immutable 'forms' (or 'ideas') as true; he can only show that empirical knowledge and belief are unsatisfactory to those who share his axioms. His Socrates is not a mystic, for he does not say (as Colin Macleod once tried to persuade me that he said), 'I've been there, so I know', but only speaks of what it *would be* like to perceive ultimate reality 'with the eye of the soul'.[19] The notion, carelessly propagated by some Platonists, that Socrates was having a mystical experience when he stood still all night at Potidea, as described in the *Symposium*, is contradicted by the text, which says that he was *thinking* about a problem and trying to solve it.[20] I myself do not share Plato's axioms, and therefore do not find his metaphysical arguments persuasive. In my introduction and commentary I made that plain, perhaps a little too bluntly. I also drew attention to passages in which the argument is vitiated by unjustified inferences, questionable generalisations and semantic slither. These passages prompted me to suggest that modem interpretation of Plato has tended to underrate the extent to which, as an evangelist for his metaphysical faith, he sometimes found rhetorical techniques a more serviceable instrument of persuasion (all in a good cause) than cool reason, and I went so far as to compare him in this respect with the forensic orators. This earned me a reproachful letter from Gerrit de Vries,[21] and I was sorry to have upset a good friend, especially one who had an incomparably detailed knowledge of the Platonic corpus, but there was more sentiment than scholarly argument in his letter, and it did not require me to change my mind. I did, however, add a paragraph

---

[19]Colin Macleod was classical tutor at Christ Church, Oxford, 1969–81. In a note to the Dundee lectures mentioned in the text below, Dover links Macleod's claim directly to the speech of Diotima in the *Symposium*; he also describes Macleod as someone 'for whose scholarly judgement I had infinite respect'.

[20]This famous passage is at Plato, *Symposium* 220c-d.

[21]Gerrit Jacob de Vries (1905–90), Professor of Greek at Amsterdam 1955–71, wrote extensively on Greek literature but was best known for his work on Plato, not least his commentary on the *Phaedrus* (Amsterdam, 1969).

to the preface of my second edition, clarifying and limiting what I had said in the first.

The crucial role of faith in Platonic philosophy is a theme which I explored further in a set of lectures on 'Faith, Reason and Authority in Greek Religion' which I gave in Dundee in 1985, and I have found no reason to go back on what I said.[22] It does not diminish my admiration for Plato as a philosophical giant or the pleasure I take in his subtlety and skill as a dramatic writer. I do not imagine I would be happy in his ideal city, but the widespread allegation that it was devised as a defence of property and nobility is superficial in the extreme and becomes untenable once we follow with adequate care the strands which run through his political thought. Plato lived in a world in which a weak city-state was sometimes laid waste by a strong neighbour and its population deported, dispersed, enslaved or killed. The fundamental question confronting anyone who wanted to construct a hypothetical state was: what structure will best guarantee it *survival* in conflict with external aggressors and internal faction? Mao often observed that it is a waste of time to formulate any kind of social and economic order unless we can also make sure that a country in which that order can be established will continue to exist. Plato and (before insanity supervened) Mao would have understood each other.

In the last few years I have had occasion to read extensively in Plato's *Laws* and have been repeatedly struck by the acuity of his incidental observations on human society; not least by the remark, in the course of horribly austere regulations on the treatment of slaves, that your devotion to justice can be truly assessed only by your behaviour towards those who are weaker than yourself and in your power. The principle is applicable equally to politics and to sex.

---

[22]SH possesses a typescript of the lectures, many of whose ideas found their way into other publications: for the thesis about the role of quasi-religious faith in Platonic philosophy (a factor Dover thought unique in pre-Christian Greek religious mentalities), cf. *The Greeks*, 2nd edn (Oxford, 1982) 123–31.

15 TRIBUTARIES 1962–

Why, Sir, I think every man whatever has a peculiar style, which may be discovered by nice examination and comparison with others.
                                  JOHNSON, *ap.* Boswell, 13 April 1778

I think it was Douglas Young who put me in touch, at the beginning of the nineteen-sixties, with Andrew Morton, the minister of Culross Abbey.[1] Our meeting inaugurated a lively family friendship which has worn well. Andrew is the least dogmatic Presbyterian minister I know (with the possible exception of his friend Jim McLeman, minister of Burghead). It takes a while to locate the granite core; in Jean Morton it is much nearer the surface, and we have happy arguments with her about morality and religion.[2]

Our friendship also began my education in statistics, which by now has gone almost as far as halfway through an elementary textbook, and in the exploitation of the computer for the study of linguistic and literary questions. Andrew's education had been scientific, and he was dismayed by the statistical inadequacy of many arguments over problems of authenticity and interpolation in the New Testament. He looked for linguistic 'fingerprints', persistent habits such as sentence-length or the proportion of monosyllabic words, which might identify an individual author and help to locate any extensive interpolation in a text by that author. The idea was not new; it was Andrew who reminded me of the passage from Boswell at the top of this page. Pioneering work was done as long ago as the middle of the nineteenth century.[3]

---

[1] Rev. Andrew Queen Morton FRSE (1919–2018) was a Church of Scotland minister and a pioneer of computerized stylometrics, which he applied especially to parts of the New Testament.
[2] Jean Morton, née Singleton, wife of Andrew Morton; they married in 1948.
[3] One of the first proposals for statistical stylometrics was made by the mathematician Augustus De Morgan in the 1850s. In Classics, a pioneer of pre-computerized stylometry was one of Dover's own St Andrews predecessors, Lewis Campbell (1830–1908), Professor of Greek 1863–92, who used statistical methods to try to establish the relative chronology of Plato's dialogues. For a historical outline, see Anthony Kenny, *The Computation of Style* (Oxford, 1982) 1–14.

I was, and remain, sympathetic to work of this kind. My first substantial article, on the chronology of Antiphon's speeches, could fairly be called statistical, however primitive it might seem to a professional statistician (I had still to learn what is statistically significant and what is not, and how one decides), because I recognised from the first that words such as 'normal', 'less', 'characteristic' and the like are statistical terms, and if one is to use them in serious argument one should back them up by precise quantification. Theological and academic hostility to stylometric studies was disheartening. Some people found it comforting to believe that every work of the Pauline Epistles was written by St Paul, although doubts about the *Epistle to the Hebrews* went back to the ancient world and had been strongly revived in Germany. G.H.C. Macgregor, professor of Divinity and Biblical Criticism at Glasgow, and a collaborator with Andrew Morton in several books, was one of those who recognised that relevant evidence can come in all shapes and sizes, but Malcolm Knox disapproved of my involvement and referred sneeringly to 'counting the commas in Herodotus'. Madge Webster lost some of the respect I had always felt for her when she told me, 'If a question needs mathematics to answer it, it is a question in which I am not interested.'[4] How can one know in advance, when one poses a question, what is going to be needed to answer it?

Many kinds of counting and calculation are best done by computer, once the texts have been put into machine-readable form, and Andrew entertained the ambitious idea of building up a library of Greek texts in that form in Edinburgh. Sidney Michaelson, director of Computer Science at Edinburgh University, backed the idea with great enthusiasm and so did Mortimer Wheeler, who was Secretary of the British Academy.[5] There were, of course, complete indexes and concordances of some Greek authors already in existence, compiled the hard way fifty years earlier, but there were still many gaps. I recalled that Wade-Gery had once asked me, with reference to a passage of Strabo whose interpretation was of some historical importance, whether *sun* ('with') always meant 'plus' in Strabo or could mean 'including', and I had to tell him that in the absence of a Strabo index no one could say.[6] I got a £300 grant from the Academy to make a machine-readable text of Strabo; there already existed a programme for arranging all the words of a text in alphabetical order and giving a precise reference to each instance. Unfortunately, it proved impossible – impossible, at any rate, for £300 – to recruit enough tape-punchers and proof-correctors to complete the job, and I found that Sidney's ebullient optimism was one side of a coin of which disorganised unpracticality

---

[4]Amy Marjorie (Madge) Webster FBA (1901–67), wife of the classical scholar T.B.L. Webster, was a Hellenist in her own right, publishing as A.M. Dale on Greek metre and other topics: see the British Academy memoir of her by R.P. Winnington-Ingram, *PBA* 53 (1967) 423–36.
[5]Sir Mortimer Wheeler (1890–1976, Kt 1952), a distinguished and flamboyant archaeologist, was Secretary to the British Academy 1949–68. Cf. the further reference to him on p. 189.
[6]On Wade-Gery, see p. 97 with note.

was the other. The Edinburgh library of Greek tapes flitted into the world of dreams, and a few years later all such projects were eclipsed by the Thesaurus Linguae Graecae, born and reared on the Irvine campus of the University of California. It is now possible, with an Ibycus terminal and a couple of discs, to key in any Greek word and any Greek author and read on the screen all the passages in which that word occurs in that author. (I made good use of Ibycus at Stanford in 1989 and 1990.)[7] The Thesaurus text of a given author is the text of one particular edition, and it would be nice if it included (as it could have done) variant readings and plausible emendations, but maybe one can't have everything all at once. Thanks to the co-operation of the Computing Department at Oxford I have print-out concordances of Herodotus, Thucydides and Xenophon; they take up four feet of shelving and are monstrously heavy to handle, but I have had occasion to bless them.

Andrew went on to develop a technique for detecting composite authorship and interpolation, the cumulative sum ('cusum') chart, which has been used to good effect in detecting forged confessions on which wrongful convictions have been based. Having made some experiments with Greek and English texts,[8] I have no doubts about the validity of the method, but 'proof' is a strong word, and I prefer to think in terms of the accumulation of probabilities.

Mortimer Wheeler set up a Computer Committee in the British Academy, and soon after I became a Fellow I was appointed its chairman.[9] Colleagues and friends who know that to this day I have not learned to use a word-processor must find that comic. The fact is that although I understand what happens under the bonnet of my car I find it impossible to conceive what happens inside a computer, and I don't like to use a machine that I can't understand. Or so, at least, I persuade myself; but there must be a fault in my sentiment, because my failure to comprehend the telephone, the television set and the combination lock does not deter me at all from using them. Perhaps I am simply in thrall to the manual typewriter on which my life's work has been done.

Anyway, the function of the Computer Committee was to assess whether projects in the humanities which would involve computers deserved grants from the Academy's research fund. The first thing I did was to circularise all Sections of

---

[7] Ibycus was an early personal computer designed to operate the Thesaurus Linguae Graecae database of Greek texts; the TLG project was launched in 1972 and has in the meantime become freely available online (http://stephanus.tlg.uci.edu/). For Dover's position as an annual visiting professor at Stanford University during 1987–92, see pp. 321–5.

[8] The experiments in question are to be found above all in Dover's final book, *The Evolution of Greek Prose Style* (Oxford, 1997), where his statistical methods were influenced in part by Jill M. Farringdon, with contributions by A.Q. Morton et al., *Analysing for Authorship: A Guide to the Cusum Technique* (Cardiff, 1996).

[9] Dover was elected FBA in 1966: see p. 189.

the Academy, asking them what jobs they wanted done.[10] I expected a flood of requests for indexes and concordances, arranged by each Section in order of priority. I received absolutely nothing; not one Section even bothered to acknowledge receipt of my circular.

From a psychopathological standpoint this was understandable. The publicity given to the Mortonian enterprises was undoubtedly brash ('the computer proves ...'), the definition of 'style' implicit in 'fingerprint' stylometry was exceedingly narrow (in some recent work it still is), stylometric tests occasionally (for example, in the case of Plato's *Seventh Letter)* made the problem worse, difference of genre within the works of one author raised doubts about the validity of the sampling, and although many authors were demonstrably consistent in their linguistic habits over a long period, we cannot easily assess the probability that a given author will be consistent over n years or, indeed, that s/he will be consistent at all (this is where the analogy with fingerprints is weak). Academics have a certain tendency to assume that nothing worthwhile can come from a source which has produced something questionable, and we missed the opportunity to take the lead, 'thinking big', in the establishment of a corpus of machine-readable texts.

The Computer Committee nevertheless received a trickle of applications, which from the first revealed that our machinery was cumbrous. The Committee could not itself decide that a project was important; only the relevant Section could say that. And the Committee did not have the expertise required for the decision on the practicability of computerising the project; for that we had to co-opt a computer scientist. In the end we recommended our own disbandment, and from then on the applicant for a grant had to make hrs own arrangements for computerisation before applying. This has worked well.

From 1962 to 1968 I was co-editor of *Classical Quarterly,* and one day in 1964 I received an article discussing, and, I think, solving, a problem in a poem of Alkman. The author, whose learning evidently extended beyond Greek literature to horse-breeding, horse-handling and the archaeology of Eastern Europe and Central Asia, was a certain George (not Georges) Devereux, and he wrote from the École des hautes études in Paris.[11] I had never heard of him, and, not knowing much about the École, assumed that he was a post-graduate research student. We corresponded a bit after acceptance of his article, and I took the opportunity of a short stay in Paris, where I was looking at some Aristophanes manuscripts in the Bibliothèque Nationale, to go and see him. He turned out to be a man in late middle age, born a

---

[10] The Academy's Sections are its subject groups: see p. 190.
[11] George Devereux (1908–85) was born György Dobó in what is now Romania. Having acquired a PhD in anthropology at Berkeley (1936), after the Second World War he became a psychoanalyst. Devereux was director of Section VI of the École 1963–81.

Hungarian in Transylvania. Having become an unwilling subject of an enlarged Romania in 1918, he went to Paris on leaving school and studied physics and Malay; his original ambition to be a pianist foundered on an injury to one arm. Then anthropology, and an assignment to study the Sedang-Moi of northern Vietnam; preparatory work took him to Berkeley, and after the Sedang-Moi he studied the Mohave people of California, among whom he felt happy and at home. One product of his Mohave days was a massive book on the psychiatric beliefs and practices of the Mohave;[12] another product was his whole-hearted conversion to orthodox Freudianism, and he practised as a psychoanalyst until in 1963 he was appointed director of studies in Ethnopsychiatry at the École des hautes études.

Reading Dodds's book *The Greeks and the Irrational* aroused his interest in the Greeks. He learned the language properly, of course; nothing less would have satisfied him.[13] I doubt if there was any language, science or technical subject that did not come easily to him, although I don't think he would ever have made a historian. His speed of absorption was extraordinary, and so was his power of recall; he could tell you at once what was *not* in a book in which you thought you had read it, and he would be right.

His most important book, *From Anxiety to Method*,[14] which he gave to Audrey after our first meeting with him, is (or should be) of compelling interest to anyone concerned with anthropology, psychiatry or the behavioural sciences; a cascade of illuminating and provocative examples of interaction between observer and observed – yet at the same time overloaded with explanations in which the recurrent 'obviously', 'must be', and the like startle anyone but an orthodox Freudian.

In 1971 he applied for a Visiting Fellowship at All Souls, and I backed him for that. He was already a good friend of Dodds – whom he admired as a psychoanalyst manqué – and I judged that six months in Oxford would give him what he needed to complete his book *Dreams in Greek Tragedy*, while his own fertility in ideas and range of expertise would (if heeded) broaden other people's views of the ancient world. All Souls consulted Vernant,[15] who described George as 'brilliant but mad', and they took the risk. I have never really known how George and All Souls got on together, and I have not dared to inquire, in case the relationship was bad and they thought it was my fault for recommending him. He declined the invitation of one

---

[12]*Mohave Ethnopsychiatry and Suicide* (Washington, 1961).
[13]Dodds, *MP* 186, mentions that it was he who persuaded Devereux to teach himself Greek in mid-life; cf. ibid., 98, for a further reference to their friendship.
[14]*From Anxiety to Method in the Behavioral Sciences* (The Hague, 1967): its central idea is the application of the psychoanalytical concept of 'countertransference' (i.e. unconscious emotional reactions by the analyst towards the patient) to the nature of observation in the social sciences. The book makes reference to the work of both Dover and Dodds.
[15]Dover SN indicates that he was later unsure whether All Souls had consulted the classicist Jean-Pierre Vernant or the anthropologist Claude Lévi-Strauss.

don[16] to a cock-sucking session, but that was the only thing he ever told me about Oxford. Catherine was an undergraduate at St Hugh's at the time, and he invited her to dinner in All Souls one evening. She found the atmosphere hostile, but whether that was because she was his guest or because she was female I cannot say.

Dreams in Greek Tragedy was a subject on which he had given a lecture in St Andrews to an audience of uniformly sceptical classicists and psychologists. He chose as his topic for the lecture three Euripidean dreams (*Rhesus, Hecuba, Iphigenia Taurica*) in which he discerned a common structure indicating as 'a basic latent theme ... the "primal scene": the child's anxiety-distorted experience or fantasy of sexual relations between the parents'.[17] And 'the recurrence of the same theme in three tragedies implies not only the conflict's persistence *in Euripides' unconscious*, but also its partial sublimation, since he expressed it in the form of great poetry'. Now, I am not in the least disturbed by the fact that the psychodynamics implicit in 'psycho-history' and psychoanalytical literary criticism often trace the roots of works of genius back to between navel and knee, because I accept George's analogy between psychodynamics and chemistry: the more stinking manure you dig into a rose-bed, the more exquisite the colour and scent of the roses. My fundamental objection to the psychoanalytical approach had always been methodological: its glibness in treating almost anything as a symbol of almost anything else and its insistence on explaining the causation of an event in terms of inference from a hypothetical covert sequence when an available overt sequence is fully adequate as an explanation. However, some weeks *before* I heard George's hypothesis about the Euripidean dreams expounded I had a most bizarre dream (punch-line: 'Never walk under a giraffe!'),[18] in which I was a child being taken to the zoo by my old Aunt Miley. Every ingredient of the dream, without residue, was explicable in Freudian 'primal scene' terms – except that 'primal' is a bit misleading, because it brought into my mind an incident which occurred when I was about twelve – and I was dumbfounded when I heard George's analysis of the Euripidean dreams. It was something which I simply could not dismiss, and it was the chief reason why I advised Blackwell to publish *Dreams in Greek Tragedy*, while warning them that it could provoke derision and hostility.

In 1972 George and I thought it would be a good idea to collaborate on my projected book on Greek homosexuality. One day, however, while we were discussing this project, he growled, 'I hate queers!', and I realised, dejectedly, that our collaboration was not going to be easy. The trouble was that by that time George hated too many things: baroque music, Catholics, the Chinese, feminists, Greens ('eco-freaks'), George McGovern, and Plato ('proved' by his *Cratylus* to be

---

[16]Dover SN claims that this was the historian A.L. Rowse (1903–97), fellow of All Souls 1925–74.
[17]This and the following quotation are both found on p. 300 of Devereux's book.
[18]Readers interested in speculating about the dream might wish to take into account a footnote on giraffes in *GH* 99 n. 79.

schizophrenic).[19] When Catherine stayed for a few days in the Devereux household in Paris she soon became weary of his obsessive railing. Fortunately, George withdrew from collaboration on the grounds that he needed to turn out books which would sell in thousands to the intellectual public in France and Germany, in order to leave reasonable means of support to his young wife. As it happened, Jane Devereux left him soon afterwards, but by that time it was too late for us to resume collaboration.

Dreams in Greek Tragedy was published in 1976 and slaughtered in a full-page *TLS* review by Bernard Knox, for whom both George (until then) and I had a very high regard.[20] Knox naturally dealt severely with the psychoanalytical explanations which the book so consistently preferred to explanations suggested by everyday conscious experience. In a protesting letter to the *TLS* George made, I think, a serious mistake by referring to Poincaré's dictum that 'two explanations which account equally well for a given phenomenon are equivalent' and saying that there are 37 independent proofs of Pythagoras' Theorem, all of which are 'right'. When I contributed, a few years later, to a volume of essays on 'The Ethnopsychoanalysis of George Devereux', organised by Hans Peter Duerr, I pointed out that the *mathematical* question, 'On Euclid's postulates, is the square on the hypotenuse of a right-angled triangle equal to the sum of squares on the other two sides?', is of quite a different kind from the *historical* question, 'What proof of Pythagoras' Theorem was I taught at school in 1931?', and questions about the causes of human action, thought and feeling, every particle of which has a location in time and space, are necessarily historical.[21] George pointed out to me, in friendly but melancholy terms, that I had confused 'alternative' explanations with the complementarity which was the essence of his own approach. I could only tell him that he himself had not observed the distinction in his letter to the *TLS*, because he had gone straight from Pythagoras' Theorem to Freud's alleged discovery of 'complementary phenomena'. I dare say I may have misunderstood something. By that time he was very ill with emphysema, and he died before we could develop the argument further.

I am far from believing that Freudian psychodynamics tell the whole story, but equally far from believing that they do not tell some part of it. I am compelled (as

---

[19] Devereux had converted to Catholicism in 1933, the year in which he changed his name.

[20] Knox's review, entitled 'Clytemnestra on the couch', appeared in the *TLS* for 10 December 1976, pp. 1534–5; Devereux's very long, angry letter in reply did not appear till 1 April [sic] 1977, p. 403. For a brief but pointed dismissal of Devereux's views, see William V. Harris, *Dreams and Experience in Classical Antiquity* (Cambridge Mass., 2009) 96.

[21] The article in question, published in German, was 'Homosexualität in Griechenland und die "Inspiration"', in H.P. Duerr, ed., *Die wilde Seele. Zur Ethnopsychoanalyse von Georges* [sic] *Devereux* (Frankfurt am Main, 1987) 47–63. Since Devereux died in 1985, the discussion recounted in the following sentences suggests that Dover must have shown him the article in draft.

a rational being) to believe that on one occasion I made a comically obvious mistake which was generated by a subconscious wish on a matter of importance,[22] and that on three occasions I had dreams which translated unconscious wishes and fears into symbols which I understood (to my lasting benefit) within ten minutes of waking up. On one other occasion a dream answered a trivial question for me and in doing so raised (it seems to me) far-reaching issues in our understanding of the arts. I had been trying, without success, to recall a passage of Greek text on which someone had confused the standpoint of the writer with the standpoint of the person written about. My dream two nights later was about a rowdy wine-and-cheese party in Scotland, a sort of Conversazione of Kirriemuir,[23] which inspired me to improvise some verses. A critic whom I did not know objected severely, 'The second line doesn't scan.' I defended myself: 'But the man is Scottish, and he might pronounce "mouthful of ..." as "mouthfu' o", which, with synizesis, could scan as two syllables.' My critic was unimpressed: 'The verses are *about* a Scotsman, but they're not *by* a Scotsman, they're by you.' On waking, I remembered what I had been seeking two days earlier. I had argued that Thucydides must have been mistaken over the location of the Bay of Terina, because he says that Gylippos was driven out to sea by a *north* wind while crossing it. A.D. Nock[24] at Harvard dismissed my argument on the grounds that it's very hard, in a storm at sea, to be sure where the wind is coming from; and I pointed out that Thucydides, while writing *about* a man in a storm, was not himself storm-tossed while writing his account. The remarkable aspect of the dream was that my unconscious mind perceived and abstracted a structure, a relationship, from a memory not accessible to me and constructed a new complex of events which exhibited that relationship. It seems to me that this kind of perception is highly relevant to the appreciation by one culture of the art and literature produced by another. When a contemporary audience sees a Greek tragedy, it may find a great many of the ingredients, taken one at a time, alien; it is the structure, the interrelation of the ingredients, which makes the complex intelligible.

---

[22] The matter was a wish to give up smoking; the 'mistake' involved leaving a shop without picking up a packet of cigarettes just purchased there.
[23] A play on a bawdy Scottish folksong about an orgy, 'The ball of Kirriemuir', with Conversazione, i.e. a (supposedly) cultured debate, forming an ironic adjustment to the title.
[24] Arthur Darby Nock (1902–63), educated in England, spent most of his career as Frothingham Professor of the History of Religions at Harvard 1930–63: see the article by W.M. Calder, *DBC*, ii 717–19. Dover got on well with Nock during his 1960–1 visit to Harvard and admired him greatly.

16 THE PUBLIC 1964–1980

It is now more than a hundred years since classicists began to lament the decline in the part played by Greek and Latin in our education system.[1] At Balliol I had no anxieties on this score. The supply of good pupils seemed inexhaustible, and in Oxford as a whole, at any given time, there were some five hundred undergraduates reading Mods or Greats. My first years at St Andrews were no less encouraging; by the early sixties I had over ninety students in my Department. A downward plunge then began; the number of pupils in Scottish schools taking Higher Greek halved, and although the decline in England was not so rapid, it was inexorable.

Bad reasons often advanced for studying Greek are: that translation makes the pupil think logically, that we cannot understand our civilisation unless we study its origins, and that we cannot use our own language 'properly' without knowledge of the Greek component in our vocabulary. All this, I fear, is bunk.[2] Language and logic have very little to do with one another; the advantage conferred by hard work spent on translating is not logicality but sensitive antennae, and that purpose would be served as well by the study of Chinese or Japanese as by Greek, perhaps better. It is patently untrue that we cannot effectively pursue a mode of thinking without knowing that it was also pursued two thousand years ago. As for the use of English, words do not have 'real' meanings, or even 'original' meanings, unless we apply that term to the oldest meanings that we can trace historically; words mean, at any given time, what the people who use them intend them to mean.[3]

---

[1] Dover may have been thinking partly of the debates which began in 1870 on the compulsory Greek requirements for Oxbridge entrance; the requirements were abolished in 1919–20. Latin was then less threatened, but its requirement was abolished in turn in 1959–60: see C. Stray, *Classics Transformed: Schools, Universities, and Society in England 1830–1960* (Oxford, 1998) 271–97.

[2] Dover was unusual in rejecting all the conventional 'defences' of Classics indicated in his text; he had previously discussed this subject in a 1985 lecture entitled 'What are the "Two Cultures"?', printed in *G&L* 314–26; for discussion of Dover's stance on this issue, see Halliwell's chapter in *S&C*.

[3] Dover consistently denied that words have 'real meanings' rooted in their etymologies: compare e.g. *G&L* 45.

The good reason for studying Greek is that it is a peculiarly interesting and worthwhile compartment of human history; and I use 'history' in its broadest sense, to cover linguistic behaviour as well as artistic, religious, social, economic, political, scientific and philosophical behaviour.[4] 'Interesting and worthwhile' because Greek culture, while similar enough to ours to be intelligible,* is also different enough to make us reflect critically on ours; and because it produced abundant literature and works of art which appeal profoundly to those to whom art and literature appeal at all. The bold assertion that Greek literature is better than English, French or Russian would be absurd; to assert that it will stand comparison is quite enough. I believe passionately that a civilisation which studies only non-historical – that is to say, non-human – subjects is a mutilated civilisation. I am content that Greek should take its chance among many other historical subjects, but not content with an education system which makes access to it difficult. If you care *enough* about what is said in another language, you will learn that language in order not to be always at the mercy of translators.

What was to be done? Any attempt to re-introduce compulsion would have been self-destructive; at St Andrews, where until 1960 it was hard for an Arts student to avoid taking at least one course of Latin, we well knew the difference between volunteers and conscripts. It would also have been a betrayal of the faith that the classical languages could stand on their own feet. What was needed was a removal of obstacles, and that meant, first, the designing of courses, both at school and university, which would be simultaneously attractive and efficient, and secondly, propaganda aimed at the creation of a favourable climate of public opinion.

In 1965 I was appointed a member – as representative of the universities – of the Scottish Certificate of Education Classics Panel, whose task was to overhaul the Latin and Greek syllabuses at Ordinary and Higher levels. Of the other three members of the panel, two were very experienced Classics teachers and one a schools inspector. Our problem was simply described but not simply solved. It was perfectly possible to make the subject more attractive by making it easier. That would mean that a student who came up to the university with Highers in Greek and Latin and wanted to continue with them would be starting at a lower level of competence; and the onus would be on the university to ensure that the lower starting-point did not entail a lower competence on graduation. I accepted that, because I thought the universities should accept the challenge, and I acknowledged

---

*Not all scholars agree; I have seen Greek civilisation described as 'unimaginably alien'. It all depends on which aspects of a culture one regards as relevant to the judgement on similarity and difference. [EDS *Louis MacNeice wrote in his poem* Autumn Journal *(1939), part IX, 'It was all so unimaginably different / And all so long ago'. But Dover later thought he was (also) half-remembering the description of classical Greek mentalities as 'astoundingly alien' in Ruth Padel,* In and Out of the Mind *(Princeton, 1992) 10.*]

[4]For Dover's conception of 'history', see ch. 31.

that the Higher course in any subject should not be tailored solely to the minority which would go on with that subject, but should also be rewarding for those whose last acquaintance with the subject it would be. It was crucial for the future of Classics that pupils should get a favourable impression of it; at the same time, crucial that we should never deceive them into thinking that they knew more than they did. Learning a language entails *sooner or later* a great deal of hard work, and if we made things easier in the short run we must on no account pretend that the long run would be equally easy.

I found myself at odds with my colleagues on the panel over three issues, and there was a further change to which I consented with misgivings. One issue was the introduction of prescribed texts; I disagreed with that because it was well known that weak pupils, both at school and at university, would sometimes learn an English translation of a text pretty well by heart, spot a key word in a piece which confronted them in the examination, and simply draw on their memory. A second, never resolved, was our disagreement about what pupils of sixteen or seventeen could be expected to understand and discuss. When I showed the panel the paper on book vii of Plato's *Republic* which I had taken in the old Higher Certificate at seventeen, they were incredulous, and I was told that I was 'living in a different world'. The third issue concerned the incorporation of a non-linguistic 'topic' in the examination; it seemed to me that the specimen questions, however worded, all added up to 'Write down everything you can remember about . . .'. The remaining issue, and the most difficult, was 'comprehension tests'. When we look something up in a Greek or Latin text, we do not translate the whole page, but home in on the words which tell us what we want to know. In a comprehension test the examinee is confronted by a passage and asked not to write a translation of it but to answer questions about its content. A good test of this kind can be set, but the specimens produced for the panel's scrutiny did not show enough skill on the setters' part.

I was embarrassed by the fact that I was also a member of the Classics panel of the Scottish Universities Entrance Board. Changing hats between one meeting and another is not too hard, but wearing both at the same meeting is impossible, as I discovered at an adversarial meeting of the two panels. The chairman was Christian Fordyce, who could be all charm and wit in dealing with his intellectual equals but could also be grotesquely boorish.[5] When the members of the SCE panel came in, he was looking out of the window and smoking his pipe; without a word of greeting he said abruptly, 'Well, let's begin', and we did. He argued that the best way of showing whether one comprehends a piece is by translating it – which sounds a truism, but is not entirely true. I was prepared to defend comprehension tests in principle, but could not defend the specimens before us. Jessie Knox, a member of

---

[5] On Fordyce, see pp. 130–1.

the SCE panel, told me afterwards that this was the most disagreeable and embarrassing meeting she had ever attended.

After a year or two the SCE Board went ahead with the changes; there was nothing the universities could do to stop it. Whether the changes did anything to slow down the decline of Greek in schools, I cannot say, but certainly a pass in Higher Greek in 1975 did not mean what it had meant twenty years earlier; I could tell that, because I found I was regularly setting my second-year class work which I had once set to the first. This did not worry me overmuch, because the few who had strong academic ambitions leaped ahead, and the rest got a modicum of Greek – and with it, in nearly all cases, a liking for the subject – which otherwise they might have missed entirely.

Existing textbooks for beginners in Greek lagged a couple of generations behind comparable books for modern linguists, because their authors failed to understand the difference between a reference grammar and a language-learning book. In consequence, the beginner had to absorb a mass of rare inflected forms before being introduced to the simplest Greek texts, and features of fundamental importance, such as word order, were treated as an afterthought. The need was for a book which would teach first what the learner was likely to encounter first and most often. For my own Department I wrote a new beginners' course-book in accordance with that principle; it required the learner to construct hrs own reference-grammar by extracting the necessary data from examples (20–30 per lesson) of two- or three-word sentences accompanied by both literal and idiomatic translations.[6] But something on a national scale was needed, and in 1974 the Joint Association of Classical Teachers launched an extremely successful appeal to fund the designing of a new beginners' course. I was one member of the large Advisory Panel; Peter Jones was the director of the project.[7] Since we now were aiming at older learners, we decided that a ration of 'adult humour' was desirable. The project team tackled this with gusto, and their first draft of the opening lessons showed a physiological and anatomical bias which, as Desmond Lee remarked,[8] reminded

---

[6]Dover's course, distributed to students in stencilled booklets, made heavy demands; it represented 'the sort of course he himself would have liked had he been an adult beginner' (Elizabeth Craik, in S&C): cf. Dover's own precocious ability as a teenager to reconstruct the grammar of a language on the basis of analysing specimen texts (pp. 51–5). But some students were nonetheless appreciative: Eric Cambridge, nearly forty years later (personal communication with SH in 2010), had 'never forgotten the sheer intellectual thrill' of the beginners' course with Dover, for all its linguistic challenges.

[7]Peter Jones (1942–, MBE 1983), who had previously been a Classics schoolteacher and was later a senior lecturer at Newcastle University, went on to become a nationally important figure in promoting wider social and educational access to Classics. JACT had been founded in 1963 by a group of school and university teachers of Classics committed to reform of syllabuses and teaching methods in the subject.

[8]Sir Desmond Lee (1908–93, Kt 1961), a classical scholar by training, was, among other things, headmaster of Winchester College 1954–68 and President of Hughes Hall, Cambridge, 1973–8.

the learner that in many respects the Greeks were like the rest of us but failed to tell hrm that they also invented Tragedy, defeated the Persian invasion, and built the Parthenon. Compromise was easily achieved (though I vetoed the sentence, 'But hark! Someone is farting', on the grounds that it was an insufficiently realistic conversational utterance). The course begins with very simple, repetitive, artificially constructed dialogues in a Greek setting and gradually progresses, with decreasing simplification and omission, to real Greek texts. Published in 1978 under the title *Reading Greek,* it had sold 60,000 copies in the English-speaking world by 1992.[9] Where *are* all those people who thought they were going to learn Greek?

After writing the departmental course, which I was confident would teach first-year university students, in one-third of their time, more Greek than most of them would have known if they had done Greek at school, I redesigned the first year as a whole so that the beginners could be fed into the main stream at the end of the year and start off the second year level (more or less) with the others and expect to complete an honours degree in Classics in the normal four years. One or two did; sadly, from one point of view, or encouragingly, from another, the very best students I had in the beginners' class were people already committed to honours degrees in other subjects.

Having thus straightened out the bottom end in 1967–8, we all turned our minds to the top end, introducing a one-year post-graduate diploma in certain specialised areas of Classics and a two-year M.Litt. by examination. Hopes of building up a substantial graduate school were not realised, because a graduate who contemplates coming to a particular university tends to choose one where a graduate school already flourishes, but we got a few. More important was the institution of a joint honours course in Classics and Ancient History (1968) and one in Biblical Studies with Greek or Latin (1970). The latter was not easy to get through the Board of Studies because the classicists looked down their noses at the divines (Adrian Gratwick reminded me that theology differs from Arts subjects in that the existence of its object of study is disputed).[10] The case for Classics and Ancient History was much clearer. Ancient History, of which Geoffrey Rickman[11] was now in charge, was flourishing and expanding to meet an increasingly enthusiastic demand, and there were not a few students, linguistically weak, who could get a respectable Second in Classics and Ancient History but would have got

---

[9]The book was published in a second edition in 2007 and is still in print as of 2023. For its importance within the context of reduced teaching of Greek in secondary schools, see James Morwood's comments in *OC* 241.

[10]Adrian Gratwick was appointed to a lectureship in Latin in St Andrews in 1966 and spent the remainder of his career there (retiring as a Professor of Latin in 2007); he was an outstanding scholar of early Roman comedy.

[11]Geoffrey Rickman (1932–2010) had been appointed lecturer in Ancient History in 1962; he was subsequently Professor of Roman History 1981–97 and elected FBA in 1989: see his British Academy memoir by John Richardson in *BMF* XI.

a Third in pure Classics and for that reason would have hesitated to try for honours in Classics at all. Among my own motives (mixed, as usual) for promoting the joint honours courses I think that a desire to keep up numbers in Classics at all costs predominated. The obvious 'cost' was acquiescence in the award of Seconds to students who were good historians but bad linguists. I was willing to pay that price, because something is better than nothing; and since they did their best and I was fond of them all, the payment didn't hurt.

The principle that something is better than nothing underlay our decision in 1975 to start a first-year class in Classical Culture, with Greek and Latin texts in translation and a good ration of the visual arts and intellectual, social and religious history. My main object in promoting this course was to make a contribution to moulding the climate of opinion at the end of the century. If students found the course interesting and rewarding, it was more likely that when they themselves were parents of students they would give good advice on choice of courses. If the idea got around that the course was a soft option, it could easily be stiffened by increasing the quantity of prescribed texts. The first year of Classical Culture was my last year at St Andrews, and it encouraged me greatly: an enrolment of over sixty, including many medievalists and art historians, from whom we often had more perceptive and stimulating essays than from our own Classical pupils. I was doubtful about extending Classical Culture to a second-year course, and dead against ever allowing it to appear, under any name or disguise, as an honours course.[12] When I was no longer present to fight that battle, it was lost.

In the Introduction to a commentary on Book VI of Thucydides which I produced in 1964 I wrote: 'I have no sympathy or respect for the currently fashionable view that Classical scholars should spend more time in entertaining the public and less in trying to discover what the Greek authors actually said.'[13] I am surprised I said that, but there it is. Perhaps I wrote it in a moment of irritation with someone (Moses Finley?)[14] who denigrated textual criticism. It did not represent my view as a teacher, because I gave just as much encouragement to students who did not like textual problems as to those who did. Moreover, while I was in Greece in the spring of 1963 I thought in some detail about the possibility of writing a book, to be called

---

[12]Similar attitudes were held by Dodds: see *MP* 175–6.
[13]The sentence appears in the Preface to both school editions of Thucydides Books 6 and 7 published by Dover in 1965.
[14]Sir Moses Finley (1912–86), an American-born ancient historian, spent most of his career in Cambridge, where he was Professor of Ancient History 1970–9 and Master of Darwin College 1976–82. He and Dover represented very different kinds of classical scholarship (cf. p. 337), but the present surmise is unfair, since Finley was on record as calling 'the fashion of sneering' at such things as textual criticism 'wholly unjustified': see his 'Crisis in the Classics', in J.H. Plumb, ed., *Crisis in the Humanities* (Harmondsworth, 1964) 21. Cf. D. Jew et al., eds, *M.I. Finley: An Ancient Historian and his Impact* (Cambridge, 2016).

Process and Product in Classical Studies, which would explain to the general public how Classics as an academic activity actually works – a sort of Classical *Double Helix,* only (I hope) easier for the uninitiated reader.[15] I started work in 1968 on *Aristophanic Comedy,* which was designed from the first for the Greekless reader with an interest in drama or the ancient world or both.[16]

In the summer of 1977 I had a visit from a BBC producer, Christopher Burstall, who was planning a set of programmes on the Greeks and wanted to know if I would be interested.[17] I was, and we started work later that summer. I can't pretend that a desire to evangelise was my only motive; somebody told me that Kenneth Clark had made a million from *Civilisation* – that is to say, from the book that went with the programme;[18] the BBC does not pay its contributors extravagantly – and even a decent fraction of that was an enticing prospect. Christopher had made other programmes which I admired, and I began in a confident mood, but when I was asked to draft a synopsis of four fifty-minute programmes I soon discovered that while Christopher knew virtually nothing about the Greeks I knew even less about television. Clark's *Civilisation* had been founded on the visual arts. I was neither an art historian nor an archaeologist, and hardly any of the things that interested me most about the Greeks lent themselves to presentation in a visual medium. Thrashing out problems in about 140 hours of talk in the summer of 1978 we decided that in addition to what was devoted explicitly to buildings, statues and vase-paintings and to the staging of excerpts from Greek plays, everything that I had to say about Greek history, ideas, values and attitudes must be said at places in the Greek world chosen not merely to provide attractive 'wallpaper' but as being directly and patently relevant to whatever topic was being discussed. Some of my wilder ideas were quickly discarded, such as being lowered by helicopter on to the summit of Mount Olympus for a discussion of Greek religion (very expensive, and the cloud-cover is notorious).

In September Christopher and I, with Denis Moriarty, the assistant producer, went on a reconnaissance of sites in Sicily and Greece, and Audrey joined us in Athens. Revision and rehearsal of our dialogue went on continuously, all day and half the night. It was decided that neither of us should speak directly to the camera; all our utterances would be either dialogue or voice-over, and we would do all in our power (which in the end proved not quite sufficient) to prevent dialogue from degenerating into a succession of feed-questions from Christopher and didactic answers from me.

---

[15]J.D. Watson, *The Double Helix: A Personal Account of the Discovery of the Structure of DNA* (1968).
[16]See the earlier reference to this book on p. 121, with the note there.
[17]Christopher Burstall (1932–2009) was a pioneering figure in the history of TV arts documentaries: see the obituary by Leslie Megahey, *The Guardian,* 10 July 2009, p. 37.
[18]Clark's *Civilisation: a Personal View* was published in 1969, to accompany his celebrated thirteen-part TV series of the same name and the same year.

Between September 1978 and March 1979 we went through another 160 hours of rehearsal and revision, try this and try that, and since I had by that time become President of the British Academy[19] I was beginning to find that if I was not to neglect the job I was being paid to do at Corpus there was no waking hour which could decently be allotted to relaxation. In March we went off to Sicily and Greece for filming, and I was immersed for a month in a milieu which was by turns rewarding and frustrating, exciting and exasperating. I soon became aware that I was watching over the incubation of mutual hostilities, from which I could distance myself easily enough. It was not so easy to shrug off the time wasted on arguments about working hours, the availability of hot meals, and demarcation; on one occasion the morning was spent (how could they argue *so long*?) over the problem of putting black drapes behind a statue in a museum, because none of the crew were scenery-people, and God forbid that non-union creatures such as the producer and I should put up drapes. Practical difficulties of a less philosophical nature did not worry me, which was just as well, because they were numerous. It was found that when I wore shirts of artificial fibre with a microphone pinned under my tie a crackling sound was recorded, and that meant wearing only cotton shirts, easily enough washable but needing ironing every time. Background noises constantly intruded; Vespas, aircraft, quarrels, children or a gust of wind which came through in sound like a drum-roll. Spring is the tourist season in Greece, and all the well-known sites were swarming with conducted parties of a dozen nationalities. Our Greek helpers, Maria Powell and Tony Vasilopoulos, patiently braved complaint and resentment in their efforts to clear a space and enforce silence for our filming. I shall not forget Tony's stern cry, 'Silence, s'il vous pleut!'; since Greek loan-words from French normally replace *eu* by *ai*, he must have thought that *pleut* was correct and *plait* an error. It was common for a take to be spoiled because a bit of fluff or other debris had been left on the inside of the lens by the rolling film. At the end of the take the lens would be inspected from the outside, and the cry, 'Hair on the gate!' meant that that take must be repeated. Now and again either Christopher or I would lose the way in the dialogue, or hesitate a moment too long, and scrap the take with a despairing 'Oh, *shit!*'. If Christopher, to keep me on my toes, changed without warning the order of points we had rehearsed, or put in a question which we had not rehearsed at all, it might throw me, but more often it worked well and stepped up the spontaneity of the dialogue. It was very rare for the first take to be satisfactory; three takes were normal, five or six not unknown, and on one occasion nine were needed. If at the end of a twelve-hour day there was ten minutes' worth of usable film 'in the can', it was a good day. I soon got used to this; a fourth take was depressing, but then I reminded myself that sounding fresh and lively when one doesn't feel it is a technical job which simply must be done.

---

[19]In 1978: see pp. 226–7.

Later in 1979 the excerpts from drama and other dramatised bits and pieces were done in the studio at Ealing, and the four programmes went into the cutting-room. There they were for a year while Christopher and the film editor put them into shape. It was a shape which gave me increasing uneasiness, and when I saw the 'rough-cut' I jotted down a number of coarse and vivid comments on my note-pad. And yet, through lack of confidence in my own judgement, I communicated none of these adverse reactions to Christopher, but continued to assure him of my contentment. This was partly through a recognition that what was done was done, partly because there were some things which I now thought bad ideas but had commended at the time of the filming, but mainly because I felt I had to be guided by Christopher's assessment of what made appropriate television for BBC 1.† I ought to have made more fuss about the costuming and make-up of the actors; they were all perfectly groomed, with Persil-white clothes, and the real Greeks were not like that. I had suggested at one stage that Socrates should pause in the middle of a philosophical sentence to hawk and spit noisily, but the suggestion did not find favour.

The preview of one programme in August 1980, attended by television critics and various others, was ominous, because at the buffet which followed they seemed more inclined to talk about the weather than about what they had seen on screen, and when I saw the first programme transmitted it was with friends who relapsed into embarrassed silence. Although Christopher and I had agreed at the start that neither of us would speak directly to camera, he had evidently decided during those months in the cutting-room that the programmes needed a long introduction in which he did speak to camera. Those of my colleagues in Oxford who had watched that first programme told me that they had switched off within the first quarter of an hour. Among the critics, Clive James spoke of 'this truly awful series'; Joan Bakewell was the only one who perceived the difficulty of presenting non-visual material in a visual medium.[20]

Christopher regretted my disappointment and sought to comfort me by telling me that my own part in the programmes came very well out of the 'ratings', as measured by the BBC's normal sampling methods. I dare say it did but I had not expected otherwise. I was not camera-shy, I knew my subject, and I had plenty of experience in engaging the attention of an audience. Henry Farrar, the splendid cameraman who filmed us in Greece, told me when we parted company that I was

---

† Kenneth Cavander tells me that he once threw a mug of coffee at a screen that was showing a rough-cut, with the robust declaration, 'This is shit!' Not my style; but perhaps it ought to be, sometimes.

[20] Clive James' scathing review, originally in the *Observer*, 28 September 1980, p. 48, strangely makes no mention of Dover himself, only of Burstall: cf. his *Glued to the Box:Television Criticism from the Observer, 1979–82* (London, 1983) 121. Joan Bakewell's review, *The Times*, 12 September 1980, p. 8, was more urbanely negative; she remarked that ideas are 'hard to televise'. Sylvia Clayton was not alone in suggesting, in *The Telegraph*, 26 September 1980, p. 13, that the programmes would have been better if presented by Dover himself, 'an affable expert', instead of Burstall.

the most professional contributor he had ever worked with, and any compliment containing the word 'professional' is enough to keep me happy for a decade. But much as I relish an ego-trip, I had hoped above all to make programmes which would earn the respect of the critics and excite interest in the Greeks. Alasdair Milne, then head of BBC television, whose view of the quality of the programmes was harsher than mine, gave me lunch and sympathy and offered me the possibility of doing some programmes on another subject. I contemplated organising a series on Language, but it turned out that such a programme had been done three years earlier; no one at the BBC seemed to have remembered that. Years later I took part in Channel Four's *Greek Fire,* an enterprise spoiled for me by George Steiner's preposterous statement that Aristotle believed that women do not have souls (beware of gurus when they have attracted enough deference to make them reckless) and recently in a radio series *Greek as a Treat,* but I have no ambition to become involved in anything on a large scale.[21]

Since the end of 1980 I have met many people who enjoyed *The Greeks* and got something out of it, so it seems that my melancholy reaction to its failure with the critics was not wholly justified. The book I wrote to go with the programmes did not sell well, but I had an absolutely free hand in writing it. It is not a systematic exposition, but passes from one topic to the next through a chain of associations which was formed essentially in the making of the programmes. I am not discontented with it.[22]

---

[21] The 1990 Channel 4 series *Greek Fire* was accompanied by a book with the same title by Oliver Taplin (cf. p. 307); George Steiner's blunder was repeated in at least one newspaper article about the series (Peter Lewis, *The Sunday Times*, 18 March 1990). The BBC radio series *Greek as a Treat* was broadcast on Radio 4 in April-May 1993 and again produced a book, Peter France, *Greek as a Treat: an Introduction to the Classics* (London, 1993).

[22] The first edition of Dover's book *The Greeks* (BBC Books, 1980) had an Introduction by Christopher Burstall which was dropped in the revised edition published by Oxford U.P. in 1982. The book contains many striking formulations of Dover's views; it was judged 'intriguing' and 'stimulating' by Bernard Knox, *Backing into the Future* (New York, 1994) 237, 'still well worth reading, not least for its chapter on Syracuse' by Paul Cartledge in his obituary of Dover, *The Independent*, 16 March 2010, p. 42, and 'very popular and original' by Donald Russell in *KJD* 166.

17 FRUITION 1966–1968

In July 1966 I was elected a Fellow of the British Academy. The Academy, founded in 1901 (nearly three and a half centuries after the Royal Society, which was for scientists)[1] appeared to have as its principal business the filling of vacancies by new elections, the administration of some public lectures established by private endowment and benefaction, and the publication of those lectures in its annual Proceedings. It occupied constricted premises in Burlington Gardens, which contrasted strikingly with the palatial home of the Royal Society in Carlton Terrace. The Secretary (Sir Mortimer Wheeler)* received a modest allowance for expenses, but no salary. Wheeler himself, in his history of the Academy from 1949 to 1968, has given the impression that until he and Sir Charles Webster (President 1950–54) shook it up the Academy was a collection of inactive and complacent old men, and that view was certainly shared by many who were outside it.[2] Perusal of the Annual Reports in the Proceedings seems to me to give a rather different picture. From the first the Academy formulated long-term projects which, in company with the academies of other European nations, it recognised as outstanding needs for the advancement of research in the humanities. The very slow progress of some of these projects and the elimination of others were in part caused by the dearth of properly qualified scholars who were sufficiently free of other commitments, but more than anything by the shortage of funds from British sources. Until 1962 successive British governments were simply not interested in furthering progress in the humanities.

---

*I first met Wheeler when he was the brigadier commanding 12 A.A. Brigade at Salerno and I was a junior officer. He had a reputation for unbelievable success and speed at getting young women into bed. [EDS *This first meeting belongs to September 1943: cf. Wheeler's own memoir,* Still Digging *(London, 1955) 163–5. See Dover's earlier references to Wheeler on pp. 172–3.*]

[1] The British Academy received its Royal Charter in 1902, some *two* and a half centuries after the founding of the Royal Society (1660).
[2] Mortimer Wheeler, *The British Academy 1949–1968* (London, 1970).

Any academy, any institution whose existing members choose new members, is vulnerable to the charge that it is a club of the like-minded, who will look askance at newly developing subjects, keep out unorthodox brilliance and (at worst) bring in their own pals. In the case of the British Academy, I can think of three or four Fellows, over the last forty years, in whose election personal ties and consequent overestimation of their scholarly merit may have mattered more than objective assessment of their work; not a significant percentage. Lack of response to new subjects can be more serious, but at least since the nineteen-sixties the British Academy has proved itself aware of that. Curiously enough – curiously, that is, to those who are accustomed to exaggerate the role of Classics in nineteenth-century Britain – by 1966 the increase of the number of Sections to twelve from the original four (History and Archaeology; Philology; Philosophy; Jurisprudence and Economics) had actually created a bias in favour of the ancient world, a bias against which Fellows in other fields were beginning to rebel. One Section was now concerned with Ancient (i.e. Greek and Roman) History, another with Classical languages and literatures, and a third with Archaeology, while all medieval and modern history was lumped together in Section II and English and other European languages and literatures in Section VI. In 1992 Section II became three sections and so did Section VI; there are eighteen sections in all.[3]

The hardest problem lies within a section. When it comes to assessing the value of someone's contribution to a subject, the existing members of an academy are likely to be the people least unfitted to do it. Who else will? The candidate's methodology may be unfamiliar and uncongenial to them but if its results are fruitful, that will do hrm good. Yet behind the assessment of an individual lie assumptions about the relative importance of different topics, periods, texts and problems *within* the subject. If an X-ologist is being considered for election and there are only Z-ologists in the section concerned with that subject, there is a danger that they may give priority to one more Z-ologist. After all, though some of the Z-ologists began the study of Z because they found it suited their temperament and predilection, others did so because they were intellectually persuaded of its importance, and none of them is at all likely to rate its importance low. This danger has not always been eluded.

There are inevitably people who are aggrieved that they have not so far been elected. One of them lobbied me, when I was President, on his own behalf; I discouraged him from such an approach and advised patience, because I was fairly sure that before long he would be elected on his merits, as indeed he was. I know of two others who are inclined to suspect that they have been in effect blackballed by an 'enemy'. In one case the suspicion is not absolutely unjustified, but the aggrieved party has unfortunately identified his 'enemy' incorrectly; in the other

---

[3] The figure has meanwhile risen to twenty-one (as of 2023).

case, the decisions on the quality of the candidate's work have been a consensus reached by fair discussion, but that is not easy for him to take.

If 1969 had passed and I had *still* not been elected I would have felt fairly aggrieved myself, and even by 1966 I was beginning to feel that it was about time. My hardback publications were *Greek Word Order* in 1960 and commentaries (1965) on Thucydides VI and VII which were abridgements of the full-scale commentary still awaiting publication. *Greek Word Order* was my most original contribution to my subject, and the abridged Thucydides offered the promise that the full version would mark a very considerable advance in our understanding of the problems in those two books. Among my twenty-odd articles, eight had made original contributions of some importance on a wide range of topics, of which two could be labelled 'history', five 'literature', and one ('Eros and Nomos')[4] could be called, I suppose, 'historical sexology'. I could look forward to the appearance of three hardbacks in 1968. On Thucydides, as it turned out, I was too optimistic, because Tony Andrewes' commentary on Thucydides V, which would appear in the same volume as my VI and VII, took longer than either of us had thought it would, and the volume did not appear till 1970, but at least I knew by 1966 that if I dropped dead the publication could go ahead without revision. *Clouds* went to press at the end of 1966; and I was beginning another book, with every prospect of completing it in the course of 1967.

This book was to be on Lysias. I had been invited in 1963 to give the Sather Lectures in the University of California some time in the academic year 1966/7, and I chose the winter quarter, January to March 1967.[5] They had hoped (as I learned some years later) that I would lecture on Aristophanes, but they did not say so at the time, so that they had no good grounds for vetoing Lysias. I was now reviving a project which had attracted me in 1948 but was set aside in 1949.[6]

In Roman times 425 speeches were attributed to Lysias; that is to say, 425 had been listed under his name in the catalogue of Greek literature which Callimachus compiled at Alexandria early in the third century BC. Dionysius of Halicarnassus, a literary critic and historian at the end of the pre-Christian era, regarded 192 of the attributions as wrong. In a few cases he had sound historical reasons but too often his reasoning was subjective and circular, to the effect 'Lysias is identifiable by a uniquely attractive style, which (unfortunately) cannot be defined or described; such-and-such a speech lacks that style, and is therefore identifiable as non-Lysian.' The clue to what had happened in the transmission of Lysias is provided by a remark made by Dionysius in another context: Isocrates' adopted son denied that

---

[4] See the earlier reference to this article on p. 162.
[5] The Sather Lectures were instituted in 1913–14 and became one of the most prestigious such series in Classics: for their early history, see Sterling Dow, *Fifty Years of Sathers* (Berkeley, 1965).
[6] For Dover's original interest in Lysias, during the brief period of his doctoral work, see p. 105.

Isocrates had ever written speeches for the lawcourts, but Aristotle (more than half a century before Callimachus) had observed that 'many bundles' of lawcourt speeches by Isocrates were in circulation in the book-trade. Galen, the great medical writer of the second century AD, describes in an essay 'On his own Books' how he overheard at a bookshop an argument about the authenticity of a book being sold under his name, and he goes on to describe how other people have passed off as their own (with omissions, additions and changes) works which he himself had written. Throughout the ancient world doubts could always exist about the authenticity of a work, because, in an age before the printing-press, the 'publication' of a work was the moment at which the author lost control of its circulation by allowing someone else to take a copy of it. Galen's concern was with people who tried to enhance their own reputation by falsely claiming to have written good books; Aristotle's remark about Isocrates shows us the other side of the coin, the bookseller's attempt to achieve higher prices and better sales by falsely attributing mediocre works to great names. I was pleased to learn from Robbins Landon (though not in time for the Sather lectures) that in the music trade at the beginning of the nineteenth century at least 160 symphonies were on sale as Haydn's, though he certainly did not write that number.[7] In September 1966 a papyrus was published which consists of fragments of an ancient catalogue of Lysias' works, giving titles and short summaries; it includes one speech which up to then had always been known as a forensic speech of Isocrates. This papyrus was an agreeable confirmation that I was thinking on the right lines.

When I arrived at Berkeley in January 1967 I had written the first of six lectures in prospect, and I had some idea of what I intended to explore in the remaining five – most obviously, the chronology of the speeches, the extent to which they exhibited a political standpoint which could be attributed to Lysias as an individual, and the possibility of separating genuine from false attributions stylistically. Before I left Berkeley I had come to the conclusion that speech XII, in which Lysias himself was the prosecutor, was the *only* one of whose genuineness we can be certain; the others, of course, may all be genuine, but there is no one of them whose genuineness we could defend with absolute conviction.

A more far-reaching idea, affecting Athenian oratory as a whole, first evolved during my time at Berkeley. An Athenian involved in a law suit was expected to speak in person, but it was up to him to decide whether to compose his own speech or to have it composed for him by someone more skilled and experienced. For that

---

[7]The American musicologist H.C. Robbins Landon (1926–2009) was the world's leading authority on Haydn, whose life and works he studied in a five-volume magnum opus (1976–80). But the information he gave Dover takes on an ironic tinge in light of the fact that he was himself fooled by a set of hoax 'Haydn' sonatas in 1993: see e.g. Jim McCue, *The Times*, 31 December 1993, p. 5, Fritz Spiegl, *The Independent*, 5 January 1994, p. 14, with full critical analysis in F. Reece, 'Composing authority in six forged "Haydn" sonatas', *Journal of Musicology* 35 (2018) 104–43.

purpose, people like Lysias were much in demand and greatly valued by those whom they helped; yet prejudice against 'subtlety' and 'cleverness', and even stronger prejudice against anyone known to have accepted money in return for writing a speech for someone else, made it unwise for the speaker in court to admit to a jury that he had sought the help of a 'consultant' and unwise for the consultant to declare his professional role ostentatiously. It seemed to me that there might be a connection between these facts and the suspect or disputed attribution of so many speeches. Suppose that the parts played by client and consultant in the composition of a speech varied from one speech to another: the client had an interest in claiming the whole thing as his own, but the bookseller an interest in treating it as the work of a famous consultant, while the consultant's own attitude would depend on his degree of satisfaction with the work and its outcome in court. If the case had failed, it could well be that neither client nor consultant would be over-anxious to assert the claim.

This argument has not been well received, and, for once in a way, I think that inappropriate attitudes of mind have affected my critics' ability to understand the argument itself. Naturally we like to construct a personality out of the works ascribed to a named author, though I myself find it easy to suppress such a liking if the reward is a more complete picture of the styles and techniques of a place and period. The legal principle 'presumed innocent until proved guilty' spills over into literary history, to the extent of implanting the disastrous principle 'presumed genuine until proved spurious' (hence the immoderate emotion generated by evidence indicating that *Prometheus Vinctus* is not by Aeschylus).[8] Adverse reaction to the crime of 'forgery' seems to affect people's reaction to 'incorrect attribution', which is quite a different matter. My notion that a given speech might be partly by a known author and partly by his (often unnamed) client seems to have been disturbing enough to obscure the care with which I had used 'might' and 'could', avoiding unjustified generalisation, and to distract attention from some of the relevant evidence. The argument 'But surely everyone would have known ...' means little when we are concerned with a society in which assertion and counter-assertion on questions of fact were the normal currency of political life, believed or disbelieved according to one's alignment.

The lectures themselves were not an unqualified success, because I packed far too much into the first one and thereby discouraged non-classicists from coming to any more. Kendrick Pritchett, who was Chairman of the Department, could see very well what had happened, and gave me heart by telling me very emphatically that what mattered most was the eventual book, not the delivery of the lectures.[9]

---

[8]*Prometheus Bound* is transmitted in the manuscript tradition as the work of Aeschylus but its authenticity began to be doubted in the mid-nineteenth century; although the jury is still out, many scholars now accept, as Dover did, that the play was not written, in its entirety at least, by Aeschylus.

[9]W.K. Pritchett (1909–2007) was Professor of Greek at Berkeley 1953–76 and chairman of the Classics department 1966–70. His *The Greek State at War* (5 vols, 1971–91) remains a work of considerable importance.

I have (and had) a great respect for Pritchett as an ancient historian, but neither of us profited from discussing history with each other. In part this was because he was distracted by an accelerating tragedy in his family, but mainly because I was on the wrong side in the bitter dispute between Pritchett and Meritt over the Athenian calendars and the possibility of translating certain dates into terms of our own calendar.[10] I knew what I had written on the subject in my forthcoming commentary on Thucydides VI, but Pritchett didn't know, and I didn't want to get involved in any discussion which would compel me to disclose it.

I was offered a tenured appointment at Berkeley, but the idea of emigration did not appeal to me. Rather on the spur of the moment I raised the possibility of negotiating with St Andrews for a joint appointment, so that I could teach there from October to May but spend the period from June to September in Berkeley for the specific purpose of producing, in conjunction with a graduate seminar there, a new edition of the fragments of Greek comedy. I put this idea to Steven Watson[11] on my return, and he was not enthusiastic; nor was I when I came to think about it more coolly. I had after all been excessively tired for much of the time that I was in Berkeley, and although I reckoned normally to spend the Long Vacation on academic work, it was a different matter to be tied for the whole of the year, maybe for a ten-year period, to a precise commitment with a regular timetable. It was a good thing that I dropped the idea of the joint appointment, because although I and my collaborators at Berkeley would have produced an edition greatly superior to what was at that time available, it would not have been comparable with the edition which Rudolf Kassel and Colin Austin have been producing in successive volumes since 1983.[12]

We were lucky in being able to rent a furnished house from the philosopher William Dennes;[13] it had a splendid view over the Bay and was within a short, though very steep, walk from a bus route down Telegraph Avenue to the Berkeley campus. We had arrived in America in time to spend Christmas with Hugh[14] in Washington – he was employed at that time by the World Bank – and took the train, via Chicago, from Washington to Berkeley. This, as it turned out, didn't have

---

[10]Benjamin D. Meritt (1899–1989) was Professor of Greek Epigraphy, Institute for Advanced Studies, Princeton, 1935–69. He is best known for *The Athenian Tribute Lists* (4 vols, 1939–53), which he produced with H.T. Wade-Gery and M.F. McGregor. Pritchett was Meritt's research assistant 1936–42; in the late 1940s his disagreement with his mentor about the Athenian calendar led to a bitter dispute which continued till Meritt's death.
[11]Principal of St Andrews: see p. 151.
[12]The German classical scholar Rudolf Kassel (1926–2020) edited the eight-volume *Poetae Comici Graeci* with the Anglo-French classicist Colin Austin (1941–2010) between 1983 and 1995.
[13]William Ray Dennes (1898–1982) spent most of his working life in the Berkeley philosophy department; he retired in 1965 as Mills Professor of Intellectual and Moral Philosophy and Civil Polity.
[14]Hugh Latimer, Dover's brother-in-law: see pp. 76 and 101.

much to recommend it, because snow delayed the train for many hours at Laramie, with the result that we missed going through the Rockies in daylight. Alan and Catherine were with us; Alan flew down from San Francisco to Los Angeles to stay with Mort Chambers[15] and his family for a few days before flying back to London in time for his start of term, but Catherine stayed with us in Berkeley and discovered, by attending the Greek beginners' class in the University, that Greek was not for her. Both children were enchanted by their first sight of California; they went for a walk down Telegraph Avenue and came back with the news, 'They've got everything! Hippies, junkies, homosexuals, prostitutes – the lot!'

That quarter at Berkeley is memorable for the occasion when the President of the University, Clark Kerr, was fired by the Regents, among whom was the Governor of the State, Ronald Reagan.[16] On campus everyone seemed to assume that the State was bent on the destruction of the University; off campus, we found it wise to hold our tongues and remember that there was a Republican under every stone. With one exception, all the faculty members and their families whom we met were opposed to the Vietnam war. The exception was frightening: a professor's wife who thought that the world was in such a mess that the Lord was bound to come within the next few years, and that we had a duty to fulfil the prophecy of Armageddon. She spoke of the 'disloyalty' of the young in a way which made me think of a Roman matron in the time of Marcus Aurelius deploring the disloyalty of young Christian converts.

Soon after our return I met Tam Dalyell[17] at a party in St Andrews and told him about the virtually unanimous opposition at Berkeley to the Vietnam war. He asked me earnestly what my American friends thought of the British Government's policy in respect of the war; I had to admit that they had never said a word about it, and I doubted whether they had any idea what it was. I myself could have taken a less unfavourable view of the Americans' intervention in Vietnam if I had thought that they could win, because I would rather have seen South-East Asia, or any other part of the world, dominated by the United States, where open criticism of public policy is frequent and strident, than by the Soviet Union or China, where it was (and in China still is) suppressed. My belief that America could not win was born when I saw a television debate from the Oxford Union in which Cabot

---

[15]Mortimer Chambers (1927–2020) was a Greek historian and papyrologist who spent most of his career at the University of California at Los Angeles. He had been taught by Dover when a Rhodes Scholar at Oxford 1949–52.

[16]Clark Kerr (1911–2003), President of the University of California (of which Berkeley is one part), was sacked by the governing body (Regents) in 1967 under pressure from Reagan as the new State Governor, who, in the wake of several years of student protests (cf. Dover's comments on pp. 199–202), had called Berkeley a 'hotbed of communism and homosexuality'.

[17]The Scottish Labour politician Tam Dalyell (1932–2017) was an MP for two Scottish constituencies between 1962 and 2005. He was noted for a fierce independence of mind and for his anti-war, anti-imperialist views.

Lodge,[18] defending American policy, spoke of the time when 'the Viet Cong would wake up one morning and decide it just wasn't worth going on fighting'. Such an idea betrayed a disastrous failure to understand Asian endurance, patience and pertinacity.† Moreover, in Giap[19] the Vietnamese Communists had an imaginative and resolute commander of genius, their morale and discipline were sustained by an ideology which inspired self-sacrifice, and they outdid their adversaries in ruthlessness. In competition for the 'hearts and minds' of a peasant population those who inspire the greater fear are very strongly placed.

In the summer of 1966 I saw *The War Game* on television, and consequently joined Civil Defence.[20] Some of my friends wondered why I chose Civil Defence rather than CND; it seemed to them that to acknowledge the possibility of any defence against nuclear attack was to compromise with nuclear strategy. My reason, though, was very simple: it had nagged at my conscience for some time that I was not using my abilities in any way for the defence of my country, and although I knew that the effect of nuclear attack on Britain would be catastrophic, the likelihood of its happening was not going to be increased by my learning how to save a few lives on the margins of the catastrophe. Through my absence in California I missed most of the basic course, and when confronted by an examination in April 1967 I had to answer most of the questions by guesswork. I fared better in the oral, particularly in the understanding of maps, and the examiner knew the reason for my deplorable performance on the written paper. 'When we get a professor joining,' he said, 'you don't think we're going to turn him away, do you?' So, corruptly, I passed, and went on to learn about chemical warfare. To my disappointment, Civil Defence was closed down altogether in 1968.

Early in 1966 we started thinking about buying a house, and had a look at one or two which were on the market. Martin Lindsay then drew our attention to a house in Hepburn Gardens, no. 49, which seemed to him, for some reason which he couldn't put into words, just the right house for us, and likely to come on the market soon because the old man who lived there was mortally ill. We had a look

---

†In 1993, when intervention in Jugoslavia was under discussion, the pacifist Lord Soper stated that Vietnam had shown the impossibility of waging war. On the contrary, the North Vietnamese showed that it was possible not merely to fight a war, but to win a decisive victory.

[18]Henry Cabot Lodge Jr. (1902–85) was an American politician and diplomat; he was US ambassador to South Vietnam 1963–4.

[19]General Vo Nguyen Giap (1911–2013), leader of the People's Army of Vietnam in the Vietnam War, was a commander of genius whose guerrilla forces had earlier defeated the French at the battle of Dien Bien Phu in 1954.

[20]*The War Game* was a BBC-commissioned drama-documentary film based on the scenario of an imaginary nuclear attack on Britain; it was shown only in certain cinemas in 1966 and not on TV until 1985, so Dover's memory is at fault: see J. Chapman, 'The BBC and the censorship of *The Wargame* (1965)', *Journal of Contemporary History* 41 (2006) 75–94. Civil Defence was a loose system of post Second World War organizations in which civilians volunteered for training.

at it after the old man was dead, bid £9,200, and this time succeeded; whether we could have got it for much less, we could not know and have never known.

The property covers about 2,000 square metres, of which about 300 are accounted for by the house, garage, drive and stone paths. The house was built in the early nineteen-twenties in a square-cut style. The kitchen was rather too big and the drawing-room too small; too little house, the average buyer would have said, and too much garden. That was why we liked it, because since we left Oxford our mild interest in gardening had gradually turned into enthusiasm. The garden at no. 49 had been badly neglected and a year of enjoyable afternoons would be needed to make it manageable. Except for a big rockery, which was in the triumphant grip of bishopweed and equisetum, it was a rather unimaginative garden divided into rectangular portions by fences and hedges, the drive lined with laurel bushes and half the back garden sterilised by macrocarpus. The bishopweed (a Presbyterian term for what Episcopalians call 'ground elder') had to be sifted out of the soil with careful fingers and a sharp eye. Nowadays I use systemic herbicide instead, against which the weed puts up such a fight that I almost admire it. But I can't admire equisetum, which lurks under rocks during the winter, rears up like a baboon's prick in the spring, and is so deeply rooted (they do say, down to twelve feet or more) that there is no way of controlling it except by ripping it up wherever it appears and putting special poisonous crystals down the hole. In time, that has worked.

The great gale of January 1968 uprooted two of the macrocarpus trees and cast them into our neighbour's garden, neatly missing his house and garage. We have had most of the others cut down, replacing them with more attractive trees. The long-term jobs were to reconstruct and re-stock the rockery and turn the rectangular lines of the lawns into curves. That took several years, because you need to live with a shape for some time before you can decide whether or not you want to change it. From the way I have written about the garden, anyone would think that we must eventually have created the kind of garden into which admiring visitors are admitted, for an entrance fee payable to a charitable cause, on alternate Sundays in summer, but in fact we have never been within a mile of that distinction. We do all our own work, except when a tree has to be cut down or a fence renewed; in consequence, at any given time twenty percent of the garden is immaculate, forty percent – mmm – promising, and forty percent chaos. We think of a garden not as a work of art which is created once and for all and after that has only to be kept from deteriorating, but as a location for continuous enjoyable activity – horticultural engineering rather than horticulture – on which we spend between us more than twenty hours a week from March to November. An awful lot of this time seems to go on weeding, mowing, moss-killing, daisy-killing, fertilising, spraying for mildew, spraying for greenfly, and then more weeding. Reconciliation to repetitious work is best achieved by putting everything into compost-heaps which will later be dug into the vegetable-bed, so that we can think of mowing the lawn as more like harvesting a crop than dusting furniture. Manipulation of shapes and colours has become our equivalent of writing fiction or poetry or painting pictures. Growing our own fruit, vegetables and herbs offers a less spiritual reward.

Just as we moved in I received a pressing invitation to take the Chair of Greek at University College London, which in the circumstances I immediately refused (I couldn't bear the thought of moving to the London area), and we also heard that Alan had been discontinued at the end of his first year at Battersea College of Technology (he was taking the hotel and catering course) because of his failure in the accountancy exams. He had learned to cook very well, and he excelled in the 'general essay' ingredient of the course, but that was all. Or not quite all; he and a girl whom he met through a school-friend's sister had fallen in love. She and Alan lived together in Chichester, working respectively as a waitress and a dustman, and later in a two-and-a-half room flat in London, she as a telephonist and he as a male char. Their living together did not worry my parents at all, but it was painfully upsetting to Cicely, who over the years had become obsessively anti-sexual;[21] I remembered now an occasion on which she had been prostrated with shock for two days because (and she herself acknowledged the reason) she had seen a neighbour walking arm-in-arm with someone else's wife in Tunbridge Wells, and she found it hard to understand how Audrey and I could bear to visit Alan and Sheila (as I will call her) in London and *set eyes on the bed*. Alan was very fond of his grandmother, and years later he told us that it was moral pressure from her that made him and Sheila decide to marry. They married in St Andrews registry in April 1968, were accepted for training as teachers at Madeley College of Education, and started their course there in September. I should add that we were very fond of Sheila and found her parents extremely congenial.

At the end of the year Catherine was offered a place for History both at York and at St Hugh's, Oxford; she chose St Hugh's, left school, and spent the time between March and October 1969 as an assistant, with rather uncertain duties, at a school in Bradford designed to improve the English of Asian children.

A crisis over University accommodation arose in 1968, and as Alan was now away for good and Catherine would be away in termtime, we took a couple of student lodgers, who had all their meals in a men's residence just down the road but slept in our house. This helped a lot to ease our transition from one kind of household to another.

---

[21] Cicely Latimer, Dover's mother-in-law: see pp. 102–3, with the Index for further references.

18 REVOLUTIONS (FRINGE) 1968–1975

What with *Humanae Vitae*[1] and the Soviet invasion of Czechoslovakia, 1968 was not a good year for the world in general. For me, it was ameliorated by the publication of my commentary on Aristophanes' *Clouds* and my book on Lysias, but aggravated by wear and tear on a vertebra which gave me a lot of pain in the neck and arm all through the autumn. I was simultaneously encouraged and disheartened by the gathering swell of student revolt which had begun on the other side of the Atlantic and crashed on European shores in 1967: disheartened by the imbecilities which vitiated the students' protests and demands, and by the obtuse complacency characteristic of academic resistance, but encouraged by those ingredients of the students' case which were anything but imbecile and by the increasing readiness of a small number of younger academics to think efficiently about the causes of the trouble and its possible cures.

During the three months at the beginning of 1967 which I spent at Berkeley (where the first, well-publicised upheavals took place in 1964–5) I had seen no vestige of student protest, except perhaps a forlorn left-over who often sat on the steps near the Sather Tower,[2] wearing a bowler hat and a buckskin jacket and gazing at the rest of us with a blank, hostile face; the only time I saw a large crowd of students being harangued by a passionate speaker, he turned out to be an evangelist. Although I cannot (one would think) have failed to read and hear about the violent confrontations which occurred in some French, German and Italian universities well before the end of 1967, I was still thinking of student unrest as an American phenomenon when I went to Rome in March 1968 – and found that I

---

[1] An encyclical issued by Pope Paul VI on 25 July 1968. It prompted widespread controversy because of its denunciation of artificial contraception.
[2] A prominent feature of the Berkeley campus, the 94m tower, usually referred to as 'The Campanile', was erected in 1913–15, the gift of Mrs Jane Sather.

had to give my seminar in Scevola Mariotti's[3] apartment, because my hosts considered it dangerous for a professor to set foot on university premises that day.

I don't remember if any academic staff were murdered during the years of trouble, though I know one professor (in Italy), much more recently, who was lucky to survive after some students had ambushed him and slugged him on the head at his house.[4] Some students were shot dead by the National Guard at Kent State University (Ohio), and there were plenty of casualties among students and police world-wide; 300 is the current estimate of students shot in Mexico City. Violence in the British universities was comparatively muted, because British students had less to be angry about. They are, in the strict sense, an élite, because they have been chosen by their universities, out of all those who have attained the minimum entrance requirements, as the people most likely to do well in university work; no one has a statutory right to go to a university. On the Continent, it is otherwise, and a common consequence is an enrolment far in excess of the numbers that the university can accommodate, teach and examine. This is not good for the tempers of those whose initial motivation is strong, and it has often pushed them into alliance with people who have the formal status of students but prefer to put their energies into activities other than study.

Another factor which tempered violence in British universities was the influence (faint in some places, but never entirely negligible) of the Oxford and Cambridge tutorial system, which took for granted the possibility and desirability of combining instruction with friendship. As my subject is not a popular one, my direct acquaintance with European universities has been limited to small departments, which are not typical. In Genoa during 1968–70 Albini's department was like a neatly cultivated garden in a swamp.[5] He expressed himself harshly about the *baroni,* and a professor in Rome, not a man ever likely to compromise over academic standards, told me that in his view the students' demands were 'ninety per cent justified'. The root of the trouble was the remoteness of the teacher from the learner, reflecting the teacher's lack of any sense of responsibility towards the average student. A formal lecture was given, the lecturer departed, and that was that. Things may not always be much better nowadays. Only a few years ago, a distinguished French mathematician visiting St Andrews was asked how he coped, given the enormous size of his classes, with students who wanted help with their individual problems and difficulties; 'I tell them,' he said happily, 'to get fucked.'

---

[3]Scevola Mariotti (1920–2000) was an Italian Latinist, from 1963 Professor of Classical Philology at 'La Sapienza' University of Rome.
[4]Dover SN identifies the distinguished Hellenist, and his good friend, Luigi Enrico ('Chico') Rossi (1933–2009).
[5]Umberto Albini (1923–2011) was a Greek scholar noted especially for his work on Athenian drama; he spent much of his career at the University of Genoa.

Although academic irresponsibility was sufficient cause for student revolt in Europe, its genesis in America was the widespread opposition of the younger generation to the Vietnam war, which quickly broadened into hostility towards the ideology prevailing in politics and business, and then towards all established institutions. In talking with American students who had taken part in protests there were occasions when I could not entirely put aside a feeling (which returned when I was at Stanford during the Gulf War of 1991) that they were not so much opposed to their government because it was waging a war as opposed to the war because it was being waged by their government. In Europe the cause of North Vietnam and the Viet Cong (who were assumed to be nice people) was taken up with enthusiasm. It was also the era of the Cultural Revolution in China, the Utopia over the horizon; the Soviet Union was in the process of demotion from its earlier utopian status, so much so that its economic system was now sometimes labelled 'state capitalism'.[6] The fusion of a conflict which everyone recognised as 'political' with an academic conflict to which most people did not give that label created a student revolution whose scale and intensity were not adequately recognised in Britain even after the events of May 1968 in Paris.

As in all revolutionary movements, a part was played by compassion and justified indignation, which found expression in millenarian fantasies. When I was assured that 'capitalism *cannot* last much longer', I recalled how often I had heard those words in 1938, and again in the early 1950s, and both times the prophecy was falsified by events.

The belief in the imminence of revolution was surprisingly widespread among young people in the period 1967–1975. In some cases it was no more than a reflex of a desire to hurt and destroy everyone who was in a position to exercise power – a desire, perhaps, for revenge on one's parents. When a student at Essex got a low mark for an essay he hissed at his tutor (a friend of mine, from whom I heard the story) 'When the Revolution comes, I shall shoot you first!' And a Vice-Chancellor who said to a student representative when faced with 'non-negotiable demands' (a favourite phrase of the period), 'Can't we talk about this as one human being to another?', was met with the response, 'I'm not interested in you as a human being.'

I read the volume of essays edited by Alexander Cockburn and Robin Blackburn under the title *Student Power*, which appeared in 1969. The contributors alternated between fiercely penetrating insights (e.g. on the absurdity of treating 'politics' and 'economics' as separable areas of study) and flamboyant irrationality (e.g. inferring, from the fact that failure-rates fluctuate between 30% and 3%, that 'the existing system of examinations is a random process of selection'). Having read the book, I re-read it and took plenty of notes. It gave me a good idea of what we might be in

---

[6] In a 1995 addendum Dover noted that state capitalism 'was actually Lenin's own term for the system he advocated in the spring of 1918'.

for, and some ideas not only for prophylactic reforms but also for reforms which I ought to have supported more actively years before.

Since the furtherance and dissemination of science and learning are the *raison d'être* of universities, I thought it best, being an English empiricist to the core and in politics more of a restless tinkerer than a revolutionary theorist, to begin with the practicalities of teaching and examining. The worst British teaching was probably never as bad as the worst European, but some of it was wretched – there existed lecture-courses which were no more than summaries of textbooks already published by the lecturers – and none was (or ever is) incapable of improvement. I admired the slogan which Sir Robert Watson-Watt[7] adopted in his scientific work, 'Contentment is the enemy.' Discussion of teaching methods was often polarised between lectures and less formal modes and concentrated on the question, 'Are lectures worth while?' But the primary question is, 'What method of teaching is the most efficient for *this* part of *this* subject with *these* students at *this* time?' Lectures may well turn out to be the right answer, especially when the available literature is unmanageably extensive and repetitious or inaccessible to students. The lecturer's job is to digest the material, isolate its essentials, present it better than it has been presented in print, and make hrs own contributions to the subject. Why not, then, put it on paper, circulate it, and devote the lecture-hours to questions and discussion (xerography has been the most important invention in my lifetime)? There is, though, one irreplaceable ingredient of lecturing: speaking *as if* one were sharing with the audience the experience of looking at a problem for the first time (Russell Meiggs used to say, 'Teaching is a branch of the acting profession').[8]

When a lecturer was appointed, it was rare, as the students frequently pointed out, to have any idea of hrs ability as a teacher, except in so far as that could be inferred from hrs interview. It was even rarer for a newly appointed lecturer to receive any useful criticism or guidance on hrs performance. This is a problem partially solved in many American universities by the unheralded attendance of professors at lectures given by their juniors and by requiring all staff to distribute questionnaires to their students. In consequence, no lecturer can be left in doubt over how hrs teaching appears to others. Generally speaking, British universities in 1969 were disinclined to learn from American practice. To attend someone else's lecture for the purpose of writing a critical report on it was felt to be not merely ungentlemanly/unladylike, but tyrannical. As for feedback, most lecturers were simply afraid of questionnaires, and this was true even of those who had least cause for fear. They were even afraid of tape-recording a lecture of their own,

---

[7]Sir Robert Watson-Watt (1892–1973), the inventor of radar.
[8]In his *Times* obituary of Dover, 9 March 2010, p. 59 (echoed in *KJD* 174), Donald Russell described him as 'a spellbinding lecturer' who (even, or especially, in formal research lectures) 'came to scorn using notes': anyone who saw Dover lecture in his prime is likely to endorse this judgement.

although, having done it myself, I could tell them how quickly and easily I had profited from it. After 1969 I made a habit of giving out questionnaires to students attending my own lectures. Staff-student councils had been instituted in many departments by then, and I circulated a draft questionnaire to mine; the students were able to add some questions which mattered to them but had been overlooked by me, and to assure me that one or two questions which I had put in didn't matter to them at all. The value of a questionnaire naturally depends on the scale of response; you can't please everybody all the time, and a response-rate of under 40% is not a good foundation for assessment of your performance. At Oxford in 1977–85 I was normally able to secure a response rate of 80%, in one year over 90%, by reminding my audience that the beneficiaries of the trouble they took to respond were the next generation of students.

In 1970 Douglas Gifford,[9] with support and encouragement from Steven Watson, took the initiative of getting newly-appointed lecturers together for discussion and guidance on the problems of teaching. Douglas himself was a little too self-deprecating, his own expositions were sometimes informal to the point of incoherence, and his enviably close relationship with his own students was rooted in his inimitable personality. Something more systematic was needed, and four universities – St Andrews, Dundee, Stirling and Heriot-Watt – formed a consortium in order to hold a four-day course at the beginning of October for all our newly appointed lecturers. Those of us who ran the course took the line that the primary objective of teaching is clarity and adequacy of *explanation;* if your students end by understanding what they didn't understand before, your teaching has been efficient, and if they don't, it hasn't. A second objective is to equip them methodologically, so that they can increasingly take over the direction of their own learning; and a third, to implant a love of enquiry – or, let's not be too ambitious, a sustainable sympathy with enquiry as a mode of existence. No one should be content to fall short of attaining the second and third objectives, but the first is indispensable. On the consortium course, each new lecturer was required to give a short lecture, which was video-taped, and then to view the tape in company with a senior critic. They mostly found that useful, but they had a poor opinion of the performance of education experts ('Why,' I was asked, 'should I be told how to lecture by someone who does it badly?'). The senior members of academic staff who acted as critics were qualified to act in that capacity only by being interested in the problem and being believed by their colleagues to be good teachers. There could certainly be thinner qualifications than that but it reminded us that wherever and whenever the serious training of lecturers started, the first trainers would be

---

[9]Douglas John (or Juan) Gifford (1924–91), born in Argentina and a specialist in Latin American studies, spent his entire career at St Andrews, where he was Professor of Spanish 1975–89; he was ordained an Anglican priest in 1981, hence 'Rev.' in Dover's index.

virtually self-appointed. It also emerged very clearly that it is difficult to assess the clarity of an exposition, and impossible to assess its adequacy, without knowing a great deal about the subject. What could be done on a general level was obviously very limited; the real responsibility for the training of lecturers must rest with departments.

It was commonly asserted by students, and no doubt widely believed, that examinations require candidates to 'regurgitate' what they have been taught and to reproduce the arguments, views and interpretations of their lecturers. This is obviously untrue of large parts of many large subjects: problems in mathematics and the physical sciences, for example, and unseen translation of languages. Even in subjects for which it could be valid – and is indeed so in some countries, where the teacher of a course is the sole marker of the examination set at the end of it – it is not consonant with my own experience in Britain. When I examined at Oxford, although I was allowed to be one marker (not, of course, the sole marker) of papers written by my own pupils, I was excluded from all discussion of the class of degree they merited. Independent marking by two examiners, and by a third if the first two disagreed significantly, ensured that no one who had given a lecture-course had the power to damn a candidate who disagreed with a line taken in the lectures. Elsewhere the appointment of external examiners, who are told nothing about any candidate until after the results have been settled, is normal practice. At St Andrews I always had an external examiner, and I have served in that capacity in five universities. I do not recall any cases of really serious disagreement between external and internal examiners, and certainly none which could not be resolved by rational discussion.

There are horror-stories, in some cases backed by hard experimental evidence, about wild divergence between independent markers of A-level English papers, and cynical jokes about the arbitrariness of the award of classes in degree examinations are propagated from time to time (most recently in August 1993) by academics who enjoy playing Yossarian.[10] There is nothing in my own experience to justify this notion, and much to invalidate it. I recall, for example, how often in the Balliol scholarship examinations Bill Watt and I, marking independently, ended up in consistent agreement on a paper in which one would have expected subjective aesthetic preference to play a crucial part. Belief in the chanciness of degree classes derives some support from the fact that however many classes there are, a few candidates will end up astride a class-boundary and have to be displaced in one direction or the other. Have to, that is, as long as the existing system of classification is taken for granted; the problem could be solved by the addition of three very small classes (I/II, II.i/ii, II/III) to the existing big four (I, II.i, II.ii, III).

---

[10]Captain John Yossarian, the protagonist of Joseph Heller's 1961 novel *Catch-22*.

As for regurgitation, this is inevitable in just one type of paper, in which the candidate is required to translate and comment on passages from prescribed texts. Prescription determines regurgitation; an argument (which I am not alone in propounding) against such papers.[11] On historical, philosophical and literary subjects I have neither sat nor set papers which could be dealt with satisfactorily by question-spotting and the recall of detail well organised in advance. There was not a single question in my six main Greats papers which did not compel me to think hard in the examination-room.

As soon as I came back from my sabbatical term in the spring of 1973[12] I was put under strong pressure by my colleagues in the Faculty of Arts to take on a second stint as Dean, on the understanding that it would be for two years only, after which Reg Christian[13] would be willing to do it. I put up very little resistance, because, in strong contrast to my earlier tenure in 1960–3, I would now have the support of an Associate Dean (for graduate students), an Assistant Dean (for the problems of individual undergraduates), a full-time administrator (Robert Douglas, with whom I knew I could work in complete harmony – and was not disappointed), and three Admissions Officers. The main attraction, though, was that as ex officio chairman of the Faculty Council and the Faculty Planning Committee I would be in a strong position to attempt a thorough overhaul of the examination system in Arts.

I had once hoped that the Scottish universities would get together on this problem, and having been for some years President of the St Andrews branch of the Association of University Teachers (Scotland) I tried in 1969 to interest the AUT(S) executive in examinations. The attempt was unsuccessful; preoccupied with issues of pay, tenure, promotion and status, they showed little awareness of what our job is all about or of what was threatening our ability to do it. Perhaps I was naive to expect otherwise, but I lost interest in the AUT and allowed my membership to lapse. It was clear that whatever had to be done in St Andrews would have to be worked out by St Andrews itself, and indeed by my own Faculty, since the Faculty of Science had different ideas.

But, of course, no measures to improve the effectiveness of teaching, no reforms of the examination system, touch the radical question with which 1968 confronted us: to what extent ought the content, character and purpose of courses and examinations to be determined by the students themselves? As soon as we say 'ought' we are implicitly distinguishing between ends and means, and it is prudent to start with the end before considering the means.

There are many subjects in which the standard of competence to be expected of a student at the end of three or four years' study is determined by the needs of

---

[11]Cf. Dover's remarks on this topic in relation to school exams on pp. 181–2.
[12]For the chronology, see p. 215.
[13]R.F. Christian (1924–2018), a major Tolstoy scholar, was Professor of Russian at St Andrews 1966–92.

society. Your qualification in engineering is not worth much if your buildings collapse and you do not know how to make them less likely to do so. A degree in a subject entitled 'German' is pointless if you can't read a page of an ordinary German text. In other subjects, though, such as anthropology, philosophy or medieval history, indication of the standard attainable by students of a given university at a given time is provided by the standard actually attained in the past and elsewhere. There is nothing arbitrary about standards which are directly observable. Factual knowledge without understanding is possible (we all know people stronger on the former than the latter), but understanding without factual knowledge is possible only by pure chance, and for that reason uncommon; popular non-fiction is quite heavily charged with nonsense which the writers would not have perpetrated if they had known more of the evidence relevant to their propositions and assumptions.

As there are many important concepts for which our language currently lacks useful words, it is difficult, without clumsy circumlocution, to avoid using the verb 'produce' and the noun 'product' in speaking of the relation between a university and its students. I dislike this, because students are not artefacts: their time at a university is just one variable (beginning at the late age of eighteen or more) in their formation. There is even less to be said for assimilating the relation between students and university to the relation between customer and supplier; the true customers are always hidden in the future, because they are the society in which the students will spend the most active and productive part of their lives, and teacher and learner have a joint obligation to serve that society to the best of their ability. Those on whom students are financially dependent share that obligation too. If an analogy with capital and labour has any relevance to university teaching, parents (and all other taxpayers) are the part-employer and the students and teaching staff jointly are the employees.

It was crucial to ask students, and go on asking them, what they really wanted, and I was depressed when some of my senior colleagues reacted as if knowing what people wanted committed us to giving it to them, when it was simply a matter of collecting the data in order to understand the situation. It was no less depressing to be told that such-and-such a way of doing things had 'stood the test of time'; the test was now upon us and time was up.

By and large, discussion of the content of courses showed the students at their worst, as when one spoke of the 'principles' of a scientific subject when what he had in mind was its economic applications. Their conceptions of 'relevance' were superficial; they wanted short cuts while simultaneously decrying spoon-feeding; and none of them, to the best of my belief, took the trouble to construct and offer for criticism a complete plan of a year's course or explain how the individual's progress in it should be assessed. Some of them gave the impression that they thought in terms of meandering, unstructured discussion of a limited range of allegedly relevant topics, and even of self-assessment. Far be it from me to tar the really acute critics (I knew some) with the same brush as the silly ones ... but it's not actually very far, because although I welcome criticism of *how* I should teach, I bristle very quickly when people who know little or nothing of my subject tell me *what* I should teach. If you want to attain a reasonable degree of competence in that subject, I know what you need to learn, and in what order; and you don't know, until your experience approximates to mine. That in no way precludes the devising of alternative options to suit different tastes and interests.

Discussion of examinations showed the students at their best. It being agreed that the purpose of examination is to provide the university with rational grounds for making a public statement about a candidate's competence, I held a very long meeting of my own staff-student council to talk about the means. I remember nothing about it except that after I had gone on rather too long about different ways of arriving at an accurate and just assessment of a candidate, one of my most able and sensitive students observed, 'But people don't want to be judged justly. They want to be judged *leniently*.' Among the students generally 'examination' and 'continuous assessment' were treated as mutually exclusive alternatives. The terminology was inappropriate, and I persuaded the Faculty to think rather in terms of 'concentrated testing' (i.e. a 'big bang' at the end of the academic year) and 'distributed testing' (i.e. lots of little assessed items spread out over the year). Each has its own signal disadvantages, which I explored in a report to the Faculty Council in 1974 and another in 1975 after the 1974 recommendations had been tested in operation. Concentrated testing is an unreal situation, because very often outside the examination-room, in ordinary circumstances, we don't rack our brains in an effort to recall a datum; we look it up. But there is an element of unreality in distributed testing also, because there are many situations in life in which we need to have a lot of material available for immediate recall. The obvious answer was a system combining both types of testing, and that is what we did: all those in the first year who got a 'certificate of distinction' or 'certificate of merit' (in American terms, a grade of A or B) on the best n of the items of work they did in the course of the year were exempted from the end-of-year examination, so that those who had failed to gain exemption still had a chance to redeem the situation by taking the examination. For final Honours the concentrated examination remained, but departments were encouraged to incorporate 'projects' and extended essays which would be subject to a viva.

By the time the new system was working we had practically forgotten the violent confrontations which had disturbed so many other universities in 1968–71 but left St Andrews an oasis in which problems were sorted out with patience, goodwill and reason. There were however two other dissensions in 1974–5, one of which led to an assault by a student on a janitor and the forcible dissolution of her stranglehold on him by my successor as Dean. That was a demand for student participation in the Senate. I was in favour of student membership of the University Court, because it seemed to me a good way of educating students in the running of institutions. The Senate's concern, though, was with syllabuses, examinations and academic failure, and I thought it wise to maintain a rigid distinction between assessor and assessed, prescriber and performer. Some years later (1982) the students' case for representation on the Senate was accepted.

The second problem was the first-year failure-rate, to which we first addressed ourselves at a staff-student forum convened by Steven Watson in April 1969. Although there are many countries in which it is taken for granted that a high proportion of students who embark on a university course will never complete it, a British university does not comfortably reconcile itself to a failure-rate higher than zero. At any university some students fall victim to psychoneurotic illness which (to judge from its incidence in the general population) could well have afflicted them even if they had not been students. Others (Oxford is no exception) leave during the first year because they discover that university work is not what they most want. There are others, too, who ought to leave because they should not have been there in the first place; set on the tramlines at school, they find the gulf between school work and university work too wide to bridge, especially if they have been discouraged at school from independent reading and thinking, and their destiny is all-round failure at the end of the first year. One significant contribution to the reduction of this category of students was the organisation (by Clark Geddes, our Director of Extramural Studies, always fertile in good ideas) of an annual 'pre-university school', in which 400–500 pupils in their penultimate school year were invited to St Andrews for a few days to learn all that we could tell them and show them about university life. A few of these pupils each year decided that it was not what they wanted to aim at, and that conclusion saved them future frustration. Another category of failure consists of students who have simply chosen to devote more time and energy to other activities than to work; the majority of those who failed in my own department admitted that frankly. The worst problem was in science, affecting particularly Scottish students whose formal qualification was passes in the Higher Scottish Certificate of Education. Since we took a lot of English students who had A-levels behind them, a qualification in many respects a year beyond Highers, the starting-point of our first-year science courses tended to be geared to them rather than to the Scots – or so, at any rate, it seemed to the Scots. Their cause was taken up, with fire and indignation, by an English student whose general hostility to the University seemed in 1975 rather dated. At the time I left St Andrews in 1976 the problem of failures in first-year science had not been satisfactorily solved.

There were by 1970 universities which had appointed counsellors, whose job it was to help individual students to cope with the difficulties produced by the interaction of alien environment, academic pressure, off-target teaching, self-doubt, love and debt. Some lecturers in the Department of Psychology, with enthusiastic student backing, urged the appointment of a counsellor in St Andrews.

If the appointment were made, it necessarily meant that an academic appointment would have to be dropped from the Faculties' shopping-list. This list was pared down each year to fit the money available, so that a request not granted one year was normally moved to a higher level of priority the following year and might take some years to reach the top stratum. It happened that Gordon Williams[14] had resigned from the Chair of Humanity in 1973 to take up a tenured professorship at Yale, and a suggestion was made that the chair should remain unfilled at least for some years, to make room for a counsellor. This was presented as a matter of life and death: it was argued that counselling by a qualified professional would necessarily reduce the failure-rate, rescue some students from despair and the abandonment of their hopes, abort nervous breakdown and prevent suicides. I did not doubt that counselling was likely, on balance, to do more good than harm; the only potential harm was encouragement of the notion that if you are at odds with your circumstances, you cannot be expected to change yourself but must demand that your circumstances be changed. It is not easy to show that lack of professional counselling (as opposed to lack of medical care or of friendship and non-professional support) has been a contributory cause of suicide, and impossible to show that there would have been more suicides if there had been no counselling. There was less room for uncertainty about the damage which would be done to Classics at St Andrews, and therefore to our recruitment of good graduate students and undergraduates in the subject, if we failed to fill the chair of Humanity, especially when we had an apparently ideal candidate (Robert Ogilvie) in view.[15] For that reason I could not consent to any list of priorities that put counselling above Latin or, for similar reasons, above any purely academic appointment already requested.

Nevertheless, it seemed to me that the least we could do as an academic community was to learn what there was to be learned from professional counsellors (accepting, rejecting or suspending judgement, in accordance with analysis of our own experience with students) and improve the quality of our amateur counselling. I therefore attended, with Audrey, a remarkable weekend conference organised by Frank Quinault at the beginning of October 1975. We had one or two professional counsellors along, but most of the time we were divided into groups in which absolute candour and absolute equality between staff and students prevailed from the first moment. The ambience might be described as 'post-flower-power'. Although it was possible before long to identify one or two individuals who had to contend with personality disorders, and although some fashionable lines, such as 'co-counselling' and the anti-psychiatry of Cooper and Laing, were plugged

---

[14]See p. 128 with note.
[15]Robert Maxwell Ogilvie (1932–81) was tutorial fellow of Balliol 1957–70, headmaster of Tonbridge School 1970–5, and Professor of Humanity at St Andrews from 1975 until his suicide in 1981. The reason for Dover's qualification 'apparently' will become clear in his note on Ogilvie on p. 232.

(obliquely) by minorities, I look back on that weekend with great satisfaction as one of the formative elements in my middle life. We decided that as we were not going to get a professional counsellor just yet we ought to do something as amateurs, and we got the use of a very small building in North Street ('the Cottage') as a 'consulting room', undertaking that two of us, according to a rota, would be there every evening. I was there about ten times in the course of 1975–6. We didn't have many clients, but the spirit of the original weekend was gratifyingly preserved. That year we ensured that we treated as important whatever was important to the client, eschewing doctrine and banning sexual and religious propaganda, whether made explicit by placards or implied by symbols. I gather that in 1976–7 this ban was increasingly relaxed.

19 RIGHT AND WRONG 1969–1983

Generally speaking, the growth of hypocrisy is proof of moral progress, for it indicates that what used to be done openly and without fear of censure can no longer be done without incurring that risk.

LESZEK KOLAKOWSKI[1]

In 1969 I was asked by the American Council for Philosophical Studies to hold a seminar which would meet in August 1970 at Colorado Springs for the benefit of young post-doctoral academics in Greek philosophy. The organisers, no doubt in consequence of the articles I had published on Plato's *Symposium,* hoped that I would offer a Platonic topic, but since 1966 I had not given a thought to Plato or any other Greek philosopher, and it was far beyond me to provide adequate philosophical fare for people who would also be having seminars with – among others – Gregory Vlastos, Bernard Williams and Gwil Owen.[2] I therefore suggested a topic with which I had briefly toyed in 1948, the moral assumptions and attitudes of the society in which Plato and Aristotle had lived, and this suggestion was accepted. How willingly or unwillingly, I never knew. I felt I was perhaps being rather impudent.

---

[1]'History and Hope', in *Marxism and Beyond,* trs. J.Z. Peel (London, 1969) 172. Leszek Kolakowski (1927–2009), a Polish-born philosopher and political scientist, Senior Research Fellow of All Souls College, Oxford, 1970–95, is best known for his three-volume critical analysis of Marxist thinking, *Main Currents of Marxism* (1978). His British Academy memoir, by Steven Lukes, is in *PBA* 172 (2011) 201–11 (available at https://www.thebritishacademy.ac.uk/publishing/memoirs/10/).

[2]Gregory Vlastos (1907–91) and Gwilym Owen (1922–82) were world-leading scholars of ancient philosophy. Vlastos was Stuart Professor of Philosophy at Princeton 1955–76, and Mills Professor of Philosophy at Berkeley 1976–87; he gave the Gifford Lectures in St Andrews in 1981 (cf. p. 229). Owen was Victor S. Thomas Professor of Philosophy and Classics at Harvard 1966–73 and Laurence Professor of Ancient Philosophy at Cambridge 1973–82. On Williams, a former student of Dover's, see p. 99 and note.

Most Greeks were not philosophers, and many treated philosophy with derision. But every Greek, like anyone else, freely used words such as 'good', 'shameful', 'honest', 'unfair' and the like, and my task would be to track down and uncover the moral assumptions which underlay everyday evaluations. Mindful of the fact that throughout my years in the Army, although I had been present on thousands of occasions on which someone expressed a favourable or unfavourable moral response to some particular action, I had never once heard anyone raise such questions as 'What is justice?' or 'What is honesty?', I was aware of the gulf between moral philosophy and morality. Moral philosophy is the investigation of the logical relation between morality and reason. 'Ethics' I decided (with Aristotle's *Ethika* in mind) to treat as synonymous with 'moral philosophy'. Morality (or 'morals') is an aspect of interpersonal relations, concerned with the choice we face between backing down and pressing on when our wishes and interests conflict with someone else's.

It might be thought that there could not have been anything new to say about Greek morality. Arthur Adkins,[3] in a well-known and influential book *Merit and Responsibility* (1960), had described what he believed to be the essential features of its historical development from Homer to Aristotle. Lionel Pearson had published *Popular Ethics in Ancient Greece* (1962) and John Ferguson *Moral Values in the Ancient World* (1958).[4] On one topic Ferguson was illuminating, but his choice of topics was rather narrow. Pearson gave due attention to writers who were not philosophers, but made no attempt, despite the title of his book, to separate the 'popular' from the idiosyncratic. Adkins's book was disquieting, because it seemed to me to construct a clear and intelligible picture of historical development only by unjustifiable selectivity in the use of evidence, ignoring complications and uncertainties. Perhaps it was arrogant of me to think that I understood better how ordinary people's minds actually work, but my irreligious upbringing, my early habituation to analysis of my parents' and relations' attitudes and motives, and above all my five years absence from academic life, gave me a certain advantage.*

None of the books I have mentioned started from what I was now convinced (dredging up from my memory tentative thoughts from the immediate post-War years) was the right point: forensic oratory.

---

*Though only in respect of a limited range of sub-cultures. Others baffle me. Throughout the John Cassavetes film *Husbands* I was constantly asking myself, 'Why does he say that? What does he *mean*? Why is he laughing? What's funny?'

[3] Arthur Adkins (1929–96) taught Classics at several British universities before holding a chair at the University of Chicago 1974–96. *Merit and Responsibility*, originally an Oxford D.Phil. thesis supervised by E.R. Dodds, constructed a highly schematic model of the history of ancient Greek moral values and their relationship to modern, post-Kantian values; for a concise critique, see C. Gill, *Greek Thought* (Oxford, 1995) 21–5. Cf. the further reference to Adkins on p. 223.

[4] Lionel Pearson (1908–88) was English-born and Oxford-educated but taught for most of his career (1940–73) at Stanford. John Ferguson (1921–89) was Professor of Classics at the University of Ibadan, Nigeria, 1956–66, and Dean of Arts at the Open University 1969–79.

We possess about 100 texts of lawcourt speeches attributed by the Alexandrian Library to one or other of ten famous Athenian orators. Some of the attributions are demonstrably wrong or at least suspect; the total number of orators represented in the corpus is far more than ten. For anyone wishing to study the career and technique of a particular orator, such uncertainty is a disadvantage, but from the standpoint of popular Athenian morality it is welcome. The verdict in an Athenian court was given by a simple majority vote in a very large jury, commonly of 501, selected by lot from among all those male citizens over thirty who wished (as, plainly, a great many did) to serve. There was no judge to give guidance on points of law, enforce rules of evidence or restrain a speaker's irrelevances. There was no possibility of appeal against a jury's verdict. Both the defendant and the prosecutor – not an official, but a citizen who chose to prosecute in order to rise in public esteem – had to speak in person. They could, however, bring forward other people to speak in support of their own case, and, of course, they could seek as much help and advice as they wished from those who had a high rate of success in such work; hence the small number of men to whom a large number of speeches were attributed. In these circumstances, in a society where documentation was sparse and the machinery for the detection of crime rudimentary, it was extremely important to make a good impression on the jury; especially important for the defendant, because Athenian law was in many respects ferocious, lavish with disenfranchisement and the death penalty. This meant that the speaker must convince the jury that he was a good, sound, patriotic, honest, tax-paying, peaceable citizen, and that his adversary was an untrustworthy, aggressive, self-seeking shirker. No one could afford to risk the appearance of adopting moral principles or attitudes other than those which his experience of life had led him to believe were shared by the majority in a very large random sample of the Athenian male citizen population.

One of the things we need to know in deciding whether or not a defendant is likely to have committed the offence with which he is charged is precisely what a modern jury is prevented from knowing: the character of the defendant as previously manifested. Equally, if we know the characters of two opposing litigants, we are more likely to judge correctly which of them is in the right. The Athenian jury was not prevented from hearing a speaker boast (truly or falsely) about his own past conduct or allege (truly or falsely) past misconduct on the part of his adversary. It was therefore common for a defendant to fend off conviction by claiming that he deserved forgiveness if his merits were weighed in the scale, and gratitude for his services to the community, of which the jury was the representative. In a modern court such considerations are supposed to operate only in the sentencing that follows the verdict (quite recently a judge made it clear that a defendant was escaping a prison sentence only because he had always given very generously to charities), but it is also not unknown for a jury to acquit when it thinks that the victim of a violent retaliation deserved to be hurt or when its sympathy goes more to the defendant than to the prosecutor (even to the extent, a year or two ago, of returning the verdict of 'Not Guilty' on a defendant who had pleaded 'Guilty'). Modern cases of this kind (and by 'modern' I do not mean merely 'twentieth-century')† strike us as odd because 'Not Guilty' is so often taken to signify that the jury believes that the defendant did not commit the crime. Athenian terminology avoided this confusion; to 'convict' was to 'vote down', to 'acquit' was to 'vote off', and a decision to 'vote off' signified 'we do not wish to punish this defendant'.

When I began to mine the riches of Attic forensic oratory I was astonished to discover that the mine had never been exploited. I found at a late stage that its presence and value had been remarked by F.R. Earp in 1929 but neither he nor anyone else had done anything more about it.[5] My first task, therefore, was to re-read the whole of Attic oratory, noting and classifying relevant passages. The second was to re-read the whole of comedy and late fifth-century tragedy in search of passages which conformed – or, more interestingly, did not conform – with the scheme of values which I drafted after reading the orators. Playwrights competed for prizes, and winning mattered a lot to them, but they did not risk their lives and property as a man in court did, and they could afford to put into the mouths of characters on stage ideas which it would have been extremely imprudent to voice to a jury. We do not know what the playwright himself thought, because he gave a character words which *that* character would have uttered in *that* situation (though often rhetorically formal and intellectualised to a highly unrealistic degree), but dramatic form (especially in comedy) gives us plenty of clues to what was acceptable in sentiment to the audience.

That was the stage I had reached by the time the seminar began at Colorado Springs, and I was able to tell my audience a good many things that surprised them, nourished as they were on moral philosophy and *Merit and Responsibility*. My commitment was over after three weeks, so we rented a car and spent ten days driving down through the deserts and semi-deserts of New Mexico, Arizona and eastern Utah, then back through the Colorado Rockies. The Grand Canyon is, to the best of my recollection, the only place I have visited which far exceeds expectations; even after seeing a thunderstorm below us and mistaking a light aircraft for a gull, we still found it hard to adjust ourselves to the scale of the scene before us. In parts of Utah and western Colorado we encountered slag-heap country, the only natural scenery that I have ever been inclined to call 'ugly'. Aspen

---

†At Memphis, Tennessee, in 1855 a woman stabbed to death a lover who had made her pregnant and then deserted her. The jury deliberated for only two minutes before acquitting her amid public acclaim when her advocate had argued that the murder was an act of divine retribution effected by 'some good angel' who put the dagger in her hand and 'guided her blow'. (Ann Jones, *Women Who Kill*, 2nd ed. [London, 1991], pp. 167f.).

[5]F.R. Earp, *The Way of the Greeks* (London, 1929).

on the last day made up for that; even our irritation, as we sat down to dinner while the clock was striking eight, at learning that we could not be served with beer or any other alcoholic drink after eight o'clock did not dim the memory of seeing a flock of humming-birds buzzing to and fro – we mistook them for big beetles – in a belt of trees at the bottom of the Cat Bells. The trip had its sentimental side. Audrey had lost the centre stone of her engagement-ring, so we bought a re-engagement-ring at a store in the Navajo Reservation; it was silver, with four uncut turquoises, and it cost six dollars. Some years later we saw a similar ring on sale in Rome for a few hundred.

By the time we got home I had decided that I would write a book to be called *Greek Popular Morality in the Time of Plato and Aristotle,* and when a representative from Blackwell did the rounds of the Scottish universities later in the year I gladly agreed to a contract. However, I still had to finish my commentary on Theocritus for Macmillan[6] (old Daniel Macmillan knew he would lose money on it, but he was determined to keep Greek afloat) and my book *Aristophanic Comedy* for Batsford. Once they were published in the winter of 1971/2 I made good progress, reading the relevant corpus of Greek literature again, more carefully and reflectively, plus Xenophon, Aristotle's *Ethics,* and whatever Plato said or implied about the popular moral attitudes which his Socrates found unsatisfactory. The modern scholarly literature, as usual, I left to the end.

By the spring of 1972 it was clear to me that I was likely to have everything in order by the end of the year, and my thoughts turned to the possibility of a sabbatical term in which I could put the book into final form. If I had stayed at Balliol after 1955 I would have been entitled to a sabbatical year, having done twenty-one consecutive terms of teaching; but there was no such entitlement at St Andrews. I got leave of absence in 1960 for four months at Harvard and for three months at Berkeley in 1967, but those were not sabbaticals, because my American employers paid me for teaching and I received no salary from St Andrews. I thought now that it would be rather nice to celebrate a quarter of a century in university teaching by taking my first sabbatical term, and that was not difficult to arrange, because there were four of us in the Department and I was willing to take an extra load before my departure and after my return.[7] Audrey and I both liked the idea of going to Italy, and an apartment in Pisa, with the splendid Classical resources of the Scuola Normale Superiore on hand, was my first idea. Italian

---

[6]Dover has not previously mentioned this commentary, *Theocritus: Select Poems* (London, 1971), his only substantial publication on post-classical Greek literature: for discussion of the book and Dover's relative lack of interest in Hellenistic literature, see Richard Hunter's contribution to *S&C*. The suggestion that *Theocritus* was unfinished in summer 1970 is at odds with the date of December 1969 in the book's Preface, so it is possible that Dover's memory is here a little approximate.

[7]The reference to 'four of us' in 1972 seems to be a slip: the Department in fact contained five permanent members of staff at this date (Dover, Ian Kidd, Robert Reid, Elizabeth Craik, Malcolm Campbell).

friends, however, suggested instead that we should go to Lucca, off the tourist track and within easy distance of Pisa. Happening to meet Ian Campbell, Professor of Latin at Edinburgh, for a few minutes on Waverley Station, I mentioned this to him, and he reminded me that his predecessor in the Edinburgh chair, Michael Grant,[8] lived near Lucca and might well know of someone who had a house to let. More than ever persuaded of the blessings that can flow from brief conversations in casual encounters, I wrote to Michael Grant, and he did indeed know a lady, Bezi Hammelmann,‡ who lived in another village near Lucca, and had a farmhouse to let. It turned out that Bezi was very glad to let to us from mid-February to mid-April, a season at which the farmhouse commonly lay empty. Everything was quickly arranged.

We put the car on the train at Edinburgh. From Nice it was an easy drive to Lucca, but heavy rain came on at sunset and we found the last stage, up dirt roads to a tiny centre of habitation called Vecoli, a little at odds with the sketch-map which Bezi had sent us. Anyway, we got the right place in the end, and next morning, which was calm and brilliant, we had breakfast on the grass in front of the house, awestruck by a panorama of hills and forests which led the eye to the snowfields on Monte Giovo and the Alpe Tre Potenze, centre-stage nearly thirty kilometres away.

This sabbatical leave coincided with a critical point in my career. Earlier in the winter a university had approached me to ask if I would be interested in appointment as its Vice-Chancellor. I had little difficulty in saying that I would not, because I could not contemplate the severe retrenchment of scholarly work which the manifold duties of a Vice-Chancellor would entail. At the other end of the scale of responsibility, I was offered a tenured professorship at the Institute for Advanced Study in Princeton. This too I declined, because I did not want to emigrate, and I did not think I would like the cloistered atmosphere of the Institute for more than the occasional short visit. A third possibility was much more inviting. Denys Page[9] was going to retire from the Regius Chair of Greek at Cambridge, and on the instigation of friends at Cambridge I decided to put myself forward as a candidate. I was beginning to feel that I needed to spend more time with graduate seminars than in lecturing to undergraduates and that my work would benefit from being constantly criticised by colleagues more numerous, and with a wider range of expertise, than would ever be possible in my Department at St Andrews (Fraenkel

---

‡She was German, and as a student in Munich during the War she had risked her life as a member of a group of young people looking after a Pole who had escaped from a death-camp.
[8]Michael Grant (1914–2004), a numismatist and historian, was Professor of Latin at Edinburgh 1948–59. He was a prolific author of books on classical topics for the general public. From 1966 till his death, Grant and his wife lived in the village of Gattaiola near Lucca in Tuscany.
[9]On Page, see n. 16 to p. 73.

had warned me in 1955, 'If you go to St Andrews, you'll become too fond of the sound of your own voice'). There was another consideration: it was obvious that my mother would soon die, and if we lived at Cambridge, near enough to Boston for frequent visits to my father, it might be possible to defer indefinitely the time when he would want to come and live with us. However, I was far from confident about the outcome of my application. Geoffrey Kirk, Professor of Greek at Bristol and Fellow of Trinity Hall, Cambridge, was obviously a very formidable rival, and I had a presentiment that he would get the job.[10] He did. I was not particularly upset, partly because the event justified my own prediction, partly because I admired what he had published. I was also freed from the hassle of finding a house, and I would not have to face the frightful spiders of East Anglia. Denys Page, on the other hand, was stupefied, and voiced his rage in a long letter to me three years later. The maintenance of confidentiality is not an outstanding characteristic of the electors to Cambridge chairs, and it was not long before I was able to reconstruct the views and arguments of all those involved.[11]

The book I had planned was divided into ninety-nine sections, and as we would be at Vecoli for ninety days I would have to finalise, on average, more than one section a day; and what would that leave us for running around to the places we wanted to see? As it turned out, I was able to complete between two and three sections a day on average, and the whole job was finished by the first week of March. This enabled us to go to Florence and Pisa, to get to know Lucca, and to spend a week visiting the Albinis in Genoa.[12] When I went back to England for a week on my mother's death in mid-March I was able to take the book with me and hand it over to Blackwell.[13] On my return a friend of ours, Inez Shipway, came to stay, and we toured further afield: Siena, San Gimignano, Certaldo and Barga. At Barga, while we were standing in the little piazza in front of the cathedral, a mass of black cloud gathered over us and a lurid yellow light fell on the snows of Monte Giovo; I hurriedly took a photograph, and by good fortune it turned out the best I had ever taken; an enlargement hung in my office in Corpus and earned me an undeserved reputation for photography.

The year and a half which I had spent on Greek popular morality consolidated not only my view of the Greek world but also my understanding of morality in

---

[10]Geoffrey Kirk (1921–2003) was Professor of Classics at Yale 1965–70, Professor of Greek at Bristol 1971–3, and Regius Professor of Greek at Cambridge 1974–82. His earlier publications were chiefly on pre-Socratic philosophy, his later ones on Homer.
[11]Dover came to believe that he had been in effect blackballed by one of the electors, his friend and rival Hugh Lloyd-Jones; cf. pp. 137–8 with notes there. Many years later, in 1984, Dover would himself be an elector for the Regius chair: see n. 12 to p. 316.
[12]On Umberto Albini, see p. 200 above.
[13]Dover's mother died while he was writing the Preface to *GPM*, which he then dedicated to her memory; cf. p. 3 with note.

FIGURE 9 Vecoli, 1973. Much of *Greek Popular Morality* was typed at the table on the grass.

general. As my concern was with our experience of morality in our responses, judgements, choices and dilemmas, and not in philosophical theorising about it, I paid a good deal of attention both to introspective analysis of my own experience and to reflection on the world in which I have lived. For me, a good world is a world in which people are honest, patient, reliable and helpful (virtues which often entail a degree of humility and, on occasion, self-destruction). Truthfulness, a virtue to which I respond with inordinate warmth, is a bridge between 'heart' and 'head' (or rather, between 'guts' and head, to use a term common to English idiom and New Testament Greek);[14] a rickety bridge, seeing that totally unfounded beliefs can inspire virtue and heroism, but I do not entertain any expectation that my moral reactions, or anybody's, will form a tight rational system.[15] When I consider what it is my 'duty' to do, what is the morally 'right' thing, I identify it as that course of action which will make some immediate contribution, however small, to the creation of a good world. How people can see their moral duty clearly and yet not

---

[14]The Greek term in question is σπλάγχνα (*splanchna*), literally 'innards': it can be used semi-metaphorically, like English 'heart', for the seat or source of strongly instinctive emotions, and not only in New Testament Greek.
[15]Cf. n. 11 to p. 55 for Dover's analogy between the unsystematic nature of morality and the constantly changing nature of language.

do it has been regarded by some philosophers as a puzzle. It is not in the least puzzling. I may see my duty, but I shall not do it unless *my desire to do it* is strong enough to overcome fatigue and all the other desires and fears (I include embarrassment and shyness among fears) which conflict with it. Acknowledgement of duty cannot in itself create desire of the strength required, any more than knowledge that speeding is illegal and fornication sinful can ensure universal compliance with secular and religious laws. I once asked Gwil Owen[16] whether, as a philosopher, he gave some thought to what he *ought* to do when confronted with a moral dilemma. 'Oh yes,' he said, looking serious, 'I do. But then,' – his face brightened – 'I usually do something different!'[17]

It is only in the artificially purified air of philosophy that a clear distinction can be drawn between 'strictly moral' judgements and judgements determined by aesthetic responses, loyalties, feuds, habits, comfort and fear. We have only to reflect for a short while on our engagement in ordinary life to see that. What is more, if people have an unavoidable aesthetic reaction to me, that reaction often motivates denigration or dismissal of my opinions in cases where an identical opinion expressed by someone impeccably presentable would be taken seriously. So, a history of moral philosophy is one thing, but a history of the operative evaluations in a given society something quite different.

The very large moral content of Christianity, Judaism and Islam has generated a widespread belief that morality had its origin in religion and remains dependent upon it. Accordingly, many who (not without reason) deplore moral deterioration in our time believe that matters would improve if more people were Christians and could thus give persuasive answers, in terms of ultimate reward and punishment, to the crucial question, 'Why *should* I?' That may well be so, but saying in effect, 'If you believed in God, and in a God who issues such-and-such commands, you *would* behave better' can hardly have much effect on anyone who does not already hold such beliefs, nor – except by creating some confusion between the truth of a belief and the effects of a belief – can it implant belief. In our own culture the issue is further complicated by increasing awareness that the conscience and sensitivity on which our morality depends cannot be reconciled with belief in a God who inflicts eternal retributive punishment. Introspection also persuaded me that whereas motives for doing wrong are often pure and simple, motives for doing right may very commonly be mixed. If that is so, cynical interpretation of an apparently altruistic action as self-interested is less appropriate than recognition that altruistic and self-interested motives can run in harness. This is commonplace in Greek literature.

---

[16] See n. 2 to p. 211.
[17] In the 1995 addenda, Dover noted: '*Teaching* the difference between right and wrong is not difficult; the problems begin when those who have understood the difference prefer and choose wrong.'

The Greek and English evaluative vocabularies do not contain any one-to-one equivalences. It is therefore essential to look (as I did) at every passage of fifth- and fourth-century literature which contains an evaluative word, in order to get a good feel of the semantic field of each one. As is to be expected, there are some oddities on the margins of the field. Reckless name-calling, common in forensic oratory and often portrayed in drama, tells us no more than its modern equivalent; 'temple-robber!' and 'tank-arse!', uttered in explosive rage, do not make specific allegations of sacrilege or sodomy. What is much more important is the evaluative implications of passages in which the speaker's effort to make a good impression on the jury is not manifested in application of favourable words to himself, but in narrative, in which all the nuances accumulate to convey the desired impression.

Sometimes Greek appears to lack a word which in English is of considerable moral importance. 'Conscience', for example, has no equivalent noun in Classical Greek, and if we look at passages containing phrases which the lexicon equates with (e.g.) 'it is on my conscience', we find that they refer to the fear of detection and (human or divine) punishment. It would be rash to conclude that the Greeks did not have the experience of shame and disgust at actions of one's own which one would blame and despise in others. There are in fact passages which show familiarity with that experience, but they do not use a noun which can be translated 'conscience'. The French and the Italians are equally acquainted with the experience, but their languages do not differentiate, as English does, between 'conscience' and 'consciousness'. We should always beware of deducing character from language.

Greek morality was no more systematic than anyone else's, if by 'systematic' we mean 'composed of interdependent parts' or 'derived all from a single principle', or both. There is no contradiction between total rejection of the First and Second Commandments and scrupulous observance of the Fifth and Ninth. Certain beliefs about gods were very widely held by the Greeks, particularly the belief that Zeus punished fraud, dishonesty and corruption, but there were no commands enshrined in a text regarded as divinely inspired. The belief that gods were themselves morally good was by no means universal; it was assumed by Xenophanes, about 500 BC, who recognised that his assertion entailed rejection of many myths as false, and to Plato it was axiomatic, but ordinary people entertained strong doubts about it, especially when their prayers were not answered. The notion that all gods are moral delinquents and morality a human construction is to be found among the Sedang-Moi, a south-east Asian people studied by George Devereux,[18] and approximations to that, in varying degrees, are not uncommon.

During 1968–72 I took part in several conferences of Scottish teachers of Religious Education; originally, perhaps, as a token agnostic, but latterly, I like to think,

---

[18]On Devereux, see esp. pp. 174–7.

because I was the only agnostic they knew who was interested enough in religion to come and discuss it for as long as anyone wished.[19] I never attacked religion in the style of Margaret Knight,[20] but acknowledged it as an ingredient of life which often has salutary effects but derives its power from beliefs which involve some serious contradictions and do not rest on adequate evidence; one pious teacher, I learned, regarded my approach as 'exceptionally dangerous'. I must confess that I was horrified by the crudity of thinking of these teachers. It seemed to me axiomatic that religious education, aimed at enabling children to understand religion and how it works, should be clearly separated from moral education aimed at enabling them to understand morality. I found that the teachers could not comprehend the possibility of this separation, or indeed distinguish between education and indoctrination. One proclaimed that her job was 'to bring children to Christ', and another was deeply shocked by the idea that St Luke's Gospel could be studied and discussed as one studies and discusses Plato's *Phaedo* ('Plato is for criticism, the Gospels for acceptance').[21] None of them seemed to have paid any serious attention to the definition of 'morality' or to have felt any curiosity about its origins, a matter on which far more light is thrown by animal ethology than by theology. Although most of them had gone through at least a one-year course of philosophy and logic in their student days, they found it hard to grasp the fact that the effect of a belief on the life of the believer is a different issue from the truth or falsity of the belief, and they used expressions such as 'the meaning of life' without making the important experiment of translating these expressions into an imaginary form of English which did not have the word 'meaning'. Their imagination stopped short of telling them what an agnostic view of life actually feels like. A man on the staff of the *Times Educational Supplement (Scotland)* confided to me his conviction that religious education was 'an insult to the children's intelligence', and he gave me space for a full-page review of a new committee report on *Moral and Religious Education in Scottish Schools*. I did my best to make my point about the independence of morality from religion, but I don't know if anyone was persuaded.[22] The notion that our moral experience itself constitutes evidence for the existence of God is not easily shaken, despite the complete adequacy of the alternative explanation of morality: as members of a social species we are *both* competing

---

[19] Dover called himself a 'genuine agnostic', often explaining the point by reference to the fifth-century BC thinker Protagoras, who opened his work *On the Gods* by saying, 'As regards the gods, I cannot know either that they do or do not exist' (B4 DK): see *ICNA* 98.

[20] Margaret Knight (1903–83) was lecturer in psychology at Aberdeen University 1948–70, a proponent of 'scientific humanism', and a severe critic of Christian values; her books included *Morals without Religion* (1955).

[21] Dover quotes this remark in a letter home of 28 September 1963, so the present paragraph clearly amalgamates recollections from different periods.

[22] The review in question appeared in *The Times Educational Supplement (Scotland)* for 31 March 1972, p. 2.

individuals desiring victory and success, *and* co-operative individuals, anxious for affection, gratitude and integration into society. Each of us occupies a point on a graph between behaviour which promotes the cohesion of society and behaviour which promotes its disruption; and since a human being's range of possible responses to any given situation is a great deal wider than that of other creatures, few of us occupy the same point on the graph all the time.

The sustained dialogue with Christians helped me to sort out my ideas on the relation between religion and morality in the Greek world but an unexpected event in the summer of 1969 was even more helpful. Gordon Williams was in America at the time, and I had a letter from Nan Dunbar (at Somerville) telling me that Gordon had fallen in love with a young American woman and wanted a divorce from Mary.[23] Nan, who knew both Gordon and Mary well, was deeply upset by the news, and I suppose my reply was insensitively lacking in an indication of surprise or shock. This generated an exchange of letters, mostly very long and sometimes a little virulent, ranging over the entire field of morality, religion, free will and the like, which lasted most of the summer. (Nan and I have one thing in common in addition to a love of Aristophanes: we both like to have the last word. She won.) I don't think there was a single point, even of marginal relevance, on which either of us effected a change of mind in the other. That fact in itself was instructive; even more so was what seemed to me an extraordinary and elusive flexibility in the relations between religious faith, moral judgement and personal loyalties. I treated the whole affair as a 'case-history', remembering occasionally that I was not a detached observer but part of the case.

Greek Popular Morality was published in 1974, and an Italian translation appeared in 1983. The translator, Livio Rossetti, is a professor of ancient philosophy at Perugia; he tidied up some wrong references, scrupulously sent me his translation in instalments for criticism, and we cleared up the last difficulties in the course of two memorable days in a remote valley at the top of the Val D'Aosta.§

To my mind the most worthwhile outcome of my work was establishment of the importance which Greek society attached to a virtue which rates no mention in Plato and little in Aristotle but figures much more conspicuously in forensic oratory and fourth-century comedy: the virtue of the person who is *epieikēs* and *philanthrōpos*, a 'nice' person whose relations with others are characterised by

---

§I had equally good fortune (though not, alas, in the Alps) with Suzanne Saïd who translated *Greek Homosexuality* into French, but on other occasions I was not given anything like enough time to scrutinise translations before they went to press. Once or twice I did not see the translations at all, with the result that they contain gross mistakes. On Japanese translations, pass.

[23] For Gordon Williams, see n. 2 to p. 128. Nan Dunbar (1928–2005), who had previously taught at St Andrews (1958–65), was a tutorial fellow of Somerville College, Oxford, 1965–95. Her massive edition of Aristophanes' *Birds*, commissioned by Dover for the Oxford series of commentaries on Aristophanes (see p. 117) and worked on for forty years, appeared in 1995.

kindness, sympathy and a reluctance to insist on legal rights (the conflict of 'niceness' with 'justice' poses a problem for Aristotle).[24]

I did not expect to return to the subject, but after Adkins had published a long and highly critical review of my book in 1978 I re-read his *Merit and Responsibility* and was seized with pedagogic zeal to protect young scholars from the influence of what I now regarded as a very misleading account of Greek moral values (Jacqueline de Romilly's *La Douceur dans la pensée grecque,* which came out in 1979, would have afforded some protection, but it was lamentably neglected in the English-speaking world). I therefore composed an article on the interpretation of passages of epic and tragedy in which one character expresses a value-judgement on the behaviour of another. This went through four drafts, one of which benefited from criticism by a philosopher, and appeared in 1983.[25]

Those who devote their time to the study of Greek society are sometimes suspected of admiring it indiscriminately. Some of the blame for this must fall upon an old-fashioned idealisation of Pericles and Socrates which was blind to the ruthless imperialism of the former and the absence of compassion in the latter. This idealisation was facilitated by the comforting notion that women and slaves didn't really have such a bad time, after all. In fact, slavery and suppression of the individuality and potential of women have been general characteristics of all human society; the first glimmers of doubt about both were the product of Greek originality and scepticism. If the historian is to be confined to cultures which score high on *all* counts, there will be no history.

I greatly doubt whether my own view of society has been formed by the Greeks, though it may have been fortified by the discovery that on many matters they thought and felt as I do. I have always tended to put the interests of the community above those of the individual. Rhetorical questions such as 'What's wrong with greed?' (Ivan Boesky) and 'Why should an individual's sense of duty to the community be greater than to his family?' (Jean Denton) seem to me to be answered by the words in which they are formulated; it is rather as if we asked 'Why shouldn't the angles of an equilateral triangle be unequal?' Lacking any sense of the 'sanctity of life'‖ I would be quite happy to see capital punishment extended to the perpetrators of any long-planned and well-organised crime, including fraud. I do not agonise over 'diminished responsibility', because I know that the proportion of cases on which we can take a defensible decision either way is extremely small.

‖*Innocent* life is sacrosanct and the duty to protect it compelling. Respect for the life of even the worst-behaved humans seems to be an aberration of post-Enlightenment Christianity. [EDS *In a 1995 addendum, Dover wrote:* 'An American friend hopes I am not a Pro-Life activist. I am not, though I do have some misgivings about abortion.']

[24]For further discussion of *GPM*, see the contribution of Chris Carey to *S&C*.
[25]'The portrayal of moral evaluation in Greek poetry', *Journal of Hellenic Studies* 103 (1983) 35–48, reprinted in *G&G* 77–96.

I do not like rules of evidence which prevent a jury (unlike anyone conducting an enquiry of any kind in any other walk of life) from taking every relevant consideration into account. I do not warm to the causes taken up by Civil Liberties. I see no good reason why I should not be compelled to carry an identity card, and I would spurn the 'right' to hold an undisclosed account in a bank overseas. Maybe I've said enough, but don't blame the Greeks.

20 ELEVATIONS 1970–1993

If you didn't have a Chancellor, how could you have a Vice-Chancellor? And then where would you be?

HAROLD MACMILLAN[1]

I was elected President of the Hellenic Society from 1971 to 1974, President of the Classical Association for the year 1975, and chairman of the Classical Journals Board from 1975 to 1978. At the beginning of 1977 I was knighted for services to scholarship. Honorary doctorates of Birmingham, Bristol, Durham, Liverpool, London, St Andrews and Oglethorpe (Atlanta) followed, agreeably supplemented by honorary membership of the American Academy of Arts and Sciences and the Royal Netherlands Academy. Election to the presidency of the Joint Association of Classical Teachers for 1985–7 filled the last space but one on the shelf of Classical trophies; the last was the award of the Kenyon Medal of the British Academy in 1993.

In 1970 I was appointed a member of the Leverhulme Research Awards Advisory Committee for a seven-year term, and when that expired, reappointed for a further five years.[2] The Leverhulme Trust makes a prodigious contribution, insufficiently recognised by the public, to the furtherance of research in the humanities, sciences and social sciences. Some of this is on a grand scale – grand, that is, for the humanities; scientists use quantitative terms differently – and nowadays often channelled through the British Academy; the Advisory Committee is concerned with the many hundreds of applications each year for more modest support.

---

[1] This frequently repeated remark is associated with Macmillan's time as Chancellor of Oxford University, a position he took up while still Prime Minister in 1960 and held till 1986.

[2] Asa Briggs, *The Story of the Leverhulme Trust* (London, 1991) 173 says that the exceptional length of Dover's service, at Briggs' own recommendation as Chairman, was eleven years (1970–81); cf. 249. He describes him as 'the ideal member ... well informed about everything ... a shrewd and conscientious judge'.

FIGURE 10 Leverhulme Trustees and Research Awards Advisory Committee, c. 1972. In front row, Asa Briggs third from left, Bill Holford far right, Helen Gardner next to him. In back row, Anthony Blunt third from right.

In April 1978 we were on the point of leaving for Italy, where I was scheduled to lecture in Bari and Padua, when I had an unexpected visit from Isaiah Berlin.[3] As a member of the Council of the British Academy, I was well aware that the process of choosing the next President had begun. Isaiah had in fact consulted each Council member individually earlier in the year, when his own inclination was for either Helen Gardner or Eric Turner,[4] and I was opposed to both: to the former because my experience as her colleague on the Leverhulme Research Fund Committee had caused me some misgivings about her judgement, and to Eric Turner because in 1974, when I had circulated a strictly confidential memorandum to the Council of the Hellenic Society on the organisation of the Congress in

---

[3]Sir Isaiah Berlin (1909–97, Kt 1957), an influential historian of ideas who spent most of his career in Oxford, was Dover's predecessor as President of the British Academy 1974–8. For correspondence of his relating to Dover's election, see Isaiah Berlin, *Affirming: Letters 1975–1997*, eds H. Hardy and M. Pottle (London, 2015) 69–70.

[4]Dame Helen Gardner (1908–86, DBE 1967) had been Merton Professor of English Literature at Oxford 1966–75, and Sir Eric Turner (1911–83, Kt 1981) Professor of Papyrology at University College London 1950–78.

Madrid that year, he gave a copy of it to Juliette Ernst, the secretary of the Fédération internationale des études classiques. She accepted my criticisms (which were rather bluntly expressed) with more grace than I had any right to expect, and her revenge – ensuring that I was put on to the organising committee of the next congress, to be held in Budapest in 1979 – strengthened a mutual respect which Eric Turner's grotesque indiscretion might have destroyed. I do not know whether his action proceeded from stupidity or from malice, but it seemed to me to rule him out as president of an academy. Now Isaiah told me that I myself was the choice of the majority of Council members. I groaned and said, 'Oh *why* do people think I can do that sort of thing?' Isaiah waved his hand dismissively, 'Nothing to it! Nothing to it!', and, after a moment's thought, 'You can leave the seating plan at the Annual Dinner to your wife.' I could not possibly take the decision then and there, but promised him that I would give him an answer as soon as I came back from Italy. I did not actually give the matter a moment's thought while we were away, because I recognised, after the first shock had passed, that I could not refuse.

There was only one ingredient of my three-year presidency which made me feel out of my element: I had to acquire *full* evening dress for the Annual Dinner and for the annual dinners of the Royal Society and the Royal Academy. The company on all those occasions was friendly, congenial and interesting, but I have never reconciled myself to the idea that it is necessary to put on peculiar clothes in order to enjoy a dinner.

Britain has as yet no Humanities Research Council.[5] The role played in other countries by such a Council has always been played here by the Academy, but with a budget which limits its scope; when I became President, the annual grant from the Department of Education and Science was just under £1.6 million, over half of which was earmarked for the maintenance of the Schools and Institutes overseas (predominantly archaeological). It was my hope that the Academy would turn into an institution taking an increasingly positive and creative role in the promotion of research in the humanities, and in my address to the AGM at the end of my first year I pleaded for a 'shift of initiative from applicant to Academy', because at present 'the greater part of the financial support which we give to research ... is a response to initiatives taken by others'. The change from a passive to an active role has indeed occurred, but by 1978 it had already begun, to an extent which my rankling disappointment over the reception of my memorandum on computational studies (p. 174) prevented me from perceiving, and I can claim no credit except for supporting other people's good ideas and not saying, 'Oh, that would never do!' There had been a cataclysm of change in the administration of the Academy in the few years before my presidency. Derek Allen, a good scholar and a man of charm

---

[5]This changed in 1998 with the creation of the Arts and Humanities Research Board ('Council' as of 2005).

and integrity but (to my mind) neither hard-headed nor innovative, moved from the Secretaryship to the Treasurership in 1973 and died in 1975. His successor as Secretary, Neville Williams (from the Public Record Office), died suddenly at the beginning of 1977. Peter Brown (from the School of Oriental and African Studies) arrived as Assistant Secretary in 1975. Williams' successor was John Carswell, who had been chief executive officer of the University Grants Committee. John showed his mettle straight away by bringing off an ingenious negotiation which enabled London University to fill the Chair of Papyrology at University College when Eric Turner retired (I am not sure it really wanted to fill it, but it was argued into a corner). John also set his sights on the creation of Academy-funded readerships and professorships which would make it possible for good academics to devote a period of two or more years to uninterrupted research without financial detriment to their universities. Such a scheme would of course require higher funding from the D.E.S., and that has come about, with generous reinforcement from the Wolfson Foundation and the Leverhulme Trust.

Financial management of the Academy's funds had also taken a more businesslike turn before 1978, with the setting up of a Standing Committee on Schools and Institutes overseas and a Major Projects Review Committee. The first meeting of the latter which I chaired was rather disagreeable; the other two members were Alec Cairncross and Freddie Ayer,[6] and I was unprepared for the philistinism which induced Ayer to question the utility of the Lexicon of Greek Proper Names (he managed to create a joky philosophical pseudo-problem out of the difference between an onomasticon and a prosopography) and the Episcopal Acta (his hatred of religion played a part there). Cairncross's good sense saved the situation, as no doubt it has saved many others, but, of course, both of them had a point: over seventy per cent of the money the Academy spent on its Major Projects went on the study of the ancient and medieval worlds, and it was legitimate to question our priorities. The fact was that the Sections concerned with Classical, medieval and (ancient) oriental studies knew what they wanted, and those concerned with modern history and modern languages appeared not to know.

The accommodation available to the Academy was derisory. It did not in fact possess any premises of its own, but was allowed the use of rooms which belonged to the Royal Society of Chemistry in Burlington House. Office-work was sometimes done in corridors, and confidential business discussed in the corners of rooms in simultaneous use for other purposes. John Carswell persuaded the Property Services Agency to find us something better, and they came up with a building in Cornwall Terrace, on the southern Outer Ring of Regent's Park; the D.E.S. was also persuaded to extend it by adding a lecture-room and to increase our grant by an

---

[6]Sir Alexander Cairncross (1911–98, Kt 1967) was, among much else, head of the Government Economic Service 1964–9 and Master of St Peter's College, Oxford, 1969–78; for Ayer, see n. 11 on p. 98.

amount which would cover the rent and rates. When John and I first went to look at the building, driving towards it from the east, my heart leapt at the sight of the splendid façade at the western end of Cornwall Terrace, but sank again when I found that nos. 20 and 21, the Academy's future home, constituted a much less impressive affair, set back a little as if cowering from its neighbours. However, it was all that was on offer, and infinitely better than our foothold in Burlington House. The move took place after the end of my presidency. Now the premises in Cornwall Terrace are proving inadequate and some Fellows ask why we can't have premises more like those of some foreign academies, notably the Lincei in Rome. The answer to that question is that the Property Services Agency is short of palazzi.[7]

After twelve years on the Leverhulme Committee, four years on the Research Funds Committee of the Academy, and several years on other Academy committees which dealt with a large field of applicants for research grants, conference grants, congress subventions and the like, it seemed to me that one way and another I must have had as much as anyone else this century to do with the direction and character of research in the humanities in Britain. Not, of course, single-handed, except – in the eyes of disappointed applicants it must seem a formidable exception – at the first stage of the Leverhulme applications, when each of us was individually responsible for massive elimination in a given group of subjects. There is no alternative to short-listing, and the most striking feature of the process is the frequency with which a list drawn up by committee members who do not have professional competence in the subject concerned coincides with that drawn up by those who do. In 1983, when Corpus and two other colleges, in conjunction with the Department of Physical Chemistry, were seeking to make three appointments in chemistry, I found that in a field of 150 applicants my own top two were included in the top four favoured by the Department. I can claim an even better record in picking philosophers and historians, though when it came to mathematicians, theoretical physicists and computer scientists I was so far out of my depth that I preferred to offer no opinion.

One day in January 1981 I was in St Andrews to give a lecture, and in the evening had dinner in Deanscourt with Gregory Vlastos, who was Gifford Lecturer that year, Ian Kidd, and a few others. Conversation turned on the recent death of the Chancellor, Lord Ballantrae, and the need to elect a successor. The Chancellor of St Andrews (as of many other British universities) is elected by a postal vote in which all living graduates are entitled to participate; s/he holds a ceremonial position, without executive power, office, staff, pay or perquisites; there is no retiring age, and if any of the electorate wished to compel a Chancellor to resign I do not know

---

[7]In 1998 the British Academy in fact moved to new and more 'palatial' premises in Carlton House Terrace, adjacent to the Mall and close to the Royal Society.

how they could set about it. None of us came up with any plausible name, and Gregory, waving his hand toward me, said, 'What about Kenneth?' We all laughed heartily at this courteous pleasantry, and I forgot all about it until a few weeks later Kenneth Silver, a Classics teacher in the Borders, asked if he could nominate me and told me that Leitch Adams[8] was willing to second the nomination. I thought, 'Well, why ever not?', and agreed. There were two other nominations, both of men who had strong family connections with the University: the Marquess of Bute, whose great-grandfather had been Rector of the University and one of its most generous benefactors, and the Earl of Crawford, whose father had also held the Rectorship and was remembered with affection and admiration by everyone who knew him for his support of the arts in St Andrews. I was disconcerted when I saw the paragraph which Silver composed, in advocacy of my candidature, for the voting paper, because even after tactful modification by David Dorward, whose duty it was to organise the election, it still read like a publisher's blurb, and I hoped no one would think I'd written it myself; the other nominators rightly confined themselves to austere statements of their candidates' careers. However, I was elected as the candidate with the largest number of votes, though my majority was not absolute.

It was a sobering as well as gratifying moment. I could not claim to be the first person with an academic background to be Chancellor of a Scottish university, because Alec Cairncross had been elected at Glasgow in 1972, but I was the first Chancellor of St Andrews who was not a duke, a peer or an archbishop. My opponents were a Scottish Catholic peer and a Scottish Protestant peer, and an agnostic English parvenu had somehow wriggled through the gap. I recalled a passage which had stuck in my mind from the opening page of my predecessor's autobiography, in which he expresses his intense, lifelong love of the house in which he was brought up. It is inconceivable that I, or my father, or my grandfather, could ever have felt affection for the houses in which we lived as children. We always hoped and worked for something better.

My first duty as Chancellor was to accompany the Chancellors of Glasgow and Aberdeen to Holyrood Palace to present the Queen with loyal congratulations on the engagement of Prince Charles. It would be difficult to devise a more empty and pointless ceremony. The following year the Queen and the Duke of Edinburgh visited St Andrews,[9] and it was my duty to represent the University during the twenty minutes that they were on our premises. It is conventional in annual reports and the like to treat a royal visit as if it were a moment of ecstasy, but for anyone who bears any responsibility for its organisation it casts a long shadow of gloom

---

[8]James Whyte Leitch Adams (1909–83), a classical alumnus of both St Andrews and Oxford, was Professor of Education in Dundee 1955–80.
[9]On 1 July 1982.

and terror for months beforehand. On the occasion of the Queen's visit to St Andrews a combination of my nervousness and incipient deafness with the noise made by the cheering children prevented me from hearing anything she said, so I replied to what I thought she had probably said, and I dare say she wrote me off as half-witted.

The Chancellor has the right to appoint one member of the University Court, known as the Chancellor's Assessor. Ballantrae's Assessor had been Alan Baxter, a lawyer whom I knew quite well, and I would have been happy to keep him but for the fact that Steven Watson had taken against him bitterly when he bought a house in South Street which Steven had wished the University to buy. It seemed to me desirable that there should be friendly relations between Principal and Assessor, and when Alan offered me his resignation I accepted it. I had my eye on Robin Buchanan-Smith, who had been University Chaplain for five years and was now the owner-manager of Eriska Hotel on the West Coast. I knew him to be realistic, energetic, innovative, and a man who could handle Steven well. To my great relief, he yielded to my importunity, and during his four years as Assessor he kept me well (and amusingly) posted on what happened, and was likely to happen, on the Court.

There was one extra consideration which helped to determine my choice of Robin. Mike Urch, the Chaplain, was leaving for a parish, and at a time when the University was faced with financial retrenchment it was inevitable that the need for a chaplain should be questioned; there was, after all, no shortage of ministers of religion in St Mary's[10] or of parish churches in the town. It was well known that I had no religion, and I had some reason to suspect the existence of a fear that I would exert myself behind the scenes to suppress, or at least reduce, religious activity in the University. I judged that my appointment of a Presbyterian minister as my Assessor would reassure people that I was more concerned with individuals than with abstract principles; and such a reassurance gave me the freedom to express the opinion, should it be invited, that at a time when the University was unexpectedly faced with a serious cut in its annual grant, it could dispense with the services of a full-time chaplain. Robin shared my opinion. I was installed as Chancellor of St Andrews on 17 October 1981, and I was allowed to suggest the names of three people to receive honorary degrees on the occasion. I thought it would be invidious to make so narrow a selection from among my fellow-Hellenists, so I settled on Anna Davies, Professor of Comparative Philology at Oxford, and the film-maker Ken Loach:[11] the former because I admired her for her combination of learning, acumen and common sense, and the latter because some

---

[10] The University's Faculty of Divinity; cf. n. ∥ to p. 130.
[11] Anna Morpurgo Davies (1937–2014), of Italian Jewish descent (and married to the ancient historian J.K. Davies 1962–78), held the chair of comparative philology 1971–2003 and was especially noted for her work on Mycenean Greek. The socialist-inspired films of Ken Loach (1936–) have won him numerous awards.

of his films, notably *Kes* and (made for television) *The Price of Coal*, seemed to me to portray realities with an integrity usually lacking in the cinema. For the third place I suggested a few historians and scientists, from whom the Senate selected, to my pleasure, Leland Lyons,[12] who had just retired as Provost of Trinity College, Dublin. I don't know whether the Senate has ever turned down a candidate proposed by a Chancellor or a Rector (the Rector in a Scottish university is elected by the students for a three-year term in office), but I came near to attempting a blackball in 1961 when Snow[13] had been elected Rector and put forward the name of Mikhail Sholokhov. Snow assured me that Sholokhov was revered by all young Soviet writers as the doyen of Russian literature; so we honoured the crafty Cossack, he charmed everyone (the headmaster of the local school found him to be 'pure gold'), and it was only later, when Daniel and Sinyavsky were put on trial, that Sholokhov was revealed as a Stalinist lackey of the worst kind. And, of course, Snow's assessment of his standing among Soviet writers was totally wrong.

Not long after my Installation Robert Ogilvie was found dead in his office in the Department of Humanity; he had shot himself. *The Times* had no obituary ready in stock, so I wrote one, in which I spoke only of his virtues.*

By convention the Chancellor of a University nominates its Principal a Vice-Chancellor,† and I had no intention or desire to violate this convention. But problems can arise when both of them live in the same small town and the Chancellor, often wrongly assumed to be responsible for the actions of the University Court, becomes a target of complaint and criticism; or worse, when s/he is lobbied and expected to intervene in matters on which the existing Acts of Parliament give hrm no right at all to intervene. I have a good working agreement with the present Principal, Struther Arnott,[14] that we do not consult one another

---

*I feel I ought not to conceal the fact that my true view of him is very harsh. In the first draft of this book I wrote two pages here about the last five years of his life. I have now deleted the passage, and people who admired him are free to suppose that my judgement of him must be founded on eccentric, even perverse, criteria. [EDS Dover wrote the Times *obituary of 13 November 1981, p. 12, in which he naturally remained silent about his adverse view of Ogilvie. The material deleted by Dover, relating to a number of aspects of Ogilvie's personal life, survives in the Dover papers at Corpus Christi College, Oxford.*]

†Knox was a candidate for the Chancellorship in 1973. He told Edward Ullendorff that if he were elected he would not consider himself bound to appoint Steven Watson as Vice-Chancellor. [EDS *On Knox and Watson, see p. 151. Edward Ullendorff (1920–2011) was a Swiss-born linguist who taught semitic languages at St Andrews 1950–59 and subsequently held chairs in Manchester and London.*]

[12]Francis Stewart Leland Lyons (1923–83) was Professor of Modern History, University of Kent, 1964–74, and Provost of Trinity College Dublin 1974–81.

[13]C.P. Snow (1905–80), government scientist and novelist, was Rector of St Andrews 1961–4; see note to p. 334 on his controversial 'two cultures' thesis. The Russian novelist Mikhail Sholokhov (1905–84) was awarded the Nobel Prize in Literature in 1965, but controversy continues over charges against him both of plagiarism and regarding his political behaviour under Stalin.

[14]Struther Arnott FRS (1934–2013), a distinguished molecular biologist, was Principal of St Andrews 1986–2000: see his Royal Society memoir by Sir Dai Rees at https://royalsocietypublishing.org/doi/10.1098/rsbm.2015.0011

FIGURE 11 At Installation as Chancellor, 1981, with Leland Lyons, Anna Davies, Ken Loach and Steven Watson. *Photo: Peter Adamson.*

except in cases in which we would do so even if we lived four hundred miles apart. Steven Watson and I did in fact live four hundred miles apart for the five years between my election and his death, but there was one matter on which I felt so strongly that I sought and found a legitimate way of putting to him an argument in complete conflict with a decision of the Court.

Twice a year the General Council meets in St Andrews with the Chancellor in the chair. All graduates of the University (the Chancellor's electorate) are members of it, and so are the academic staff, no matter where they graduated. It cannot tell the Court what to do, but it has a statutory right to transmit requests and observations to the Court, and the Court has an obligation to take these into account. In 1981 the University Grants Committee, cutting the annual grant to St Andrews much more drastically than anyone had foreseen, recommended the closure of the Departments of Archaeology, Linguistics, Music and Theoretical Physics. The Faculties, Senate and Court acquiesced. I could not quarrel with the closure of Archaeology, because our effort to keep it going as an independent department had not come off; and I had no opinion on Theoretical Physics. The closure of Music, however, seemed to me a disaster, because although it was comparatively expensive it cemented town and gown together. The closure of

Linguistics, although less disastrous, angered me; the report of the Court's Restructuring Committee seriously misrepresented the intentions and hopes entertained by the Faculty of Arts when the department was created and Jan Mulder was the first appointment to it in 1964 (I was there), it could not be claimed that Linguistics was peculiarly expensive (why not close the Faculty of Divinity instead?), and I had a suspicion – for Linguistics is a notoriously schismatic subject – that the UGC might have received prejudiced advice. It occurred to me that if someone at the General Council gave notice of a motion deploring the proposed closures and secured a hefty majority vote, I would be bound, as Chairman of the Council, to transmit its views to the Court and would also be free to support them by arguments as cogent as I could construct. I pointed this out to people who implored me to intervene, and they took the hint. The Council meeting in January 1983 was quite unlike the meetings of a decade earlier, which were apt to consist of a few rows of old faithfuls who got through the business in five minutes, listened politely to the Principal's address, and went off to lunch. This meeting was packed to the limits of the hall by university staff; the motion got its majority and explicitly invited me to intervene with the Court, so I wrote a letter which my duty as chairman required me to write. It had no effect, of course; Steven told me privately that he 'didn't care a bugger about the General Council'.‡ My great regret, throughout the whole business, was that the University had not given enough thought during 1980 to the question of which departments should go if closures became inescapable. Had it done so, it would have been able to put a firm counter-proposal to the UGC and would not have been forced into flabby acquiescence.

In 1981 I was made a member of the Prize Committee of the Balzan Foundation, an international trust which each year offers three prizes of scale and academic standard comparable with the Nobel prizes; not, however, comparable in public esteem, especially in Britain, because Nobel got in first and 'Nobel prizewinner' lodged itself firmly in the language as an honorific epithet. Balzan differs from Nobel in three important respects. Although in the course of twenty years it has twice given a prize for 'humanity, peace and the brotherhood of mankind', it has no commitment to a regular 'peace prize'; this avoids the absurdity of honouring retired terrorists and the considerable risk that some recipient of a peace prize may subsequently turn nasty. It gives no prizes for creative literature, and therefore escapes ridicule and censure by literary critics. What is most important, it covers (by contrast with Nobel) the whole range of humanities, sciences and social sciences. Each year it announces the three subjects in which the following year's

---

‡It may seem odd that the replacement of (metaphorical) 'fuck' by 'bugger' was often felt to be a creditable act of self-restraint, but, of course, unvoiced consonants (e.g. /f/, /k/) are more brutal than voiced (e.g. /b/, /g/).

prizes will be given, and invites academies and universities throughout the world to make their nominations; as a rule, between twenty and thirty nominations for each subject come in, and the committee is divided into three subject-committees to deal with them.

As the Foundation's administrative offices are half in Bern (finance) and half in Milan (prize committee), it was commonly believed in the British Academy that the whole thing was an 'Italian racket', a peculiarly unjust view (now discarded, I hope), given that during my years on the committee only five out of forty prizewinners and four out of seventeen committee members were Italian. I noticed that it was rare for an academy or university to nominate anyone of a nationality other than its own; but there were some noteworthy exceptions, and committee members sometimes produced nominations on their own initiative without regard for nationality. Of the forty awards there were only four with which I myself disagreed – in one case strongly enough to abstain from voting on it[15] – and a further four for which I would have accepted a runner-up as readily as the winner; and if that gives an impression of a committee ruled by reason and harmony, the impression, while not absolutely true, is nearly true. I value my years on the committee for the wisdom and humanity which were so conspicuous in some of its members.

The Foundation did everything in style, putting us up in the Hotel Cavour in Milan (accommodation so-so, but cuisine splendid) and inviting us with our wives to the prize-giving ceremonies, which were held alternately in Bern and Rome. None the less, in 1991 I had a ten-year itch (Lord Jenkins[16] recently declared in a radio interview, 'No one is any good in a job after ten years'), and since I was in a very low state that summer with 'post-viral syndrome', a legacy of Californian flu at Stanford, I decided to resign. Much of the proceedings in sub-committees and of the conversation at mealtimes was in French, and I had become increasingly depressed and humiliated by my failure to understand spoken French on a level with my French-speaking colleagues' ability to understand spoken English. If I had been feeling physically fitter I would probably not have worried about that.

---

[15]This was the case, as Dover SN reveals, of the Lithuanian-French philosopher Emmanuel Levinas (1905–95), whose work, in the tradition of phenomenology, Dover considered to be 'mere incantation'. Levinas was awarded the Balzan Prize for philosophy in 1989.

[16]Roy Jenkins (1920–2003), a Labour MP 1948–76 but a founding member of the Social Democratic Party in 1981. When Dover was writing *MC*, Jenkins was Chancellor of Oxford University (1987–2003). See the further reference to him on p. 256, with note there.

21 DOVERS 1972–1982

Remember me.
I have forgotten you.
　　　　　　　　　　　　'ROSIE PROBERT' in **DYLAN THOMAS**, Under Milk Wood [1]

The last time my parents came to stay with us in Scotland was in the autumn of 1972, and a photograph I took of them shows my mother, deeply lined and screwing up her eyes against the sun, holding on to my father's arm as if she were not sure of standing upright without it. The last time I actually saw her was towards the end of that year. When I asked her (as one does) how she was, her eyes opened brightly, her mouth formed a wry smile, and she said, 'I want to die.' I couldn't say anything except 'Yes, I know', because I did know, and in her condition I would have felt the same. She was constantly choking, her voice was faint and dragged slowly, and any meal was a struggle for her. My father coped with looking after her and the house and the cookery better than I would have expected (and an admirable help came in twice a week), but I once heard him from the next room inveighing against my mother for not making a more successful effort to speak clearly; 'They just won't come and see us!' he said, with panic in his voice. She didn't answer; she had given up rational self-defence.

　　It was obvious to us that she was likely to die before he did. Years earlier we had promised them that whichever of them died first, the other could come to live with us. Why we were so rash, we found hard to recall; perhaps we felt that we were so fortunate in most ways that we ought to take on a burden or two, although we were violating a rule which we normally treated as important, never to make a promise to a parent.* In any case, it probably looked at the time as if my mother would be

---

*We have always respected this rule in our dealings with our children.
[1] Rosie Probert is the voice of blind Captain Cat's dead lover as heard in his nostalgic dreams of life at sea; Cat responds with tears and 'Come back, come back': Dylan Thomas, *Under Milk Wood. A Play for Voices* (London, 1954) 71.

the survivor, and although her health might give us problems her character would not. My mother died in March 1973, while we were at Vecoli.[2] When I went back to England for a week I found my father oscillating between a state which he described as 'unspeakable anguish' and a glimmering of ambition to pick up some threads which he had had to drop while looking after my mother. He even learned a Chopin nocturne which he had not played before, but interest in the piano did not last him long; his technique, which sounded pretty good by my standards, was lamentable by his, and he had for so long been accustomed to thinking of the performance of music as a means of earning the applause of other people that he could not reconstitute it as a bridge between himself and the composer. In the autumn of 1973 we were called on to redeem our promise. He sold his Boston house and most of his furniture and moved in with us.

It was during that summer that Alan's marriage to Sheila fell apart.[3] My first reaction to this astonishing news was totally selfish; they were nineteen when they married, I had defended them against all accusations of imprudence, and now I was proved wrong. Anyway, Alan took off for Scotland, secured a job as an administrator of the Theatre Workshop in Edinburgh, and moved rent-free into a house at East Linton whose owners were abroad. There he was soon joined by Wendy Clark, and from that day to this they have been held together by an unfaltering love.[4] Alan thought, as he told me later, that we might be so upset by all this that we would sever connections with him, at least until we had cooled down after a year or two, but we did not think a rigid moral line would serve any useful purpose. We liked Sheila, were sorry for her and admired her fortitude, and indeed kept in touch with her from time to time, but we also liked Wendy and found much to admire in her too. Alan had the idea that once the divorce was through Sheila would marry a certain mutual friend of theirs. Whether this was acumen, clairvoyance or reckless guesswork on his part, I don't know, but Sheila did marry the man; they have lived happily, had two children, and have now emigrated.

Wendy bore our first grandchild, Rebecca ('Beki'), in 1974, and they soon had to think about moving, because the owners of the house at East Linton would soon return, and the salary which the Theatre Workshop paid Alan was largely devoured by the cost of commuting to Edinburgh. Fortunately, they had made a lot of friendly contacts at East Linton, and since Alan was able and willing to turn his hand to a wide range of jobs in farming and building they had a spell in a farm cottage and then were given the basement flat of Hopes House, on the edge of the Lammermuirs, in return for looking after the owner's horses; Wendy (like Sheila)

---

[2]See the earlier reference to his mother's death on p. 217, with note there.
[3]See p. 198 for this marriage.
[4]Dover SN records not only that the marriage eventually ended in 1999 but that this was 'the most tragic thing that has happened to me', a comment to be compared with what he originally wrote at *MC* 26 about 'tragic anxieties' in relation to one's children.

has a way with horses. At this point their ambitions for the future tied in nicely with an idea of our own. After Audrey inherited some healthy investments from her mother we contemplated turning money and paper, ephemeral and untrustworthy things, into solid land. It now seemed sensible that Audrey should buy a bit of ground with a dilapidated cottage on it, turn the cottage over to Alan to rebuild, pay him a subsistence wage for doing so, and then let him and his family live there for as long as they wished. She went off with Wendy's parents to look at a few sites in Wales, but on all of them the land was obviously unproductive. A site in Ayrshire was a bit better, but bare and ugly, and at one in Angus, which we looked at together, bog-cotton was the most conspicuous vegetation. Then Alan picked up the news that Glendeuglie estate, on the edge of Glenfarg (eight miles from Perth), was going to be auctioned off in parcels. We had a look at the houses which stood on three of the parcels. One had a sitting tenant who might or might not live some years more, one was rather extensive and bound to be costly, and the third, Barley Mill, was hardly more than a ruin. At first sight we ruled out Barley Mill, but Alan saw that it was actually the most promising of the three and likely to be sold for little more than the price of the land on which it stood. Much of this land was impenetrably covered with tall comfrey and nettles, a more encouraging sight than bog-cotton. It would qualify, as we learned on a visit to the planning department in Perth, for an improvement grant to cover the cost of bringing in electricity and water. Alan had managed to get a large caravan on indefinite loan, and they would live in that on site while Alan put in plumbing and wiring and a damp-proof course, raised the roof, replaced most of the timbers, and built an extension, facing all the new parts with granite from the impending demolition of Glendeuglie House. To our delight, Audrey's bid was accepted, and Alan, Wendy and Beki moved in with their caravan in November 1977. They lived cheerfully in conditions at which a Spartan might have blenched, getting all their water from a standpipe which on occasion had to be thawed out by gripping it in thickly-gloved hands, and more than once, that first winter, waking up with ice around their lips. Since Alan also had to clear the land, grow fruit and vegetables, nurture hens and Muscovy ducks, and top up his subsistence income by doing temporary jobs for local farmers, it was two and a half years before they could settle into the house, by which time Nicholas, our second grandchild, had been born. There remained the problem of earning a living, and it took some years more – years of risk, anxiety, debt, and alternating excitement and discouragement – before that problem was solved by the expansion, from minuscule beginnings, of their fashion-designing and dress-making business.

In 1973 I told my father nothing about Alan beyond the bare minimum of fact, and even in the following years I avoided discussing Alan with him, because Alan's resilience and acquisition of practical skills meant nothing to him by comparison with the neglect of opportunities to achieve the respectability of a white-collar career. On the few occasions when he tried to prod me into expressing indignation and disappointment, I would not be drawn. He was, of course, delighted to be a great-grandfather, but Beki, in most ways a happy and peaceful baby, always cried when he tried to hold her, and he did not care for babies who were less than angelic. Over the years, long before my father came to live with us, I had come to realise how much more strongly I sympathised with the young than with the old. This inclination grew as I myself moved onwards through middle age, and his presence in the house reinforced it.

To begin with, he was so grateful for being rescued from solitude that everything we did and said was right in his eyes. He made many friends of all ages, and seemed to most of them a wise and benevolent old man. None the less, he had not lost his capacity for creating a tense and disagreeable atmosphere. He ceased to play the piano, lost interest in history, rarely looked at television, and was indifferent to the garden (in which he never sat). It puzzled him still that for me work was not just a means of earning enough money to enjoy leisure.

When we moved to Oxford in 1976 he broke into tears and laughter at the sight of the drawing-room, which measured thirty feet by twenty, in the President's Lodgings. All his life a big drawing-room had been his Holy Grail.

I am aware in writing all this that I am in danger of lapsing into a catalogue of grievances. Let me therefore simply say that my father's attitude to other people – my

FIGURE 12 Percy Dover (father) and Lillian (Dover) Lipscombe (aunt), Glen Clova, 1975.

students, my colleagues, our friends – was irreconcilable with ours, and I was not able to relax and disregard it.

Soon after our arrival in Oxford he needed an operation to remove stones from his gall-duct, and afterwards a curious leakage of material somewhere inside him twice prostrated him with a very high temperature, delirium and rigor. On each of these two occasions the doctor asked us, 'Do you want me to treat him?', a very reasonable question when the patient is 85. On the first occasion we said 'Yes' automatically, because we were quite unprepared for so direct a question, and a death-sentence calls for some reflection. So he was taken into the Radcliffe, and a dazzling cocktail of antibiotics brought him back from the edge. The second time we would have undoubtedly said 'No', but for the presence of a district nurse who seemed to us keen on rescuing him and might have been a whistle-blower (it was only later that I realised that the doctor must have known that she was not). So again he went into the Radcliffe. On the third evening that I visited him there I could see and hear for myself that his breathing was much more normal. I was on my way to Eton to give a talk to classicists in Buckinghamshire schools, and I remember that journey as one of the low points of my life; I felt like a prisoner who is sentenced afresh the day before he is due for release.

From hospital he was sent for a fortnight's recuperation to St Luke's, a private nursing-home in Oxford, and the doctor pointed out to me that if we wanted him to stay there it was a great deal easier to take the decision now, while he was in, than to put him back there after he had come out. This idea was very attractive, and financially manageable. He had paid me, on his insistence, £600 a year while he had been living with us, and the accumulated £3,000, plus interest, would last for ten months at St Luke's, without touching his savings. He had a pension of £2,500 a year, the interest on his building society accounts currently amounted to £2,000 a year, and we could make up the rest by investing what I was going to make from television in 1978.[5] By chance, it fell to Audrey to break the news to him, because it was on her visiting day (one of us visited him daily) that he talked of his return to the Lodgings. He took our decision very badly, and when I saw him next day he was lying on his bed with his eyes closed as if knocked out. I demonstrated to him that he would not be, as he envisaged, 'homeless and penniless' by the end of the year, and promised him that he could come back to the Lodgings for odd days and, if he felt up to it, come to St Andrews with us in the Long Vacation (to which his response was 'Bugger St Andrews!'). It was fortunate for both of us that Audrey had fought and won the battle, even though it had a very bad effect on her blood-pressure; she did not suffer from the irreparable metal-fatigue which the first twenty years of my life had caused in my machinery, and she could be tough where I might have weakened. Alan rang me up to give me his moral support, and I told

---

[5]Evidently advance payment for the BBC series *The Greeks*: see pp. 185–8.

him, 'When I'm that age, whatever I may say, don't on any account have me to live with you.' He laughed and said, 'Well, we'll wait and see'; but I meant it, and still do.

My father never reconciled himself to St Luke's, and never ceased to regard his stay there as 'incarceration'. He stayed all the time in his own room and made no attempt to strike up a friendship with any of the other patients. Their occasional tentative conversations with him at brief meetings in the corridors seemed to him only to show that they were tedious people (many of them were not), and the notion that he might try to make *their* lives more interesting did not enter his head. Once when I was visiting him he said, out of the blue, 'I do wish I were not such a *coward*', but I couldn't get him to enlarge on that. One afternoon in early December 1978 I found him put to bed because his heart was beating rather slowly and feebly. He was more serene, cheerful, relaxed and humorous than he had been for years, and I enjoyed my visit. That night his heart slowed to a halt, and in the morning he was dead.

Aunt Lillian and Uncle Cyril came over to Oxford for the cremation, and only a few days later Cyril himself suddenly died.[6] Audrey went down to their house in a village near Eastbourne and brought Lillian back to us for Christmas and the New Year. Lillian had always paraded her dread of solitude and declared she would 'go mad' if Cyril died. She did. There was no lack of neighbours willing to help, but she locked her doors, frenzied with fear, and would let no one in. So the neighbours soon decided she was impossible to help; the house was sold, and she was admitted to a geriatric hospital. There she took against everyone, especially her fellow-patients, and imagined that Cyril was still alive, flirting with the nurses. When I visited her she told me about this indignantly, declared that she had cut Cyril out of her will, and confided in me that she had suspected him of infidelities ever since he had admitted that he was too old for sex with her. So that was Cyril's reward for fifty years of patience and good humour; I felt that I was looking into the gates of Hell, and I could not wait to be rid of the older generation of Dovers.

Naturally she wanted to come and live with us; 'I'd be willing to sleep on a chair in the kitchen!' she declared. Equally naturally, we were not willing even to contemplate it, especially after we discovered that she had telephoned our housekeeper, Irma Couling, in our absence and extracted from the good-hearted Irma an assurance that as far as she was concerned there was no problem. It was sad, because when I was a child Lillian and I had hit it off extremely well and had a lot of laughs.† The hospital, anxious not to keep her, found her a place in a private nursing-home, which she didn't like, then in another, which she liked even less, and in a third, where she soon died, convinced that the nurses invaded her room at

---

†She was the only really fat person I knew – prodigiously, impossibly fat, it seemed to me, but that was long before I had been to California.

[6]Cyril Lipscombe has not in fact been mentioned previously; for aunt Lillian, see p. 31.

night, danced there, and tortured her for fun. She had made a will in which I was the chief beneficiary, but she altered this because I did not visit her often enough, and left the lion's share to a nice old couple who visited her much more often. I didn't begrudge the change, because they had earned it and the money would make more difference to their lives than to mine. The journey between Oxford and Eastbourne was tedious and time-consuming, but I dare say we would have managed to make it more often if her conversation had been anything but a recital of grievances and delusions. One can pay too high a price for money.

So much for the older generation. In the younger we had a cause for rejoicing over and above the birth of Beki and Nicholas. After her degree in history at Oxford Catherine trained as a National Health Service administrator, and in 1977, when she was working in Northampton General Hospital, she and a newly-arrived Indian doctor from Kerala fell in love. He was already married to a wife in India, from whom he was seeking a divorce, so they moved in together. However, this gratifying turn of events did not develop quite as we expected; the divorce hung fire until we introduced them to an Australian graduate student, whom they befriended, and when we came back from our trip round the world in 1982[7] we learned that the Australian was moving in and Catherine was moving out. The divorce went through, the doctor married the Australian, and they went off to her country.

---

[7]See pp. 272–6.

22 COLLEGE AND UNIVERSITY 1975–1986

Nothing ever happens in colleges.

                                                              H.W. GARROD[1]

One evening towards the end of 1975 I received a telephone call from Robin Nisbet, who had been a pupil of mine at Balliol in 1948–9 and was now Professor of Latin at Oxford and a Professorial Fellow of Corpus Christi College. Derek Hall, who succeeded Frank Hardie as President of Corpus in 1969, had died in office, and the College was looking for a new President. Would I be interested? If so, I would be welcome to come down to Oxford for an interview, without commitment on either side. I was greatly surprised by this message, because the possibility that anyone at Oxford might think I was the right sort of person to be head of a house had not occurred to me, and although I had greatly enjoyed managing a Faculty in harness with my teaching and research, I had little idea of what managing a college entailed. However, the prospect was worth exploring, if only out of curiosity, and I wrote Robin what I called a 'negative manifesto', setting out reasons for which the College might decide after all that it didn't want to pursue the matter. These reasons included my unwillingness to attend religious services except for weddings, funerals and ceremonial occasions; the fact that although I was very happy with committee work which had something directly to do with the organisation of teaching, research and education in general, I was apt to be bored by discussion of the price of carpeting or heating-systems; and the need to adjust the accommodation in the President's Lodgings to take account of my father's inability to go up and down stairs. I learned in reply that the problem of my father's accommodation was soluble, that no one minded my agnosticism enough to rule me out, and (although

---

[1] H.W. Garrod, 'On growing old', in *Genius Loci and Other Essays* (Oxford, 1950) 15, a collection Dover may have found his way to via its (sometimes supercilious) essay on 'Autobiographies'.

I inferred later that the Bursar must have suffered some disquiet) that my strongly academic orientation was welcome. Audrey and I were invited down to Corpus in December; we stayed with the Leppers, and while Audrey met some of the senior Fellows' wives, I was interviewed by Robert Gasser, the Acting President, dined with the Fellows, and was formally interviewed by them in the Senior Common Room.[2]

The only part of the conversation at dinner which I recall concerned the Scottish universities' consortium for the training of new lecturers,[3] about which I was enthusiastic. When we came to the after-dinner interview, the proceedings opened with a question put to me by Robert: how did I see the job of President in the years to come? I had an urge to reply: 'Look, there is a job that you want done. Tell me what it is that you want, and I'll tell you whether I think I can do it. Then you can decide whether *you* think I can.' I thought it would be rather rude to say that, but I diffidently broached a question which had been in my mind: how long and how seriously had the College considered whether a college needs a full-time president rather than a part-time office which would be held by a Fellow for a three-year or five-year term? This was, of course, stalling while the other half of my mind was formulating a positive answer to Robert's question. The answer I gave was that I regarded a college not as a club, but as an instrument for the advancement of science and learning; probably (I have forgotten much) I gave some indication that I was less interested in inter-collegiate rivalries than in how a college could best serve the ends of the university of which it was a component. I also said that I would regard it as essential to the performance of my job to know everyone in the College, so far as that was humanly practicable. I thoroughly enjoyed that evening, because since I already had a reasonable job and was not desperate for change, I was interviewing the Fellows while they were interviewing me.

Anyway, I seem to have gone down well, because next morning a delegation of senior Fellows came to tell me that the job was mine if I wanted it. I did not feel that I could give an immediate answer, but promised to telephone in a day or two. On the way home, before catching the night train, we called on Eric Handley[4] at the Institute of Classical Studies to seek his opinion (which he couldn't really give) on whether the cause of Greek would be better served by my staying at St Andrews or moving out of a professorial chair into the presidency of an Oxford college. Now we had a difficult decision to take. One thing for sure was that we must keep our St Andrews house, not only for my eventual retirement from Oxford but as a

---

[2]F.A. (Frank) Lepper (1913–2005) was tutorial fellow in ancient history at Corpus 1949–80, Robert Gasser tutorial fellow in Chemistry 1959–82.
[3]See pp. 202–3.
[4]Eric Handley (1926–2013) was Director of the Institute of Classical Studies in London 1967–84 and Professor of Greek at University College London 1968–84; for his later appointment to the Regius chair of Greek in Cambridge, see n. 12 to p. 316.

refuge in the Long Vacations from the stiflingly overcrowded south of England. That could be managed if we furnished the house cheaply and sparsely and let it each academic year to people coming to St Andrews on sabbatical leave. The change of job was not so easily decided, but I became aware that in my heart I was not really looking forward with unalloyed pleasure to another fifteen years of routine teaching at St Andrews. Moreover, I was making mistakes; I had recently introduced some changes, at both first-year and fourth-year level, which unrealistically assumed that students could learn by analogy and example much more than in fact most of them can.[5] In short, I was beginning to lose my grip as a teacher, and I needed to pull up my roots and start life afresh. So I rang Corpus, said Yes, and was elected. Audrey, while not all that fond of Oxford as a place, could see the pros and cons clearly, and was prepared to fall in with my own choice. My election seemed appropriate to colleagues in the Classical world, since Corpus had an exceptionally high reputation in Classics. We moved into the President's Lodgings in September 1976.

There was a time when the headship of a house was regarded as crowning a career in academic life or public service. That is no longer so; during my ten years at Corpus five heads of houses left (without being pushed) for other jobs, three of them reverting to professorial chairs, and colleges seeking to replace heads who left or retired were sometimes rebuffed by the candidate of their first choice with a polite equivalent of 'Don't be ridiculous!' The status of the President of Corpus in the early years of this century is reflected in the size of the Lodgings, extraordinary for so small a college. When P.S. Allen was President (1924–1933) he needed all those bedrooms for weekend entertaining, at which it was not uncommon for twenty people to dine at his table.[6] The disproportion between College and Lodgings was reduced first by new building for the accommodation of junior members* and then, during the presidency (1950–1969) of Frank Hardie,† a studiously unpretentious man, by the conversion of a dozen rooms of the Lodgings to other useful purposes.

I inferred from my experience as a Fellow of Balliol under two different Masters that the distinctive feature of the Presidency of Corpus would be accountability

---

*Although the statistical table in the *Oxford University Calendar* has now for many years used the word 'students' to cover both undergraduates and those working for advanced degrees, general usage, up to the time I left Corpus, preferred 'junior members'. I have called 'senior members', for brevity's sake, 'dons'; 'fellows' will not do, because some dons (e.g. college lecturers with temporary appointments) are not fellows of colleges.
†In the University volume (1954) of the Victoria County History of Oxfordshire his brother Colin is erroneously listed as President.
[5]This seems to reflect, in part, the unrealistic nature of Dover's Greek coursebook for beginners, though that had been in use for almost a decade: see note to p. 182.
[6]For Allen's Presidency, see *CCH* 365–9, for Hardie's, 385–93.

without power, and I was not mistaken. Frank Lepper once told me, 'Remember, it's *your* college. Whatever goes wrong, *you* get the blame.' One thing that went wrong in my first year or two was that Corpus lost its high place in the Norrington Table, an annual exercise which rated the colleges in order by the ratio of Firsts to Seconds to Thirds gained by their undergraduates in university examinations. As in some other small colleges, the offices of President and Tutor for Admissions were combined at Corpus (not so now), but that did not mean that the power to admit or reject rested with me; it rested with the Tutors in the subjects concerned, and if the applicants they picked disappointed them in the end, they could not blame me. Indeed, they did not; but the coincidence of a new President and a fall in academic ratings made me a little sensitive, lest anyone outside the College think I affected its academic ethos adversely.

I once overheard Trevor Aston[7] saying at dinner, 'The great thing about being a Fellow is that you can tell the President to go to hell.' This is true. The President cannot hire or fire, nor can he command. All decisions of significance are taken by majority vote at College Meetings: that is to say, meetings of the Governing Body, which consists of all Fellows, except Honorary, Emeritus and Junior Research Fellows. The President is Chairman of the Governing Body and of all its standing committees. However, Trevor's forthright summary of the constitutional position leaves out of account the President's *auctoritas,* the weight which his wishes and views carry. I was able to exploit that, more effectively than I had dared to hope, at the very start. Most male colleges had been very slow to admit female guests; at Balliol, when I left it in 1955, there was no occasion on which a woman could sit down in Hall or in the SCR as the guest of a member of the College.[8] Over the years, things had changed a bit; by 1976 colleges normally admitted female guests, but rather grudgingly. At one college Fellows were allowed to bring women other than their wives as guests any time, but their wives only on one evening a week; the reason (or so we were told by a friend who seemed to think we would find it amusing) was that one wife drank a bit too much; the fact that some of the Fellows also drank too much and behaved foolishly or offensively was not, it seems, taken into account. When we arrived in Corpus, we discovered that the entertainment of female guests in College was a recent innovation, and that a rule of 'no wives except on Tuesdays' was in force. Audrey hit the roof at that, not least because she had been given no warning of it, and I wrote a memorandum to the then Master of Common Room, Brian Farrell (no one could be less of a male chauvinist than he is), pointing out that rules were hardly appropriate to such matters as the invitation of guests. As the rules stood, I could bring in a boring and offensive male guest as

---

[7]The book's first reference to a figure (at this date a Senior Research Fellow of Corpus) who will later have a lurid spotlight thrown on him (ch. 26).
[8]Cf. Dover's earlier thoughts on this subject on p. 135. SCR is the Senior Common Room.

often as I liked, and indeed 'an illiterate prostitute picked up in a bar, but not the person to whom I am married'. At a meeting of the SCR, from which I absented myself, the restrictive rule was dropped.

On one other occasion I did not rely on rhetoric, but took an 'administrative decision' rather in the spirit of *Darkness at Noon*.[9] The College was plagued by a gang of unapproachable, smelly, mangy stray cats; they preferred shitting in our garden to anywhere else, and the toms marked their territories pertinaciously all over the College. Shortly before our arrival an attempt had been made to trap them, but an old College servant who fed them affectionately released them from the traps first thing in the morning. So, with the connivance of the Steward, I brought in a Pest Control man (at the College's expense) and had them all trapped and shot on the spot. After that the College smelled better. Next year a plague of wall-voles ate most of our spring bulbs.

In chairing the proceedings of the Governing Body I was determined that no Fellows should ever have cause for complaint that business had been hustled through and that they had not had a chance to put their arguments forward. This was easy; experience with the Arts Faculty Council at St Andrews had shown me that I had the patience to chair a meeting for four or five hours, if necessary. At the same time, no one should be allowed to ramble out of control, and in order to ensure that decisions were reached in a logical sequence it was important to brood over the agenda beforehand and think of the arguments likely to be used at the meeting. Occasionally I circulated a memorandum of my own before the meeting, without (save in one case) declaring my own opinion. I never voted unless the votes of the others present were equally divided and a casting vote was necessary.[10] To the best of my recollection, there was only one question of importance on which a casting vote was called for; that was on a proposal, early in 1986, that the College should cease to bank with Barclays because of its heavy investment in South Africa. Fortunately, I had expected the hung vote and had prepared and rehearsed an explanation of why, after five months of reflection on my experience in South Africa and the conversations I had had there, I was voting in favour of the proposal.[11]

Some members of the Governing Body were Professorial Fellows, useful critics but understandably reluctant to intervene in matters which did not directly concern them, the College's academic and economic relations with its junior members. Among the other Fellows, most were good at running things within the

---

[9] A novel, first published (originally in German) in 1940, by the Hungarian-British author Arthur Koestler (1905–83): Dover is alluding ironically to the work's dark depiction of the nature of dictatorial power.
[10] Dover followed this same principle when President of the British Academy, not without consequence where the 'Blunt affair' was concerned: cf. pp. 282–3.
[11] Dover's trip to South Africa in 1985 will be recounted on p. 320 (cf. 295).

framework we had inherited but not greatly inclined to contemplate modifications of the framework itself. The two most fertile in ideas were, in their different ways, Trevor Aston and Brian Harrison, and contributions came increasingly from Andrew Glyn and Jennifer Hornsby.[12] Brian Campbell, despite many deeply conservative predilections, was always adaptable, and often imaginative precisely because his predilections were not donnish.[13] My job was to nudge good ideas forward when they were originated by others and to sustain them against adverse criticism – notably the completion of the *Biographical Register 1880–1974* and the solid historical articles in *The Pelican*[14]– and also to sow the seed of new ideas and tend its growth; a combination of the roles of seducer and midwife. I had no inclination to be a Master of Porterhouse.[15]

One great change, the admission of women, had effectively been settled before my arrival.[16] Corpus had already changed its statutes to admit women Fellows and graduate students. Five colleges had gone mixed ('co-residence' was the formal term) in 1974, and it had been agreed that if there were more than five wanting to go mixed in 1979 they would be selected by lot. The decision had to be taken not later than the summer of 1977, so that the admissions procedures for 1978, governing the 1979 entry, could be publicised in time. The meeting of college representatives began on the assumption that the earlier agreement on five at a time would hold, but this assumption was suddenly invalidated when University College declared that it proposed to go mixed anyway, whatever the result of the ballot. The immediate reaction of other colleges, led by St John's, was to cry indignantly that if Univ was not going to abide by the agreement there was no reason why *they* should. The collapse of gradualism without a dying twitch was the most dramatic event I witnessed in my ten years at Oxford.‡ In the following month all the men's colleges except Christ Church, Merton and Oriel set in motion the change of statutes required for the admission of female undergraduates. Our

---

‡A warning to all (auto)biographers. On the whole subject of the attention paid to the possibility of co-residence at the time (1964–65) of the Franks Commission I was given totally false information by someone whose accurate knowledge I had every reason to trust, and it was only good luck that led me to the relevant documentation. The firm intention of New College to admit women had been formed by the end of 1964, and was known to Franks and to the Hebdomadal Council. [EDS *The Franks Commission was set up to review many aspects of the organization of Oxford University and its colleges (cf. further references on pp. 253, 258); its chairman, Lord Oliver Franks (1905–92), was Provost of Worcester College. See A.H. Halsey in HUO 721–36.*]

[12]On Aston, see p. 291 below; Brian Harrison (Kt 2005) was tutorial fellow in modern history and politics 1967–2004, Andrew Glyn the same in economics 1969–2003, and Jennifer Hornsby the same in philosophy 1978–94.
[13]Campbell was fellow and Estates Bursar (cf. p. 257) of Corpus 1972–89.
[14]*The Pelican Record* is the Corpus college magazine; the *Biographical Register*, an initiative of Trevor Aston's (*CCH* 405), was published in 1988.
[15]Porterhouse is a fictional Cambridge college in the 1974 novel *Porterhouse Blue* by Tom Sharpe.
[16]For a full account of this issue, see *CCH* 398–404.

debate on the issue at Corpus was perfunctory, as no one now was prepared to argue against the change. After a year Christ Church and Merton fell into line, and Oriel followed. All the colleges except St Hilda's are now mixed.[17]

Quotas being ruled out on legal grounds, there was no way we could ensure a fifty-fifty mix, and the shift in the habits of applicants and their schools took time, so that for some years after 1978 our female entry was between thirty and forty per cent of the total, and it is only now (1993) that it has reached fifty per cent. To speak of the 'civilising effect' of women on the College may sound patronising, but it is also true; the hard-drinking, glass-breaking rugger-club set dwindled away. Inevitably there have been sexual problems. While I was merely annoyed, on an annual inspection of College premises, to see that the plaster on the wall above one woman's pillows had been pulverised by the constant impact of her energetic lover's head, I was more perturbed by a woman who was completely thrown off balance by the transfer of a man's affections to another woman on the same corridor, and by a man who had to take a year off because he was obsessed by a woman who had no time for him. That kind of trouble is more manageable when the two people concerned live in different colleges. The effect on the cleaners was also regrettable. Some were widows with a right to be jealous, and they were not well disposed towards young women who did not sleep alone; and one did not have to be a widow to resent the behaviour of men who would leave a loaded condom on the floor for a cleaner to tidy up. Those, however, were intercollegiate problems before any colleges went mixed.

In the popular perception of Oxford colleges there are three persistent ingredients: colleges are rich, they spend their money on luscious food and wine, and the Fellows (unmellowed by the food and wine) are smoothly spiteful towards each other. Well, the third of these beliefs may once have been true of Corpus; when Frank Lepper was offered a tutorial fellowship in 1939 the then Warden of New College (H.A.L. Fisher) advised him not to take it, because Corpus was such a quarrelsome college. I can see what he meant. There were at that time only eleven fellows, among whom Phelps detested Veale, and the mathematics tutor, Pidduck, formed so unfavourable an opinion of his colleagues that he took all his meals in his room and ceased to attend meetings.§ I have heard the presidency of Sir Richard Livingstone described as a 'slipshod tyranny', but although 'slipshod' is fair enough (when he died, it was hard for his successor to work out from pencilled

---

§Pidduck had a wonderful death. Having gone up Scafell Pike, he came down a little way to eat his sandwiches, seated himself comfortably against a rock, and died. It was a while before other walkers realised that the man apparently sitting still and admiring the view was dead. [EDS *Further information on the three fellows named in Dover's sentence can be found via the index of* CCH.]

[17]St Hilda's too went mixed in 2008, leaving Newnham College, Cambridge, as the only single-sex college remaining in Oxbridge.

notes on scattered scraps of paper which applicants for the following year were accepted and which rejected), I find it difficult to think of Livingstone as any kind of tyrant.[18] In my own time there was widespread dislike and distrust of Trevor Aston, and by the end he and I were enemies. I had a brush or two with John Bramble and Don Wild, in which more forethought and sensitivity on my part would have been desirable.[19] Brian Campbell and I avoided, by humour or silence, the potential conflicts which our radically different views of the world outside the college might have generated, and as both of us were products of the same South London middle-class milieu we often found ourselves in agreement – not always shared by some of our more tolerant colleagues – on what constituted dishonest or dishonourable behaviour on the part of junior members. As for the other Fellows, I naturally had my preferences and reservations, but never the slightest inclination to say, as one head of house said to me during his first year of office, 'You know, some of my Fellows are mad. I mean, literally, *mad*!'

As for wining and dining, the food was not extravagant, most of us drank wine very sparingly (and some not at all), and in any case drink was paid for by the drinker. There was no High Table at weekends, and on a weekday it was unusual to see as many as a dozen Fellows and guests at High Table. What was called by some the 'ritual dance' of port and dessert in the SCR after dinner became infrequent and vanished in 1982. Lunch, not dinner, was the meal at which most of us met and talked shop, a pattern of change already conspicuous at Balliol when I left there in 1955.

Corpus had no Annual Feast; Corpus Christi Day was celebrated by our sister college in Cambridge with a splendour which made me feel, when I attended as a guest, that I was rapt into another world. During my first term I was invited to the annual dinner of the Skinners' Company, of which a Corpus man, Richard Holroyd Pearce, was Master that year. It was a grand occasion, and plainly it was up to me to invite the office-bearers of the Company to a comparable occasion in College. Since there was none such, I could not and did not, an omission for which I was loudly upbraided by Pearce at a Gaudy some years later.

Colleges began life with endowments, which have increased in value over the centuries, and they now derive wealth from their investments and their ownership of farms, offices and shops, supplemented by benefactions and the product of appeals. There is a correlation between wealth and age, but the comparative poverty of the newer colleges has been partly rectified by transfer of capital from rich to

---

[18]Sir Richard Livingstone (1880–1960, Kt 1931), a classical scholar who preached a kind of Christianized Hellenism, was President of Corpus 1933–50; he had been Vice-Chancellor of Queen's University, Belfast, 1924–33: see the article by C. Stray in *DBC*, ii 585–7. For Dover's view of him as not taking the Greeks sufficiently on their own terms, see *G&L* 285–6.

[19]John Bramble was a tutorial fellow in Classics 1970–86, Don Wild a biochemist and, at one stage (cf. p. 257), also Domestic Bursar of the college.

poor, through an annual tax, recommended by the Franks Commission in 1966. The letting of college accommodation to conferences and summer schools during vacations is a comparatively minor source of income; more important are the college fees payable by all junior members – that is to say, by the education authorities which pay fees and grants – over and above University fees.[20] The justification for college fees is threefold: in the first place, the salary of a tutorial fellow does not all come out of the salaries element in the annual grant made to the University, as is normal elsewhere, but in part from the college, and the salary of a Junior Research Fellow entirely from the college; secondly, while all universities have to deal with the problem of maintaining their premises – a crippling expense when, for instance, new fire regulations have to be obeyed – the maintenance of very old buildings costs more than most, and what was once purpose-built has to be adapted to purposes not envisaged in earlier centuries; and thirdly, colleges are necessarily uneconomical, being each a small unit with its own library[|] and its own administrative and domestic staff. One other consideration, often overlooked, should be added: whereas universities in general are forbidden to subsidise the feeding and housing of their students, there is no such constraint on colleges. It was certainly College policy in my time at Corpus to charge room-rents far below the going rate in the city and to keep the inevitable annual increase in charges down to the level of the annual increase in the student's maintenance grant. I am thankful that retirement saved me from having to deal with that problem after 1986.

In terms of wealth, Corpus is a middling college, able to keep up a steady building and renovation programme which by the end of 1986 had affected every corner of the College. The three most important changes were the creation of a new Senior Common Room, the moving of the College Office, and the conversion of the President's Lodgings to other uses. The third of these changes was Keith Thomas's decision, and no business of mine, but it corresponded to ideas which I had from time to time entertained as an armchair architect.[21] The move of the College Office was the only revolutionary change which I initiated myself, getting out of the armchair and taking up a steel rule – though, not surprisingly, it needed the talent of Geoffrey Beard[22] to find a neat and imaginative solution to what seemed the one stumbling-block. The new SCR originated in a general feeling

---

[|]The three-tier library system, comprising college libraries as well as the university library and faculty or departmental libraries, is one of the great selling-points of Oxford and Cambridge.

[20]Needless to say, there have been major changes in student funding and fees since Dover wrote this account.

[21]Sir Keith Thomas (1933–, Kt 1988), previously a fellow of St John's College, Oxford, 1957–86, was Dover's successor as President of Corpus, 1986–2000; for the change of Lodgings in his time, see *CCH* 427, with 408 for the change of College Office mentioned by Dover.

[22]The College architect; cf. p. 302.

among the Fellows, and was by no means unanimously approved, because several thought that the available money could be better spent on the endowment of senior scholarships for graduate students and other ways of furthering research. I could sympathise with them, but nevertheless put my weight behind the project, for a reason whose validity was, I think, eventually demonstrated. The old SCR was all very well for a Fellowship of a dozen, but now that there were thirty of us it was quite inadequate – arrive for lunch at five past one, and you might have to queue for a seat – and it made us peculiarly reluctant to elect Visiting Fellows and give unrestricted lunching rights to College lecturers. That kept us too much of a closed community. Once we had enough rooms, and they were big enough, attitudes changed, and we became far readier to welcome visitors of all kinds, an interesting illustration of the dependence of the moral on the material. The price we paid for rejoining the world was the loss of three undergraduate rooms, but this loss was offset by the conversion of Beam Hall, on the other side of Merton Street, to undergraduate and teaching rooms when Thomas Charles-Edwards moved out.[23]

The old College Office was the anteroom to the old President's Study. It was approached by an exceptionally steep staircase, something of a deterrent to any 'senior citizens'¶ who wanted to see me, and immediately inside the door were three steps which sometimes caught even young visitors unawares. It was narrow, with a door at the far end connecting with the office of the Senior Tutor's secretary, and the traffic flow problem was acute. My Study (which I never used as a study, because it could not have taken all my books) was dark and gloomy, with very restricted views. I could not help feeling that it was designed to intimidate, as if mine were a royal presence, though the analogy which occurred to me more readily was a spider lurking at the bottom of a funnel web.[24] I had a strong desire to be more obviously accessible. Apart from that, the Library was (as usual) short of space, and a massive old door, to which only the Librarian and I had keys, connected my Study with the west end of the Upper Library. Just at the time when I was due to present an ad hoc committee with my plans for moving the whole office complex to ground-floor rooms in the Front Quad, I received a lawyer's letter telling me that a substantial bequest from the estate of Sir Llewellyn Woodward was on its way 'for the benefit of the College Library'. This would pay nicely for the incorporation of the old President's Study in the Library, and no one voiced opposition to the move of the offices, including mine, to the convenient and preeminently accessible location which I had chosen for them. By comparison with the majestic offices of most heads of houses, my bright new room was

---

¶I do not like the expression (or the euphemism 'elderly'), but I have already used 'old' twice in the preceding sentence.

[23]On Charles-Edwards, see n. 3 to p. 292.

[24]It is pertinent that Dover was an arachnophobe; cf. pp. 40 and 273.

undeniably humble, even grotty, but it suited the relationship I wanted to establish with the junior members of the College. Moreover, with a ground-floor view of the front quad I was able to notice who went around with whom. Noticing is always helpful. The head of an institution can never know too much about those who belong to it.

Student troubles were a thing of the past in 1976, and none of us had any occasion to fear sit-ins or egg-throwing. In one respect the morality of the students had taken a downward turn: theft of books. The College Library was open day and night, without invigilation, and there had been a time, well within the memory of several Fellows, when book losses were negligible. By the end of the nineteen-seventies the annual book-check was revealing an alarming rate of loss, and when the total reached 1,100 we resorted to electronic tagging, which activated an alarm if a book was improperly removed without being de-magnetised by an invigilator. One or two of the more determined criminals circumvented that by surreptitiously dropping books out of the Library windows on to the flower-beds. The book-thief was careless of the needs of other people, some of whom might be wanting the same books for the same essay, but the solidarity of students against authority was such that we never got the co-operation we might have had. The notion of collective punishment, which is the other side of the coin of solidarity, was accepted a couple of generations ago but out of the question nowadays; rightly so, in my view, but collective inconvenience as a consequence of unattributable crime is a fair imposition. Apart from book-theft, there were occasional deliberate dishonesties, such as by-passing gas-meters, and plenty of thoughtlessness; the morally sturdy young woman who plastered all her walls with posters and cards presumably just didn't know what improperly used blu-tak can do to plaster. Vandalism was rare – and convicting the culprit even rarer. Once upon a time (I am told) a Dean could assume that wrongdoers would own up and accept their punishment. Now they don't if they can avoid it. The College provides for appeals against the Dean's rulings, and in my second term I had to convene a disciplinary committee to hear such an appeal. The proceedings lasted from two in the afternoon until midnight, with a break for dinner. One thing I learned was that a judge, unlike the chairman of a meeting in which errors and confusions can be sorted out in a relaxed way, cannot afford to let his attention wander for a moment. Once an appeal has been made and the whole affair moves on to the judicial plane, rules of evidence, which have little to do with the reasoning we employ in real life, come into force, and a college is neither trained nor equipped for the detective work needed to make a conviction stick. A year or two later I had to advise the Dean (both of us gnashing our teeth) to drop a charge of dangerous vandalism because if the suspects appealed there would be no hope of proving the case against them.

For some time the Junior Common Room had entertained the ambition to be represented on the Governing Body and take part in its decisions. I found it amusing to recall that at Balliol in 1938–40, in a JCR of which Edward Heath, Roy Jenkins and Denis Healey were officers, the notion that undergraduates might participate in the government of the college was never voiced.[25] Anyway, I was in sympathy, and since a college is not responsible for syllabuses and examinations my objection to the admission of students to the St Andrews Senate did not apply.[26] I produced a long memorandum on the pros and cons of the JCR's request (the language of 'non-negotiable demands' was passé by that time), but the cons outweighed the pros in the minds of my colleagues, for there was only one vote in favour of the request. A year later, however, we agreed to have an undergraduate representative on the Internal Management Committee and the Buildings and Furniture Committee. This worked so smoothly and uncontentiously that it seemed to me appropriate, after another year had passed, to put my weight behind a renewed request from the JCR for representation on the Governing Body itself. Knowing that our sister college in Cambridge had already taken that step, I rang up Duncan Wilson, the Master, to ask him how it worked. 'I think,' he said, 'that the undergraduates have had a very civilising effect on the Fellows.' I was heartened by that, but did not report it, as it would have leaked and would not have improved the Master's relations with his Fellows. This time the vote in favour of the JCR was substantially larger, but still a minority. The JCR Committee was downcast, and asked me if they should resign, because they had been elected on a promise that they would secure representation, and now they had failed. I persuaded them not to resign, giving them an elementary lesson in politics: one can promise to try one's utmost, but one cannot promise to succeed. The next year's JCR President wrote in his annual report, 'One more push . . .', and the push broke through in 1983, when the Presidents of the JCR and MCR and the Secretary of the JCR were admitted as non-voting members at College Meetings. It was accepted on both sides that some items of business, essentially those which concerned the academic progress, character, finance or health of an identifiable individual, should be reserved for the Fellows alone, and it proved quite practicable to dispose of reserved business either before the junior members arrived or after they had gone.

The Third Estate of a college is the staff,** those who operate the Lodge, kitchens and offices, tend the gardens and repair or clean the premises. They are the

---

**Everywhere else 'staff' means Professors and lecturers (as in 'staff/student ratio') – what the Americans call 'faculty'.

[25] Of these three future politicians, Edward Heath (1916–2005) went on to be Conservative Prime Minister 1970–4, while Roy Jenkins (see the earlier mention on p. 235) and Denis Healey (1917–2015) both, among much else, served as Chancellor of the Exchequer in a Labour government. The three overlapped at Balliol in Dover's first year, 1938–9: E. Heath, *The Course of My Life* (London, 1998) 47. Healey was the only one of the three who read Classical Mods and Greats: see his *The Time of My Life* (London, 1989) 24–46. For a reference to Dover in Jenkins' own autobiography, see *A Life at the Centre* (London, 1991) 33.

[26] For the objections in question, see pp. 207–8.

responsibility of the Domestic Bursar, and their day-to-day organisation rests with the Steward. When I arrived at Corpus, Brian Campbell, who had been appointed as Estates Bursar, was doubling as Domestic Bursar. From 1978 to 1982 the duties of Domestic Bursar were taken over by Don Wild, who had to combine them with the teaching of biochemistry; not really, to my mind, a happy arrangement for a scientist, especially at a time when bursarial responsibilities were increased by a continuous building programme, and I contrived to shift him out of the Domestic Bursarship once I was sure that we were all happy to elect him to a tutorial fellowship in Biochemistry and that a reorganisation of the Bursary, promoting Brian's very able secretary, Pat Heavens, to be Assistant Bursar, was going to work.

The staff were capable of rising to an occasion superbly, as they did when Oxford was submerged in snow on the day of the Gaudy in January 1982, but much of the time friction was generated by antipathies between individuals and departments. Norman Beech, who had been the Assistant Accountant in the Bursary, was promoted to Steward at the end of 1976, and his admirably even temper was severely tried by the unwillingness of some staff who had known him as an underling to accept him as a boss. (In 1987 he moved to a happier atmosphere as Steward of Wadham, and the domestic side of Corpus was reorganised with the appointment of a Domestic Bursar from outside Oxford.) I found throughout my time that an element of conflict was built into the College – built into any college, I suppose – by the fact that the Bursar felt bound to stand up for the staff in any disagreements between senior members, junior members and staff. I don't see how he could have done otherwise, but for a keeper of the peace, which is what I was supposed to be, such conflicts posed problems which I could not easily resolve. The staff themselves were inclined to regard the junior members as spoilt and unreasonably demanding. I dare say they thought the same of the dons but did not feel free to say so.

One welcome consequence of the admission of junior members to the Governing Body and some of its committees was a diminution of the functions of the Joint Committee, on which Fellows, junior members and staff were represented, under my chairmanship. There was no recurrent occasion (twice a term) which I dreaded more, for several reasons. Most of the JCR's complaints concerned food, but the Manciple (in charge of the kitchens) was not a member of the committee; I doubt if he would have come if invited, and in any case his uncompromising forthrightness might have raised the temperature too high. A partial solution of that problem was found in the setting up of a Food Committee which relieved the Joint Committee of the need to argue (e.g.) over the satisfaction of vegetarians. That still left problems. Some (by no means all) Fellows reacted to suggestions and requests from the JCR with immediate 'Ah, but ...!' objections, not infrequently cast in facetious or sarcastic terms, which made me curl up; I had learned years before that if you wish to cause students to take a second cool look at what they have said you must absolutely resist any temptation to sarcasm or facetiousness.

People sometimes found it hard to distinguish between serious listening and craven concession. Once Fellows had got their initial response out of their system, they often proved helpful, constructive and ready to compromise, but it was a pity that progress had to start on the wrong foot, and there were occasions when the patience and courtesy of the junior members earned my respect. I found it hard to combine chairmanship of a committee made up of three interest groups with representation of one of those groups, the Governing Body, and I told my colleagues that the job of representation must be left to those Fellows who served on the committee. On a couple of occasions, when tension between the Steward and the President of the JCR developed, I had to rule that it was impossible for a committee to take sides between Oh-no-you-didn't and Oh-yes-you-did, and a waste of time for it to try. One way and another, not a nice committee.

The headship of a house does not in itself necessarily confer any significant degree of power in the management of the University. The heads of houses collectively decide who is to deliver the Bampton Lectures on theology; not an exacting task, as things go, but not without interest when there is an argument, as there once was, over whether a candidate regarded by some Christians as heretical was the right person to deliver lectures intended by their founder to confute heresy. (My sympathy on this occasion was with the Christians, on legal grounds.) Heads of houses also meet each term at the Conference of Colleges, a body created by the Franks reform. Designed as a forum for the exchange of ideas on matters of common concern, it came in my time to assume real power.

Despite the paucity of their functions *ex officio* in the management of the University, heads of houses are apt to find themselves appointed to a variety of committees. I was a Curator of the Bodleian Library until 1983, a member for two years of the committee on ad hominem promotions, a member of the Oxford and Cambridge Schools Examination Board, and co-chairman of that Board in 1984–6 (the chairman at the Cambridge end was, by coincidence, the Master of Corpus Christi College, Cambridge). The Curators of the Bodleian, whose remit covered all other University (but not college) libraries, met every week in termtime, and much of our energy, especially after 1981, was devoted to the problem of money; the potential cost of the conservation work that needed to be done was gigantic, acquisitions ran at the rate of a kilometre of shelving a year, the staff numbered over four hundred, and we were constantly faced with the need to leave vacant posts unfilled, reduce opening hours and cut acquisitions. When the pressure of my work for the Committee on Undergraduate Admissions gave me a perfect excuse for resigning from the Curators at the end of 1982, I did so with relief at being released from the need to participate in unpopular decisions which unavoidably detracted from the status and usefulness of one of the world's greatest libraries.

The Conference of Colleges was more congenial, because tight finances impelled it in what I regarded as the right direction. Each college had always been accustomed to determine the level of College Fees which it charged, but at the end of the nineteen-seventies the Research Councils became restive at having to pay, on behalf of each graduate student whom they supported at Oxford or Cambridge, about a thousand pounds a year more than they would have to pay at other universities, although the focus of the graduate student's life was often not the college but the laboratory or the hospital. The Department of Education and Science and grant-awarding education authorities in general thereupon began to stir and growl as they realised that whereas university fees were fixed nationally, in agreeing to pay college fees they were in effect signing a blank cheque. The Conference of Colleges appointed a committee to negotiate with the Department of Education and Science over the level of college fees and the rate of future increases permissible in the light of inflation. Christopher Ball, Warden of Keble,[27] was our principal negotiator, and he instilled a salutary fear in us by menacing predictions of drastic governmental intervention if we failed to make a rational case for our present fee levels and to agree to keep within a narrow band, applicable to all colleges, for all future increases as determined by annual negotiation with the DES. We did as he advised; a very significant reduction of college autonomy, and an increased recognition that colleges are components of a university.

An even more important step was taken in 1981 in respect of college size. The size of Oxford's undergraduate population was fixed by the University Grants Committee, but since each college decided independently how many undergraduates it would admit for a given year, it was impossible to guarantee that the total permitted to the University, i.e. the sum of the colleges, would not be exceeded through ambitious expansion on the part of one or two of the components of the sum. The only remedy was to set a target figure for each college. The Conference of Colleges appointed a committee which tackled this job, listening to some pleas for special consideration and doing its best to take fair decisions on them. Eventually the list of targets was accepted; I was not happy with the figure for Corpus, because it seemed to me that we were working slightly below capacity, but given the constraints under which the committee had operated I could not reasonably make any fuss. The whole exercise was of a kind which would have been unimaginable a generation earlier.

A third blow at college autonomy was in preparation at the time of my departure and did not fall until afterwards. When a University lectureship was to be combined with a tutorial fellowship in a college, representatives of the college and the faculty (or laboratory) interviewed the candidates jointly and reached agreement on their choice. There were, however, many University lectureships which were not intended to include tutorial responsibilities. The applicants for these posts were given to understand that, if appointed, they would be offered a college fellowship. Often they

---

[27]Sir Christopher Ball (1935–, Kt 1988), Warden of Keble 1980–8 and later Chancellor of the University of Derby 1995–2003.

were; but not always, and colleges received each year a melancholy list of people who were entitled to fellowships but had been left on the shelf for a long time, sometimes for so long that any college which contemplated offering one of them a fellowship might well wonder what was wrong with someone that nobody, it seemed, wanted. The problem of entitlement was taken seriously and handled beautifully, by the Vice-Chancellor (Sir Patrick Neill),[28] who persuaded the colleges to clear the list by accepting the allocation of a couple of new Fellows apiece. Maybe some colleges thought it monstrous that Fellows whom they had not chosen themselves should be wished upon them. Maybe, for all I know, some of the people on the entitlement list were malevolent, boring or crazy; but in that regard the colleges' own choices had not always attained perfection.

There was one other area of Oxford's activity even more sacred and mysterious than college autonomy; the relation between teacher and learner. My experience with the Scottish consortium and my acquaintance with the procedures of American universities convinced me something could be done to improve the standard of teaching at Oxford, and my first step in that direction was to make use, in the lecture-course I myself gave, of a detailed questionnaire to be completed by those attending. Naturally I hoped that I was setting a precedent. The next step was to persuade the University to accept responsibility for the systematic and continuous improvement of teaching. I sent a memorandum to the General Board in September 1980, setting out both the arguments for doing something (including a suggestion that Oxford should never be content with anything less than the highest standard of teaching in the world) and a detailed scheme for doing it. I was bidding high, challenging the gentlemanly ethos of Oxford with brutal Americanisation. A meeting with the Appointments Committee of the Board in January 1981 was good-natured and helpful, and I appreciated the force of objections to some aspects of my proposed scheme, but the Board was not willing to go beyond giving encouragement to newly-appointed lecturers to submit voluntarily to a modicum of professional training. However, one positive outcome was the setting up of a Committee for the Training of University Teachers, whose first meeting, as chairman, I convened in October. We decided that the 'modicum' should consist of a couple of days before term in January and another couple in April; that these days should be constructed round video-tapes of 10–15 minute lecture-slices, each tape to be followed by detailed criticism; that we needed outside help, for general guidance on principles from people professionally concerned with educational techniques; and that we needed in addition the presence at each lecture of a member of the Faculty concerned, who would be prepared to take part in the criticisms,

---

[28]Sir Patrick Neill (1926–2016, Kt 1983), a distinguished lawyer, was Vice-Chancellor of Oxford 1985–9 and Warden of All Souls College 1977–95.

because if one knows nothing of, say, theoretical physics one is not in a position to form an opinion about the clarity or adequacy with which a point in that subject is expounded. These courses – if that is not too grand a word – began in January 1982.

We were too slow (our fault, and mainly mine) to co-operate closely with the OUSU Education Committee, which had produced at the end of 1980 an important survey of student criticism of teaching at Oxford; it was not until 1983 that we were able to recruit a substantial number of students for the audience at the video-taping sessions, and only in 1984 that we co-opted a student as a (non-voting) member of the Committee. We did not press hard enough for the inclusion in our course of graduate students who were aiming at an academic career. However, each year we formed a better idea of what to do next time. The professional help was unstintingly given by David Warren Piper and his colleagues at the University of London's Centre for Staff Development in Higher Education. Much of what they said was excellent, but some of it was aimed too low, designed to help those teaching students much more naive and much less articulate than one finds at Oxford. One of my colleagues justifiably grumbled about one video, 'They weren't talking about Chekhov, they were talking about their personal experiences in setting about writing an essay on Chekhov.' It takes only one such incident to put people off a project which they don't really like in principle anyway, and those who were put off don't seem to have had what I would regard as an intellectual's proper reaction: 'It shouldn't be quite like *this*, but now suppose . . .' There were, of course, a few who gave the project unreserved support, notably my Corpus colleague Ron Hill,[29] who had for years devoted some of his time to helping new lecturers in the sciences to improve their technique, Nevil Johnson (Nuffield), and David Robey (Wolfson), who was the most active member of the Committee. It seemed to me essential, as I had emphasised in my original memorandum to the General Board, that training should be the responsibility of Faculties, but there was not enough enthusiasm to go round. The whole notion that lecturing could and should be improved encountered resistance of a kind and degree unworthy of rational beings, and nowhere more than at a meeting of my own Sub-faculty in May 1981. The older members of the Sub-faculty seemed to think that inviting feedback on lecturers entailed a commitment to currying favour with ignorant, lazy or loony students. I came away from the meeting disheartened, but I was glad to learn afterwards that a core of more promising sentiment was taking shape among the younger lecturers. Reform, as usual, lies with the fledglings.

Everything done or said so far, except for the 1979 OUSU report, concerned lecturing, and even in my memo to the General Board I had not dared to speak of tutorials. There were undoubtedly some dons who regarded tutorial technique as incommunicable and their own technique as sacrosanct. In 1979 I attended a

---

[29] Tutorial fellow in Physics at Corpus 1959–90.

seminar on tutorials organised by the Department of Educational Studies; only seven or eight people turned up, including the invariably sensible Ron Hill, and I noted that the most penetrating and interesting comments came from two members of the Faculty of Engineering. In Corpus, by keeping my ear to the ground and putting together scraps and the implications of scraps, not least from undergraduates who chose to talk about their personal problems to me rather than to their Tutors, I formed a strong impression that the favourable assessment which some Tutors made of their own relations with their pupils was not always justified. What I could have done about that without breach of confidentiality, I do not know; but, thank goodness, Brian Harrison took the initiative in 1985 by designing a very full and detailed questionnaire in which undergraduates could say what they thought about their tutors. No one was required to reveal hrs identity, but only hrs subject. No one except me saw the completed questionnaires; we got a 55% response, with no funnies, and I made a digest for all Tutors, question by question, without identifying any of the individual targets of criticism, after which I destroyed the completed forms. I also gave a large selection of remarks which appeared on the forms, again without clues to identification. I find I have forgotten all those remarks except one, which occurred several times, to the effect that some Tutors were too ready with commendation and insufficiently exacting.

A few Fellows of colleges played a part in local politics as city or county councillors, and there were choirs and societies in which dons mixed with non-dons, but most of the time Town and Gown went their own ways; or at any rate, Gown went its way while Town tried, not very hard, to find one. My only excursion outside the ivory tower was as an active promoter of the appeal for the conversion of St Paul's Church in Walton Street into a performing arts centre, and as a member of the governing body of the Oxford Area Arts Council. That Arts Council had made itself a limited company; prudently, as it turned out, because it went into liquidation in 1986 when the County Council,[30] for unusually bad reasons, withdrew its annual subsidy. The St Paul's Church Appeal never reached its target, because although personal contacts brought in some generous donations from far afield, individuals, firms and institutions in Oxford itself were almost without exception apathetic. It may be that music and drama in Oxford had for so long flourished as University activities that there was no real market for them in a purely civic context. It was the second time that I had been associated with an unsuccessful appeal, and it made me wary of appeals in general. If Corpus in 1975 had told me that it was looking for a fund-raiser, I would have turned down the job. Some people are very good at it, and fully deserve the gratitude of the beneficiaries; but it just isn't my line.

---

[30]Dover SN suggests that this may have been the City Council.

23 STYLE 1977–1994[1]

I analyse it and scream with pleasure.
ESA-PEKKA SALONEN, on Haydn's contrapuntal technique[2]

Heads of houses at Oxford (they order things differently at Cambridge) cannot be employed by the University as professors or lecturers, though they are allowed to supervise (as I did) postgraduate students who are writing doctoral dissertations, and to put on lecture-courses if invited to do so by the relevant Faculty. I offered a short course of seven lectures on the history of Greek prose style, and this was welcomed. I gave the course in alternate years, from 1977 to 1985, and made use of its essential points in one or two lectures in German universities in 1983 and a couple of seminar-meetings at Cornell in 1986. By the time I went to Stanford in 1988[3] I had formed the firm intention of writing a book, *The Evolution of Greek Prose Style*, which would not attempt to follow the entire history of the genre down to the end of the Eastern Roman Empire but would concentrate on the ways in which, beginning about 500 BC (the transmission of poetry in writing began long before then), prose was moulded into an art-form of which Plato and Demosthenes, less than a century and a half later, were incomparable practitioners. At Stanford I ran a graduate seminar on the subject for a whole quarter, and for the first time (lecture-audiences are passive) benefited from operating with a team able and willing to address itself to such fundamental questions as 'What *is* style?'[4] During

---

[1] It is unclear why this second date is not 1997, i.e. the year of publication of *The Evolution of Greek Prose Style*.
[2] Salonen (1958–) is an internationally renowned classical conductor as well as a composer; Dover's choice of epigraph is designed to contradict the misconception that stylistic analysis in inimical to aesthetic responsiveness.
[3] For Dover's annual visits to Stanford during the academic years 1987–92, see pp. 321–4.
[4] In the eventual book, Dover actually thanks six graduate students by name (p. vi); on his Stanford teaching, see also p. 323 with note 8 there.

the winter quarters of 1988–1990 at Stanford I was mainly concerned to complete my edition of Aristophanes' *Frogs*, but by the beginning of 1992 that was off my hands, and I was able to exploit the immense resources of the Green Library in order to bring myself up-to-date on stylistics in general. In working through this mass of theoretical material I was encouraged when I found much (especially in Enkvist and Jakobson)[5] which I had already derived from study of the Greek language and reflection on English, but disappointed at finding nothing at all which had not already occurred to me, nothing that justified me in changing my mind, and very little which even seemed to make any adjustment of formulation desirable.

When I first lectured on Greek prose style in 1977 it was not quite the first time I had addressed myself to the subject; I had given three pages to it at the end of *Greek Word Order* in 1960 and devoted a good deal of thought to the main methodological issues in reviewing Thesleff's *Studies in the Styles of Plato* (1967).[6] I was aware, however, once I had finished writing about Greek morality and sexuality, that I was undergoing a reorientation, away from 'history' and towards 'art'. I would be reluctant to dispense with those inverted commas. After I had published *Aristophanic Comedy* in 1972 a reviewer (Jeffrey Henderson) remarked, 'Dover is not a literary critic, though he tries hard to be one.'[7] The first half of that sentence is dead right, I'm not; the second half is dead wrong, because I have never tried to be a literary critic, but always to be a historian of language and literature.[8] 'Literary history', if one is concerned with the Greeks, does not connote preoccupation with biographical details, because we know very little indeed about the lives of Greek authors, and some of the most interesting items in the history of Greek prose are anonymous. I suppose that I could be most accurately described as a historian of Greek *behaviour*, and what happened to me in the late nineteen-seventies was a decisive shift from political, social, moral and sexual behaviour to linguistic and literary behaviour. 'Joy' and 'love' are perfectly appropriate terms for my reaction to objects of study; Jane Harrison said that the morphology and syntax of the Russian verb made her 'weep for joy',[9] and Sakharov declared that what he

---

[5]Nils Erik Enkvist (1925–2009) a leading Finnish linguist, Roman Jakobson (1896–1982) an influential, Russian-born practitioner of structuralist linguistics. Dover was in general averse to 'theoretical' linguistics: see p. 52.

[6]The review appeared in *Gnomon* 41 (1969) 636–9.

[7]J. Henderson, 'Scribes, scholars and Aristophanic comedy', *Arion* NS 1 (1973/4) 530–7, at 531.

[8]Dover's other references in *MC* to 'literary criticism' exhibit a somewhat restrictive (and partly jaundiced) attitude to the subject: see pp. 176, 234, 265, 335. He takes it to be fundamentally concerned with subjective response and evaluation, not historical interpretation, a view akin to that of A.E. Housman (though Dover might not have welcomed the comparison) in his Cambridge inaugural of 2011: A.E. Housman, *Collected Poems and Selected Prose*, ed. Christopher Ricks (London, 1988) 302–5.

[9]Jane Ellen Harrison (1850–1928), classicist and anthropologist, told Gilbert Murray (see p. 68 n. 4) in a letter of 22 November 1914 that the system of verbal aspect in Russian made her 'just weep for joy': Dover will have seen the letter in Jessie Stewart, *Jane Ellen Harrison: A Portrait from Letters* (London, 1959) 156; he had quoted the same phrase in his 1976 Presidential Address to the Classical Association (*G&L* 311).

loved most of all in the world was the faint cosmic radiation that came from the uttermost bounds of the universe.[10] But now my intellectual pleasure in solving problems was steadily, increasingly, supplemented by aesthetic pleasure in the arts. At St Andrews we had been unfailing attenders at the Film Society every Sunday in termtime, and I might well have said during those years that film was the artform which affected me most deeply.* The move to Oxford broke the habit, and I turned more often to music and literature. A song-recital by Teresa Berganza in the crypt of the cathedral at Santander (with bats flitting close above the heads of the audience) and Alfred Brendel's playing of the *Eroica Variations* in the Sheldonian at Oxford can both claim the status of 'life events' in my memory. I explored the British and European classical novelists with greater passion, and began to look at some aspects of Greek literature with sharper eyes. I had always derived peculiar pleasure from Herodotus, no matter what he was talking about, and I now began to ask more insistently, 'How does he do it?' I saw an analogy between a half-page of Herodotus and a Celtic brooch in which a firm basis of symmetry is enlivened by dramatic variety of detail.

To say that you and I differ only in style is to say that we do the same thing in different ways; but what exactly is the boundary between 'thing' and 'way', between 'content' and 'form'? I was aware of a school of literary criticism which alleges that content and form are inseparable. I suspected that this was one of the fatuously extravagant doctrines which achieve popularity among critics solely because they repudiate a Classical tradition. I encountered a similar doctrine in Germany in 1983, when a research student asserted that the transposition of two words in a Greek verse made the meaning 'completely different' even though the difference could not be shown in German or English translation. The utterances 'Get out!' and 'Would they perhaps, if conditions had been otherwise, have been willing to compromise on a provisional allocation?' can fairly be regarded as *almost* completely different (not absolutely different, because they both contain the phoneme /t/), but 'completely' is a strong word and should not be abused. So far as concerns content and form, it was clear that the question which mattered was 'To what extent, and in what circumstances, are content and form separable?'

I began, as always, with my own experience. I write a lot, and I try to make every sentence not only clear and precise but also architecturally, phonologically and rhythmically attractive to those readers who share my own aesthetic preferences. In consequence, I may sometimes take five minutes or more on the verbal form of a sentence. What is going on? A few minutes ago, when I wrote the words 'content

---

*There are all sorts of other things that I might well have said – for example, that *Last Year at Marienbad* was the worst film I'd ever seen, until *Performance*, *Ghostbusters* and *L'Annonce faite à Marie*.

[10]Andrei Sakharov (1921–89), Russian physicist and winner of the Nobel Peace Prize (1975): for the remark, made to his wife, see R. Lourie, *Sakharov: A Biography* (Hanover NH, 2002) 370.

and form', I was conscious of resisting a very strong pull towards 'form and content'. The pull was created by a preference for a particular rhythmical flow, and I resisted it because 'the same thing in different ways' dictated the order 'thing ... way', and that in turn seemed to me to dictate 'content ... form'. Having drafted a paragraph, I revise it, sometimes two or three times. As a rule, my purpose in writing is to explain something; that is to say, to cause a reader to understand something. The purpose is not changed by the process of frequent revision, which addresses the sole question, 'What choice and arrangement of words are most likely to achieve my purpose?'

One does not have the access to other people's minds that one has to one's own, but much is known about the changes which authors during the last three hundred years have made in successive drafts of their own works. In ancient Greek prose literature it is possible to identify certain passages in which an author has re-used material which he himself composed on an earlier occasion for a similar though not identical purpose, and others in which he has adapted for his own purpose material originally composed by someone else. Where the re-use or the adaptation differs linguistically from the original, we have to enquire into possible reasons for the difference. Sometimes we have no idea of the reasons, and it is prudent to refrain from fantasy. Occasionally the probable reason is rhythmical preference. There is, however, one instance of adaptation which seemed to me to clarify not only the form/content dichotomy but the definition of 'style' itself. An author during the fourth century BC (perhaps it was Lysias, though the attribution to him is far from certain) composed a speech which purports to be a funeral laudation of Athenians killed in a year of war. Surveying past Athenian achievements, he follows closely (identical ordering of events, with some verbal coincidences) the account given by the historian Thucydides of a campaign sixty years earlier.[11] However, whereas the historian's account is full of military detail, the orator omits most of that detail, turns an indecisive battle into a decisive victory, and expatiates on aspects of the campaign about which the historian says nothing: the courage, discipline and resolve of the Athenians. A difference of style, certainly, but a difference in the selection of data and in the presence or absence of evaluative comment on the data selected. But there is in addition a set of linguistic differences; the historian's narrative proceeds in a succession of main clauses, whereas the orator constructs an edifice of parallel and antithetical participial clauses, each set leading to a climactic main clause. Here we can clearly distinguish between *historiographical* style and *linguistic* style; differences in the former, looked at from the level of the latter, are differences in *what* is said but linguistic style is concerned with *how* it is said. But it is also possible to look – upwards, so to speak – from the orator's narrative to the genre 'funeral laudation' and observe that in that genre one

---

[11]Dover discusses this example in more detail in *The Evolution of Greek Prose Style*, 5–10.

may either dwell on particularised events or (as in the famous funeral speech put into the mouth of Pericles by Thucydides) keep to generalisations; another distinction between 'what' (laudation) and 'how' (particular or general). There are many areas of behaviour, other than prose composition, in which similar separation of levels is applicable; a 'how' question about level 1 is necessarily answered in 'what' terms, which provoke a level 2 'how' question, and so on down until we reach the purely linguistic level, and that is the level with which my book is concerned. Failure to keep levels distinct has been responsible for much confusion (and some avoidable disillusionment) in the discussion of style.

When I was writing about Greek word order I found that the essential clue to the principle I was seeking emerged from documentary inscriptions; in the same way, it was inscriptions which provided me with conclusive demonstration that there are circumstances in which it is possible to separate form cleanly from content. There are so many recurrent ingredients of prescription and statement in documentary inscriptions for which the composers, had they chosen, could have adhered to invariable formulae, but preferred to exercise choice between alternative wordings. From that starting-point we can make a tentative foray into literature and observe that an author who often has occasion to give the names of towns, rivers and mountains may choose different ways of saying 'and its name is ...' or 'which is called ...'. Emboldened, we may launch into Plato and recognise that many of his arguments would be incoherent were it not for the synonymy of some pairs or trios of words, expressions and constructions, a synonymy which we accept effortlessly in reading him, while its artful deployment keeps us on a line of the argument while conveying an impression of 'natural' conversation.

Two further aspects of prose style seemed to me not to have received the degree of attention which they deserve. One of them emerges conspicuously from the comparison I made just now between an historian's account and an orator's account of a military event. The historian assumed that his hearers/readers were interested in the things in which he himself was interested – hence the tactical details – and not in any moralising comments which he might have been inclined to make. The orator knew that his audience was not (on that occasion) in the least interested in tactics but wanted to be reassured of the virtues of its ancestors. That much accounts for the difference in historiographical style; but the orator also knew that the audience of a funeral laudation expected certain types of word- and sentence-structure which would have struck an inappropriate note in a historian's military narrative and might have aroused in a jury mistrust of the speaker. Linguistic style cannot be divorced from the audience's expectations, and those are determined by the purpose and occasion of the utterance. The boundary between stylistics and sociolinguistics is – or if it is not, should be made – a fuzzy one.

The second matter is quantification. We are commonly told that a given phenomenon occurs 'often' or 'rarely' in a given author, or that it is 'characteristic' of hrm. Such statements are likely to be true if they are made by experienced readers, but they can be untrue (I once made a bad mistake of this kind about Thucydides, of all people, but fortunately not in print), and it is salutary to remember that all words such as 'most', 'more', 'frequent' and the like, are vague statistical terms. 'Often' should provoke the challenge, not only in stylistic but also in political and social questions, '*How* often?' I had to devise techniques for meeting that challenge, in the hope of answering it in terms which would be both precise and informative (answers which are precise but miserably uninformative are just too easy). I expect – but I haven't finished the book yet – to find that passages which lodge in our memory as brilliantly or deplorably characteristic of an author represent the extreme development of tendencies which are also statistically characteristic of that author. The attempt to achieve genuinely informative quantification has been extraordinarily tedious, because it has entailed a great deal of counting by hand, then scrapping the lot and re-counting on a different basis, and then usually scrapping the fresh count and starting again on a third basis. The use of a computer was out of the question, not just because I am afraid of computers, but because the conversion of the texts to machine-readable form would have required such heavy and thoughtful enrichment before they could be turned over to a programmer that it was quicker to work with pencil and paper.[12] This had the further advantage that repeatedly working over the same texts prompted a great number of new questions and lines of enquiry which would not have occurred to a computer.

I recall a genre of *New Statesman* competition in which the setter wrote a passage in the style of a certain author on a subject quite alien to that author, and competitors, thus deprived of any clue in the subject-matter, had to decide what author was being parodied. A similar game was sometimes played in the television programme *Face the Music,* a theme from one composer played in the style of another, the competitors being required to identify the 'other'. The importance of parody for stylistics has been somewhat underestimated, and its most interesting aspect is the ease with which we can sometimes get the right answer without being able to put our finger on any particular phenomenon in the piece and justify our answer in communicable terms. It is equally remarkable that an experienced listener who cannot play any musical instrument and may lose hrs way in following a score can nevertheless often identify correctly the composer of a piece s/he has not heard before.†

In writing about Greek prose style I was frequently tempted to use musical analogies, but I became increasingly nervous of doing so. How does one distinguish between form and content in music? Are Beethoven's violin concerto and his transcription of it for the piano (adding a rather banal part for the left hand and

---

†I have frequently done that. The piece *reminds* me (can't say how) of A, but the melodic invention is not as *good* (what do I mean?) as A's, so B is the likely candidate (e.g. A= Sibelius, B = Nielsen).

[12]Compare (and contrast) Dover's earlier remarks on computerized stylometrics, pp. 171–4; by the 1990s, computers could have assisted his work greatly if he had not been so 'afraid' of them.

retaining the same orchestral parts throughout) two different forms imposed upon the same content? And how about the visual arts? What name do we give to that which two portraits of the same person have in common but do not share with a portrait of someone else? I have little doubt that in any art-form a use may be found for the terms 'form' and 'content', but the uses in two different arts might not be analogous, and it would be imprudent for me to venture far from language.

24 EXCURSIONS 1979–1984

It was fortunate that by the time I became President of the Academy I had overcome the fear of flying which had rather restricted my mobility in the thirty-odd years since the War. This fear originated, I suspect, in my experience in the anti-aircraft defence of airfields in Africa and Italy; I so often saw crippled aircraft crash on landing that their fragility made a much deeper impression on me than their power. I flew from Boston to Newark and back in 1960, and across the United States in stages after we left Berkeley in 1967, because there was no other way of keeping my promises to lecture at Austin, Norman and Pennsylvania State College, but I wished all the time that there *had* been another way. In 1978 I realised that there was no escaping air travel if I was to participate, within the limits set by my Oxford commitments, in the television filming in Greece and Sicily. Flying out to Catania via Rome I concentrated my mind on aerodynamics – I had taken the trouble to find out how and why an aircraft stays up – and ever since then I have taken delight in seeing the world from the air. No more clammy hands on take-off; even a certain smugness when I travel with friends who become tense during turbulence or at touch-down.

I was invited to lead a party from the Academy to China in October 1978, but, much as I would have wished to go, it seemed to me quite impossible to be absent from the College in the first ten days of the academic year; so Isaiah Berlin agreed to go in my stead.[1] However, another opportunity to visit the Far East came almost at once, when I was invited, together with the presidents of many academies in the world, to the celebrations of the centenary of the Japan Academy in January 1979. It was the only occasion on which I have ever flown first class (paid for by the Japanese); the weather was perfect all the way, and over the Arctic ice-pack and the mountains of Alaska I marvelled at the emptiness of the world. Membership of the Japan Academy was limited to 150 for humanities and sciences together, in a nation of over

---

[1] Dover makes a double error here: the Academy delegation to China was in October 1979 not 1978 (so 'almost at once' in the next sentence is confused), and Isaiah Berlin withdrew at a late stage because of illness; see Dover's 1980 Presidential Address, *PBA* 66 (1980) 79, for both details.

a hundred million, so that a formidable degree of eminence was required for election, and it did not come early in life. The proceedings of the centenary celebration were slow and solemn, including the presentation of a congratulatory address from each academy. We were introduced to the old Emperor, and each of us had to make a little speech to him, to which, I noticed (my knowledge of Japanese is rudimentary), his reply usually began *watakushi mo*, 'and I for my part ...'. As the nations were lined up in alphabetical order, by the time UK was reached I gave up all hope of uttering anything very original; on my left USA and USSR had my deepest sympathy. We were taken on visits to Kabuki plays, the great Buddha of Kamakura, and a museum containing manuscripts which showed how just before the xenophobic centuries began Japanese mathematicians and scientists were profiting from their acquaintance with the Dutch. And, of course, there were some splendid meals.

At the end of 1979 the Belgians were celebrating the hundred and fiftieth year of their existence as a nation. An invitation arrived from the Dutch-speaking academies in Belgium to a week's worth of celebrations in Brussels, and about a fortnight later an invitation to a similar get-together came from the French-speaking academies. As I had already accepted the first invitation, I asked one of my Vice-Presidents, Owen Chadwick,[2] to accept the second. I hope he and his wife had as good a time as Audrey and I did. The core of the celebrations was a series of non-lectures on non-subjects (e.g. 'the contribution of Belgium to theoretical linguistics'), but the parties made up for that. At the first reception we noticed on arrival that while all the Europeans were caught up in a greeting-frenzy a black man and a yellow man were left talking to one another in isolation. Thinking it was time to make them feel welcome, we joined them. The black man was a professor of surgery from Sierra Leone, and the yellow man was Huan Xiang, Vice-President of the Beijing Academy of Social Sciences (which in China comprehends historical subjects as well). I made his acquaintance again when a delegation from Beijing visited the British Academy in the spring of 1980 to arrange a scheme of regular academic exchanges between our two academies;[3] he was very friendly, and promised that I would be invited to visit China and give some lectures there.

At the same time Masaaki Kubo[4] in Tokyo University told me that the Japan Science Foundation hoped to invite me to lecture in Japanese universities; invitations came from Princeton and Toronto; and I had a standing invitation from my one-time student Alan Henry, now Professor of Classics at Monash, to lecture in Australia.[5] It

---

[2] Rev. Owen Chadwick (1916–2015) was, among much else, Regius Professor of Modern History at Cambridge 1968–83 and succeeded Dover as President of the British Academy 1981–5.
[3] Dover expressed optimism about the prospects of expanded scholarly contacts between the British Academy and China in his 1980 Presidential Address, *PBA* 66 (1980) 79.
[4] Masaaki Kubo (1930-) was Professor of Classics at Tokyo University 1969–91; he had published a Japanese translation of Dover's *The Greeks* in 1982.
[5] Alan Henry (1936–2022) had also been an Assistant in the Department of Greek at St Andrews 1959–63. A specialist in Greek epigraphy, he was Professor at Monash University 1973–96.

occurred to me that if Corpus were willing to allow me a sabbatical term (to which a President has no statutory right) I could take up all these invitations within a single period of three months. I could not decently offload all my presidential commitments in the Academy on to my Vice-Presidents, so that if I went on my world-tour at the ideal time, from late February to late May in 1982, it would be necessary for me to tell the Council early in 1981 that I would not stand for re-election to a fourth and final year of office. That was not a difficult decision. Many years later I realised that it may have been interpreted as motivated by fear that my re-election would be opposed by Fellows who disapproved of my role in the Blunt affair (see Chapter 25), or even as an admission of guilt. The affair was not irrelevant because it had undoubtedly imposed a strain on me which diminished the charms of office by comparison with a trip to the Far East, but there were two facts which made my decision particularly easy: the Academy's new premises, come what may, could not be ready for occupation before my fourth year had expired; and Council agreed with my proposal that it should nominate Owen Chadwick, absolutely ideal for the job, as my successor.

I got my sabbatical term, and left home in February 1982. Two weeks at Princeton gave us the chance to renew friendships and to spend a good day at the Metropolitan Museum in New York. The blistering heat of Melbourne was welcome after the freezing slush of Toronto (which people energetically shovelled back on the road as soon as the road-clearing machines had dumped it on to the sidewalk). A pity that I lost my birthday on the international date-line. The month in Australia was totally enjoyable from start to finish – the finish was in Perth, staying with Martin and Moia Lindsay, old St Andrews friends – and it struck us that Australia had changed its culture, through immigration, from beer and steak to vino and pasta. The only thing which would dissuade me from living there is the spiders.

We had the best imaginable approach to Japan, with Mount Fuji emerging serenely from a perfect dawn. My lectures in Japan were mostly on aspects of Greek morality, but I gave two seminars in Tokyo, each lasting from half-past two until the building closed at five, on the interrelation of the manuscripts of Aristophanes. Kubo, the professor of Classics at Tokyo, comparable in learning, acumen and imagination with the best of his counterparts in Europe (but he always publishes in Japanese), looked after us wonderfully. Having taken his first degree at Harvard, he understood English perfectly, and this was just as well, because the people attending my seminars, despite the ease with which they read English, found me hard to understand no matter how deliberately I spoke, and Kubo's services as interpreter were often required. I was puzzled later by the fact that no such problem arose in China, and I can only suggest that whereas Chinese word order has much in common with English, Japanese word order differs so radically that the listener may often become confused over English phrase-boundaries and clause-boundaries.

I was interviewed by a Japanese journalist who asked me why the Japanese should be interested in the ancient Greeks. My answer was that 'should' does not come into it; anyone is free to sample any past culture, and it is to be expected that a few will find attraction and interest in the Greeks, a few in Anglo-Saxon literature, a few in medieval Russia, and so on, just as a Westerner may find that the history and literature of Japan may engage hrs enthusiasm more than that of Europe. 'You mean,' put in Kubo, 'that children can choose their parents.' Cultural parentage, we found, was a characteristically Japanese preoccupation; well aware of the bizarre marriage of Japanese tradition with Americanisation which constitutes their present culture, some of them hankered after a *ménage à trois* through the addition of a specifically European model. It was hard to imagine the Chinese, in whose eyes the rest of the world is a benighted periphery, worrying themselves about alternative models.

We stayed in Kyoto for a few days, and opposite the university hostel in which we were lodged were ordinary houses and shops. At the corner of the block, a niche in the wall, and in the niche small clay figures wearing clean woolly hats and smiling at the posies of flowers laid before them. They were the gods of the block; move on two hundred yards, and you meet a fresh set of gods. I thought at once of nymphs and dryads, Greek immortals with very limited domains, and I was even more strongly reminded of the ancient world when I saw colour-slides of the annual spring festival at Nagoya, where a gigantic phallus is carried in procession to its shrine. Between ancient Japan and ancient Greece there is no possibility of cultural influence; it is just that similar assumptions about how the world works express themselves in similar manifestations.[6] Some years ago a poll indicated that ninety per cent of Japanese regard themselves as having no religion, but there is no lack of ritual: a Catholic wedding, presentation of sons at a Shinto shrine and at the end a Buddhist funeral.

We learned much from the Kubos about Japanese attitudes to the arts, including sloppy edges to the glaze of vases (human error establishes a rapport between maker and user), preference for 'single' over 'double' flowers (double flowers exemplify a greedy, discontented Western urge to improve on Nature), the austere beauty of gravel raked in swirls, the allusiveness of a dance movement (tracing an ideogram for a philosophical term) in a certain genre of popular knockabout mime. A taste for Noh plays needs to be acquired, and the accompanying music did nothing to remedy my long-standing lack of enthusiasm for any music that comes from east of the Bay of Bengal.

It happened that we had made the acquaintance of several young Japanese couples in Oxford, thanks to Audrey's activity in the Newcomer Club; we renewed this acquaintance, and spent a couple of days in Tokyo as guests of Michael and Ichiko Inagaki. It was hard for wives who had tasted the freedoms of Western

---

[6]Dover had already compared ancient Greek and modern Japanese religion in *The Greeks*, 2nd edn (Oxford, 1982) 57, presumably on the basis of his earlier (1979) visit to the country (pp. 271–2).

society to readjust to the predominant attitudes of their own country; one of them wept when she recalled the happiness of two years she had spent in Britain. Even the most considerate and perceptive of husbands may not always be an adequate protection against mother-in-law.

We visited Hiroshima for two days (I lectured on Byron for the British Council),[7] and on our tour of the museum which commemorates the city's destruction by the first nuclear bomb we were accompanied by an Englishman who had lived many years in Japan and knew all levels of its society intimately. After reading all the reproachful captions on the exhibits, he growled: 'When have the Japanese *ever* shown *any* mercy or compassion towards *anyone*?'[8]

The most startling culture-shock in our way round the world was the transition from Tokyo to Beijing: from noise, glare and comfort to early lights-out at night, a river of bicycles (with bells but no lights) flowing around and between sparse lorries and even rarer cars, and handcarts laden with building materials lugged along by humans. The abundance of public lavatories surprised us until we realised how few private lavatories there were.

My lectures in Beijing were (at their request) on Aristophanes and the Peloponnesian War. An abstruse subject, one might think, in a country where there were, I believe, only four old men who could read Greek; but understandable at a time when many Chinese were addressing themselves seriously to the question, 'What limits, if any, should be set to open criticism of public policy?' I was asked earnestly if I thought that Aristophanes 'went too far', and I could only say that there is no such thing as 'going too far' if what one says is true; but I was impressed by the sense of history that made my hosts consider an alien author who had been dead for two millennia relevant to their own problems. Six years had passed since the death of Mao and the repudiation of the Cultural Revolution, and now there was an uncomfortable oscillation between dogma and pragmatism. On the one hand, the response to some of our questions on political and economic matters came in almost identical words everywhere from Beijing to Canton, as if drawn from a handbook of regulations for conversation with foreigners. When we commented on the height and angry speed of the Yangtze at Shanghai, we were blandly assured that it was quite normal, and an English-speaking medical student who started to tell us about disastrous floods and landslides up-river was shooed away. Talking to one official of the Beijing Academy, I enquired what his adolescent sons wanted to do when they left school, and I was made to feel that I had asked an indecent question; one does not *want*, one goes where one is sent. Temples were show-pieces (we were surfeited with them), but it was *de rigueur* to point a scornful finger, with a forced high-pitched laugh, at people who prayed in them. On the

---

[7]This is presumably the lecture 'Byron on the Ancient Greeks' printed in *G&L* 292–303.
[8]Cf. Dover's earlier reference to the bombing of Hiroshima on p. 91.

other hand, the lively, cheerful friendliness of the students, their energy and patience in coping with a material austerity which would defeat our own students, were a delight. Our mentor from the Academy, Deng Junbing – whose husband was a diplomat – was sophisticated and perceptive. We were freely told that overhaul of the system of land-tenure was required because 'some people are lazy', and we found that comprehensive education had been jettisoned in favour of high-pressure schools for the top flight. Our general impression was that the Chinese would do whatever they judged to be advantageous, and would then label it 'socialism'. An article in the English-language *Beijing Daily* questioned the dogma that the arts should serve politics, and hovered on the edge of the question, 'What are politics *for*?' Ironically, a passage from the works of Stalin was cited in support of the writer's standpoint. (It would have been surprising, though, if a Soviet communist of later date had been invoked in any context.) Our Chinese friends disapproved of our resistance to the Argentinian attack on the Falklands,[9] on the grounds that it gave the Soviet Union an opportunity to pose as the champion of Latin America, and whatever strengthened the status of the Soviet Union was a bad thing. During the years of Soviet–Chinese co-operation the Chinese had been patronised, and that is something they do not like. The Soviets were also regarded, in Khrushchev's time, as deficient in the revolutionary zeal which the long civil war in China had bred into the People's Liberation Army. I can imagine that even Stalin turned pensive if he heard how the Chinese Chief of Staff in 1950 reacted to the threat of American nuclear attack: 'They may even drop atom bombs on us. What then? They may kill a few million people. Without sacrifice, a nation's independence cannot be upheld.'*

People unacquainted with my subject often assume that we constantly visit Greece, but that is not so. Archaeology and topography affect my work on literature so marginally that I have not *needed* to go to Greece for purely academic purposes since 1963; and although the scenery and the sites move me profoundly, I can't help having mixed feelings about the culture of the inhabitants of the country. Their vitality is enchanting, but I am put off by melodramatic chauvinism, whether it is British or Greek. I am not particularly fond of Greek food or wine and I don't swim or bask. All the same, we didn't turn down invitations, in 1982 and 1983, to free passage on Swan's Hellenic cruises in return for a few lectures by me. These cruises, organised from first to last with splendid efficiency, took us to Ephesus, Troy, Istanbul and Samothrace, none of which we had seen before, and, for good measure, to Tunis, Malta and Pompeii. On Greek and Turkish soil those of us who lectured were permitted to perform outside the entrances to sites, but everything

---

*Max Hastings, *The Korean War* (New York, 1987) 134.
[9] For Dover's own views on the Falklands war, see pp. 329–30.

past the entrance was the preserve of the professional guides. The Greek guides were excellent; the Turks amusing, but under the curious illusion that they were the direct descendants of the Hittites and Trojans. Genetically, I dare say many of them are, but the Turkish language was not heard in Turkey until after the end of the ancient world. I suppose that as a student of Homer I ought to regard the walls of Troy as the most sacred memory of those cruises. What I actually remember most vividly is the bee-eaters flitting through an olive-grove at Phaistos, Eleonora's Falcon hunting swallows off the coast of Crete and the pitiless majesty of Mount Athos as we rounded it close inshore.

Our most recent visit to Greece was to a week-long conference on Chios in 1984, devoted to lectures on all aspects of the history of the island.[10] Some lectures were given in English, others in Greek, and two young Greek women from EC headquarters gave a marvellous display of simultaneous translation through our headphones. We came close to defeating them, though, and they begged for a sight of our scripts the day before; as one of them explained, you know what politicians are going to say, but the content of a scholarly paper is less predictable. That visit to Chios was our first experience of the Aegean in May, and we delighted in the wild tulips. On a visit to Nea Moni, the convent in the middle of the island, the Mother Superior gave us beans, bread and a delectable liqueur, and said grace with an uninhibited joyousness which suggested that she had been eagerly waiting all morning for an opportunity to address God; a contrast to the mumbled or chattered grace at dinner in a college.

---

[10]The conference led to a book, J. Boardman and C.E. Vaphopoulou-Richardson, eds, *Chios: A Conference at the Homereion in Chios 1984* (Oxford, 1986). Dover's contribution, reprinted in *G&L* 1-12, was on the intriguing fifth-century BCE writer Ion of Chios (one of whose works, his *Epidemiai*, was itself a kind of memoir).

25 THE BLUNT AFFAIR 1979–1981

If your brother wrongs you, rebuke him. If he repents, forgive him.
LUKE 17.3

I had known Anthony Blunt since 1972, when he joined the Leverhulme Research Awards Committee.[1] When it was revealed in Parliament in November 1979 that he had at one time been a Soviet spy, I was totally surprised.[2] I knew, of course, that he had had a long-standing friendship with Guy Burgess, but in so far as I took any notice of rumours that he had tipped off Burgess and Maclean I assumed he was following a popular version of E.M. Forster's maxim, 'If I had to choose between betraying my country and betraying a friend, I hope I would have the guts to betray my country' – a version which expurgates the preceding seven words, 'I hate the idea of causes, and . . .'.[3] Quite a lot of friends were betrayed by the people who took up the Soviet cause and treated the Soviet Union as their adopted country. I observed that Blunt always chose vodka out of the splendid array of aperitifs which confronted us at the Leverhulme Committee lunch, and it occurred to me afterwards that it may have amused him to do so.

The news of his treachery, closely followed by the revocation of his knighthood, did not raise in my mind any question at all about the maintenance of his status as a Fellow of the British Academy, and it came as a surprise to me when I got a letter from Jack Plumb expressing the hope that 'immediate action' would be taken to

---

[1] See Figure 10, which Dover misdated in the first edition of *MC* to 1971; cf. Asa Briggs, *The Story of the Leverhulme Trust* (London, 1991) 188–9. For Dover's service on the committee in question, see pp. 225 and 229.
[2] On the facts of Blunt's espionage, see Christopher Andrew, *The Defence of the Realm: the Authorized History of MI5*, updated edn (London, 2010) esp. 261, 268–72, 436–9.
[3] E.M. Forster, 'What I believe', in *Two Cheers for Democracy* (London, 1951) 78 (with 'my friend' and 'should have').

expel Blunt, because the Academy should not 'harbour traitors'.[4] There could be no question of immediate action, because no Fellow could be expelled except by a vote at the Annual General Meeting in July, and then only on the recommendation of the Council, but at least the matter could be put on the agenda of Council (of which Plumb was a member) for its meeting on February 15th. I pointed this out to Plumb, and in reply he added a further hope, that I would 'give the Academy a strong lead'. I was certainly not going to do that; my job as chairman was to ensure that all members of Council had their say and that the outcome truly represented the considered view of the majority. The only 'lead' I proposed to give was – as in the business of my College – an insistence that everything which called for decision was decided clearly and in good time. So far as my feelings went, I would cheerfully have assisted Blunt to fall from a top-floor window, but as I read the Statutes and Bye-laws of the Academy it did not seem to me that they were about feelings.[5]

Council met, and every member (except Arthur Brown) spoke at some length. A straw vote gave 9 to 8 in favour of expulsion.[6] In accordance with the Bye-laws, I was required to invite Blunt to come to the next Council meeting and make a case for his retention; I issued the invitation, but he declined it. Some Fellows would have been relieved if I had asked Blunt to resign (as the Society of Antiquaries had done, successfully), but it went against the grain for me to ask a man if he would be so good as to consider the comfort of his executioners.

Although the whole discussion was rational and even-tempered (John Carswell[7] thought it 'showed the Academy at its best') it left me with some very disturbing reflections. One factual misapprehension, that the Queen was 'Patron' of the Academy, confused the issue briefly. The dictum that 'Integrity is indivisible', pronounced by one member, resounds agreeably but is false; whatever else Blunt did, it cannot annihilate the fact that he was a great historian of the visual arts.*

Bye-law 11(1) of the Academy provides for the expulsion of a Fellow 'on the grounds that he or she is not a fit and proper person to be a Fellow'.[8] Bye-law 27(1)(b)

---

*A few years later a Professor at Stanford, rightly eulogised at his funeral for his devotion to the interests of his students, had in fact contrived a suicidal accident when he realised that his persistent sexual abuse of a mentally handicapped boy could no longer be concealed. That did not falsify the eulogy.

[4]Like many other communications mentioned in this chapter, this letter is illustrated in *QR* (p. 12), which is itself in part based on a dossier of materials deposited with the Academy by Dover (see *QR* p. x) and should be consulted throughout for the documentary record, including the personalities involved, but will be cited very selectively in these notes. For a further analysis of Dover's handling of the affair, see Osborne's chapter in *S&C*.

[5]It is essential here to remember Dover's consistent, if exaggerated, distinction between (non-rational) 'feelings' and 'rational thought': see esp. pp. 25–6. Cf. Peter Brown's comment in *KJD* 170 on Dover's handling of the Blunt affair: 'he deprecated all concession to "feelings"'.

[6]The Council minutes (*QR* pp. 16–17) say it was 8 to 7.

[7]Secretary of the British Academy 1978–83.

[8]Dover SN notes that Bye-law 11(1) had in the meantime become 12(1): the bye-laws are available at https://www.thebritishacademy.ac.uk/about/bye-laws-british-academy/

makes it a condition of nomination for election that at least three Fellows sign a statement that '[they] are, from their own knowledge of the person proposed or of his or her work, of the opinion that he or she is a fit and proper person to be a Fellow of the Academy in accordance with Article 6 of the Charter'. Article 6 of the Charter provides that 'New Fellows shall be elected ... from among persons who have attained distinction in some one or more of the branches of scientific study which it is the object of the Academy to promote'. If we read Bye-law 11(1) in the light of 27(1)(b), and 27(1)(b) in the light of Article 6, it is obvious that misconduct which lies outside the 'scientific study which it is the object of the Academy to promote' does not constitute grounds for expulsion. F.A. Mann thought the opposite, but there are times when law is too serious a business to be left to lawyers.

Is treason so uniquely monstrous, misconduct so horrible, that it could not have entered the minds of those who framed the Charter and Bye-laws? Some said yes, but, not surprisingly, some said no; the only surprise was that there was no clear correlation between division of opinion on this issue and the political division between Right and Left, for some lifelong Conservatives thought that Blunt's treason should be forgiven and forgotten, while many Socialists (including at least two ex-Communists) were merciless. I was not happy with the idea that some crimes or immoralities are so much worse than others that the law can be brushed aside; it made me think of the alleged occasion when the Athenian assembly, discussing a Persian ultimatum, stoned to death a citizen who argued for its acceptance.[9] A good lynching may warm the hearts of the perpetrators, but it sets a horrible precedent. Not a few Fellows have behaved very badly in their private lives; and if we are going to make good moral character a condition of tenure of a Fellowship, when do we start expelling those who do not satisfy that condition?

There was, however, one consideration which furnished a decisive reason, fully compatible with the Charter and Bye-laws, for expelling Blunt. He had transferred his allegiance to a regime which deliberately falsified history and persecuted scholars who attempted to exercise independent judgement; and nothing could have been more directly opposed than that to the purposes of the Academy. It was for this reason that I favoured his expulsion; but, to my astonishment, not a word was said about it in the Council meeting. During the last twenty minutes of the discussion I fought against the temptation to raise the point myself; at the end of the meeting both Vice-Presidents and the Secretary told me that they had no idea which side I was on, and I went home satisfied that I had done my job as chairman.

But there were plenty of reasons for dissatisfaction, and I did not look forward happily to the next Council meeting. Blunt had no intention of resigning, as I discovered through Peter Lasko. Richard Cobb told me that Blunt had 'had many

---

[9] This event is recounted, in the context of Mardonius' occupation of Athens in spring 479 BC, at Herodotus 9.5. Dover also mentioned it in his British Academy Presidential Address of 1980, *PBA* 66 (1980) 83–4, but the analogy with the Blunt affair seems oblique.

letters from Fellows begging him not to resign'. Through correspondence and conversations I became aware that the majority on Council was by no means representative of the views of the Fellowship as a whole – many upright and conventional individuals told me that the matter should simply be dropped, urging that 'Blunt's folly should not outweigh his services to scholarship', even that 'Blunt has suffered enough' – and I came to the conclusion that if Council's recommendation went to the AGM it would be defeated. A few days after the Council meeting Alan Taylor declared in *The Times* that if Blunt were expelled he would resign his Fellowship.[10] A letter promptly appeared in *The Times*, over the name of Lord Beloff, suggesting that Taylor had offered Fellows a very strong inducement to expel Blunt; but the letter was not written by Beloff, and I have never discovered who the forger was.[11]

Naturally I did not know at the time, as we now know from his *Letters to Eva*, that Taylor was looking for a pretext for resignation.[12]

I reckoned that I knew by now how each member of Council would vote at the meeting on March 18th, who would abstain, and who would be prevented from attending by absence abroad; and I knew in consequence that everything might turn on my own vote. The Bye-laws give the President two votes, one regular vote as a Council member and a casting vote to resolve a tie. I had never exercised my right to vote simply as a member, believing that a chairman should vote only if everyone else's votes resulted in a tie and a casting vote was inescapable; and I was not willing to abandon this principle. When a case of homicide was tried at Athens by the Areopagus a tied vote meant acquittal, for Athena was imagined as voting for the defendant. As a lifelong student of the *Oresteia* I would have to use my casting vote in Blunt's favour.[13] In any case, there is a tradition that a casting vote should be a vote for the status quo. My vote would come as a shock to some members of Council, and I thought it prudent to warn them beforehand; so I drafted a memo, in which I incidentally revealed my own view of Blunt's guilt, and sent it to Owen Chadwick and Michael Howard for their opinions. They both thought that I should not reveal my own view, so I circulated an amended memo,

---

[10]Dover's chronology is confused: the report of Taylor's intentions (not a 'letter', *contra* QR p. 43 and Miranda Carter, *Anthony Blunt: His Lives* (London, 2001) 492) appeared later in the run up to the AGM, in the 'London Diary' of *The Times* for 24 June 1980, p. 14; the hoax Beloff letter appeared on 26 June, p. 17.

[11]Taylor himself was amused by the hoax: Adam Sisman, *A. J. P. Taylor: A Biography* (London, 1994) 390.

[12]Dover alludes to Taylor's letter of 24 November 1979 to his (third) wife, Eva Haraszti, in which he muses hypothetically that if Blunt were to resign from the Academy it 'would give me an excuse' to do so as well: A.J.P. Taylor, *Letters to Eva: 1969-1983*, ed. E.H. Taylor (London, 1991) 405. Dover's interpretation of this as a longstanding aim is questioned by Kathleen Burk, *Troublemaker: The Life and History of A.J.P. Taylor* (New Haven, 2000) 342-3, but accepted by Sisman, ibid., 393.

[13]Dover is referring to the third play, *Eumenides*, of Aeschylus' trilogy the *Oresteia*, where Orestes is acquitted of matricide on a tied vote: see *Eumenides* 733-53.

in which I emphasised that whatever decision we took, it must be one that I could defend before a possibly hostile AGM (to say nothing of the media) 'with conviction and vigour'.[14] This meant that Council must give an absolutely firm and clear statement of its reasons: if the vote was for expulsion, that treason is uniquely reprehensible, or that Blunt had transferred his allegiance to a totalitarian government inimical to the pursuit of scholarship; if for inaction, that the Bye-laws precluded expulsion; I also made a point (which in the event the Council did not take seriously) that even if we decided that Blunt was not a 'fit and proper person . . .' it was nevertheless open to us to abstain from making any recommendation to the AGM if we judged that such a recommendation on so divisive an issue would do more damage to the Academy than would be done by inaction.

As it turned out, my Vote of Athena was not needed; on March 14th I heard from George Caird that he would be unable to attend the meeting, and he was one of those opposed to expulsion. The vote was 8 to 7. This was confirmed without further discussion at the last Council meeting (May 16th) before the AGM.

When the agenda for the AGM went out they included with Council's recommendation notice of a counter-motion by Lionel Robbins and Helen Gardner, which 'deplored' Blunt's conduct but proposed that the Academy should not 'proceed further in the matter'. I prepared in advance three different press releases for three eventualities: acceptance of Council's recommendation, acceptance of the Robbins-Gardner motion, and rejection of both. The first emphasised Blunt's transfer of allegiance, the second and third pleaded the constraints imposed on the Academy by its Bye-laws.

The AGM was attended by 187 Fellows, and in the course of the afternoon a swarm of journalists accumulated in the courtyard of Burlington House. The discussion went on for a long time, until Professor L.C.B. Gower proposed that the meeting should 'pass on to the next item of the agenda'. Several Fellows jumped up to second this. Carswell murmured to me that Robbins had a right to have his own motion discussed, but I did not think that anyone has a right to have a motion discussed if a meeting declares that it does not wish to discuss it. Anyway, Robbins resolved that question by withdrawing his motion, and we straightway voted on whether to pass on. The vote was overwhelmingly in favour, 120 to 42, with 25 abstentions.†

---

†Lord Blake immediately left the meeting at a rapid pace, and it was widely assumed that his departure was an indignant protest, but he had warned me before the meeting of the time by which he would have to leave for the Lords.

[14]The amended memo, reproduced in *QR* p. 23, still hypothetically raised the question whether Blunt's allegiance to the Soviet Union intrinsically contradicted the *raison d'être* of the Academy, but did not indicate that this was Dover's own judgement. Strictly speaking, the phrase 'with conviction and vigour' related to the eventuality in which Dover had to defend a vote for *expulsion*, but the memo later stresses that he would need to be able to defend any decision without 'hesitation or equivocation'.

Three Fellows resigned from the Academy in the next few days: John Crook, Colin Roberts and T.C. Skeat. Letters, mostly hostile to the Academy, appeared in the *Daily Telegraph,* but no correspondence in the press can go on for ever. We moved up to St Andrews for the rest of the Long Vacation.

That, I thought, was that; but it wasn't.[15] The flame burst out from the embers in the first week of August. Charles Bawden resigned, and Oliver Gurney wrote to me to ask if I knew of 'a movement among the Fellows to fight the decision from the inside'; 'if so,' he added, 'I would gladly support it.' Robert Ogilvie warned me that my St Andrews colleague Norman Gash was hoping to persuade Fellows in Scotland to resign on December 31st if Blunt himself had not resigned by then. Sidney Allen wrote to me from Cambridge to say that he would do just that. My first thought was to stop the haemorrhage, and I had a talk with Gash on August 13th (whether on my initiative or his, I do not recall). The situation was as bad as I feared; not only Gash and Allen, but, I learned, also Plumb and Ian Christie were uttering the threat of resignation. Gash gave me the impression that he thought the AGM had been 'packed' by supporters of Blunt from the University of London. That was not so, for only 48 of the 187 attenders were from London, and of those 48 I knew that 11 favoured expulsion and 7 were against it; it was probably fair to assume that the remaining 30, whose views I did not know, were divided in the same ratio. (I discovered later that another passionate expeller[16] was so out of touch with reality that he had not bothered to come to the AGM, taking it for granted that expulsion would be overwhelmingly approved.) Anyway, Gash suggested that I would best serve the interests of the Academy by asking Blunt to resign.

My real feeling about the Allen-Christie-Gash-Plumb combination was the indignant resentment which one feels towards terrorists who threaten to blow up innocent passengers if they do not get everything they want. This was not entirely just, because the Academy was not a planeload of innocents but, in the eyes of the combination, the perpetrator of a crime; however, I felt as I did. A rule of procedure in dealing with terrorists is, I understand: play it cool, don't antagonise them, go along with them sympathetically until you have a good chance of frustrating their purposes. I was quite willing to put on that act, in the unhappy awareness that on occasion there is no way of saving the hostages except by concessions. Of one thing I was quite certain: the Academy's interests came first, and Blunt's interests nowhere at all. It was only mid-August, with four and a half months to go before the threatened resignations could take effect; how many more would there be? Gurney's letter haunted me, and I knew of another Fellow who had repented of his vote for absolution and was ready to join the rebels. On my reckoning, there could

---

[15] For continuation of the controversy in the course of August, see *QR* pp. 56–85.
[16] Dover identifies this person as Sidney Allen.

well be up to fifteen resignations. They could all be averted if Blunt resigned, and I thought it just possible that the four who had already resigned could be persuaded to accept re-election. It was therefore up to me somehow to cause Blunt to resign and at the same time to give as few people as possible any grounds for thinking that I was pressing him as hard as the rebels wanted me to; in short, to control the damage.

It so happened that Blunt had written to me a few days earlier to express his 'deep distress at the way the *Daily Telegraph* [was] using [him] as a stick with which to beat the Academy'. I now wrote to thank him for that, reminded him that I had not said a word to him about resignation while he was under threat, and went on to suggest that now, when there was no longer any threat to him, he might 'give serious consideration' to resigning as a means of 'healing the wound' in the Academy.[17] I had just finished the letter when I was telephoned by a man on the *Sunday Telegraph,* who asked me for my reaction to Plumb's letter to me. As I had received no letter from Plumb, I didn't know what he was talking about, and he explained that Plumb had written to me on August 11th (not knowing that I was in Scotland), declaring his intention to resign at the end of the year if Blunt had not resigned by then, and had sent a copy of the letter to the *Telegraph*. The *Telegraph* man read the letter to me over the phone. It was a hard blow because, whereas I had not thought it probable that Blunt would take my suggestion very seriously (in his position I would not have done so), it seemed to me now certain that he would not do so if he thought I had written at the behest of his fiercest adversaries. It was only twenty minutes to the last post from St Andrews, and vitally important that my letter should bear a postmark earlier than next morning's *Telegraph*; so I added a postscript to assure Blunt that I was not writing on anyone else's orders, whatever he might see in the papers next day. I also wrote rather angrily to Plumb and Allen, pointing out that the chances of Blunt's resigning were now greatly reduced.[18]

It seemed to me the right moment at which to write to *The Times,* appealing to the rebels (actual and potential) to abide by the overwhelming verdict of the AGM, and offering reasons why they should do so (it was time, by way of a change, for an intelligentsia-rousing piece in the eye-level press). For the first time, I had not brought my typewriter to Scotland, so I wrote in longhand, sent the letter to Carswell, and arranged with him that it should be typed and sent to *The Times* on the 18th if there had been no further developments by then. This went off on the 15th. Later that day Blunt rang me to say that he was indeed giving serious consideration to resigning. 'The trouble is,' he said, 'there are people who say they'll

---

[17] Dover kept no copy of this letter of 13 August: see p. 287 below; cf. *QR* p. 69, with p. 60 for Blunt's own letter of 8 August.

[18] Dover's letter to Plumb of 14 August (*QR* p. 69) is especially striking for the refusal to speak to Blunt in person, on the grounds that he did not wish to appear 'foolish or disingenuous' in Blunt's eyes or to be 'despised' by him.

resign if I do.' I exclaimed 'Good Lord!', and he half-laughed and said, 'Yes, I know, but that's what they say.' There was nothing much I could say then except to emphasise his freedom of action. Two days passed, and then another call from Blunt: he had decided to resign. I thanked him and said that 'on balance' I thought he had done the right thing.

I withdrew my letter to *The Times,* and thereupon did something idiotic, for which I have not forgiven myself: Audrey and I went off to spend the weekend in Alan's uncompleted house, which did not yet have a telephone.[19] This left John Carswell at the Academy to deal with the press. Knowing that Blunt had written to me, and that the letter in which I had sown the seed of resignation was in response to that, he drew the very reasonable inference that it was Blunt who had 'himself approached the President of the Academy about his position'. This created some misapprehensions; if I had had enough sense to estimate correctly the interest which Blunt's resignation would arouse in the press, I would have furnished John with copies of the relevant letters well in advance.

A letter of resignation from Alan Taylor came swiftly, declaring that he would have no part in a 'witch hunt'. I had always admired Taylor for his frequent clarity of perception and exposition – despite his preference for clarity over adequacy of explanation – and the sloppiness of 'witch hunt' was a disappointment; witch hunts, after all, occur when people think that something has gone wrong and look for a reason, and the Blunt case was very different from that. A *Daily Express* man, knowing of Blunt's homosexuality, asked Allen in a creepy tone of voice if there was a 'special relationship' between Blunt and Taylor. I was not tempted to any such absurd speculation, but I was disturbed by a letter from Helen Gardner, regretting that I had 'yielded to pressure from members of a minority', and even more so by one from Michael Wallace-Hadrill, who fully supported me but made an ominous reference to Fellows who 'approach[ed him]' for advice. Advice about what? I thought it best to send a memo to all Fellows, setting out the whole sequence of events and offering a rational justification for my own actions.[20] This went out on August 22nd, and I received twenty letters of support, including some from Fellows who had voted against expulsion at the AGM. Six letters were less friendly. One of them was a letter of resignation, subsequently withdrawn when Blunt himself persuaded the writer to think again.[21] Another, from an ex-Communist friend[22] whose judgement I had hitherto respected, told me 'Your conduct of the AGM did not suggest complete impartiality on the issue'; I reflected sourly that it must be

---

[19]For the 'Spartan' conditions in which Alan and his family were living at this date, see p. 239.
[20]The memo is reproduced in *QR* p. 79.
[21]The writer was Richard Cobb (Dover SN).
[22]Christopher Hill (Dover SN), who had been a tutorial fellow in modern history at Balliol when Dover himself was a fellow during 1948–55. Hill (1912–2003) had joined the Communist Party as a student *c.* 1934 but resigned in 1957 in the wake of the Soviet invasion of Hungary.

difficult to be so far up Stalin's arse for so long without suffering from some impairment of vision. Tony Andrewes, whose judgement I could never fail to respect, asked whether it is ever safe for a President to ask anyone to 'consider' anything, because the source of the suggestion necessarily lends it weight. E.H. Carr thought that to clear myself – or rather, to enable Fellows to decide whether I was in the clear or not – I needed to publish the letters I had exchanged with Blunt. That I could not do, because I had written to Blunt in longhand and kept no copy, and in any case the evidence which alone could show whether I put pressure on him was irrecoverable: the whole tone of our telephone conversations, conversations between two people who had known each other reasonably well for eight years.

In October 1980 Christie wrote a piece for *Encounter*, under the title 'A Confusion of Fellows',[23] in which what I had always regarded as the crucial issue, Blunt's covert support for totalitarian persecution of the humanities, was properly spelled out for the first time. I replied with a piece in the November number, explaining the constraints imposed by the wording of the Bye-laws and enlarging on two aspects of the matter which I thought needed to be brought into the open. One was the attitude of the non-academic public. It so happened that with the exception of a BBC producer, whose answer to the Blunt problem was a laconic 'Shoot him', no member of the public who spoke to me about Blunt was in favour of expulsion or any other punitive action (my words 'without exception' in *Encounter* were wrong; I had forgotten the producer). There are people who will find that hard to believe, because it is absolutely contrary to their own experience, but different individuals have different experiences. Those whom I knew as the fiercest enemies of Blunt were all academics, some of whom may have known that a KGB man convicted of a treason like Blunt's was stoked into a boiler-furnace by his indignant colleagues; and I must confess to having had a certain sympathy with the view that a nation which can tolerate traitors has a diminished chance of survival. The second aspect which needed emphasis was religious. One Fellow[24] told me privately that his vote against expulsion was determined by a Christian duty to forgive the repentant, but he 'did not have the courage' to say so in the debate. People find religion so embarrassing a topic that we shall never know how large a part was played by the duty to forgive, but among those who voted against expulsion I certainly recognised many whom I knew to be of strong Christian faith.

Did Blunt repent? He said that he did, and a Christian might feel a duty to believe him in the absence of evidence to the contrary, while others might be sceptical of any statement made in his own interest by a lifelong deceiver. Sir

---

[23]*Encounter*, October 1980, pp. 30–2.
[24]Dover SN identifies him as John McManners (1916–2006), at this stage Regius Professor of Ecclesiastical History at Oxford.

Douglas Logan[25] told me that Blunt alienated many of his potential supporters in London University by his 'complacency and arrogance' when he was interviewed on television shortly after the news of his treason broke. And did Blunt ever come entirely clean about his past? Or rather, did the Prime Minister come clean in her statement to Parliament? I put the question to a Fellow who, I suspected, was in a position to know.[26] 'Did Blunt do more damage than was stated in Parliament?' He inclined his head downwards about a centimetre and put his lips into a configuration which bore more resemblance to 'yes' than to 'no'. Or perhaps I was mistaken.

I never succeeded in persuading Crook, Roberts and Skeat to seek re-election to a body with which they were ashamed to be associated, though Bawden was re-elected in 1985. The nett loss, therefore, was five, including Blunt himself and Taylor. (A few years later Taylor enquired of the Secretary if there was any mechanism by which he could come back in. There wasn't, as he had by then passed the age-limit.) The damage had been controlled as well as could have been expected.

The last flicker of the Affair came in June 1981, when Taylor published a 'Postscript to the "Blunt Affair"' in *Encounter*.[27] He would not, he said, have 'revived' the matter if I had not 'set [him] the example', and he ignored the existence of Christie's piece, to which mine was a reply. His declared belief that 'intellectual liberty' was the issue at stake explains his resignation but does little credit to his intelligence.

Except for a few hours now and again during the week following August 17th, when I wondered if I had so misjudged the situation that by having any dealings at all with the rebels I had compromised my own reputation and damaged the Academy irreparably, I found the whole Affair, from beginning to end, absorbingly interesting and therefore intensely enjoyable. Disappointments, forebodings and shocks all afforded me the delights of solving practical problems. In the spring I managed to give up smoking for a couple of months, and again for three months later in the summer, so that all through the crises of July and August I was fuelled on toffee and nuts instead of nicotine, and it was only the start of term in October that caused a lasting relapse.[28] The only occasion on which any unguarded emotion in connection with the Affair broke through was in December, when I received an honorary degree from London University. Just as the party was breaking up after dinner, David Lang, rather drunk, upbraided me loudly for 'persecuting a poor,

---

[25]Sir Douglas William Logan (1910–87, Kt 1959), Principal of London University 1948–75.
[26]Sir Thomas Broun Smith (Dover SN): Smith (1915–88, Kt 1981) had held chairs in law at Aberdeen and Edinburgh and was a member of the British Academy Council during Dover's Presidency.
[27]*Encounter*, June 1981, pp. 93–4, with a reply from Dover, p. 94.
[28]See the further explanation of the temporary abstention from smoking at the end of this chapter. Dover was eventually forced to stop smoking in March 1994: see the note to p. 312.

sick old man'.²⁹ As he did not stay after launching this attack, I exclaimed 'Well, fuck you, then!' after his back, rather too loudly. Next day I wrote to him, apologising for my rudeness and hoping to put our discourse on a more rational level. He replied in sympathetic terms.

There were however some emotional stresses in other parts of my life. Not long before, it had seemed to me that an attractive young woman was making a very strong play for me. It was only the fifth time in my life that I had ever imagined such a thing; of the previous four occasions, all long ago, my imagination proved to be right in three, and on the fourth I never knew whether it was right or not. This time the signals were so intense and frequent (and we clicked instantly; you know how it is) that it remained only for me to take the last step with a decisive proposition. I hesitated, because I could see no justification for inflicting such an injury on Audrey, whose affection and support had been unfailing for more than thirty years. I cast around for a possible justification, and dredged up one occasion, during our first year at Corpus, on which she had failed to give me support which I badly needed. Perhaps that freed me from obligation. Well, no; the argument was patently sophistical and withered in the light of reason. So I passed over my only opportunity, and no doubt my last, to have an adulterous affair. A moral victory? Well, an affair would have been great fun (for me), and I was confident that I could manage it without alienating myself from Audrey; but suppose the other woman found that she could not treat it so lightly? That was a risk I was not prepared to take. On the other hand, suppose that she had not been simply (as she was) rather attractive, but dazzling, and suppose it had been easy (it would actually have been very hard) for us to meet frequently. What then? I might have adjusted my moral priorities to satisfy myself that what I was doing – whatever it was – was right.³⁰

I told Audrey all about it when the opportunity had passed and the desire had faded. I could truthfully assure her that the woman wasn't anyone she had met or was ever likely to meet.

So that was tidied up, but a different incident in the spring suggested that I was under more powerful stresses than I recognised. I was returning by train from an Academy meeting, reading a book in a crowded compartment, when I became suddenly aware that people were jumping up, seizing their briefcases and going out into the corridor. A young man on one of the seats opposite had vomited and was sitting motionless with his cupped hands, full of vomit, over his mouth. Everyone else departed hurriedly, either looking at him with fury or contempt or not looking at him at all, so that he and I were left alone. I remembered that I had one or two plastic bags in my briefcase, and I gave him one in which to empty the vomit. This

---

²⁹David Marshall Lang (1924–91) was Professor of Caucasian Studies in London University 1964–84.
³⁰À propos moral 'adjustment', Dover noted in his 1995 addenda: 'I know men who have contrived to reconcile their piety with their adultery.'

did not generate conversation, and after a little while, mumbling something about leaving him in peace and quiet, I followed the other passengers in looking for a seat elsewhere. I got one four coaches away, and was at once assailed by an inner voice commanding me to go back and look after the young man. I disobeyed; the train was very crowded, and it was a battle to get from one coach to another. After I got home I told Audrey the story, and by that time I found I was haunted by the fact that for all the other passengers the risk of contamination by a touch of vomit was more important than doing anything for someone who was taken ill. 'What's the *matter* with people?' I asked, and then burst into tears and kept repeating 'What's the *matter* with people?'

The combination of this reaction with my aborted love-affair (which at the time I was still keeping to myself, because my regret for a missed opportunity was still alive) induced me to make four rather expensive visits to a psychiatrist, who at the fourth visit confessed himself unable to find in me any symptoms of depression or indeed of any other medical condition within his province. I wondered if I had unwittingly discovered a psychological principle of 'displaced stress'; the corner of the table on which one is standing holds up, but the far corner cracks. Probably abstention from smoking was the cause of all the trouble. My main reason for giving it up was to encourage Alan to do the same, because he was smoking too much. When he gave it up overnight and showed no inclination to revert, my motive was lost, and I was back to normal by the end of 1980.

26 THE ASTON AFFAIR 1980–1985

Except for family honour or personal money matters, you should never kill. Maybe I'm not educated, but I know what I think, especially when it's true.
                    A Sicilian ex-soldier interviewed by **DANILO DOLCI**[1]

When I came to Corpus Trevor Aston was a very senior Fellow. He had been a tutorial fellow in History from 1952 to 1968; then, on his appointment as University Archivist and Director of the History of the University project, he was elected to a Senior Research Fellowship, without stipend but with rooms in College (his first marriage[2] was dissolved in 1969).

I knew from my confidential files that in the nineteen-fifties and sixties he had applied for several chairs, including one in Australia, but since then his devotion to the College seemed to have been single-minded. He combined an intimate knowledge of every stone and board of its fabric with a strikingly unsentimental readiness to accept and promote change. As College Librarian for many years he had persuaded the Governing Body to allocate the money required for the creation of an exceptional library. I valued his membership of the Buildings and Furniture Committee, because he was quick and thorough in doing his homework and fertile in ideas.

He had little respect for majority opinion when his ideas were not accepted. All the same, as late as 1979, when I knew that Thomas Charles-Edwards' term of office as Dean would expire the following summer, I seriously considered inviting

---

[1] 'The point of this quotation, which none of the numerous critics of this chapter have even mentioned, is that individuals differ remarkably in their attitude to "sanctity of life" – and are not notably open to reason. I would describe myself as "not open to reason" on my own fundamental moral choices.' (Dover SN)

[2] To Margaret Aston, neé Bridges; they had married in 1954.

Trevor to become Dean.[3] I knew from the file that he had needed psychiatric treatment in the nineteen-fifties; what the file did not tell me – nor did any Fellows, understandably preferring that I should form my own opinion in due course – was that he had also behaved in the nineteen-sixties in a way which had strained the tolerance of some of his colleagues past its elastic limit. Something of that was conveyed to me by two Fellows when I discussed with them the possibility of appointing him Dean; nothing like enough, though, to satisfy my curiosity. Two small incidents round about that time were disturbing. Once, when we were talking about collegiate life and he made a brief reference to his first marriage, I caught the gleam of a brutal and unimaginative cynicism; how coarse and violent it could be, I learned only after his death from people who had known him much longer than I. Upon his second marriage, in 1979, about which I had learned only on the grapevine, the College Secretary asked him for the date and place, for inclusion in the College Record. He forbade her to mention it, adding that the only member of the College who had known about it must have gossiped improperly, 'with what motive, I do not know'. Since a wedding is normally regarded as a happy event, the reason for gossiping was obvious enough – except to someone who would rather impute bad motives than good.

Frank Lepper was due to retire in the summer of 1980, and would have to leave 3 Merton Street, a splendid old house almost opposite the College. It was agreed that it should be let unfurnished to the Astons, even though there was a case for converting it into undergraduate accommodation, and some Fellows whose memories went back more than ten years prophesied trouble from any commercial transaction between the College and Trevor. They were proved right, but I suppose I was still in the Astonian camp, and my own advocacy secured a majority. The opportunity for a good deal of refurbishing of the house existed – I can hardly say it was 'needed', because some argued that what had been good enough for the Leppers was good enough for the Astons – but the fact that the house would be empty from July to October created a now-or-never situation. After the details had apparently been settled and the cost allocated, snowballing began; Trevor kept an eye on the work every day and constantly asked for changes and additions. A state of war developed between him and Don Wild, who was Domestic Bursar at the time, and necessarily spread to the Bursar.[4] The contractor didn't mind, because his estimate included an allowance for 'the Aston factor'. Each side thought that I favoured the other. To make peace I proposed that whatever was done to 3 Merton Street should be regarded as done for the College rather than for any particular occupant of the house; this was grudgingly accepted, and a few years later it turned out to be a decision of accidental wisdom. There was bickering about Trevor's

---

[3] Thomas Charles-Edwards was a tutorial fellow in modern history at Corpus 1971–96.
[4] The Estates Bursar was Brian Campbell: see n. 13 to p. 250. On Don Wild, cf. p. 252.

contract of lease; on one point (I forget now what it was) the College capitulated, whereupon Trevor demanded (but did not receive) a fee for 'getting the College out of a difficulty', because we had adopted his wording. Trouble, too, inevitably, over the division of the garden between 3 Merton Street and the adjacent College house, Kybald Twychen. He wrote me long letters, and I replied by letter, doing my best to get through to him by reason and candour, but without brutality. He rightly thought that any Fellow who was aggrieved or in trouble of any kind should be able to come and talk to me, and I made time for him.[5] He told me on one occasion that he always felt better after talking with me, and I was glad to hear that, but I wished that my amateur psychotherapy could have an effect which would last more than forty-eight hours.

Things got worse in 1982. When I came back from my sabbatical term,[6] he had taken against the Governing Body as a whole, apparently because it had failed, preoccupied as it was with acute problems of space, to leap with joy when he offered to give the College his grand piano. His Fellowship came up for its seven-year renewal in July; as a rule, such a renewal went through on the nod, hardly giving the Fellow concerned (who was required to leave the room for that item of business) time to close the door behind him. This time there was an embarrassing silence, until hands crept up slowly, one after another, in sufficient number to give the required majority.[7] I don't know if he had any knowledge, or even suspicion, of what had happened, but later in the summer he came to see me because, he said, he felt that all was not well between himself and his colleagues, and he couldn't understand why. I reminded him of an occasion – it was my first evening in College after my sabbatical – when he had exclaimed 'Fuck the College!' loudly enough to stop a conversation in another part of the room, and I told him that he often smelt strongly of gin by mid-morning. No one, he said, had ever seen him drunk (this was untrue) and 'I *never* drink gin!' Then he gave a sheepish laugh as his eye fell on the glass of gin and tonic in his hand, which he had chosen when I offered him a drink. It was not long before he was weeping and declaring that he was 'the worst historian in Oxford'. I was able to tell him that even among Oxford academics, who are not, by and large, the most charitable portion of humankind, I had never heard anyone question his professional competence. Trevor's mood of extreme humility and self-deprecation was very rare, and I did not encounter it again.

At the end of 1982 we had to consider what the rent of 3 Merton Street should be for the next three-year period, and we asked our agent to go over the house, after due notice, and give us his opinion. Trevor professed to have believed that the purpose of the agent's visit was to check whether anything more needed to be done

---

[5] Cf. *IPC* 97, 'after eight years of trying to do my best with him', and *ICNA* 104, 'for eight of those years he'd had a great deal of support and help from me'.
[6] The sabbatical during which Dover went on a world lecture tour (pp. 272–3).
[7] For this significant detail and its interpretation, see further on p. 300 with n. 22 below.

to the house. When he discovered its true purpose he was enraged and wrote to me to say that he had instructed his solicitors to sue the College for obtaining entry by false pretences. This was absurd, because the letter he had received in advance from the Bursar made the situation perfectly clear in the first paragraph. When he rang me to ask if he and his wife could come and see me, I told him that they could not, because now that he had instituted legal proceedings all communication about the house should be between his solicitor and the College's. He was silent for a bit, and then started: 'Surely you must admit that I was totally misled...' For once, I got angry, shouted 'No, I don't. Read the letter!', and slammed the phone down. That afternoon he dropped me a note resigning his Fellowship. Maybe I should have welcomed that and circularised the other Fellows immediately, telling them the fact without comment. I did not feel, though, that I could allow even a Trevor Aston to turn his life upside down in a moment of childish rage; so I did nothing, and next day received the expected telephone call from him. His resignation, he said, was 'the maddest thing [he'd] ever done', and he begged me to disregard it. I sent it back to him and promised I would not tell anyone else about it. I suspected that he might have played this game with my predecessors, but I did not know that he had, and I had some respect for the general rule that anyone who resigns for the first time should be given the chance to think again. A second time is a different matter.

In 1984, by which time Trevor had acquired a flat in London and a cottage in an unspoilt part of Spain, he announced his intention of giving up the tenancy of 3 Merton Street, and he asked to come back into College. Since, in addition to his work for the History of the University, he was editor of *Past & Present*,[8] he needed quite a lot of space for people as well as books. There was only one set of rooms which would do, and that only if a bathroom were converted into working space. He said he would be content to use the communal bathroom off the staircase. When the adequacy of the rooms was questioned at a College Meeting he took offence and stalked out. He got his way, but wrote me a long letter in which he berated the Governing body for persecuting him and attributed their malice to jealousy. I told him later that it was the maddest letter I'd ever had. 'Perhaps I *was* mad,' he said, and told me about his medication, which included lithium. It was characteristic of him to profess robust rationality and objectivity until there was no profit left in that line, and then to switch to an appeal for compassion on the grounds of mental illness.

The incidents to which I have devoted these peevish pages are only a sample, not a catalogue. Between May 1982 and October 1985 I had few opportunities to withdraw attention from Trevor.

---

[8] A high-profile journal of social and cultural history founded in 1952 and edited by Trevor Aston from 1963 until his death.

The scale and richness of the Corpus library are one of Trevor's two most notable memorials *(Past & Present* is the other), but they were also what in the end brought him down. Starting from the base-line of the nineteen-fifties, when it was necessary to raise an undergraduate library to a good standard, the library budget was regularly kept in line with the annual index of book-prices, and that principle was not questioned, until by the early nineteen-eighties we were spending far more than many much larger colleges.[9] What Tutors asked the Library to buy, it bought; but it bought a great deal more, at Trevor's own discretion. Observation of what was appearing on the shelves suggested that he regularly spent an inordinate amount on the history of the visual arts, ostensibly in the hope that the eyes of undergraduates would be opened. As it was hard to make a rational change in purchasing policy on the basis of mere impression, in 1982 some Fellows began to ask for a termly classified accessions list, a demand which seemed to me entirely justifiable. Trevor, however, prevaricated persistently and ingeniously. Relations between him and the library staff deteriorated to the point of breakdown. What was more important, Trevor alienated the other members of the Library Committee, who persisted in their demand for accessions lists until he ran out of excuses. The crisis came when the Committee, entertaining a suspicion (which, to my mind, was not demonstrably justified) that in formulating the budget for 1985 Trevor had suppressed some inconvenient facts about the annual index of prices, decided that David Cooper, the Assistant Librarian, should attend its meetings, as was normal for Assistant Librarians in other colleges. Rather than sit at the same table as David, Trevor resigned the office of Librarian. We framed a new statute, defining the responsibilities of the Library Committee, a 'Fellow-librarian' and a 'Librarian-in-charge', and devised a simple scheme of priorities for all proposed purchases.

Within a few minutes of arriving back from South Africa in September 1985 I learned that Trevor trouble, acute and insupportable, had broken out in my absence and reached a peak that very morning.[10] His wife had made it clear to him that she was seeking a divorce, a matter in which she received widespread sympathy. Trevor had thereupon taken an overdose and told the porter, who told the doctor, who ensured that the overdose was not fatal and, with a colleague, 'sectioned' Trevor for compulsory detention in the Warneford.[11] After a few days Trevor escaped and disappeared, but was traced by the police and brought back to the Warneford. Judging before long that the danger of suicide was past, the hospital allowed him to discharge himself, and he returned to his rooms in College. During these events

---

[9]See the further details of expenditure in *CCH* 412–13, with 404–20 for a fuller narrative of Aston's relationship to the college library, differing in emphasis at various points from Dover's.

[10]For Dover's South African trip, see p. 320. On the mounting problems involving Aston between August and October 1985, one should consult the account in *CCH* 415–18 and Ewen Bowie's chapter in *S&C*; cf. the Introduction, 9–11.

[11]The Warneford Hospital, at Headington, near Oxford, is a specialist NHS unit for psychiatric services.

his conviction that he was persecuted by a conspiracy of his enemies was greatly strengthened, and some lifelong friends – including Dick Southern,[12] a man of exceptional integrity and charity – were rejected with bitterness. The doctors who had sectioned Trevor were forbidden by him to set foot in his rooms again, and after his death I found among his papers a long narrative accusing nurses at the Warneford of insulting and unreasonable behaviour. By now the locks on the London flat had been changed, and there was an injunction to prevent him from trying to communicate with his wife. He therefore had to stay in College or go to Spain, and for a while he stayed in College, drinking a lot of whisky. On the morning of the 27th[13] he staggered out of his urine-soaked bed, fell down some stairs in the Fellows' Building, shouted frighteningly at two cleaners who tried to help him, made his way to the Lodge (attracting unfriendly looks from members of a conference staying in College) and got the Porter to ring for a taxi to take him to Heathrow; but he was too drunk to find his money or his air ticket to Spain, so he returned eventually to his rooms.

At lunchtime John Nowland, the Senior Common Room butler, took me aside. Over the years he had been marvellously patient with Trevor, because he combined a talent for tolerance and compassion with rough-spoken candour; he was certainly more supportive than any of the Fellows could have been. Now he was in a bitter mood. 'I'll look after him, but no more molly-coddling. I've told him so. It's disgusting. What would happen to any of *us*,' he asked, 'if we got drunk in public like that? How long would we keep our jobs?' I didn't answer, because we both knew. 'Well, President,' said John, 'it's *your* problem now.'

In the course of that day and the next six different Fellows and Lecturers came in to see me, and a seventh rang me up, to tell me about the state Trevor was in, because I 'ought to know'. No doubt they expected me to do something about it. Since they themselves had no idea what to do, I hope they judged me leniently when I hadn't either. I called an informal meeting of six other Fellows, in order of seniority after Trevor, people who had known him before my time, and their sentiment was expressed unanimously, promptly and ruthlessly.[14] We had to get rid of the man; we couldn't have him lurching around the Front Quad after the

---

[12]Sir Richard Southern (1912–2001, Kt 1974) was Chichele Professor of Modern History at Oxford 1961–9 and President of St John's College, Oxford, 1969–81. Dover had known Southern since the early 1950s, when they were both fellows of Balliol.

[13]The 25th, according to the contemporary diary kept by another Corpus fellow, James Howard-Johnston (mentioned in Dover's text below), as reported in Bowie's chapter in *S&C*; cf. *CCH* 415 (with 414 n. 51).

[14]For the six fellows involved in this meeting, on 27 September, see *CCH* 415. Bowie, in *S&C*, challenges the accuracy of 'in order of seniority'. One of the fellows in question, Christopher Taylor, wrote to *The Times* on 16 December 1994, p. 17, after publication of *MC*, to take issue with part of what Dover's account implies was agreed at the meeting: for further details on this vexed point, see the Introduction, n. 33.

undergraduates had come up, or using violent language in the hearing of guests or visitors, or demonstrating to College employees that Fellows could get away with bad behaviour which would not be tolerated in people with less secure jobs. Trevor held his Senior Research Fellowship by virtue of his appointment as Director of the History of the University. If, as rumour from time to time suggested, the committee responsible for that project was perturbed by the slowness of its progress, it might conceivably remove him from its direction, and his Fellowship could then be formally terminated. This, however, turned out to be a non-starter. It was, of course, open to us, under our statutes, to deprive him of the Fellowship regardless of his University appointment, but only by a two-thirds majority of those present and voting at a College Meeting. There could be no assurance of that requisite majority; out of thirty Fellows, some were Professorial Fellows who were not around often enough to know what dealing with Trevor was like, while others, especially among the younger Fellows, might be irrationally hopeful or indiscriminately compassionate. Even if the majority was secured, Trevor might win on appeal to the Visitor[15] (the Bishop of Winchester, *ex officio*), and the consequences of such a victory would be worse than the present situation. For a little while we considered the possibility of a bargain, offering Trevor an Emeritus Fellowship on condition he moved out of College. As he could not move out without finding accommodation elsewhere (if so minded, he could make that process last a very long time) and his London flat was now barred against him, there was no reason to think that he would agree to such a deal; moreover, as an Emeritus he would have dining rights, and if he exercised them often he would be frustrating the main purpose of the deal.

James Howard-Johnston urged me to consult Trevor's doctor and the two psychiatrists at the Warneford who had dealt with him, and I willingly took that advice. The doctor was inclined to doubt whether Trevor's behaviour came into a category with which medicine was expected to deal. He gave me some sympathy, and sowed in my mind the idea that something might be gained by treating Trevor as one would treat a sane and robust delinquent. Both the psychiatrists, however, emphasised that Trevor was a very dependent person – at the moment, dependent on one of them – and extremely vulnerable; a formal letter from me, whether cold or heated, threatening his tenure of his Fellowship, might push him into suicide. One of the psychiatrists told me, with fervour in her voice, how much she 'admire[d my] courage'. I was so mystified by this that I let the conversation end before I

---

[15]The euphemistic title of the person charged with ultimate authority to resolve disputes in the college. In the debate over the present chapter that followed the original publication of *MC* (see the Introduction, 11–15), John Tusa (1936–, Kt 2003), who had been very briefly President of Wolfson College, Cambridge, in 1993, wrote sardonically to *The Independent*, 29 November 1994, p. 15, to 'sympathise' with Dover by saying that 'the merest prospect of intervention by "The Visitor" is guaranteed to produce paralysis of will bordering on catatonia in any body of dons'.

could formulate the question, 'What would be an un-courageous way of dealing with the situation?' Maybe she meant that I sounded relaxed and cheerful, which was how I intended to sound. I had by then sent[16] a letter to Trevor in what I judged to be a frank and friendly tone, telling him that we just couldn't have Fellows falling around and shouting abuse at staff. I told him, as I had told him before, that I admired his energy and imagination and ambitions for the College. 'We all want,' I said, 'to see the good Trevor all the time and the appalling Trevor none of the time.' I sent a copy of the letter to the psychiatrists, and learned from one of them some weeks later that they had regarded it as a model of its genre. I was encouraged also by advice from John Bramble,[17] who was probably closer to Trevor than any of us. He had no doubt that Trevor's trouble all the time was alcohol, and emphasised that there is no cure for alcoholics until they have hit rock-bottom and cannot any longer deceive themselves about their predicament.

A couple of days later Trevor came to see me. It appeared that he had read my letter, and I was surprised at how well he had taken it. I did not realise that he had 'read' it in some curious way which allowed only the less unwelcome parts of it to filter through. He talked of his own history of mental illness, and it became obvious from the complacent way in which he expounded the difficulty of finding the right person to treat him – finding, that is to say, someone of whose theory and method he could approve – that no conception of any obligation to reduce the strain on the rest of us entered his head. A quarter of a century had passed in which he had not found a psychiatrist worthy of approval; and it seemed that so far as he was concerned the unsuccessful search could go on for the next quarter-century too. I told him that many Fellows had talked to me because they were worried about him. 'Worried that I'll commit suicide?' he asked. It was on the tip of my tongue to say, 'No, worried that you won't', but that would have been unjust to my more compassionate colleagues, and I took refuge in 'Worried about your state of mind'. We returned to his state of mind, in an unprofitable conversation which I had to bring to an end in order to get some lunch before a two o'clock meeting.

It was clear to me by now that Trevor and the College must somehow be separated, and my problem was one which I feel compelled to define with brutal candour: how to kill him without getting into trouble.[18] I recalled a story told to me

---

[16]The first printing of *MC* had 'Anyway, I sent ...', implying that this happened *after* the conversation with the psychiatrists. Dover changed the text in the second impression (1995), and explained this in an addendum (p. 264), in the light of information from James Howard-Johnston's diary (n. 13 above). The letter, which, unlike much of Dover's other correspondence with Aston, does not survive, was written a week earlier on 30 September (*CCH* 415).
[17]See n. 19 to p. 252.
[18]This disarmingly blunt sentence was quoted endlessly in the press, and interpreted diversely, during the controversy which followed the publication of *MC* in 1994: see the Introduction, 9–15, with n. 34 there for Dover's partial regret over his choice of words. In a letter to the *History Workshop Journal* 41 (1996) 262 (see p. 90 n. 16) he called the state of mind in question 'homicidal musing'.

by Frank Lepper some years before: Trevor had rung up Jim Urmson in the middle of the night and declared he was going to commit suicide that night, whereupon Jim said 'Don't be a bloody fool!' and put the phone down (that no doubt was why, when the Fellows and their wives gave a farewell dinner for the Urmsons, Trevor ostentatiously absented himself and insisted on his right to have dinner on his own in the SCR).[19] This gave me an idea: suppose he rang me and told me he had taken an overdose; could I just do nothing? I consulted a lawyer, only to learn that the law, as I might have expected, is not inclined to make things easy for those who plan to cause the death of others. I was warned that a deliberate act of omission could lead to a charge of murder.[20] I considered the possibility of declaring, if I successfully performed the crucial act of omission, that I had not for a moment taken him seriously and had judged that a dismissive reaction was the best way to bring him to his senses. I was, after all, familiar with his manipulative techniques. However, in the light of what the psychiatrists had said to me, it was obvious that such a plea would not stand up in court. There was also a question of conscience; I had no qualms about causing the death of a Fellow from whose non-existence the College would benefit, but I balked at the prospect of misleading a coroner's jury, whose raison d'être is to discover the truth.

As it happened, at our next meeting he put a dagger into my hand,[21] and I used it unthinkingly to greater effect than I could have achieved by calculation. He had re-read the letter which the psychiatrists had regarded as striking the right note, and protested vehemently against my words 'shouting vulgar abuse at College employees', declaring that since he never did such a thing he cannot have done it on the occasion to which I referred. Laboriously, I took him through the many occasions on which he had denied ever doing things which he then went on to do. We bogged down in quibbling, and I moved on to other contradictions; in particular, how he had claimed that he had been well for fifteen years, and was well now, only a few weeks after telling me that he was being treated for severe manic depression. 'It seems to me,' he said, after a pause, his voice becoming strident and bellicose, 'that allowance is made a hundred per cent for physical illness, but not even five per cent for mental illness.' I told him that what Fellows could not take was that he switched to the plea of illness only when the arguments by which he tried to wear us down had failed. At this point he said that his relations with the

---

[19] Jim (James Opie) Urmson was tutorial fellow in ancient philosophy at Corpus 1959–78. Frank Lepper: see note on p. 246.
[20] Whoever gave Dover this advice, it makes no legal sense to suppose that failure to react to a suicide attempt, as opposed to encouraging or assisting a suicide, could be construed as murder: see the discussion by Pamela R. Ferguson, 'Killing "Without Getting Into Trouble"? Assisted Suicide and Scots Criminal Law', *Edinburgh Law Review* 2 (1998) 288–314; n.b. 312 on the immediate point in this sentence of the text.
[21] For the tragi-comic misparaphrase of this clause as 'you put a dagger in his hand' in *IPC* 100, see the Introduction, n. 59.

Fellows had always been characterised by mutual affection and admiration until now, when his enemies had conspired to persecute him and were 'using' me. Indignant at such drivel, I told him of the embarrassing occasion on which his Fellowship was renewed by a small margin.[22] I can't say I felt any exultation in telling him that, but I certainly felt relief at coming out with the truth. 'You're trying to push me out of the College!' he said, his voice cracking into a squeak.[23] This was so obviously true that I didn't say anything, but walked restlessly up and down. I left it to him to speak next. Perhaps he hadn't expected that, because after a silence he muttered that I had given him 'too much to take on board' in his present situation, and swiftly left. During the next few days he sat around in the SCR talking to anyone willing to listen about the disastrous mistake the College had made in electing me President.[24]

On the night of October 16th I was rung up by a mutual friend,[25] not a member of the College, to whom Trevor had been talking a lot that day. Since her own husband had committed suicide, it caused her great anguish to hear Trevor talking the same way, and she felt that the danger-point was very close. I rang Trevor's doctor to discuss what we should do. As he had been forbidden by Trevor ever to see him again, we would have to force the door and no doubt use force also to get Trevor to the Warneford, a procedure which would be necessary if he had already

---

[22]Both *CCH* 416 and Bowie's chapter in *S&C* insist that there was no vote on this occasion, only a short pause before renewal was proposed; they do not mention that earlier in this chapter Dover himself referred to 'an embarrassing silence, until hands crept up ...' (293): that may be what he meant by the loose phrase 'small margin'. There is no doubt about the sincerity, at any rate, of Dover's memory: in an unsent letter to Aston of 29 June 1982 (in the Corpus Dover archive: see our Editorial Foreword), written just a week after the renewal of Aston's fellowship, Dover says that he had felt 'unbearably tense' on that occasion 'because I knew very well that your re-election was by no means a foregone conclusion'.
[23]See the Introduction, n. 62, for Dover's sense at the time of how 'wounding' the exchange was for Aston.
[24]In the 1995 reprint of *MC*, after the matter had been publicized by James Howard-Johnston in *The Independent* for 29 November 1994, p. 19 (see the Introduction, 11 with n. 36), Dover included the following important addendum (p. 264) about a book borrowed by Aston from the college library and found to be missing on 14 October: 'I omitted this from my narrative because I wrongly located it in 1984, and enough was enough. However, I learn from Charles Webster, Trevor's successor as Fellow-Librarian, that I wrote Trevor a letter about the book in the last few days before his death, and that I insisted on treating the loss as justifying a special enquiry by senior Fellows. As I don't remember writing the letter, and I am informed that no file copy of it has so far been found in the College, I cannot say more about its content or tone. Yet I must have sent it, because I do remember a telephone conversation with Trevor about the loss, which must have been on 15th or 16th October, and I don't think he would have rung me then unless he had had some communication to answer. The anxiety in his voice persuaded me that he had no idea where the book had gone.' Howard-Johnston's view, in the article cited above, that 'this may have been the last straw' which precipitated Aston's suicide, needs to be weighed against Dover's statement about the documents found beside Aston at his death (p. 301). Cf. the account in *CCH* 416–18.
[25]Identified as Vera Peters in *CCH* 418 n. 66. The date was corrected in the 1995 reprint of *MC*; the first impression had 'October 15th'.

taken an overdose but hardly justified on the strength of a friend's intuitive reaction to a telephone conversation. 'Trevor,' said the doctor, 'is by far the cleverest manipulator I've ever encountered.' I said that with the possible exception of my grandmother, I could say the same. We agreed that there was nothing to be done. The last person to see Trevor that night, as I learned later, was Elizabeth Rawson.[26] He promised her earnestly that he would not commit suicide.

But he broke the promise, which he had understandably made to reduce the likelihood that his purpose would be frustrated, for next morning he was found dead. I had to identify the body formally in the presence of the Coroner's officer. Beside the bed lay a desperately affectionate letter of farewell to his wife[27] and an official letter notifying him of the date of divorce proceedings. There was nothing accusatory, no outpouring of grievances except for the narrative of his escape from the Warneford.

If there was an inquest, I was not notified of it and saw no report in the newspapers.

Next morning I got up from a long, sound sleep and looked out of the window across the Fellows' Garden. I can't say for sure that the sun was shining, but I certainly felt it was. I said to myself, slowly, 'Day One of Year One of the Post-Astonian Era'. For a little while I even regretted my decision to retire in 1986. Two Fellows whom I had long recognised as the most humane of all my colleagues – one of them reacted to Trevor's behaviour in 1984 by saying, 'How awful it must be to be like that!' – told me that they could feel nothing but relief at his death.

We held Trevor's funeral service in the College Chapel, and Robin Nisbet said the appropriate things. In January we held a memorial service in the University Church, at which Alan Bullock and Rodney Hilton said more of the appropriate things; I knew that Trevor had wanted Dick Southern also to speak at his memorial service (an event which he had always taken for granted), but Dick declined, for reasons which I understood better when I heard his superb address at the memorial service for Michael Wallace-Hadrill.[28] Some time after the service for Trevor a Fellow of Magdalen told me, 'Corpus is the only college in Oxford which could have tolerated Trevor for so long.'

In the last year of his life Trevor put up a scheme for creating a small quadrangle of undergraduate accommodation in Merton Street by filling in the spaces south

---

[26]Elizabeth Rawson (1934–88) was tutorial fellow in ancient history at Corpus 1980–8.
[27]Judith herself told Paul Thompson that it was 'a beautiful love letter, conveying a sense of final peace' (see p. 263 of the article cited in p. 90 n. 16).
[28]Robin Nisbet: see note to p. 115. Alan Bullock (1914–2004, Kt 1972) was Master of St Catherine's College, Oxford, 1960–80, and Vice-Chancellor of Oxford 1969–73. Rodney Hilton (1916–2002) was Professor of Medieval Social History at Birmingham University 1963–82; Aston had been one of the editors of his Festschrift. On Dick Southern, see n. 12 to p. 296; Dover SN suggests that Southern thought Aston should not have a memorial service because he was not a Christian. Michael Wallace-Hadrill (1916–85) was Chichele Professor of Modern History at Oxford 1974–83.

of Kybald Street, and Geoffrey Beard, the architect who has done so much for late twentieth-century Corpus, produced a characteristically ingenious and attractive plan. If this plan is ever put into effect – and that is exceedingly unlikely, now that Corpus and Christ Church have collaborated in building on an Iffley Road site – I hope it will be called 'the Aston quad', or at any rate part of it 'the Aston Building'. It was his initiative and his alone.

27 ADMISSIONS 1982–1984

Anyone who wanted to be admitted to Oxford applied not directly to a college, but, like all other university applicants, to UCCA (the University Central Council on Admissions), putting Oxford as one of hrs top four preferences and also listing four colleges in hrs order of preference. UCCA sent a copy of the application form to the Admissions Office at Oxford, which in turn sent a copy to the college of the applicant's first choice. The Entrance Examination was held late in November,[1] interviews in December, and decisions were taken by Christmas. This was acceptable to UCCA, because it meant that applicants who had put Oxford first were disposed of, one way or the other, before other universities came to consider them. Cambridge followed roughly the same timetable.

There were, however, other routes into Oxford. Applicants who for one reason or another did not want to take the Entrance Examination could be interviewed in October in the hope of being offered a place conditional on the grades they obtained in A Levels the following summer. If they made a very favourable impression at interview they might be given a Matriculation Offer, requiring them to satisfy only the minimum requirements at A Level (hence the widespread gossip that 'you can get into Oxford on two E's', formally true if 'can' is given the right emphasis and intonation). Some, but not all, colleges participated in a 'Scottish scheme', offering to Scottish pupils who had a good record in the Scottish Certificate of Education at Higher grade a place conditional on their completing a course for the Scottish Certificate of Sixth Year Study. Other colleges made Matriculation Offers to pupils from Inner London schools intending to read PPE; others again operated similar schemes for pupils from designated areas for certain subjects.

---

[1] Dover does not spell out that the entrance examination was usually taken in the seventh term of the sixth form, requiring applicants to stay at school after (in England) their A levels, something easier to arrange at private than at most state schools. The abolition of the seventh-term option was to be one of the main recommendations of the Dover committee (pp. 306–7).

Though designed to increase opportunity, the growing complexity of the system came to be regarded by applicants and their advisors at school as baffling, because it made the applicant's choice of college harder; it was a matter not just of knowing in which special schemes, if any, a given college participated, but also of knowing the attitudes of individual colleges to alternative modes of application. Choice of college was taken much more seriously by applicants than it was when I left school and went where I was told; pupils in their penultimate year at school now tended to come to Oxford for a day, visit four or five colleges, interview the Tutors for Admissions, and decide on the best buy. Since our society has always cast the female in the role of shopper, the fashion for exploratory interviewing was set by the girls, but was soon taken up by boys. However sensible their decision, there were still some hazards built into the system. When we interviewed for Conditional Offers in October, we had no idea how good a field of first-choice candidates would present itself in the Entrance Examination a month and a half later; too many Conditionals, and we might find ourselves turning away better candidates in the examination; too few, and we would regret that if we had a weak examination field. The qualitative variation in that field, from subject to subject, year to year, and college to college, was wide and unpredictable. Suppose, for example, we regularly had four places available each year for a given subject; this year we might have only six first-choice candidates, four of them distinctly weak, for those places, whereas next year there might be a dozen, six of them very good. A reasonably good applicant in that subject who happened to have made Corpus hrs first choice this year would be lucky, whereas next year s/he could well be unlucky. It was not surprising that an article by a headmaster in the press spoke contemptuously of 'the Oxbridge lottery'.

At one of its meetings in 1980 the body of Admissions Representatives, a body which determines the procedures of the Admissions Office, showed itself aware of rising discontent in the schools and appointed a committee to formulate changes which might make the system more intelligible. I forget now what changes the committee proposed, but they were not accepted, and things went on as before (indeed, more so) until the meeting in November 1982, at which Keble announced that it proposed in future to hold its interviews for Conditional Offers at the same time as the Entrance Examination. There was an outcry at this, partly because it was thought to be unjust that an applicant who put Keble first and wanted a Conditional Offer should be precluded from having a second shot in the Entrance Examination, if unsuccessful at hrs interview for the Conditional, but mainly because most of us were possessed by a surge of feeling that could be expressed as, 'Oh, for Christ's sake, no more complications!' The outcome of that meeting was the appointment of a committee with a remit

> to review all the procedures by which undergraduates are admitted to Oxford, and to aim to arrive at a simplified procedure which will command the unanimous agreement of colleges (or the agreement of the great majority).

I was one of the fourteen people appointed to that committee, and as the senior head of house on it (the other two were Norman Crowther-Hunt, Rector of Exeter, and Christopher Ball, Warden of Keble) I was its provisional chairman. I had a different idea, and entertained the hope that I might persuade Rex Richards (Warden of Merton) to take on the chairmanship; he combines acumen, pertinacity and tact to a rare degree, he had proved an outstandingly good Vice-Chancellor, and – to my mind, an important consideration – he had been free of Admissions business and could look at our goings-on with fresh eyes. However, I did not succeed in persuading him, so I remained chairman of the committee.

Between December 1982 and the beginning of June 1983 we held twenty-seven meetings. The last three, beginning at five or half-past, went on until midnight or after; we completed our report and published it on June 3rd, the Admissions Representatives recorded their straw votes on its proposals later in June, and the substantive vote came towards the end of October. In the course of our work we held two meetings with representatives of Cambridge colleges, because it seemed to us advantageous from the schools' point of view that Oxford and Cambridge should move in the same direction at the same time. The Cambridge people learned plenty about the way our thoughts were going, but we learned nothing at all about theirs. That was partly because Cambridge did not have, as we did, a body of Admissions Representatives with authority over the colleges, but mainly, I suspect, because they wanted to wait and see what we did, in order to devise a different procedure which might appeal to schools more and so divert good applicants from Oxford to Cambridge. They did just that in 1984, adopting a two-stage process of a type which we had considered and rejected. Some schools like it, but the statistics since 1984 do not suggest that there has been any significant redirection of strong candidates from Oxford to Cambridge.

When I told colleagues the terms of my committee's remit and came to the words 'which will command the unanimous agreement of colleges', the usual reaction was laughter at the very idea that colleges would ever agree unanimously about anything. I had to admit that it was an unusually daunting remit. Committees are commonly required to recommend what they think should be done, but mine had to recommend what it thought other people would think should be done. It would have been very easy for a small group of like-minded people to devise an admissions system of dazzling simplicity which would be abhorrent to all colleges, but it would have been a waste of time, and in any case we were not, when we began, at all like-minded; we had to become so, and that took twenty-seven meetings spread over six months. On a couple of occasions Crowther-Hunt seemed to be irritated by Peter Neumann,[2] and I once felt a little annoyed at Christopher Ball when he warned us portentously of what might follow from our

---

[2] Peter Neumann was tutorial fellow in mathematics at Queen's College, Oxford, 1966–2008.

failure to get on faster but made no suggestion as to how we should do so. Otherwise, from beginning to end of what became an exhausting process, we worked together happily, constructively, sometimes with reasons for laughter.

I thought at the beginning that we might send out a questionnaire to all colleges, asking fundamental questions such as 'Do you want to set a written examination to (a) all applicants, (b) some applicants, (c) no applicants?', and going on from there to a breakdown into more detailed questions, but Crowther-Hunt thought that this approach was 'too philosophical', and the others agreed. So we simply asked all colleges what changes they would like to see made. We wrote also to teachers' organisations and other universities, and made it known that we welcomed letters from individuals and schools. Altogether we received 158 communications, and everything went into a digest updated weekly. We also spent time on statistics which showed, among other things, that applicants who had been accepted in their fourth term in the sixth form performed just as well in their final examinations at the University as those accepted in their seventh term, after A Levels.

Since all of us had extensive experience of operating admissions procedures,[3] visiting schools and answering applicants' enquiries, it was not surprising that of all the hundreds of suggestions made to us there was only one (the idea that the Entrance Examination might be moved from November to June) which was new to any of us. We were struck by the fact that no category of respondent, whether it was colleges, maintained schools or independent schools, was able to offer a united view. Some heads thought that such-and-such a change would increase our field of applicants fourfold, others that it would make no difference at all. Some colleges were in favour of making everyone take a written examination, some wanted it abolished altogether. And so it went on; depressing, in one way, but from another point of view, liberating. It was up to us to work out, by painstaking discussion, in the light of the best information available to us, the probable consequences of any given change. The most intractable difficulty lay in the interdependence of our decisions and therefore of our recommendations. We could not decide what to do about A until we knew what we were going to do about B, and B all depended on C, but C could not be decided except in the light of the decision on A. For three months we tried to find the right point at which to cut into this chain and string it out into a linear sequence. At one stage I was so concerned about what I felt to be my own inability to find that point (what, after all, are chairmen *for*?) that I offered to resign; but there was no rush of volunteers, so I stayed. Eventually one of our firm preferences, once agreed, had a domino effect, and everything was straightforward from then on. We were able to recommend (with dissent recorded

---

[3] Dover had had experience of admissions both as Tutor for Admissions at Balliol (pp. 125–7) and as Dean of Arts at St Andrews (pp. 147–8).

by only one member on one of the recommendations) that only applicants in the fourth term of the sixth form should be admitted to the Entrance Examination; that all others, plus any fourth-term applicants who so wished, should be selected on interview and record, without examination; that all offers, of whatever kind, should be made at the same point in the year, December; that all applicants should be permitted to express a preference for up to three colleges, in order, but should also be entitled to say 'no preference'; and that applicants who did so should be allocated to colleges in a way which would equalise, as far as possible, the ratio of applicants to places.

There was a moment at which I felt rather sick: one member of the committee said that he wouldn't dream of admitting an applicant whom he did not think he would enjoy teaching. I thought of my days as a professor at St Andrews, when I never knew, until I went into my lecture room on the first day of the year, who my pupils would be, and that hadn't worried me in the least; if anything, it made life more interesting. I hope I was able to sow in a corner of my colleague's mind the notion that it is essential to look at the whole process of university admission from the standpoint of the applicant and to concentrate on getting into the university (forget about colleges) as many as possible of those who both wish and deserve to be there.

When the report came out, Oliver Taplin[4] and I held a press conference in Magdalen. It was not a success; a man from the *Oxford Mail* turned up, no one else. The range of subjects about which the papers declare that the public has a right to know evidently did not include a simplification of Oxford's admissions procedures. What did crop up before, during and after the deliberations of the committee was the fact that forty per cent of Oxford applicants from independent schools are accepted, but only thirty per cent of those from maintained schools, with the consequence that not far short of one half of all British undergraduates at Oxford come from the independent sector. In the final examinations, however, the difference disappears; at any rate, in 1982 the ratio of firsts, seconds and thirds was identical for both sectors. This suggested that the admissions procedure might not be very good at sorting applicants who had been intensively prepared for the Entrance Examination from those whose potential, comparatively undeveloped at the stage of application, was none the less equally high. My committee was criticised (and still is) for not addressing itself to that question. Our defence against the criticism is twofold. In the first place, no matter how important and urgent the desirability of giving a fairer deal to the maintained sector, that was not the problem we were told to solve by the body which appointed us; if I'm hired to decorate a drawing-room, I don't submit plans for turning it into a dining-room. Secondly, there is no way in

---

[4]Tutorial fellow in Classics at Magdalen College, Oxford, 1973–2008; later, Professor of Classical Languages and Literature 1996–2008.

which an adjustment of the ratio between the two sectors could be *guaranteed* except by the imposition of quotas which treated the category of school from which an applicant came as more important than the applicant's own abilities; and I, for one, was not willing to recommend that. The best way to make an adjustment of ratio probable – as opposed to guaranteeing it – had long been known and put into practice: visits to schools by former pupils now at Oxford, and Open Days on which pupils could come and meet undergraduates and tutors. We didn't need a committee to discuss that; the colleges themselves, and the Oxford University Students' Union, were doing all they could. To my mind, one of the most important relevant data emerged from the statistics my committee collected: in five sample areas of England, both urban and rural, north and south, the percentage of university applicants from maintained schools who made Oxford or Cambridge their first choice lay between 5% and 8%, whereas the corresponding figure for the independent sector was 17–35%. There are plenty of good departments in universities up and down the country, plenty of schools in which no teacher has an Oxford or Cambridge degree and many of the strongest pupils may be encouraged to go elsewhere.

When our report was submitted to the Admissions Representatives it enjoyed a degree of success which six months earlier had seemed inconceivable. We made nineteen recommendations, but three of them could be subdivided, so that the true total was twenty-four. Four were accepted unanimously, seven by a majority of 27–1, and eight more by majorities between 26–2 and 20–8.* Three underwent minor amendment, and two were rejected. Neither of those rejected was particularly important to me, but I suspected that there was trouble lurking in the narrow majority by which our recommendation that 'no statements by any college about preference for one mode or another should appear in the prospectus' went through, and in fact individual colleges later decided that they would openly express preferences in respect of certain subjects. It had become apparent to us in the course of our work that although it is a college, in all cases, which takes the final decision on the acceptance or rejection of an applicant, when it comes to preferences for one mode of selection over another an individual Fellow is likely to agree not with the other Fellows of hrs own college but with people in the same Faculty who are Fellows of other colleges.

One of our recommendations which went through on the nod (27–nil, with one abstention) was that entrance scholarships and exhibitions should be entirely dissociated from admission procedures and awarded for meritorious performance at the end of the first or subsequent years of an undergraduate's course. This was grief to the older generation of dons and schoolteachers, who attributed it to savage and reckless egalitarianism on the part of my committee.[5] I could well

---

*I have simplified by treating an abstention as a vote against.

[5] For one example of a complaint about Dover's own 'egalitarianism', see the review of *MC* by Max Beloff in *The Times Higher Education Supplement* for 23 December 1994, p. 21, with the Introduction, 16.

remember, though, that it was seriously discussed in Balliol thirty years earlier, and it must have been discussed since then in other colleges also. No one dared to make the first move, for many schools which sent their best pupils to Oxford liked to be able to publish a list of winners of entrance awards in their annual reports and would direct those good pupils towards colleges which continued to offer awards. The summer of 1983 was the first occasion on which the colleges held hands, took a deep breath and jumped together.[6]

---

[6] The recommendations of the Dover committee were implemented from the start of the academic year 1985–6. For a brief appraisal of the changes against the background of larger trends, see Michael Brock, 'The University since 1970', in *HUO* 739–74, at 753–6.

28 BEST BEFORE 1983–

We have now entered upon a new phase of the struggle.
JEFFERSON DAVIS after the fall of Richmond[1]

I had the idea that after my father had died I might at last be free of the recurrent spells of physical feebleness and tiredness which had so robustly defied all impertinent attempts at diagnosis that they were pretty plainly psychosomatic.[2] For a couple of years it seemed that my prediction was right, because I was in good shape throughout 1979 and 1980. I had a bad spell in the spring and early summer of 1981, then a long remission broken only by one day in 1982, our last day in Australia. After the work of the Dover Committee was completed in June 1983 we went off to Germany, where I lectured in Hamburg, Göttingen, Cologne and Konstanz. I was conscious of a pressure which came near to defeating me while I was composing and translating my lectures. The weather was very hot in Germany and just as hot when we returned, and after term was over and we had come up to St Andrews I felt in a more wretched condition than I had experienced since my brief collapse in 1959.[3] Swamped with self-pity, I spent hours lying in the shade in the garden, sometimes tearful, sometimes unable – and this was a completely new experience for me – to find relaxation in academic work. Sleeping was no problem; I went to sleep at night in a matter of seconds, and woke much later in the morning than I wished to. The trouble was weakness in the limbs, shortness of breath, irregular beating of the heart, a feeling of emptiness in the torso, and a relentless hissing in the ears. Things improved later in the summer, when Catherine came up

---

[1] From the final proclamation, issued in the dying days of the US Civil War (4 April 1865), of the Confederacy President, Jefferson Davis: full text at https://jeffersondavis.rice.edu/archives/documents/people-confederate-states-america. Dover's choice of epigraph resonates sardonically with the chapter's account of physical and psychological decline.
[2] The personal side of Dover's narrative picks up from the death of his father in ch. 21. For his view of the 'psychosomatic', cf. p. 154.
[3] See p. 154 for this episode.

to St Andrews for a week and she and I walked up Mount Keen from Glen Esk, I in the lead by a big margin on the way up and she in the lead by a bigger margin on the way down. Mount Keen is a short and easy walk by Highland standards; I could not doubt that an era in my life was over and that from now on fatigue would be my normal condition and spells of fitness a lucky break. That is how it has turned out. The first week of our stay at Cornell in 1984 and the first fortnight of our month at Pietermaritzburg in 1985[4] were spoilt (though not for anyone except ourselves, because I always come to life in a lecture-room and in company which I don't wish to bore or embarrass) by a physical weakness so intense that I often imagined myself dropping dead on the way to the Department. I had a thorough medical examination in 1983 and again (from a champion diagnostician in Oxford) in 1986; and in 1991, after a short attack of flu at Stanford left me desperately enfeebled, I underwent every test that the Palo Alto Clinic could think of. The resultant diagnosis was Post-Viral Chronic Fatigue Syndrome, a (comparatively) concise label for 'You are radiantly healthy, and it's too bad that you feel ill all the time'. That summer my own doctor decided to treat me as if I were suffering from depression, and put me on paroxetine for several months. This raised my general level of well-being a significant stage, at which I remained. The causes of my occasional straying on to a higher or lower level are mysterious; sometimes, perhaps, physical exertion, sometimes lack of exercise, sometimes working late and sometimes not ... a warning not to confuse causation with coincidence. I drink coffee immoderately (a litre a day, half of it decaffeinated), smoke in moderation (a hundred Extra Mild a week),[5] and drink alcohol only as a host or guest. I don't criticise doctors for not yet finding the cure I need, any more than I criticise palaeontologists for not yet knowing at what stage of hominid evolution articulate speech developed, or physicists for not yet finding the ultimate particle.

At Cornell I switched from ill to well after spending twenty-four hours in bed over a weekend, and at Pietermaritzburg the switch came when I was taken for a stiff walk in the Drakensberg by Geoff and Valerie Chapman. They remarked that they didn't know anyone else of our age who could have done the walk, and we welcomed the compliment, but it was my swansong. I knew that I would never now do four two-day walks (sleeping rough) which I sadly, so often, wish I had done when my legs bore me well: Ossian to Dalwhinnie via Ben Alder, Kinlochewe to Poolewe via A' Mhaighdean, Cairn Toul from Carn Ban Mor, and Creag Meagaidh by a route which I studied on the map and looked at from below. The Drakensberg was Audrey's swansong too, because arthritic stiffness in her knees keeps her away from gradients; and her regret is as deep as mine.

---

[4]The Cornell and South African trips are both described in the next chapter.
[5]Dover was required by his doctor to stop smoking in March 1994 in advance of an operation on his abdominal aorta.

Well before I paid my first visit to Cornell – in fact, before the end of 1983 – I came to a decision about my date of retirement. I was entitled to stay in office until 1990, by which time I would be seventy, and I began to feel that that was rather late in the day. I therefore decided that I would go in 1986, and in order to give the College as much time as possible in which to seek my successor I made my decision public at the beginning of 1984. Wear and tear had something to do with the decision; the level of energy and concentration I had sustained in the course of chairing the Committee on Undergraduate Admissions seemed somehow to have used up my reserves, Trevor's bad behaviour was getting worse, and there were some underlying problems on the domestic side of the College which I did not think I could solve. It was not that I disliked administration; there were days when I came into my office after breakfast with an eager appetite for the morning mail and an almost arrogant confidence that whatever problems it raised would be at least manageable, mostly soluble, and all interesting. I could not deny, though, that I wanted to spend more time on research. Three books of which I was the author, and two of which I was co-author, had been published since I arrived at Corpus, but two of those five had been completed before the end of 1976, and in the other three I was, so to speak, living off my fat. Of seventeen articles which I published during 1976–1983, nearly half had been prepared in the previous year or two. Remembering how surprised I had been at my interview in 1975 when I found that the Fellows had not formulated any kind of job-description for the presidency, I thought it would be helpful to them if I gave them a written analysis of the job I had found myself doing, and after keeping a careful check on my expenditure of time over three sample periods I discovered that I had been spending one third of my time on academic research and publication (my working week, counting College-related entertaining as work, consistently came out at fifty-five hours, exactly the result I had got from a similar analysis at St Andrews some years earlier). I began to consider the possibility that I would find three thirds nicer than one third. Another consideration was that I was receiving invitations from America and Canada for fairly extended visits in term-time, and I could not tell them, 'Okay after September 1986' before I had said anything to the Fellows about the way my thoughts were going.

Discontent with my physical feebleness has been greatly aggravated by deafness. I became aware in 1983 that my hearing was deteriorating, because Audrey could hear bird-song which I could not, and Catherine, who at the time was 'house governor' of the ear, nose and throat hospital in Grays Inn Road, arranged for both of us to be examined by her favourite audiologist. We were both rated sub-normal and given hearing-aids, which have certainly improved matters for me (Audrey seems really not to need hers), but they are disastrously unselective at noisy parties. The worst of it is that there are many people with whose voices I have no problem at all, but others whose speech comes through to me only as a meaningless murmur. The second category includes people whom I like and with whom I would gladly talk more, but embarrassment drives me to avoid conversation with them. This degree of deafness has extinguished my last hope of making significant progress in foreign languages before I die. In some quarters I have a reputation as a good linguist, because I can read eight languages, have an elementary knowledge of several more, understand the grammatical structure of a great number, and have given intelligible, even (at times) elegant, lectures in Italian, French, Spanish, German and Dutch. But in fact I fail on the basic test of linguistic competence, because except in Italian (during some periods of my life), and except on academic subjects, I have great difficulty in understanding what is said to me at normal speed. If the speed is reduced, the difficulty vanishes and I understand everything, but I still cannot follow what foreigners say to one another. I have seen many foreign films since I was eighteen, and latterly a fair number of foreign television programmes, but my ability to understand the dialogue remains exactly where it was sixty years ago; that is to say, I understand nothing whatever except 'Yes', 'No' and some exclamations. If I tune in my radio to a French station and light on a discussion, I recognise French by its sound-pattern, but after listening for several minutes I may still be unable to decide whether the topic is political, scientific or artistic. An irrepressible 'If only...' always flitted about in my mind: if only I could saturate myself in film and radio and television, one day I might break through. That day will not come now, and I find myself increasingly debarred from understanding any form of my own language except a clearly articulated standard South English, Standard Scottish or Standard American. Much television – particularly comedy, thrillers and eye-witness reports – and long sequences in films have become a meaningless noise, and even live theatre is often unrewarding. In 1990 I went to a performance of *The Winter's Tale* at Stanford. The actors were British, and distinguished, but they favoured the throwaway style which is now customary in performing Shakespeare. After a bit I caught the words 'many thousands', which reassured me that the play was being performed in English and not, as I had been tempted to think, Vietnamese. After that I occasionally caught 'Bohemia', 'sir' and 'madam', but that was all. My erroneous belief that the principal young female character in *The Winter's Tale* is called 'Imogen' did not help.

Perhaps this lamentable shrinking of my comprehension is not just a matter of bad hearing, but an aspect of a general, long-standing obtuseness. Many years ago I read *The Owl Service*,[6] which was written, I believe, for teenagers, and I remained totally baffled by the 'explanation' which the last chapter purported to give. In the film of Isabel Colegate's *The Shooting Party*[7] Aline and Cicely looked so much alike to me that I thought they were the same person, and that Charles was the same

---

[6] A 1967 novel for young adults by Alan Garner.
[7] Colegate's novel was published in 1980; the film adaptation (dir. Alan Bridges) appeared in 1985.

person as Tibor. This made some of the plot hard to follow. Well, it can't be helped. I have always needed a little longer than most people to sort out what I take in.

Of all the symptoms of advancing age the most dreadful by far is decline in sexual vigour. I suffered my first attack of impotence soon after my sixty-first birthday, in circumstances which are curious and instructive. When Geoffrey Parker wrote an obituary memoir of Sir George Clark for the *Proceedings of the British Academy* he submitted his draft to Lady Clark, and she was strongly of the opinion that it misrepresented her husband's view on a matter of some importance. The problem was brought up to me, as President of the Academy, by Maurice Keen, and I discovered that Clark had left in the keeping of the Academy, for the benefit of any future obituarist, a thirty-page memorandum in which he made the views he had held at different stages of his career quite plain. Parker had very properly used this document.[8] It occurred to me that it would be a good idea if I deposited in the Academy a similar document about my own life, because there were many matters on which it would be much more useful for an obituarist to know my attitudes and sentiments from this direct testimony than to infer them from patchy impressions retained by other people, especially on matters on which tact, embarrassment or shame kept me silent in my lifetime. So I put the document together, a page or two at a time, over a period of weeks, sent it off to the Academy to be kept under seal until my death,[9] and was then stricken by impotence. This was an experience for which nothing had prepared me, and I thought that maybe it was statistically normal at sixty-one. After a couple of months things came right quite suddenly and inexplicably. Audrey suggested that in composing a document for use in my own obituary I was in effect drawing a line under my life and saying, 'That's it. You're finished', and it was not surprising that it took my central nervous system two months to recover from the shock of so disagreeable a message.

My sexual potency was low during my period of excessive fatigue in 1983, but that seemed so obviously a reflex of my general condition that it did not cause me anxiety. In the spring of 1984, however, after our return from a congress on Chios,[10] I again became impotent at a time when I was otherwise feeling fit. Whereas at sixty-one I had accepted my fate with melancholy resignation, the recurrence of the same trouble at sixty-four turned my thoughts not simply to suicide in general but to the practicalities of alternative methods of suicide. This may seem to some readers an abnormally strong reaction, but until people are more willing to talk about their experience of impotence we do not know what is

---

[8] Parker's memoir of Clark was published in *PBA* 66 (1980) 407–25.
[9] This did not, however, prevent the Academy from incompetently losing the document, which could not be found when Dover's memoir came to be written in 2010–11.
[10] See p. 277 for this event.

normal.* I recall reading that your first fuck makes you feel that you have 'joined the human race', and it is to be expected that impotence should make you feel that your humanity has been withdrawn. I also felt that inability to sustain an erection was the cruellest insult I could cast at my wife (Gandhi did not mind insulting his wife in that way, but I do).[11] On the last day of April I went up to London to attend a lunch-party at the Academy with Peter Brooke (then Minister of State for higher education) and a dinner-party for Conor Cruise O'Brien. I think I was reasonably lively company at both meals, and during the afternoon I had a profitable talk with Eric Handley about the candidates for the Regius Chair of Greek at Cambridge,[12] but all the time that I was on my own I was rehearsing in my mind a jump out of the train on the way back to Oxford.

Instead of jumping, I went to see my doctor next day (as everyone should do when assailed by suicidal feelings) and was cheered up by his exposition of the irregular, intermittent nature of impotence; no one, it seems (and it is interesting that this was news to me), can ever say with assurance, 'That was my last fuck'. Audrey, although she had to cope with signs that the antidepressant currently prescribed for her was not working, was flawlessly supportive, and it was thanks to her, not to any inner resources of my own, that later that summer, at sixty-four, we had some of the best fucks of our life. Since then, ups and downs; having been accustomed all my life to giving myself an erection simply by turning my thoughts the right way, I have now had to come to terms with a recalcitrant and unimaginative penis, but my doctor's implicit prediction has been vindicated by periodical flares, infrequent enough to be ticketed with place-names and dates in our memory (e.g. Fresno 1990, Genoa 1993) but nevertheless sufficient to keep optimism alive.

I have sought, but have not found, aspects of old age which compensate for its ills. There just aren't any – except, maybe, a complacent indifference to fashion,

---

*I regret having to admit – well, no, I don't have to, but I choose to – that there had been five previous occasions in my life on which I had given serious attention to suicide as an escape route; on four of those occasions, escape from a humiliation which in prospect seemed unbearable. None of the five had any sexual dimension, nor was I in peril of any prosecution or blackmail. My father talked so readily of suicide that I suppose I took it for granted as an option always available. Once when I was about ten and we were on holiday at Paignton I deliberately dashed out of a sidestreet and across a main road without looking. This action was not caused by unhappiness but by a feeling that I *must*, just once in a way, exult in doing something that was absolutely forbidden. I never did anything like that again. Years later, some of my students told me about similar actions in their own childhood or adolescence; they called it 'attempted suicide', but 'suicidal risk' would have been a more accurate description. [EDS *For one of the earlier occasions when Dover had contemplated suicide, see* IPC 111–12. *On 'exulting' in doing something forbidden, Dover wrote in a 1995 addendum: 'But at any age I would have recoiled with loathing from the deliberate destruction of a useful and beautiful object, an act by which the adolescent Mathieu in Sartre,* L'Age de raison (p. 64), *achieves "liberation".'*]

[11]Presumably an allusion to Gandhi's decision to take a vow of celibacy in 1906 without prior consultation with his wife: M.K. Gandhi, *An Autobiography*, trans. M. Desai, ed. T. Suhrud (New Haven, 2018) 344.

[12]For Eric Handley, see n. 4 to p. 246: Dover and Handley were both on the board of electors for the Regius professorship, but Handley later withdrew and was appointed to the chair himself.

FIGURE 13 Previous frontispiece (cropped). Kenneth and Audrey in their St Andrews garden, May 1990. *Photo: Joy Russell (wife of Donald Russell).*

because people no longer seeking employment or promotion have less to fear. And maybe, just possibly, some events which can make the heart leap at any age, such as the appearance of buds in March on a deciduous shrub, make it leap a fraction higher in the old. Joy in the maturing of one's grandchildren simply slots into the place previously occupied by joy in one's children. And when I am told (as in an absurd book by Alex Comfort, which I read at Cornell in 1984) that I am 'the same person' as I was forty years ago, I recognise the assurance as the most banal of truisms; I do not need to be told that my body, in which my thoughts and feelings and recollections occur, is a spatio-temporal continuum. The fact that a few people don't age as most of us do has no more relevance to a particular individual than the fact that a few people can conduct a Strauss opera from memory or ride a bicycle on a tightrope.

29 AT LARGE 1984–1992

In 1984 Cornell appointed me a Professor-at-Large. It sounded as if I were being cast in the role of a lurker in the bushes on campus, but it meant that I was allowed to go there for a fortnight in three of the following six years and on each occasion give three or four lectures or seminars in return for startlingly high remuneration. An apartment in the centre of the campus was available to us, less than a quarter of a mile from the Classics department; the University Library is superb, and the rural scenery of up-state New York enchanting, especially in the fall. We were entitled to free meals at all the dining-places in the university, and in 1984 the Hotel School just across the road from our apartment was a very good eating place. Sadly, it was shut for reconstruction on our two subsequent visits, 1986 and 1988.

At the end of our first visit we went to Atlanta, where I was given an honorary doctorate by Oglethorpe University. I owed that honour to a historic link between Corpus and the state of Georgia: James Oglethorpe, founder of the colony of Georgia and a successful fighter against the French (from Louisiana) and the Spaniards (from Florida) had been an undergraduate at Corpus, and we had entertained in College people who came from Georgia to look at his portrait. It must be admitted that although he matriculated, he then went off to central Europe as aide-de-camp to Prince Eugen, and his brief appearances in Oxford did not earn him a degree. Despite that, he was presented by the College for the degree of Master of Arts, and maybe he deserved it more than most, because as Member of Parliament for Godalming he exerted himself in the cause of prison reform at a time when the barbarity and dishonesty of prison superintendents were intolerable. I learned a lot about him when I was invited to give the address at a service accompanying the unveiling of his memorial tablet in the church of Godalming, and all that I learned was heartening. After the Forty-five he was court-martialled for failure to cut off Prince Charlie's retreat from Lancashire into Scotland. The court-martial acquitted him of dereliction of duty, but malevolent suspicion that he might share the blatant Jacobite sympathies of his family remained. Not surprisingly, he left the army, to become in old age a respected friend of Johnson, a vigorous critic of the British handling of the disaffected American colonies, and the initiator of friendly relations with the first American ambassador in London.¹

The President of Oglethorpe was an admirer of Sir Richard Livingstone's writings on education, and I had some difficulty in concealing my ignorance of them.² I had an uneasy feeling that the occasion was meant to elicit from me a mellifluous and 'inspirational' address, and they may have felt a little let down by my unscripted (though by no means shapeless) talk on ways in which the American system was superior to the British. I hope, at least, it was good for their morale.

There was no jaunt to America in 1985; instead, we spent a month at Pietermaritzburg, where I lectured in Geoffrey Chapman's department,³ and rounded that off by a few days in Cape Town, Stellenbosch and Witwatersrand. There were, no doubt, people who thought we should not have accepted an invitation to South Africa, but I took advice on that from a Zulu research student at Corpus and some white South African friends, one of whom had escaped from house arrest half-hidden by a false beard and got across the border into Botswana. Even if they had advised us not to go (they did not), I doubt if I would have heeded them, because I am not short of curiosity, and I like to know what it is that there is a fuss about. Academic society in Pietermaritzburg, however, was not a representative sample of South Africa; the way English-speakers there talked about the government in Pretoria made me think of Parisians in Occupied France, and one woman married to a man who lived in Bloemfontein told us that half the conversations she had in Pietermaritzburg would have been impossible in Bloemfontein. All the same, it was not uncommon to meet academics who spoke Afrikaans at home but were fluent in Zulu, Sotho, or both. In the Oude Kerk at Stellenbosch, when I noticed Treurnicht's name in the list of its former pastors, my host said, 'That was in the days when he was a Christian', and indeed the congregation had lately acknowledged publicly that apartheid was a sin.⁴ Audrey was able to visit an African township adjoining Pietermaritzburg, in company with a Zulu social worker; I stayed away, having been advised that an adult white male would not be well received. We left South Africa less apprehensive about civil war between blacks and whites than about a fundamental lack of solidarity in the black community. As the appalling fate of Rwanda and Burundi has shown, in respect of tribal savagery many Africans are no better than the white inhabitants of south-east Europe and the Caucasus. Reverence among the Zulus for the memory of

---

¹On Oglethorpe and Corpus, cf. *CCH* 234–5; Dover mistakenly makes him MP for Godalming instead of Haslemere.
²On Livingstone, cf. p. 252 and note there.
³Geoffrey A.H. Chapman (1942–2014) was an Oxford-educated classicist who emigrated to South Africa in 1967 and became Professor of Classics at Natal University, Pietermaritzburg; in 1988 he returned to England to pursue a career in schoolteaching.
⁴Andries Treurnicht (1921–93) was a right-wing South African politician, a diehard defender of apartheid, whose early career had been as a preacher in the Dutch Reformed Church.

Shaka's military genius is all very well, but Shaka travelled the same road as Hitler, Stalin and Mao into the darkness of sadism and paranoia, and it would be salutary if the Zulus followed the example of the Oude Kerk and expressed public repentance for the sufferings they inflicted on other black peoples.[5]

Since there was much work to be done on the Lodgings in the Long Vacation of 1986, the College was anxious that we should move out as soon as possible, and we arranged to move on July 1st. Catherine and Jan Lord, the housekeeper of the Lodgings, went up to St Andrews a day or two beforehand to make sure that the St Andrews house was habitable and stocked with food by the time we arrived (we had had some alterations made, and the mess was likely to be considerable). We reckoned that loading-up at Oxford would take two days and the vans' journey to Scotland a whole day, so that the moving-in would not begin until the morning of the fourth day. Accordingly, we planned to spend the second night in a hotel at Oakham and arrive in St Andrews on the evening of the third. However, at mid-morning on the second day the moving men announced that they had got everything in and would be at Carlisle that night. Adjusting ourselves with abandon to this total change of plan, we jumped in the car and set off. I drove as far as Carlisle, where Audrey took over. I twice had to restrain her, though with regret, from exceeding ninety miles an hour on the A74. That wasn't really an expression of exuberance over escaping from Oxford as such, but we did feel an extraordinary sense of liberation from obligations and responsibilities. Alan had suggested to me that I should speak not of 'retirement' but of 'going free-lance', and that has, after all, proved an accurate description of my life since 1986.

In the autumn of that year we were able to respond to a number of invitations by making a transcontinental trip which began at Sackville in New Brunswick, continued to Calgary (where the chairman of the Classics department was a former St Andrews pupil of mine, John Yardley), then for a week at Victoria University on Vancouver Island; the return trip gave us two nights and, inevitably, a lecture by me at Stanford and culminated in our second stay in Cornell. At Stanford I was asked if I would like to spend a whole quarter there for each of five successive years. Being uncertain over how tired I was going to feel how much of the time, I settled for three, though in fact after our third winter there I gladly took on the other two. We didn't look forward to the hassle of letting our house, but as things turned out we were able to lend it to people we knew, or to people known by others whom we knew, simply on the basis of their paying the gas, electricity and telephone during their occupancy. Since we chose to go to Stanford for the period between the New Year and the end of March, there was no serious setback to our

---

[5]Shaka (1787–1828) was a Zulu chieftain whose military exploits during 1816–28 created a Zulu empire in SE Africa.

gardening routine, though we realised in 1993, when the aconites, snowdrops and crocuses came up, what we had been missing.

During our first quarter at Stanford the University found us an apartment ten minutes walk from a campus bus stop in one direction and three minutes from a supermarket in the other. In each of the following four years we rented a house in southern Palo Alto, an area of seraphic respectability. Our landlady was a doctor's widow, Alicia Ames, who flitted south, even to Mexico, for the three months which were wintry by Bay Area standards. By comparison with houses in the immediate neighbourhood (one of which changed hands for two million dollars while we were there), her house was a shack, but it suited us well; the rent was low (as rents in those parts go), it was close to the Caltrain station, a campus bus-stop, and the shops in California Avenue, public transport was good in the daytime, and a nearby friend lent us a car for going further afield and attending concerts and plays on campus in the evening. One way and another, we were better suited there than we would have been by renting a house in the residential expanses of Stanford itself.

Our visits to Stanford made it possible for us to see something of other universities, either while we were there or on the way home: Whitman College (Walla Walla), Fresno, Santa Barbara, Los Angeles, Tucson, San Antonio, Ottawa, McGill, Columbia, Middlebury. The most bizarre was Deep Springs College, perhaps the smallest college to be found anywhere (five faculty, twenty-five students, some of the latter and one of the former being of high calibre). It is a speck of human habitation on the High Desert east of the Sierra Nevada, and one reaches it by a very long car journey from Las Vegas (where we gambled with two dollars' worth of quarters, and lost the lot), passing on the way the second most famous brothel in the world. The Davis campus of the University of California we visited not from Stanford but after our last stay in Cornell in 1988. They worked me hard at Davis (eleven lectures and seminars in five days), but from there we rented a car and enjoyed a wonderful few days at Yosemite, encountering on the journey the variegated surprises of inland California.

We made so many good friends among the faculty and students at Stanford that an abbreviated catalogue would be invidious, and it is best to name no one. Teaching was a joy, particularly the first and the last graduate seminars that I held,[6] and on three occasions I gave an undergraduate lecture-course on *Greek Values, Attitudes and Beliefs*, which was attended by about ninety people, including scientists and engineers who wrote some very perceptive term-papers. I cannot speak with equal warmth of the Administration, which at its lower levels was forgetful and confused (rather like American banks) and at higher levels beset by unrealistic ambitions.

---

[6] His first Stanford graduate seminar was on Greek prose style: see p. 263 with n. 4 there. His last was on Aristophanes' *Frogs*: see Dover's 1993 edition, p. vi, with glowing praise of his Stanford students and the thought that 'the future of classical studies may perhaps be brighter in the United States than in Europe'.

Maybe I am a little soured by its refusal in 1992 to give tenure to a valuable member of the Classics department, a refusal grounded in an unwillingness of the Deans to consider the coverage which a department must have if it is to attract students. It was alleged that Stanford didn't like to give tenure to people who were not 'among the top half-dozen in their fields in the world'. The short rejoinder to that could often be, 'Look who's talking!' One might also ask, what is a 'field'? 'Zoology' or 'the respiratory system of *Artioposthia*', or some point in between, and, if so, what?

In recruiting new faculty – I spent rather more time than I would have wished to spend on search committees – Stanford is undoubtedly hampered by the fact that the price of houses in the Bay Area is so high that it is hard to attract first-rate people from further east except by offering salaries larger than the university can afford to pay. It is also hard for any Classics department in an American university to find candidates in the home market who have what I would regard as a good knowledge of Latin or Greek. That may shock people who went through a Classical education like mine, but it is one side of a coin whose other side shines brighter. Among my graduate students at Stanford there were few who had first arrived at a university with the intention of specialising in Classics. Most of them had sampled the subject during their first semester and decided 'This is for me'. A system which allows people to do that is crucial to the survival of the Classics, and to say that Classics departments in British universities 'ignore it at their peril' is to make not – as those words usually make – a minatory prophecy but a statement of present fact. They do ignore it,[7] and they are imperilled. Mobility of orientation, like mobility of employment, is more conspicuous in America than in Britain. One consequence of the American approach is that when they embark on graduate school they are capable of bad linguistic mistakes, their recall of vocabulary is weak and their ability to translate simple English into Greek or Latin poor by the standards of a British sixth form.[8] But if they are highly intelligent, strongly motivated and passionately interested in the subject – and my Stanford graduate students possessed those virtues – their ignorance (sometimes mistaken for stupidity by thoughtless British critics) does not matter, because when they are not sure of something, they look it up. The trouble starts when they are secure in their profession and stop looking things up. Even that does not always matter, because it is possible to have very good ideas and follow them up effectively while making a few incidental linguistic mistakes which in no way affect the argument.[9] But sometimes it does matter, because an argument which rests on mistranslation, misinterpretation or failure to assess relevance is a waste of everybody's time, and the worst American publications in Classics outstrip the worst that Britain and

---

[7] Much less true in 2023 than it was in 1994.
[8] This last reference-point for linguistic standards is no longer applicable in the way it was during Dover's own education and earlier career.
[9] Cf. the similar but more general point about mistakes and their implications on p. 137.

Europe can produce. It is a relative matter; I once listened to a paper by a distinguished British ancient historian which collapsed (as he admitted) when it was pointed out that he just hadn't looked at the apparatus criticus on the passage which was crucial to his argument, and I saved another (even more distinguished) from making a fool of himself in print through a simple mistranslation of a passage in a late Greek author. This sort of thing is particularly important when an ancient historian or historian of ancient literature is entranced by a theoretical schema derived from sociology or metahistory and batters the evidence into submission.

Stanford has high admission standards, and the level of intellectual competence in general protects the student-body from infection by -isms and anti-isms which assail rationality on many American campuses. During my first two quarters there, however, a fuss arose over the definition and content of a course in 'Western culture'. There seemed to be confusion on both sides. Writers who live in Central or South America, a few thousand miles west of Europe, and use those modern forms of Latin which are called 'Spanish' and 'Portuguese' were not regarded as Western. The Bible was treated as a Western text, though if the terms 'Western' and 'Eastern' are to be allowed any relevance to the ancient Mediterranean basin, there are few works as uncompromisingly Eastern as the Bible. So far as I am concerned, the terms are not relevant. The Greeks used 'Europe' and 'Asia' in a geographical sense (extending 'Europe' indefinitely northeast of the Black Sea), but they would have been surprised to be lumped together under the label 'European' with the inhabitants of Spain and the Alps from any other point of view. The more we find out about the eastern Mediterranean in the Bronze Age and the Archaic Age of Greece, the more numerous and significant the strands of a cultural continuum appear. As for race, the Greeks were aware that if you go far enough south you meet black people, and if far enough north, people with fair hair and blue eyes, but nothing in Greek literature suggests awareness of any physical differentiation eastwards and westwards, from Portugal to Iran.

The onslaught on 'Western culture' originated in a desire to compensate for the historic injustice of racism, but confusion of acquired culture with genetically determined race has been disastrous. I am allowed to entertain an adverse opinion of the behaviour of an individual; why may I not entertain an equally adverse opinion of a culture in which that behaviour predominates because it is admired and inculcated? Gilbert Murray's reaction to Arnold Toynbee's Reith Lectures was: 'He wilfully ignored the fact that our Western or Christian civilisation is *better* than that of Asia or Africa' (the inclusion of 'Christian' is strange, coming from a man who found Assisi 'mad').[10]

---

[10]See Duncan Wilson, *Gilbert Murray OM 1866–1957* (Oxford, 1987) 392 (a book Dover had reviewed: n. 18 to p. 6), where 'better' is not italicized; for the reference in 'mad', see ibid., 140. The 1952 BBC radio Reith Lectures by the historian Arnold Toynbee (1889–1975), on 'The world and the West', created controversy by their critique of Western civilization's aggressiveness. Toynbee had previously (1913–42) been married to Murray's daughter Rosalind. Dover cannot have admired Toynbee's best-known work, *A Study of History* (1934–61), which would have fallen foul of his dislike of would-be comprehensive 'theories' (see p. 337) and of 'metahistory' (pp. 324, 336).

Anyone who said that to a student audience nowadays would probably be vilified as a racist and pelted with dung; but although it is clear from correspondence that Murray did not shake free of belief in a correlation of skin, hair and face with intelligence and virtue, he could have shaken entirely free and still have drawn harsh contrasts between cultures.

When I had gone round the National Museum in Mexico City, it occurred to me that every sculpted face I had seen there, with the exception of a superb statuette of a wrestler, expressed ferocity, rage, hatred, fear or pain. My imagination took flight to Olympia, and rested there.

In the summer of 1989 we paid a short visit to Israel, where I had not set foot since the days when it was Palestine. I gave some lectures at Tel Aviv and Jerusalem, and we were entertained by good friends in Haifa and Beersheba; glimpsed Bonelli's Eagle near the tomb of Ben Gurion, but, alas, no sign of a hyrax, which I rate second (after the red panda) among the endearing furry animals by which the world is enlivened. I have always been aware of a conflict between heart and head in contemplating Israel. During its wars my heart was with the Israelis, because I admire their unique combination of brains and guts. My head is with the Palestinians, because although I see little to choose intellectually between believing that God composed the Koran and invoking a Bronze Age legend as a justification for grabbing other people's land, it is the latter which in our day has caused more misery. Our visit to Israel did nothing to resolve this inner conflict; throughout our time there, we were more strongly reminded of South Africa than of anywhere else we had been.

Our third trip to Stanford had a delightful sequel. Friends and colleagues had got together to publish a volume of essays in my honour, to be completed in time for my seventieth birthday in March 1990. The enterprise was organised by Elizabeth Craik,[11] and a couple of days after our return from Stanford that year we were invited to a reception in London, where a leather-bound copy was presented to me. I could not help remembering how Juliette Ernst, for so long the editor-in-chief of *L'Année philologique*,[12] hated commemorative volumes of this kind and inveighed against them because of the inordinate trouble they gave to bibliographers. They do indeed; but I had never refused to contribute to one myself, because I would not have liked the honorand to think I didn't admire hrs work, and I can't pretend that any scruples about bibliographical efficiency diminished my pleasure in being given the honour. I was particularly pleased that the volume begins with a felicitous

---

[11] Elizabeth Craik studied as a St Andrews undergraduate with Dover 1956–60 and later became a member of the Department of Greek: see n. 15 to p. 133, with her contribution to *S&C*.

[12] The most extensive bibliographical index of publications in classical scholarship.

prologue in Greek by Donald Russell.[13] At the same time the Hellenic Society decided to appeal for contributions to establish a fund bearing my name, to which research students and young lecturers could apply when they needed money for books, photographs, microfilms or visits to libraries. I was consulted about the scope of the work which I would like to see supported from this fund, and I decided that it should be for the editing or exegesis of Greek texts of any period from the Bronze Age down to the middle of the fifteenth century. I am glad to say that the appeal was successful and is serving its purpose.

Opposite Donald Russell's prologue in the honorific volume there is a caricature of me drawn by one of my St Andrews students, Fred Hepburn, in 1976, when I was lecturing to the Honours class on Aristophanes' *Birds*. The picture (of which I have had a copy hanging in my study ever since it was drawn) represents me as a human-headed bird; whether raptor or owl, I cannot say for sure, but its talons are frightening. The image was appropriate, because over the years Audrey and I have become devoted admirers of birds, and when we left Corpus our parting gift from the Fellows was a good pair of binoculars. We are not, I am glad to say, twitchers; we relish the sight of a rarity, but it is the behaviour of birds which most interests and attracts us, and we can observe that best (often from the kitchen window) in our own garden, which we have year by year made into a place more interesting to them as well as to us. Maybe this is the Dunroamin[14] syndrome; or maybe not, because after 1990 we began, for the first time since the children were small, to take real holidays for their own sake instead of trips abroad in which we fitted a day or two of holiday around my commitment to lecturing. This new-found hedonism has taken us in one year to the Auvergne and in another to the Dolomites, and I think the appetite may grow.

---

[13]On Russell, see p. 106 with note there.
[14]A pseudo-Gaelic place name, punning on 'done roaming'.

30 THE THATCHER AFFAIR 1985

What is a Mercedes or a four-course lunch, compared with ideological happiness?

GENERAL ILIE CEAUŞESCU[1]

At St Andrews, and no doubt in most universities, suggestions for the award of honorary degrees are made by a committee to the Senate. The Senate's discussion, like the committee's, is subject to strict rules of confidentiality, only the positive decisions are recorded in the minutes, and those decisions are final; no one who is not a member of the Senate has any opportunity to express an opinion. At Oxford the system is different: the proposals made by the Hebdomadal Council are put to Congregation, of which all resident Oxford MAs are voting members, so that there is no possibility of keeping the debate confidential.

It was proposed at the end of 1984 to confer an honorary doctorate on Margaret Thatcher, the Somerville graduate who had been Prime Minister since 1979. This accorded with a tradition of honouring any Oxford graduate who occupied that office. The proposal aroused widespread indignation in the academic community, and I was asked to add my signature to a flysheet urging Congregation to reject the proposal. I signed, in common with 274 others, for three reasons.

The most important reason was that the relation between universities and government had changed a great deal since the days when a graduate's achievement in reaching Downing Street could be treated as a triumph in the 'outside world', rather as a school would treat the award of an international prize to one of its former pupils. The outside world is no longer outside. Universities are now very

---

[1] We have been unable to identify a source for the (ironic) ascription of this sentiment to the Romanian general and politician Ilie Ceauşescu (1926–2002), younger brother of the communist dictator Nicolae Ceauşescu (1918–89).

heavily dependent on the state, and a Prime Minister, especially a Prime Minister who dominates hrs Cabinet and takes some pride in inflexible adherence to principle, is in a strong position to determine the direction and scale of academic developments. In these circumstances an honorary degree looks disquietingly like a bribe, a bid by a university to establish a friendly relationship which it hopes will cause it to be more favourably treated than other universities in competition for a bigger share of the cake. The obvious answer, suggested some years earlier, was to stop giving degrees to people who have power for good or ill over universities.

Secondly, I agreed with the authors of the flysheet that conferment of an honorary degree is a very strong expression of admiration, and at a time when the country was deeply divided it was inappropriate to behave in a way which would seem to other universities a declaration of political allegiance by Oxford. It was suggested in the Congregation debate that other universities couldn't care less what the 'fat cats' of Oxford and Cambridge did. From conversations afterwards in several universities I judge that suggestion to be at best a half-truth; if we had conferred the degree, it might possibly have been shrugged off as thoughtless adherence to tradition, but the refusal made many people adjust their perception of Oxford – perhaps for the worse, outside academic circles, but inside for the better.

My third reason was that I shared the general academic view of the Government's ethos, which seemed at times ostentatiously philistine, impatient with all studies which did not obviously lead to the prompt creation of wealth, unfriendly to those which generated fundamental criticism of existing social structures, and unaware of the ultimate dependence of the 'applied' on the 'pure'. This was not a new phenomenon in British history, but it was new in our lifetime. Or it seemed so, perhaps because philistine statements by members of Parliament and members of the Government were cheered on by a fiercely anti-intellectual section of the press. I once told Robert Jackson, when he was responsible for Higher Education in the Department of Education, that such pronouncements generated widespread fear and mistrust of the Government in universities, and he dismissed them as insignificant ('Oh, well, Norman *Tebbit*...!');[2] but revelation of the attitudes and sentiments of those who have power is never insignificant to those over whom the power is exercised. Any government has a right to withhold money from activities which it ranks low in importance, but the exercise of a right is often wrong, and a government cannot expect to be honoured by its victims. 'Victims' is a melodramatic word (though not so melodramatic as wails about 'penal' taxation), and a tasteless word when the real

---

[2]Norman Tebbit (1931–) was a prominent member of Margaret Thatcher's government; as Minister for Trade and Industry (1983–5) he had defended cuts in the education budget by sneering on one occasion at the study of subjects such as Egyptology and anthropology. In a diary piece in the *London Review of Books*, 4 June 1998, W.G. Runciman recalled being told by Tebbit in the 1980s that the universities 'have let down the country'.

victims are the unemployed, most of whom had lost their jobs in consequence of policy decisions taken miles above their heads. I did not suffer from the delusion that I had a solution to the economic problems of this country, but it seemed to me that an obsessive concentration on the lowering of the inflation rate, combined with an addiction to low income-tax, obscured from the Government the obvious, immense and enduring damage which very high unemployment, especially among successive batches of school-leavers, would inflict on our society. Privatisation came to be treated as a panacea, just as nationalisation had once been a socialist panacea. 'Choice' became an incantation, and central controls, derided as 'the nanny state' when they were designed for the restraint of predators, were unhesitatingly adopted and extended as an instrument of governmental power. Since I deeply mistrust panaceas, slogans and spells, and believe that government, like education, should in the main consist of continuous tinkering and tuning, interspersed with the floating of radically new ideas in order to gather and reflect on people's reactions to them, I considered that when invited, as a member of Congregation, to vote on the proposed honorary degree, I must on balance vote against it.³

On balance, because I was by no means a hostile critic of everything that the Prime Minister had done. Even her notorious dictum, 'There is no such thing as society', although a wild shot, at least implied recognition of a genuine target. The major trade unions had lost my support in 1972–4 when I reflected on the attitudes underlying utterances by their own spokesmen, which I scrutinised for implications just as I would have scrutinised, with a historian's awareness of the need to read between the lines, passages of the Greek orators. The leaders of the long dock strike, given the opportunity to put their point of view in *The Times*, merely exhibited a reverence for traditions which they found congenial, totally excluding any consideration of the question: how can the loading and unloading of ships best be organised in the interests of the community as a whole? I was also a firm supporter of the Falklands war. In the run-up to Congregation an imbecile and understandably anonymous flysheet which appeared on notice-boards in Oxford common-rooms castigated Thatcher for 'going to war' over the Falklands, and for authorising an attack on 'a retreating ship' (the Argentinian cruiser *Admiral Belgrano*)⁴ at a time when it looked as if a negotiated settlement might be brokered by the United States. This was an unhappy example of the chronic failure of the British Left to understand war.* The

---

*One might compare Ken Livingstone's notion that the prospect of interminable guerrilla warfare in Britain would be a more effective deterrent to invasion by a hostile power than our nuclear weapons – a notion which neglects the obvious fact that an island of sixty million acres inhabited by fifty million people is an ideal target for short-term toxic chemicals. [EDS Ken Livingstone (1945–), a Labour politician who, prior to 1994, had been prominent on the Greater London Council and an MP from 1987.]

³For a brief account of the political background to the vote in January 1985, see D. Cannadine, *Margaret Thatcher: A Life and Legacy* (Oxford, 2017) 70–1.

⁴The sinking of the *Admiral Belgrano* on 2 May 1982, with the loss of 323 lives, became, as Dover intimates, the subject of protracted controversy about the ethics of warfare.

Falklands war began at the moment when an Argentinian soldier carrying a weapon and willing to use it stepped ashore; that *is* war. The direction in which the bows of an enemy warship happen to be pointing at the moment of encounter cannot justify letting it go. The idea that our declaration of an 'exclusion zone' round the Falklands, within which all shipping would be in danger, implied abstention from attacking an Argentinian instrument of war wherever it might be found had never occurred to me, nor should it have done. As for peace formulae, negotiations could well be prolonged by Argentina while its forces strengthened their defensive positions on the islands day by day, and to permit that would have been inexcusable. I was not surprised when an Argentinian admiral in a widely published television interview admitted that if he had been in the shoes of the British submarine commander he too would have attacked the *Belgrano*.

To return to the debate: Peter Pulzer[5] wanted me to speak in it, but I had already invited some undergraduates to lunch that day and was unlikely to be free before three o'clock; I gave hospitality precedence over participation in a debate to which I could hardly have contributed anything that had not already been said by someone else, and I had no doubt that the proposal would be defeated by a large majority. Thus I got to the Sheldonian too late for a seat and joined the overflow in the basement, listening to the debate relayed from above. The proposal was in fact defeated by 738 votes to 319; as the *Guardian* pointed out, the percentage in favour was the same as the percentage of the British electorate which voted Conservative in 1983, a datum which suggests that Oxford is not really so odd a place. I had two interesting encounters afterwards. A historian who needed access to Downing Street archives had been afraid to sign the flysheet and no less afraid of being seen to vote No.[6] Another friend who had come with the intention of voting Yes told me that he was so disenchanted by the speeches on his side that he left early without voting.

It so happened that I was the only reigning head of house to sign the flysheet. I learned later, from its principal organiser, that five other heads of houses had expressed strong sympathy with it but in the end did not sign. The motives of four of them are not known to me; the fifth, I understand, was dissuaded by his Fellows on the grounds that he would be blacklisted by the Government and would never again be asked to serve on any advisory committee (the long-standing and widespread belief that Thatcher was more vindictive than any of her predecessors was one of the most striking aspects of the whole affair). Herbert Hart, the retired

---

[5]Peter Pulzer (1929–) had just become the Gladstone Professor of Government and Public Administration at Oxford and was a fellow of All Souls College. He published a retrospective essay on the Thatcher affair, 'The Oxford vote', in the *London Review of Books*, 7 March 1985 (reprinted in N. Spice, ed, *London Reviews: A Selection from The London Review of Books 1983–1985* (London, 1985) 13–20), which provoked a highly animated exchange of letters in subsequent issues.
[6]Dover SN identifies Margaret Gowing (1921–98), Professor of the History of Science at Oxford 1973–86.

Principal of Brasenose, was a signatory, but the media do not seem to have observed that, and on the day of the debate Robin Day invited me to contribute over the telephone to 'The World at One'. I explained my point of view, and he asked, 'Well, who *would* you give honorary degrees to, then?' I said, 'The sort of person we normally give them to, scientists and scholars and artists.' At that he ended the interview, without putting the awkward question, 'What about the President of Italy?', who was also receiving an honorary degree.

The Times had a leader next day under the title 'Sale of Honours',[7] suggesting that Thatcher would have had her degree if she had conspicuously favoured lavish funding of Oxford. This was clever rhetoric, and I gave the writer full marks for skill at his trade, but it is sad to see the reading public deliberately misled. *The Times* compensated a few days later by printing a thoughtful article by David Watt on the alienation of the professional classes from the Government.[8] The most peculiar reaction was an article by Lord Beloff in the *Daily Telegraph*, putting the blame on sinister Marxists who had conned well-meaning, unworldly dons into following their line. He described me as 'hitherto only known to the public as the author of the standard work on Greek homosexuality', rather as the *Observer*, in covering the Blunt affair, had said that I was 'chiefly known as an expert on Thucydides' who was now 'desperately trying to hold the Academy together';[9] it is, I suppose, a populist tenet that a classical scholar is necessarily disqualified from understanding, let alone managing, an issue in 'real life'. I had already exchanged letters with Beloff, and had made the point that I was cheered to see the company in which I found myself; I had in mind, for example, Henry Harris, Denis Noble and Michael Atiyah.[10] Beloff observed that I was also in the company of the *Morning Star*, and he advised me to scrutinise the credentials of my partners. I thought he was mistaken in assuming that if A and B want the same thing the validity of A's arguments for it is affected by the motives and character of B. It occurred to me six or seven years later that I was vulnerable to the same criticism. There was an amusing sequel to the *Telegraph* article: an Oxford historian, himself in favour of the degree, wrote me a vicarious apology for it, remarking that 'it is rather unpleasant to have allies of such a kind' and ending 'I dare say you have

---

[7] *The Times*, 30 January 1985, p. 13, with supercilious criticism of Dover's own supposed reasoning.
[8] 'Does Oxford speak for the nation?', *The Times*, 1 February 1985, p. 12.
[9] Beloff's article, 'What happened to Oxford?', appeared in *The Telegraph*, 1 February 1985, p. 20; the *Observer* article to which Dover alludes (clearly from memory) was Laurence Marks, 'Daggers drawn among the dons', 24 August 1980, p. 9 ('Dover ... an authority of [sic] Thucydides ... hoping desperately to prevent the academy from tearing itself apart').
[10] Three of Oxford's most distinguished scientists of the time: Sir Henry Harris (1925–2014, Kt 1993), Regius Professor of Medicine 1979–92; Denis Noble (1936-), Burdon Sanderson Professor of Cardiqvascular Physiology 1984–2004; Sir Michael Atiyah (1929–2019, Kt 1983), Royal Society Research Professor 1973–90 (and, among much else, winner of a Fields medal for mathematics, 1966). All three had signed the flysheet (p. 327).

some pretty shady allies too'. Of course; it is hard to think of any issue of importance in which one does not have shady allies.

Many other letters came in, some complimentary, some vituperative. They included a daft letter from a Conservative MP, demanding my resignation from the Chancellorship of St Andrews. I answered everyone (mostly in longhand) politely and rationally, and had the pleasure of causing a retired Wing-Commander to cool down. An old lady rang me up and reproached me for discourteous treatment of the first woman to become Prime Minister, all the more discreditable because Oxford had elected a 'notorious war criminal' (Macmillan) as its Chancellor.[11] I did not pursue the question of our Chancellor's responsibility for the indiscriminate return of Russians and Jugoslavs to their unforgiving fatherlands in 1945, but could only agree that the first woman to become Prime Minister deserved honour simply for getting there, and regret that other considerations were of overriding importance. That regret beset me intermittently until the autumn of 1993, when it was finally laid to rest by Lady Thatcher's revelation of her personality in a series of television interviews.

---

[11] For Macmillan's Chancellorship, see the epigraph to ch. 20.

31 A HISTORY MAN

I would prefer to write this chapter in Greek, but the reader might not like that. Contemporary English is laden with ambiguities which make it hard to speak of history, art and science without supplementary explanations and definitions.

I use the word 'history' to denote an activity, the activity which Herodotus called *historiē*: trying first to find out, then to understand, but with a restriction (and here my 'history' differs from his *historiē*) to what humans have done, said, written, thought and felt. I don't add '... in the past', because those words would be otiose; what is not past is not available for our investigation, though it is natural enough that we should use the term 'the present' in speaking of states of affairs which we expect to continue beyond the time at which we are considering them. The political acts of governments and the belligerent acts of armies constitute a fraction of what the human race has done, but they are so often assumed, in popular usage, to be the essential subject-matter of history that I cannot describe myself as a 'historian' without risk of being misunderstood. I must, however, take that risk. I have never neglected to investigate the actions of governments and rulers, armies and fleets, but I have given rather more time to attitudes and assumptions (the parents of spectacular political events, as of much else), to the arts (particularly literature) and to the languages which are the medium of literature.

When I was at school, 'Is history a science or an art?' was a weary topic set for essays, and I don't suppose anyone would have got high marks for explaining that it is neither. In English, 'science' (unlike the cognate words in Romance languages and the German *Wissenschaft*) denotes the study of how things work when they are events and not human actions. History is plainly not that; but the investigation of, say, the conditions on which a slave was manumitted in the late Roman Empire has more in common with investigation of the properties of a metal than either of them has with the composition of a tune or a picture. What the historian or scientist does is to find out about something which is there already, whereas the artist causes something new to be there. Some confusion is caused by the use of the word 'history' to denote the narrative of events in writing. Herodotus, again, provides an implicit distinction of some importance, because his opening words are: 'This is the exposition (*apódexis*) of the investigation (*historiē*) made by Herodotus'. If he had never written a word, he would still have been a historian by virtue of his activity in investigation. Conversely, a popular writer who puts together a historical narrative by reading existing narratives covering the same ground is not a historian; s/he has produced an *apódexis* of other people's *historiē*. 'Art' is another semantic disaster. We use the word in the singular most commonly to denote painting, drawing and sculpture, and, in a more sophisticated register, to cover music and literature as well; in the plural with the article, 'the arts', with much the same denotation as the sophisticated use of 'art'; but in the plural without the article, as in 'Faculty of Arts', for the study of human activity of all kinds (and in some universities, of philosophical problems also). 'Art' and 'the arts' have generated 'artist' and 'artistic', but 'Arts' has no corresponding agent-noun or adjective. It is not surprising that scientists who are talented musicians, painters, designers or poets regard themselves as bestriding what Snow called the 'Two Cultures'.[1] They are half right, in so far as human activity which is not exclusively or primarily concerned with overt bodily movements on a large scale can be roughly divided into 'inquiry' (history and science) and 'creation' (art); but within 'inquiry', the difference between history and science is so important that I would rather speak of three cultures than of two. I think I began to formulate and preach this doctrine about thirty years ago, but I did not expound it properly until in 1985 I was invited by Rougemont School to give a public lecture and chose 'What are the "Two Cultures"?' as my subject.

I did not face squarely the question, 'What is literature?' until I became an organiser and part-author of a small book for the general reader, *Ancient Greek Literature,* which Oxford published in 1980. In writing the chapter on science and philosophy I treated the literary status of some items in the Hippocratic corpus of medical works as 'doubtful', and I firmly banished the philosophical writings of Aristotle from the category 'literature'. How thoughtless I was, I realised a few years later as my plans for writing a book about Greek prose style took shape. To begin with, although a distinction between 'poetry' and 'prose' is easily and unambiguously expressed in Greek, it did not have words, within the category 'prose', with which to draw a distinction between what is literature and what is not. Furthermore, I recalled that as long ago as 1945 I had been moved to profound aesthetic admiration by the elegance, force and clarity of a military despatch and by the same qualities in a technical description of a manufacturing process. And it is certainly not just austere historical curiosity which has brought me back time and again, all these years, to reading Herodotus, Thucydides and Plato. Yet whatever I may say about

---

[1] On Dover's acquaintance with C.P. Snow, see note to p. 232. On Snow's controversial 'two cultures' thesis, see S. Collini's Introduction to C.P. Snow, *The Two Cultures* (Cambridge, 1993). The 1985 lecture of Dover's mentioned in the text was published in *G&L* 314–26 and is discussed in Halliwell's contribution to *S&C*.

my own 'profound aesthetic admiration' is only an autobiographical statement and therefore of restricted interest. It is the authors who matter; what were they trying to do, and what were the expectations of their original audiences? Critics for whom 'intentionalist' is a naughty word will not think much of those questions, but I can't say that that worries me.[2] I have paid attention to such critics, but my attention has not been rewarded by insights which have been of the slightest use in answering the questions which interest me. I do not consent to being told by other people what *ought* to interest me, and I have no patience with literary critics whose writings resemble incantation rather than rational communication.[3] Perhaps this is because I consider that it is people who 'mean', and words are only the instrument by which they do so. Of course, as an English-speaker I constantly refer to the 'meaning' of a word, but that is an abbreviated way of referring to what people usually meant when they used the word; were that not so, would translation be possible?

The history of Greek literature is the history of an interaction between tradition and innovation, and once the extant works are located in place and time and (integrating our history of literature with the history of Greek society) the relation between a work and its occasion or function understood, it is possible to formulate demonstrable hypotheses about the expectations of an audience, the author's perception of them, and the ways in which innovation engendered new expectations. For me, a by-product of this study was the formulation of a possibly idiosyncratic answer to the question, 'What is art?' The more I brooded over the styles of the citations from the earliest philosophers and theoretical scientists and on the other side over Plato's philosophical writings, the more obvious it became to me that art is not a labelled shelf on which we firmly put some whole books while excluding others, but an activity which may be sustained throughout the writing of a book but may also be intermittent, even fragmentary. It is, in fact, the activity of caring about the look or sound of what one produces. That predominates in music, painting and sculpture, even to the exclusion of other ingredients. A poem is a poem, and a novel is a novel, if its author says so. It may be a lousy poem or novel, but that is quite a different matter. A widespread confusion equates art with good art and prompts people to say, 'That's not art', when they would say, if they were clearer-headed, 'That is worthless, incompetent art.' The activity which I call 'art' may manifest itself in extremely trivial ways. I come into a room, see a picture hanging askew, and straighten it; why?* Or having put on a dark suit and a

---

*Explanations in terms of social conditioning may well be true sometimes and to some extent, but have no relevance in the present context; and we must not forget the aesthetic preferences displayed by non-human creatures, as described in Desmond Morris, *The Biology of Art*. [EDS *The subtitle of Morris's book, published in 1962, is 'a study of the picture-making behaviour of the great apes and its relationship to human art'.*]

[2]For Dover's view of attempts to avoid 'intentionalism', cf. *G&L* 62 and *The Evolution of Greek Prose Style*, 13 n. 15 ('[M]y approach to all utterance is pragmatic and resolutely intentionalist').

[3]On Dover's attitude to 'literary criticism', cf. n. 8 to p. 264.

cream-coloured shirt, I spend a couple of minutes on choosing a tie to go with that. It is rather more important if I spend a day in translating a passage of Greek poetry, trying one way after another to transfer the power of the original into English; but how is it possible to find any sharp point of division between that and the straightening of a picture, when both exemplify the activity of caring how something that I do sounds to those who hear it or looks to those who see it?

The contemporary shift of focus from author to reader, from what the author meant by his words to what they 'mean to' any of us (are *we* all that interesting?), has had its effect on attitudes to history, generating the notion that statements about the human past are the fictions of individuals, classes or cultures.[4] Some of the causes of this effect are irrational, some are dishonest, and their reasons for decrying objectivity are, as a rule, amusingly obvious. Sometimes the trouble is a simple failure to distinguish between the reliability of historical statement and the validity of historical investigation. Of course there are plenty of errors in historical narratives (as there are in scientific expositions), but the perception and demonstration of error are themselves historical activity. Scepticism about the possibility of making true historical statements can only seem comic to a scholar who has seen so many hypotheses, including emendations of texts, confirmed by subsequent discovery. Moreover, since a present-tense statement about human behaviour is a generalisation derived from the speaker's knowledge (or complacent ignorance) of past events, it is itself a historical statement, only superficially disguised; a generalisation about historians has no claim to immunity from any of the criticisms that may be directed against the historians.

There is, however, another side to the question. There usually is, and in this case it is something which ensures an indefinite lifespan for history as an activity. Undoubtedly historical narratives carry an ideological charge in so far as the author imports, consciously or unconsciously, implicit evaluations; *how far*, is the question that matters. Certainly also the material that an author selects for treatment or discards as insignificant tells us much about hrmself, hrs milieu and hrs expected public; *what* it tells us, *how much* it tells us, are called 'metahistorical' questions, but their *historical* character cannot be concealed just by a change of label. In October 1993 I took part in a day-long seminar on metahistory at the Open University, in which the crucial point was made by the sociologist Stuart Hall:[5] granted that a historian, confronted by his chosen material, poses and tries to answer questions about it, *where do the questions come from*? I recalled a striking

---

[4]Dover had in mind here the work of Hayden White (1928–2018), American theorist of historiography as 'metahistory': in an addendum to the first edition of *MC*, Dover said he was surprised how hard Arnaldo Momigliano (cf. p. 105) found it 'to come to terms with the historiographical critique of people like Hayden White'.

[5]Stuart Hall (1932–2014) was an influential Jamaican-born cultural theorist, Professor of Sociology at the Open University 1979–98.

illustration. In the index to the three massive volumes of Werner Jaeger, *Paideia: The Ideals of Greek Culture* (1939–45) there is no entry at all for Slaves and Slavery.† Well, one couldn't drag them into absolutely everything (though I expect Moses Finley‡ would have managed to do so even if he had written an article on the syntax of the Greek verb), but in a book on the ideals of Greek culture the omission would be unimaginable in the nineteen-eighties. I am aware that the questions which arise in my mind when I am confronted with a problem in Greek history nowadays are not all the same as those which would have arisen in 1948.

The trouble is, questions which matter to me at a given time may not be answerable, because the evidence is simply not there. Making good the deficiency by imposing 'must have...' in accordance with theories seems to me neither honest nor rational. That is one reason why I am likely to remain an Anglo-Saxon empiricist hospitable to ideas but hostile to any theory which boasts of its own comprehensive power.[6] Another reason is my considered refusal to separate interpretation of my own experience from the recovery of the experience of others, no matter how remote in time and place.

If I address the enquiry, 'Where do the questions come from?' to myself, I can give a threefold answer. Some of them are simply dictated by their own object. Confronted by (for example) a new text – by which I mean a text new *to me*, however long it may have been known to others – I know that it came into being at a certain time and place, and I know that it is a human act, not a natural event. What I don't know in advance is the answers to the four questions fundamental to the identity of any such act: where? when? who? and why? A second category of questions comprises those which are raised by other people and communicated to me. Among questions of that kind there are some which I have a professional obligation to pursue, in order to explain them to learners, or a moral obligation, for the sake of being helpful and encouraging. There is a third category of questions: those that are prompted by my own interests, character and experience. Many of them are explicable by reference to what I have in common with others of my age, region, class and education. But not all; like every other individual human, I am prepared from a unique recipe.§ I cannot

---

†The late John Sullivan drew my attention to this. I had not noticed it; but I had so rarely had occasion to look at *Paideia*. [EDS *John Patrick Sullivan (1930–93): an English classicist who emigrated to America and was Professor of Classics at the University of California at Santa Barbara 1978–93. Werner Jaeger (1888-1961) left Germany in 1936 and held chairs at Chicago and Harvard; he was the proponent of an idealized and much-criticized Greek neo-humanism: see the article by W.M. Calder in CSBA, 211–26.*]

‡As this is not the only unfriendly reference I have made to the late Sir Moses Finley, I must in fairness also record my view that when he first set foot in Cambridge his pertinacious raising of new, imaginative and important questions was a great stimulus to historical studies in Britain. [EDS *See also our note to the earlier reference to Finley on p. 184.*]

§It should not be forgotten that in South Africa Abraham and Constand Viljoen, identical twins brought up together, have achieved prominence in opposed political parties. I expect, though, that it *will* be forgotten, in order to make life seem simpler than it is.

[6]For Dover's self-description as an empiricist, cf. p. 202.

expect to explain why what interests me most does so. I notice that I don't ask metaphysical questions – What is Art? What is Morality? and the like – although I've never taken a conscious decision to avoid them.⁷ I identify particular questions first and only then consider what definitions of art, morality, etc., will be useful for the purpose of answering those questions. Perhaps I make the process sound arbitrary and chaotic; but there is no chaos, only an increased clarity in communication, if we declare and explain our arbitrary priorities and choices in terms which remove misunderstanding.‖

‖The first footnote in the book (p. 24) refers to a recent event of which the superficial significance is sexual but the deeper significance is not. The same can be said of my last footnote. Early in the nineteenth century a woman in Yorkshire, Anne Lister, was a very active lesbian who recorded her exploits in code in her diary. The code was deciphered in the nineteen-twenties by members of an antiquarian society; they were deeply shocked, and locked the diary away. Recovered in 1984, it was used for a television programme in 1994. The critic John Naughton, writing in the *Observer Review* of 8 May 1994 remarks: 'The question which nagged in the mind was not about the prevalence of lesbianism in 19th-century Yorkshire, but about Miss Lister's code and how it was cracked', and he suggests that history is 'a record of what one age finds interesting in another'.

⁷For a much stronger statement of aversion to metaphysics, see the Introduction, 4 with n. 11.

32 EPIMETRON[1] 1994

A good friend who read several portions of the book last week saddened me by saying that he vividly recalled my adverse criticisms of other people but could not remember any compliments that I paid them. He admitted that I praise much more often than I blame, and we agreed that we are up against the way memory works. Anecdotes about stupidity and malice impress and amuse, anecdotes about wisdom and charity rarely do so; that is one reason why I have left out a few score anecdotes I would have enjoyed telling. The predictions of political pollsters and weather forecasters are nearly always right, but it's the ones that are wrong which we remember. That being so, it must be very easy for any reader of this book to persuade hrmself that people of such-and-such a category – say, Oxford dons, Classicists, the Scots, what you will – are an unworthy lot. If you form such a conviction, never let it rest without asking: '*Compared with whom*?' And don't allow that question to lie around unanswered.[2]

---

[1] An ancient Greek word meaning 'additional measure'; no English usage is recorded by the *OED*.
[2] The addenda which followed here in the original 1994 edition and (a longer list) in the 1995 reprint have been incorporated, with a few minor exceptions, at the appropriate points in the editorial annotations to the text.

INDEX

[This is a revised and expanded version of Dover's original index; it covers the main text as well as, very selectively, the editorial notes, but not the Introduction.]

abortion 223 n.‖
Adams, Leitch (J.W.L.) 230
Adkins, Arthur (A.W.H.) 212, 223
admissions, university 75, 147–8, 250, 303–9
adultery 222, 289
Aeschylus 69, 71, 193, 282
Aesop's fables 39
aesthetic responses 55, 76, 116, 165, 204, 219, 265, 334–5
agnosticism 159, 220–1, 230, 245
Alam Haifa 85
Alamein 79–80, 82, 84
Albini, Umberto 200, 217
alcohol 24, 40, 60, 215, 293, 296, 298, 312
Alington, Cyril (Very Rev. C.A.) 158
All Souls College, Oxford 175–6
Allan, Donald (D.J.) 98
Allen, Derek (D.F.) 227–8
Allen, Jack (J.F.) 141
Allen, P.S. 247
Allen, T.W. 133
Allen, Sidney (W.S.) 284–5, 286
ambitions 24, 56, 57, 110–11
Ames, Alicia 322
ancient history 88, 96, 128; *see also* history
Andocides 114
Andrewes, Antony 119, 191, 287
anthropology 49, 167, 175
Anthropos (journal) 52
Antiphon 106, 114–15
arachnophobia, *see* spiders, fear of
Archilochos/us 55 n.12, 74 n.19, 121–3,
areal linguistics 53

Aristophanes 117–18, 120–1, 166, 174, 185, 199, 215, 264, 273, 275; in Plato, *Symposium* 161–3
Aristotle 99, 188, 192, 211–12, 222–3, 334
army, experience in 79–91
Arnott, Struther 232–3
art(s) 37, 55, 75, 86, 178, 180, 185, 263–5, 269, 274, 276, 333–6
Association of University Teachers (AUT) 205
Aston, Trevor (T.H.) 87 n.11, 90 n.16, 248, 250, 252, 291–302
Atiyah, Sir Michael 331
atrocities (in war) 90–1
Auchinleck, Sir Claude 84
Austin, Colin (C.F.) 194
Australia (visit to) 272–3, 311
Austronesian languages 53, 55–6
autobiography, nature of 23–7, 250 n.‡
Ayer, Sir Alfred ('Freddie') 98, 104, 228

Bach, J.S. 35, 48
Bakewell, Joan 187
Ball, Sir Christopher 259, 305–6
Ballantrae, Lord (Bernard) 229, 231; autobiography of, 230
Balliol College 69, 71, 75, 102, 104, 107–11, 125–9, 135, 179, 248, 256
Balogh, Lord (Thomas) 104–5, 127
Balzan Foundation 234–5
Barbour, Robin (Very Rev. R.A.S.) 69
Barley Mill 239
Barnes, Leonard 110

Barrett, Spencer (W.S.) 72, 128, 137 n.26, 138 n.27
Bawden, C.R. 284, 288
Baxter, Alan (A.G.L.) 231
Bean, George (G.E.) 67–8, 69–71
Beard, Geoffrey 253, 302
beauty 110 n.28, 130, 159, 163–4, 274, 316 n.10
Beazley, Sir John 115 n.†
Beck, Maximilian 75 n.23
Beech, Norman 257
Beethoven 36, 265, 268
Beijing 272, 275–6
Belgium 272
belief, *see* religion
Beloff, Lord (Max) 282, 308 n.5, 331
Bennett, Alan 165 n.*
Berganza, Teresa 265
Berkeley, University of California at 121 n.22, 157, 192–5, 199, 215, 271; *see also* Sather Lectures
Berlin, Sir Isaiah 226–7, 271
Bernal, Martin 121
Bernanos, Georges 158
Bible 36 n.3, 44–6, 48, 52, 324
birds 21, 48, 129, 215, 277, 313, 325, 326
Blake, Lord (Robert) 283 n.†
Bleek, Dorothea 51
Blunt, Anthony 226, 273, 279–90, 331
Bowra, Sir Maurice 72–3, 128, 137 n.26
Bramble, John (J.C.) 252, 298
Brendel, Alfred 265
'Brideshead syndrome' 75
British Academy 133, 172–3, 189–90, 226–9, 235, 271–2, 279–90; Cromer prize 56; Kenyon medal 225
British Empire 109–10
Britten, Lord (Benjamin) 23
Brooke, Peter (P.L.) 316
Brown, Arthur 280
Brown, Jimmy 88
Brown, Maurice 41
Brown, P.W.H. 228
Brown, William 78 n.28
Browning, Robert 53
Buchanan-Smith, Robin (Rev.) 231
Bullock, Lord (Alan) 301
Burn, Andrew (A.R.) 69
Burstall, Christopher 185–8

Burton, Reggie (R.W.B.) 137 n.23
Butler, Lionel (L.H.) 146
Byron, Lord (George) 275

Caird, George (Rev. G.B.) 283
Cairncross, Sir Alexander 228, 230
Cairngorms 132
Caithness, George (G.S.) 155
Callan, H.G. ('Mick') 123, 134
Cambridge University admissions 305
Campbell, Archie (A.D.) 149
Campbell, Brian (B.G.) 250, 252, 257, 292 n.4
Campbell, Ian (I.M.) 216
Campbell, Lewis 171 n.3
Campbell, Malcolm 215 n.7
Canada 313, 321, 322
capital punishment 223
capitalism 60, 201
Carnegie Trust 131
Carr, C.T. 149–50
Carr, E.H. 287
cars 111, 153
Carswell, John (J.P.) 228, 280, 283, 285–6
Cartledge, Paul 165, 188 n.22
Case, Thomas 135
Cassavetes, John 212 n.*
Cassino 81 n.6, 82, 83
Catholicism 62, 159
Cavander, Kenneth 187 n.†
Chadwick, John 68 n.3
Chadwick, Owen (Rev. W.O.) 272–3, 282
chairmanship of committees 146, 154, 173, 255, 257–8, 280–2, 306
Chamberlain, Neville 64, 78
Chambers, Mortimer (M.H.) 195
Chancellorship of St Andrews University 229–35
Chapman, Geoffrey and Valerie 312, 320
Charles-Edwards, Thomas (T.M.O.) 254, 291–2
Cheape, Alexander 144
China 67 n.2, 195, 201, 271–6
Chinese language 179, 273
Chios 70, 277, 315
Chomsky, Noam 52
Christian, Reg (R.F.) 159 n.*, 205
Christianity 43, 47, 134 n.**, 158–9, 219, 222, 223 n.l, 258, 287, 324; *see also* religion

Christie, Ian (I.R.) 284, 287
Cicero 108
circumcision 49, 62
Civil Defence 196
Clark, Sir George 315
Clark, Lord (Kenneth) 185
Classical Culture, undergraduate course in 184
Classical Quarterly (journal) 174
Classics 42, 55, 69, 75, 95–6, 108, 127, 179–85, 190, 209; good/bad reasons for studying 179–80, 273–4; Oxford syllabus in 125, 128, 137; survival of 179–80, 322 n.6, 323; in USA 323–4
classification, linguistic 53–5
Cleghorn, Rhoda 147
Cobb, Richard (R.C.) 281, 286 n.21
Codrington, R.H. 52, 54
coffee 157, 312
Cole, G.D.H. 110
Colorado 211, 214
comedy, Greek 105, 117, 118, 162, 194, 214, 222; *see also* Aristophanes
communism 53 n.8, 63, 76–8, 87, 88, 196, 276, 281
'composition' (Greek and Latin) 68–9, 75, 98, 108, 115, 136, 267
comprehension tests 181
computers 171–4, 268
Conservative Party 59–60, 78, 87, 140, 281, 330, 332
content and form 115, 265–9
Cooper, David 295
Corbett, Patrick (J.P.) 127
Cornell University 135, 263, 312–13, 317, 319, 321, 322
Corpus Christi College, Cambridge 252, 256, 258
Corpus Christi College, Oxford 245–62, 291–302; admission of women 250–1; bursars and staff 256–8; Governing Body 248–9, 255–6, 257, 258, 291, 293; junior members 247, 249, 252, 253, 255, 256, 257–8; library 253, 291, 292, 295, 300 n.24
Couling, Irma 242
counselling, university 208–9
Craik, Elizabeth 182 n.6, 215 n.7, 325
Crook, John (J.A.) 284, 288

Crowther-Hunt, Lord (Norman) 305–6
Curtis, Katharine 158
Czechoslovakia 64, 65, 76, 199

Dalyell, Tam 195
Davidson, Francis 44
Davies, Anna 231, 233
Davis, University of California at 322
Day, Sir Robin 331
deafness 231, 313–14
Deanship (of Arts Faculty, St Andrews) 137, 146–50, 205–7
debt 60
Deep Springs, Ca. 322
defamation 26–7, 166
definitions 99, 338
deformity, *see* funnel chest
Demosthenes 263
Deng Junbing 276
Dennes, William (W.R.) 194
Denniston, J.D. 72–3, 114 n.*, 117
depression, economic 62; psychological 97, 155–60, 290, 299, 312, 316
de Romilly, Jacqueline 223
Devereux, George 156, 174–7, 220
De Vries, G.J. 168
diaries 24
Dick, Marcus (M.W.) 127
Dickens, Charles 76, 110
Dik, Helma 117
Dodds, Eric (E.R.) 49 n.11, 72–3, 78 n.28, 128, 130, 138, 159, 175, 184 n.12, 212 n.3
Dorward, David (D.P.) 230
Douglas, Robert 205
Dover, Alan (son) 107–8, 154, 195, 198, 238–9, 241, 286, 290, 321
Dover (née Latimer), Audrey (wife) 49, 101–3, 107–8, 129–30, 131, 134, 138, 153–60, 175, 185, 209, 215, 239, 241–2, 246, 247, 248, 289–90, 315, 316–17, 320
Dover, Beki (granddaughter) 238–40, 243
Dover, Catherine (daughter) 22, 107–8, 176, 177, 195, 198, 243, 311–12, 313, 321
Dover, Clara 29
Dover (née Healey), Dorothy (mother) 22, 32–3, 36–8, 40, 43–6, 57, 59, 76, 99–103, 112, 160, 237–9

Dover (née Gadsby), Eliza (paternal grandmother) 30–1, 301
Dover, Henry (great-grandfather) 29
Dover, Henry James, 'Jim' (grandfather) 29–31, 35, 39 n.9
Dover, James (I, great-great-grandfather) 29
Dover, James (II, great-granduncle) 29
Dover, Lillian (aunt), *see* Lipscombe, Lillian
Dover, Nicholas (grandson) 239, 243
Dover, Percy (father) 31–2, 34, 35–9, 40, 43, 46, 57, 60, 64, 99, 100, 107–8, 111–12, 160, 237–8, 239–42, 311, 316 n.*
Dover, Wendy (née Clark) 238
dreams 38–9, 155, 157, 176–8
Duerr, Hans Peter 177
Duke, Alison 153
Dunbar, Nan 222
Dundee University 130, 143–4, 147, 149, 150–1, 169, 203; *see also* Queen's College, Dundee
duty 21, 46, 86, 218–19, 223, 287

Earp, F.R. 214
Edmonds, J.M. 118
electro-convulsive therapy (ECT) 97, 155
Eliot, George 36 n.4, 110
Enkvist, Nils Erik 264
entomology, love of, *see* insects
epigraphy, *see* inscriptions
Ernst, Juliette 227, 325
Eros/eros ('sexual love') 161–5, 191
escape (from family tensions) 35–42, 56; (from humiliation) 316 n.*
euphemism 26, 89, 254 note ¶
examinations 204–7, 305–7
experience, limited value of 82

Fabre, J.-H. 40
failure-rates, university 208–9
Falconer, Alec (A.F.) 148–50
Falklands war 276, 329–30
fantasies 24 n.*, 83, 111, 165, 176, 201
Farrar, Henry 187–8
Farrell, Brian (B.A.) 248
fear 36, 38–9, 46, 94, 109, 220, 271; *see also* spiders, fear of

feelings *contra* beliefs/reasons 25–6, 49, 280, 325
Ferguson, John 212
films 76, 212 n.*, 231–2, 265, 314
Finley, Sir Moses 184, 337
Fondation Hardt 12
Fordyce, Christian (C.J.) 130–1, 181–2
forgiveness, Christian 46, 279, 287
Forster, E.M. 279
Foucault, Michel 55
Fraenkel, Eduard 67, 72–4, 105, 116, 128, 130, 137 n.26, 138, 216–17
France and the Second World War 61–2, 64, 65, 76, 320
Franco, General 62
Fränkel, Hermann 122
Franks Commission 250 n.‡, 253, 258
Freud, Sigmund 25, 31–2, 156, 175, 176–8; *see also* 'primal scene'
Fulton, Lord (John) 127 n.§
funnel chest 25–6, 48, 58, 86, 89 n.13, 110 n.28

Gadsby, Arthur, Eliza (née Lloyd), Harry, Kate 30–1
Gandhi 316
Gangtown 40, 41, 59
gardening 111, 119, 197–8, 322
Gardner, Dame Helen 226, 283, 286
Gash, Norman 284
Gasser, Robert (R.P.H.) 246
Gauldie, Sinclair 146
generals, attitudes to 84–5
Germany and the Second World War 61–5, 76–8, 80–4, 87
ghosts 39
Gifford, Douglas (Rev. D.J.) 203
Glyn, Andrew (A.J.) 250
God, Judeo-Christian 27 n.‡, 43, 45–7, 49, 83, 134 n.**, 156, 158–9, 219, 221; *see also* Christianity and religion
gods, Greek 220
Gomme, A.W. 96, 118–19, 130
Gomme, Phyllis 119
Gow, Andrew (A.S.F.) 74
Gower, L.C.B. 283
Gowing, Margaret (M.M.) 330 n.6
Grant Michael 216
Gratwick, Adrian (A.S.) 183

Gray, Dorothea 113
Greece, landscape of 69, 276–7
grief 59
Grimm's Fairy Tales 38
Guest, Lord (Graham) 141
Gurney, Oliver (O.R.) 284

Hall, Derek (G.D.G.) 245
Hall, Stuart 336
Hammelmann, Bezi 216
Handley, Eric (E.W.) 246, 316
handwriting 58
Hardie, Frank (W.F.R.) 247
Hare, R.M. 104
Harris, Sir Henry 331
Harrison, Sir Brian (B.H.) 22, 250, 262
Harrison, Jane 264
Hart, Herbert (H.L.A.) 330–1
Harvard University 119, 137–8, 154, 178, 215
Headlam-Morley, Agnes 135
Healey, née Millson, Annie (maternal grandmother) 32
Healey, Lord (Denis) 127 n.§, 256
Healey, Gilbert (uncle) 33
Healey, Harry (I, maternal grandfather) 32
Healey, Harry (II, uncle 'Shane') 33, 34, 41–2
Healey, Rt. Rev. Kenneth (uncle) 33, 34, 43, 111
Heath, Sir Edward 256
Hegel, G.W.F. 75
Henderson, Jeffrey 264
Henry, Alan (A.S.) 272
Hepburn, Fred (F.C.) 134 n.16, 326
heredity *vs* environment 88
Herodotus 96, 172, 173, 265, 281 n.9, 333–4
Hertford scholarship, Oxford 75
Highlands, Scottish 129, 131–2, 312
Hill, Christopher (J.E.C.) 286 n.22
Hill, Sir Ian 154
Hill, Ron (R.W.) 261–2
Hilton, Rodney (R.H.) 301
Hiroshima 91, 275
history, Dover's conception of 98, 180, 333–8
Hitler, Adolf 59, 61, 63, 64, 78, 321
Holford, Lord (William) 140, 141, 143

Holladay, James (A.J.) 104
Homer 55 n.13, 122, 167, 212, 277
homosexuality, Greek 161–9, 176, 331
Honeyman, A.M. 148–9
honorary degrees 225, 231, 288, 319, 327–9, 331
Hornsby, Jennifer 250
Howard, Sir Michael 282
Howard-Johnston, James (J.D.) 296 n.13, 297, 298 n.16, 300 n.24
Huan Xiang 272
Hubbard, Margaret 137 n.22
Hunter, Lord (J.O.M.) 140, 142–3

illness 49–50, 58, 80, 154, 157–8, 311–12
impotence 315–16
Inagaki, Michael and Ichiko 274
independent schools 306–8
inscriptions 21, 96, 98, 114–16, 117, 121, 267
insects 21, 30, 39–40, 42, 120
intellectuals 23, 86, 96, 261
intentionalism 335
Ireland scholarship, Oxford 98
Irvine, Sir James 130
-isms, dislike of 324
Isocrates 105, 191–2
Israel 325
Italy 65, 80, 83–4, 88, 90, 94–5, 102, 155, 200, 215–16, 226–7, 271
Ivens, Walter (W.G.) 52

Jackson, Robert (R.V.) 328
Jaeger, Werner 337
Jakobson, Roman 264
James, Clive 187
James, Robert (R.L.) 67, 69
Japan 36, 62, 83, 179, 271–5
Jenkins, Lord (Roy) 235, 256
Jesus Christ 46
Jews 49, 58 n.2, 61–2, 64, 65, 86, 159 n.*
Johnson, Nevil 261
Joint Association of Classical Teachers (JACT) 182, 225
Jones, Peter (P.V.) 182

Kassel, Rudolf 194
Keen, Maurice 315
Keir, Sir David Lindsay 97, 126–7, 130

Kenny, Sir Anthony 159 n.10
Kerr, Clark 195
Kidd, Ian (I.G.) 81 n.6, 132–3, 161, 229
Kirk, Geoffrey (G.S.) 217
Knight, Margaret 221
knighthood 225
Knox, Bernard (B.M.W.) 177, 188 n.22
Knox, Jessie 181
Knox, Sir Malcolm 129–30, 140, 141–3, 149, 150–1, 172, 232 n.†
Kubo, Masaaki 272, 273
Kyoto 274

Labour Club, Oxford 76
Labour Party 88
Ladd, Tony (C.A.) 150
Landon, Robbins (H.C.R.) 192
Lang, David (D.M.) 288–9
language(s) 49, 51–6, 179, 220, 314; *see also* linguistics
Lasko, Peter 281
Lasserre, François 121–2
Last, Hugh 97
Latimer (née Andrews), Cicely (mother-in-law) 61 n.l, 102–3, 111, 129, 140, 160, 198
Latimer, Hugh (brother-in-law) 76, 101, 103, 194
Latin 41, 42, 67–8, 68–9, 98, 106, 108–9, 133–4, 179–81, 209, 323
Latte, Kurt 74
lecturing 114, 132, 202, 216, 261–2
Lee, Sir Desmond 182–3
Lemmon (née Latimer), Helen (sister-in-law) 103, 108
Leonardo society (Balliol) 110
Lepper, Frank (F.A.) 246, 248, 251, 292, 299
Levens, Robert (R.G.C.) 117
Leverhulme Trust 225–6, 228, 229, 279
Levi, Anthony 159 n.10
Levi, Peter 159 n.10
Levinas, Emmanuel 235 n.15
libraries 51, 52, 90, 253 n.l, 258, 264, 291, 295, 319
Lindsay, Lord (A.D.) 95, 127
Lindsay, Martin and Moia 196, 273
Lindsay, W.M. 73–4

linguistics 52, 53, 76, 116, 267, 272; *see also* language(s), stylistics
Lipscombe, Cyril 242
Lipscombe, Lillian (née Dover, aunt) 31, 240, 242–3
literary criticism 176, 191, 264, 265, 335
Livingstone, Ken 329
Livingstone, Sir Richard 251–2, 320
Lloyd-Jones, Sir Hugh 74 n.19, 136, 137–8, 217 n.11
Loach, Ken 231–2, 233
Lobel, Edgar 136
Locarno 102
Logan, Sir Douglas 288
Lord, Jan 321
Lorimer, W.L. 129, 132
lynching 281
Lyons, Leland (F.S.L.) 232–3
Lysias 105, 108, 191–3, 199, 266

Maas, Paul 74, 116
McClelland, Grigor (W.G.) 154
Macleod, Colin 168
McFarlane, Ian 160
Macgregor, Rev. G.H.C. 172
MacKinnon, Donald (D.M.) 103–4
McLeman, Jim (Rev. James) 171
McManners, John 287 n.24
Macmillan, Daniel 215
Macmillan, Harold, 1st Earl of Stockton 137, 225, 332
Mann, F.A. 281
Mann, Thomas 110
Mao Zedong 169, 275, 321
Marchant, E.C. 114
Mariotti, Scevola 200
masturbation 24 n.*, 32, 47, 164–5
Matthews, Alistair (A.F.M.) 70–1
meaning(s) 179, 335, 336
Mee, Arthur 38, 39
Mehta, Ved (V.P.) 138
Meiggs, Russell 96–7, 106, 130, 202
Menander 118, 119
Meritt, Ben (B.D.) 97, 194
metahistory 324, 336
metaphysics, aversion to 168, 338
Mexico 200, 322, 325
Michaelson, Sidney 172
middle class 60, 61, 87, 93, 252

Miles, Dame Margaret 95 n.*
Milligan, Stephen 24 n.*
Millson, Bessie ('Miley': grand-aunt) 33–4, 40, 176
Milne, Alasdair 188
Mitford, Terence (T.B.) 71, 134, 159
Momigliano, Arnaldo 105, 336 n.4
Mono-Alu 53–4
Montgomery, Lord (Bernard) 84–5
morale, military 81–2, 83, 84–5
morality, general 39, 40 n.10, 46, 47–8, 55 n.11, 212, 217–20, 221–2, 281, 289, 291 n.1, 338; Greek 211–20, 223; of students 255
Moriarty, Denis 185
Morton, Andrew (Rev. A.Q.) 171–3
Morton, Jean 171
Mosley, Oswald 59 n.6
Mulder, Jan 234
Munich Agreement 64–5, 76
Mure, Geoffrey 97 n.‡
Murray, Gilbert (G.G.A.) 68, 72, 118, 264–9, 324–5
Murray, Lord (Keith) 142–3
music 76, 265; *see also* Bach, Beethoven, Nielsen, Sibelius
Mussolini 60–1, 65, 90 n.§
Mynors, Sir Roger 127
mystical experience, Dover's 158; Socrates' 168

Nagoya 274
National Health Service 111
Nazis 60–2
Neill, Sir Patrick 260
Neumann, Peter (P.M.) 305
Nielsen, Carl 268 n.†
Nisbet, J.W. 148–9
Nisbet, Robin (R.G.M.) 109, 115, 245, 301
Noble, Denis 331
Nock, A.D. 178
novels, Dover's unfinished 110
Nowland, John 296

Oakden, J.P. 150
O'Brien, Conor Cruise 316
Officer Cadet Training Unit (OCTU) 79–81, 85

officers 85–6
Ogilvie, Robert (R.M.) 209, 232, 284
Oglethorpe, James, and Oglethorpe University 225, 319–20
old age 316–17
Olympia, sculptures at 69, 325
oratory, Greek 192–3, 161, 168, 192–3, 212–14, 220, 222, 266–7, 329; *see also* Andocides, Antiphon, Demosthenes, Isocrates, Lysias
Ordinary degree 148
O'Shea, Hilary 165 n.*
Ovid 108
Owen, Gwil (G.E.L.) 211, 219
Oxford Area Arts Council 262
Oxford and Cambridge Schools Examination Board 258
Oxford University, admissions system 303–9; Conference of Colleges 258–9; Congregation 327–30; Curators of the Bodleian 258; heads of houses 245, 247, 252, 254, 258, 305, 330; *see also* Classics, Oxford syllabus in; Corpus Christi College, Oxford; PPE; Regius Chair of Greek, Oxford; training of university teachers; tutorials, Oxford; women at Oxford

Pacific linguistics 51–6, 123
pacifism 46, 64, 96 n.†
Page, Sir Denys 73, 117, 122, 136, 216, 217
Papuan languages 53, 55
Parker, Geoffrey (N.G.) 315
parody and stylistics 268
Parry, Adam (A.M.) 119
Past & Present (journal) 294–5
Paton, H.J. 98
Pauline Epistles 46, 172
Pearce, R.H. 252
Pearson, Lionel 212
Pericles 223, 267
Phelps, William 251
philosophy 75, 96, 98–9, 103–4, 127, 128, 161, 163–5, 167–9, 211–12, 214, 218–19, 221, 334, 335
Pidduck, F.B. 251
Pietermaritzburg 312
Platnauer, Maurice 117

Plato 69, 99, 106, 169, 174, 181, 211, 215, 220, 221, 222, 263, 267, 334; *Phaedrus* 161, 164, 168 n.21; *Symposium* 161–5, 167–9
Plumb, Sir John 279–80, 284–5
poetry, Dover's 110
Poland 64, 65, 77, 86
political views as student 59–62, 76–7, 109–10
Powell, Maria 186
PPE (Philosophy, Politics and Economics) 95, 127, 128, 303
precocity 26, 182 n.6
prescribed texts 71, 109, 113, 181, 184, 205,
'pre-university school' 208
Price, H.H. 98
'primal scene' 32, 47, 176; *see also* Freud
Pritchett, Kendrick (W.K.) 193–4
privatisation, Thatcherite 329
prose/poetry distinction 334
prostitution 93
Proust, Marcel 110
psychiatry 31, 97 n.‡, 155–6, 175, 209–10, 290; and Trevor Aston 292, 297–9
psychodynamics 25, 176–8; *see also* Freud
psychosomatic, the 154, 311
Pulzer, Peter (P.G.J.) 330

Queen Elizabeth II 137, 230–1, 280
Queen's College, Dundee 129, 131 n.11, 150
questionnaires, student 202–3, 260, 262
Quinault, Frank (F.C.) 209

race 41, 55, 62, 65, 87, 324
Rawson, Elizabeth 301
Ray, Sidney Herbert 52, 54
Read, John 141
Reagan, Ronald 195
Regius Chair of Greek, Cambridge 216–17, 316
Regius Chair of Greek, Oxford 72–3, 111, 130, 137–8
religion 43–7, 158, 219, 220–2, 274; *see also* Catholicism, Christianity
religious education 220–1
research 123–4, 229, 313
residences, student 146

retirement 313
Richards, Sir Rex 305
Rickman, Geoffrey (G.E.) 183
right and wrong, *see* morality
Robbins, Lord (Lionel) 283
Robbins Report 144–5, 150
Roberts, Colin (C.H.) 284, 288
Robey, David (D.J.B.) 261
Rommel, Erwin 84–5
Rose, H.J. 128, 129, 143
Ross, David 155
Rossetti, Livio 222
Rowse, A.L. 176 n.16
Royal Artillery 77, 79
Russell, Donald (D.A.F.M.) 106, 107, 202 n.8, 317, 326

sabbatical leave 205, 215–16, 273, 293
Saïd, Suzanne 222 n.§
St Andrews University 128–38, 139–51, 207–10; General Council 233–4; Classics Departments 132–4, 182–4; *see also* Chancellorship, Deanship
St Paul's School 37, 42, 48, 58, 67–9
Sakharov, Andrei 264–5
Samuels, Michael (M.L.) 77–8
Sangro, battle of the 85
Sather Lectures 117 n.12, 121 n.22, 191–4; *see also* Berkeley, University of California at
Schenk, Hans (H.J.) 136 n.‡‡
science 39, 62, 86, 98–9, 104, 121, 147, 165, 180, 333–4; departments of, St Andrews, 139–44
Scotland, *see* Highlands
Scottish Certificate of Education 148, 180, 208, 303
Scottish education 147–8, 179
Scottish Universities Entrance Board 181
Scruton, Roger 166
selectivity, autobiographical 24
Semitic languages 49
Senio, river 90
sex 31–2, 45, 47–8, 55 n.11, 93–5, 100–1, 102, 163–4, 165, 169, 198, 251; *see also* Eros, Freud, homosexuality, impotence, masturbation
Shaka, King 321

shame 40, 77, 93, 315; Greek experience of 212, 220
Sharp, Thomas 139
Shipway, Inez 217
Sholokhov, Mikhail 232
Sibelius, Jean 76, 129, 268 n.†
Silver, Kenneth (K.G.) 230
Simpson, Pat 156
Skeat, T.C. 284, 288
Smith, Adam 63 n.¶
Smith, Norton (J.N.) 149–50
Smith, Sir Thomas Broun 288 n.26
smoking 178 n.22, 288, 290, 312
Snell, Bruno 122–3
Snow, Lord (C.P.) 127 n.‡, 232, 334
socialism 60, 62, 87, 110 n.25, 276, 329
Socrates 120, 164, 187, 223; in Plato 163–4, 168, 215
Soper, Lord (Rev. D.O.) 196 n.†
Sophocles 69
South Africa 249, 295, 312, 320, 325, 337 n.§
Southern, Sir Richard 296, 301
Soviet Union 63, 76–7, 78, 84, 87, 110, 195, 199, 201, 232, 276, 279
Spengemann, William 27
spiders, fear of 40, 217, 254, 273
Stalin, Josef 63, 78, 90–1, 140, 232, 276, 287, 321
Stanford, Bedel (W.B.) 116 n.8, 117
Stanford University 173, 201, 235, 263–4, 321–5
statistics 171–3, 268
Steiner, George 188
Stirling, Sir James 146
Stirling University 145, 203
stoicism, personal 58–9, 77, 80
stress 289–90
Stretton, Hugh 105
student participation 207–8
student revolt 199–202
style, linguistic/artistic 106 n.§, 153, 161, 171, 174, 191, 193, 263–9, 334–5
stylistics 106, 171–4, 192, 264, 267–8
suicide 23, 156, 209, 315–16; *see also* Aston, Trevor
Sullivan, John (J.P.) 337 n.†
Swan Hellenic cruises 276
Szasz, Thomas 156

Taplin, Oliver (O.P.) 188 n.21, 307
taxation 63, 328–9
Taylor, Alan (A.J.P.) 158, 282, 286, 288
Taylor, Christopher (C.C.W.) 296 n.14
teaching, nature of 68, 74, 81, 85, 89, 97, 108, 123–4, 132, 133, 136, 145, 182–3, 184, 200, 202–4, 207, 247, 260–1; *see also* training of university teachers
Tebbit, Lord (Norman) 328
television 185–8
textual criticism 71, 96, 114, 133, 184, 336
Thatcher, Lady (Margaret) 288, 327–32
Theocritus 215
theory, aversion to 23 n.4, 27, 218, 264 n.5, 272, 324, 337
Thesaurus Linguae Graecae 173
Thomas, Sir Keith 253
Thucydides 64 n.11, 69, 83 n.8, 88–9, 96, 113, 118–20, 173, 178, 184, 191, 194, 266, 267, 268, 331, 334
Tolstoy, Lev 88 n.‡, 159 n.*, 110
Tolstoy, Nikolai 90
town and gown, in St Andrews 134, 140, 233; in Oxford 262
Toynbee, Arnold 324
trade unions 329
tragedy, Greek 75, 178, 214, 223
training of university teachers 202–4, 246, 260–1
translation 69, 98, 133, 137, 162, 179, 180, 181–2, 184, 204–5, 220, 221, 323–4, 325, 326, 336; *see also* 'composition'
Trenkner, Sophie 153
truth(fulness) 26–7, 37, 165, 218, 275, 299, 300
Turner, Sir Eric 226–7, 228
tutorials, Oxford 98, 103–4, 108–9, 114, 200, 261–2; St Andrews 132
'Two Cultures' thesis 179 n.2, 334; *see also* Snow, C.P.
Tylor, Sir Theodore 126

Ullendorff, Edward 232 n.†
unemployment 328–9
University College London 104, 162, 198, 228
University Grants Committee 140, 228, 233, 259,
Urmson, Jim (J.O.) 299

vase-painting, Greek 115 n.†, 166, 167
Vasilopoulos, Antonios 186
Veale, Sir Douglas 251
venereal disease 94
Vergil/Virgil 46, 69
Vermeule, Emily 166
Vernant, J.-P. 175
Vietnam war 195–6, 201
Vishinsky, Andrei 63
Vlastos, Gregory 211, 229
'voices', hearing 49, 102, 158

Wackernagel, Jacob 116
Wade-Gery, H.T. 97, 172, 194 n.10
Wadham College, Oxford 107, 108–9
Walker, Ernest 104–5
Wallace-Hadrill, Michael (J.M.) 286, 301
Warren Piper, David 261
wartime service, *see* army, experience in
Watson, Steven (J.S.) 151, 203, 208, 231, 232 n.†, 233
Watson-Watt, Sir Robert 202
Watt, David 331
Watt, Bill (W.S.) 72, 98, 127, 128, 129, 204
wealth 111
Webster, Sir Charles 189
Webster, Madge (A.M. Dale) 172
Weldon, Fay 142 n.*
Wells, Frederick (A.F.) 72
Wells, H.G. 76
Wemyss, Lady Victoria 145
Werner, Alice 51
Wester Ross 48, 159; *see also* Highlands
'Western' culture, controversy over 324–5
Wheeler, G.C. 53–4

Wheeler, Sir Mortimer 172, 173, 189
White, Hayden 336 n.4
Whitting, Philip 67–8
Wilamowitz-Moellendorff, Ulrich von 73, 74
Wild, Don (D.G.) 252, 257, 292
Williams, Sir Bernard 99, 211, 109
Williams, Sir Edgar W. ('Bill') 104–5, 130
Williams, Gordon 53, 128, 136–7, 154, 160, 209, 222
Williams, J.W. 130
Williams, Mary 222
Williams, Neville (N.J.) 228
Wilson, Sir Duncan 256
Wimpee 40, 45, 59
Winkler, Jack 159 n.10
Woozley, Tony (A.D.) 137
women at Oxford 248–9, 250–1
word order, Greek 55, 115–17, 182, 267
Wright, John (J.N.) 134 n.**, 143, 144, 149
Wright, Erskine (T.E.) 130–1, 133–4
writing-systems 41–2

Xenophanes 220
Xenophon 96, 120, 173, 215
xerography 202

Yardley, John (J.C.) 321
Yosemite 322
Young, Douglas (D.C.C.) 73 n.*, 132–3, 171

Zaehner, R.C. 136 n.‡‡
Zulus 320–1